CRACKED ICE

An Insider's Look at the NHL

STAN FISCHLER

NTC/Contemporary Publishing Group

Library of Congress Cataloging-in-Publication Data

Fischler, Stan.
      Cracked Ice: an insider's look at the NHL / Stan Fischler.
         p. cm
      ISBN 1-57028-219-6
         1. National Hockey League—History.   2. Violence in sports.
      I. Title.
      GV847.8.N3F563   1995
      796.962'64—dc21   98-41999
                                            CIP

For Simon, Ben, and Shirley
—the starting team

Interior design by Hespenheide Design

Published by Masters Press
A division of NTC/Contemporary Publishing Group, Inc.
4255 West Touhy Avenue, Lincolnwood (Chicago), Illinois 60712-1975 U.S.A.
Copyright © 1999, 1995 by Stan Fischler
Printed in the United States of America
International Standard Book Number: 1-57028-219-6
99 00 01 02 03 04 LB 18 17 16 15 14 13 12 11 10 9 8 7 6 5 4 3 2 1

CONTENTS

PREFACE

I saw my first hockey game before the Japanese bombed Pearl Harbor.

I earned my first paycheck in the hockey business before Toe Blake's Montreal Canadiens launched their first dynasty by winning five straight Stanley Cups.

And I haven't stopped writing about the ice game since.

In the 44 years since I began writing professionally about the National Hockey League, I have experienced innumerable changes.

The advent of the goalie mask was one such change. It began when I watched Jacques Plante's mug get dismembered by an Andy Bathgate blast at Madison Square Garden, an event that traumatized me.

Despite the damage done to Plante, I subscribed to the Toe Blake Theory that goalies should remain maskless. As more netminders chose to save their faces, I felt that a wonderfully intimate aspect of pro hockey was disappearing.

Then came protective helmets, curved sticks, and the slap shot, all of which bothered me. But nothing was more disturbing than NHL expansion from 6 to 12 teams in 1967–68.

That was a killer. Only one who had been raised on the six-team NHL could possibly imagine the sudden quality decline when the new expansion teams actually became high-grade versions of American Hockey League clubs. The 1968 Stanley Cup final between the Montreal Canadiens and the brand-new St. Louis Blues set hockey back light-years as far as I was concerned, yet somehow, The Game survived.

In time, expansion teams flexed their muscles, and by 1974 the Philadelphia Flyers had won their first of two straight Stanley Cups.

Then came the birth of the World Hockey Association, raids against the NHL, international matches with the Soviet Union, and the inevitable NHL-WHA merger.

As startling as all of these changes may have been, each had a positive element that left me without rancor. How could I rail against goalie masks if they save a netminder's life? Who was I to tell Stan Mikita not to wear a helmet after Bill Masterton was killed because he wasn't wearing headgear? Where did I come off criticizing expansion or the WHA when it was the latter that enabled me to get my first broadcasting job?

It was all progress, and I eventually came to understand that—for the most part—progress was leading to The Game's betterment, although I'll always maintain that the curved stick was an egregious mistake.

But a new element and emotion intruded when the National Hockey League Players' Association called its first strike in 1992. Hockey liberals, pro-unionists, and the anti-Alan Eagleson Brigade might have called the walkout progress—particularly because it was directed against John Ziegler's misguided regime.

I do not stand among them. Liberal on some issues, conservative on others, I regarded the strike among the most nauseating events of my hockey journalistic career; and I still do. Etched in my memory forever is a discussion I had with union leader Ken Baumgartner.

Make no mistake, I've always liked Baumgartner as a person and considered him a valued player for the New York Islanders for about a dozen games. But on this night when Baumgartner attempted to rationalize the runaway salaries that he and some of his colleagues were making, then I knew big-league hockey was in big trouble. Not long after that, my old pal Kevin Lowe launched a similar peroration about "underpaid" hockey players.

"Dammit," I said to myself, "this guy believes it as much as Abraham Lincoln believed 'The Gettysburg Address.' "

Later that evening, my hockey colleague—now with ESPN—Vic Morren and I walked out of the Plaza Hotel toward the Columbus Circle subway station in Manhattan. An early spring dusk was falling over New York City as we strolled through the perimeter of Central Park.

"Something awful is happening to the game of hockey," I said to Morren.

"I know what you mean," he replied.

"It's greed-to-the-radical-fifty," I went on, "and unless the NHL can put the lid on it, hockey as we know it is never going to be the same."

It never was. Incredibly, the union scored a TKO over Ziegler and the NHL ownership while salaries climbed and climbed and climbed. A fourth-line player such as Troy Crowder, who wasn't worth $100,000 on the best day he ever had, suddenly was demanding twice that amount and wound up being a coveted commodity by the Detroit Red Wings despite his innumerable shortcomings.

From time to time both NHL executives and agents would insist to me that runaway inflation simply could not continue without a big-league hockey version of the Wall Street crash of 1929 that led to the Great Depression of the 1930s. Yet almost blithely the likes of Bruce McNall, Neil Smith, and Michael Shanahan, to name a few, tossed money at stickhandlers as if it were growing on trees.

I watched these episodes with a mixture of awe and downright fear until the Great Lockout of 1994–95. Now wealthier than they ever had been, NHL players seemed oblivious to losses being suffered by many teams. Union boss Bob Goodenow betrayed a crass insensitivity to small-market teams such as Quebec, Winnipeg, and Hartford. Player representatives such as Bruce Driver simply refused to believe owners like John McMullen when they attempted to open the books and show them that, yes, they were taking a fiscal beating.

The lockout stunned me to the very core, both professionally and emotionally, because I knew that it signaled one of the most dramatic changes our favorite game ever endured. What's more, I believed implicitly that the changes it wrought would do to the NHL's fabric what World War I inflicted on Europe's political mosaic when the armistice was signed in 1918.

When the lockout began in October 1994, I suggested to Don Broad, then with McGraw-Hill Ryerson, that a book chronicling major league hockey's turbulent period—from the 1992 strike through the lockout—would be a valuable addition to any history of the game.

"The lockout should be over in a week or two," I told Broad over lunch early in October 1994. "Even if it goes as long as a month, the changes in hockey should be profound."

Broad agreed, and the concept for *Cracked Ice* was born. Like the generals who predicted that the Great War of 1914 would end in a matter of weeks, we were unable to believe that the lockout would go on and on and on, past Christmas 1994 and through New Year's Day 1995.

As I began writing the manuscript, I realized that to make a coherent history of the turbulent period, I could best do it through my own eyes and that I should fix a starting period. I chose the John Ziegler presidency because I had covered it closely since its inception and also because it impacted directly on events of the 1990s through to the present.

I decided to follow the Ziegler years through the 1992 strike, his demise as president, and the subsequent rump administration of Gil Stein leading to the Gary Bettman era. In that period, I had come to know and very much like Bruce McNall, who would impact the NHL the way the San Francisco earthquake reverberated through California. Because of my experiences with these and other major hockey characters like Alan Eagleson, I decided to personalize the history and tell the NHL story through my eyes, biased though they may be.

Originally, I had planned to end the book with one chapter after the lockout ended. Everything seemed to be in order until the 1995 playoffs began and a seemingly foreign entity known as Nashville began intruding into the picture.

Nashville as an NHL site? It seemed impossible to anyone who had followed hockey as long as I had. Yet this was part and parcel of the new NHL era—one where luxury boxes became more important than ordinary seats, where venerable arenas such as Chicago Stadium were replaced and the new ones named after corporations, and where players were traded not because of a stickhandler's skill, but rather because of what the player was earning or wanted to earn.

Nashville's bid to steal the Devils from New Jersey was symbolic of hockey in the 1990s, and I found myself right in the middle of this arresting story that was filled with characters that central casting couldn't have produced in Hollywood.

Thus, I decided that yet another chapter would be about the Nashville–New Jersey tug of war. And it was, except that the story began to take on a life of its own with dramatic twists and turns that became mind-boggling to one who had thought he had seen just about everything in four decades on the NHL beat.

Instead of one chapter, Nashville–New Jersey became an entire section of the book simply because it deserved to be and because the suspense it generated was even more gripping than the lockout, which had plenty of drama in its own right. As it happened, the Devils remained in New Jersey, and Nashville finally obtained an expansion team—the Predators—which began its first season of play in 1998–99.

Between resolution of the Nashville–New Jersey conflict, and the Predators' opening night in October 1998, a number of other traumas rocked the NHL.

The Whalers left Hartford following the 1996–97 season, moving to North Carolina. Although the club—renamed the Carolina Hurricanes—eventually would play its games at a new arena in Raleigh, temporary headquarters were established in Greensboro. Attendance was ignominiously low.

Compounding the NHL's embarassment was the John Spano fiasco on Long Island, which unfolded before my eyes. A year of New York Islanders rebuilding was wasted until it was discovered that Spano lacked the funds necessary to run a major league hockey club.

Even after Spano was exposed the Islanders controversy persisted, exploding in a chain reaction of frustrating events that continued through the autumn of 1998. One day it seemed as if new ownership, headed by billionaire Howard Milstein, had put the team back on track. A day later the Islanders, Nassau County, and the SMG company, which manages Nassau Coliseum, were fighting it out in New York State Supreme Court.

Just when I thought the Islanders' chapter had come to a logical conclusion, I was back in the Mineola courthouse, covering the proceedings and preparing yet another addition to the chapter.

All of which is a long-winded way of saying that I'm bringing you a Fischler-eye-view of hockey from the first seat on the roller coaster. It has had its ups and downs, for sure, but it has been one hell of a ride.

I hope you like it.

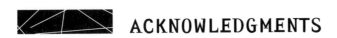 **ACKNOWLEDGMENTS**

When I undertook the writing of *Cracked Ice* I anticipated that considerable research would be necessary, although the book is essentially based on my own experiences through the administrations of three National Hockey League leaders.

Once the outline was in place, St. John's University student Rick DaCruz became my part-time librarian and a major domo in charge of researching relevant articles.

In the beginning our focus was on the Lockout of 1994–95 and, frankly, we anticipated that it would be over and done with in a matter of one to three weeks. But it grew like the fabled Topsy and so did the hours which Rick invested in the project, not to mention the mountain of clippings which reached such great proportions that they had to be transferred from my Manhattan office to larger quarters at Casa DaCruz in New Jersey.

To say that Rick had a Herculean task on his hands would be an understatement, but he remained unflagging in his pursuit of relevant material even after his graduation. Because DaCruz's time was limited, it was imperative to add other researchers. David Kolb, Dave Harsanyi, Keith Fernbach, Ann Marie Lynch, and Anna Horton were especially helpful.

The updated edition completed during the 1998–99 season, also required considerable assistance from various quarters.

As always, Adam Schwartz of the NHL public relations department was there when help was needed as was Chris Botta of the Islanders, John Rosasco of the Rangers, and Rick Minch of the Devils.

Our staff at Fischler Hockey Service, headed by Jon Scherzer, performed nobly and well. Deep bows are in order for G. P. Aroldi, Christina Attardo, Thomas Berk, Andrew Buzin, Dan Saraceni, Darren Siegel, Amy Spencer, and Beth Zirogiannis. No doubt we've forgotten some notables. To those we can only say "Sorry!"

We would be remiss if we failed to deliver special kudos to those who saw the merit in an American—as differentiated from Canadian—version of the book. Tom Bast originally ran with the idea. Ken Samelson followed up along with Chad Woolums. Last but certainly not least, our thanks to Julia Anderson, Senior Project Editor at NTC/Contemporary Publishing Group, for her patience, fortitude, and guidance in seeing this special project through to completion.

A DONUT AND A DISAPPEARANCE
The Decline and Fall of John Ziegler

It is far too simplistic to assert that one incident contributed to the decline and fall of John Ziegler as NHL president. Of this I speak firsthand, having followed Ziegler in my journalistic capacity, from the beginning to the end of his presidency.

Ziegler's enforced departure was caused by several elements and incidents, including the power-loss of his chief supporters, Alan Eagleson and Bill Wirtz, as well as his apparent capitulation to union boss Bob Goodenow following the 1992 players' revolt.

But one tremulous episode among the many set off the avalanche that eventually buried Ziegler under a mountain of bad publicity. Future hockey historians will refer to it as "The Donut Incident," although there were no crullers involved, as far as Ziegler was concerned.

The unforgettable mess developed, as many hockey messes do, from the fire of a heated Stanley Cup playoff game. The New Jersey Devils, who never before had been in a postseason tournament, had gained a berth on the final night of the 1987–88 season, edging the New York Rangers.

From a league viewpoint, this was not a happy event. Even during the Ziegler regime, the Rangers were regarded as the jewel of American-based NHL franchises: the club right smack in the middle of the world's media capital; the one that could produce considerable positive ink by doing well in the playoffs. For the "Broadway Blueshirts" to miss the playoffs completely was not exactly a disaster, but certainly akin to one.

For the Devils to edge them out was even more onerous because New Jersey's owner, John McMullen, from time to time had been one of Ziegler's critics.

The Devils not only reached the playoffs, they proceeded to upset the favored Islanders and Capitals in rounds one and two, respectively, before meeting Boston in the semifinals. The Cinderella Devils were given little chance of toppling a Bruins' club led by the inimitable Raymond Bourque on defense. I expected New Jersey to go out in five games tops.

However, coach Jim Schoenfeld had turned his squad into believers and managed to leave Boston after the first two games with an even split. It now was Friday night at Byrne Meadowlands Arena, game three, with emotions beginning to run high. In terms of artistry, the third match would be rated a three on a scale of one to ten.

I was, as usual, covering the games for SportsChannel New York, the cable service that broadcasts both the Islanders' and Devils' matches. During the contests at Byrne Arena, I had a very strategic location—directly between the rival benches at ice level. I could see the whites of both coaches' eyes, particularly Schoenfeld, whose eyes were popping out over what he considered inept officiating.

Although Schoenfeld's club was overwhelmed, 6–1, referee Don Koharski did not help matters. To the Devils' fans his work had a distinctly pro-Boston edge.

Schoenfeld later candidly allowed that he suspected his players would lose after the third shift of the first period, but he was still seething at the end. Instead of following his players into the dressing room—directly opposite to our television studio—Schoenfeld remained at the players' bench. At game's end, referees use the same ramp to reach their dressing room, so the Jersey coach figured the longer he waited the more likely he could deliver an eye-to-eye repudiation of Koharski's work.

Even before the game had ended and Schoenfeld began his vigil, waiting for Koharski to come off the ice, I had removed myself from between the benches because I had to get into the SportsChannel studio for postgame interviews. The following description of events comes from several eyewitness accounts and published records of what was said and done.

The consensus among some pro-Devils observers is that Koharski could have defused the whole incident and forever have avoided the fracas that ensued. Instead of plunging headlong into the cauldron by skating over to Schoenfeld, Koharski could have kept his distance, remaining at center ice for a longer period and motioning Schoenfeld into his locker room. There was no rush for Koharski. He didn't have to flee the arena; all he had to do was wait it out, even if a half-hour was required.

Moreover, the NHL's security chief, Frank Torpey, was standing next to Schoenfeld and was in an ideal position to usher the enraged coach into the vomitory exit and out of harm's way.

Koharski eventually skated directly toward the players' bench, where the encounter with Schoenfeld was as inevitable as the *Titanic* hitting the iceberg. Linesmen Ray Scapinello and Gord Broseker accompanied the referee. Schoenfeld's coaching aide, Doug McKay, was with him as the Devils' big, redheaded leader confronted Koharski with flowing invectives.

Koharski brusquely continued forward, but Schoenfeld managed to get himself in front of the referee again. "You f—— walked right into me," Schoenfeld reportedly yelled. "I'm standing there and you stepped on my f—— foot."

At this point McKay intervened, trying to place his left arm between the coach and the referee. One report noted that Scapinello ran toward Schoenfeld but bumped McKay, who then bumped Koharski. The alleged inadvertent blow pushed the referee off the rubberized runway and against the wall.

At least two witnesses present, who had no connection with the league, insist that at no time did Schoenfeld lay a hand on Koharski. But the referee, according to one report, shouted at the coach as if Schoenfeld was the culprit: "You're gone now! You're gone. You won't coach another f—— game." By this time the full-fledged melee was taking place right outside our interview room.

Now aware that Koharski was implying that the coach had manhandled him, Schoenfeld shot back, "You f—— fell and you know it. You know you fell. I didn't touch you. You're full of s——. You're crazy. You're crazy."

Koharski continued snapping, "You're gone," with a postscript that he hoped the incident was on tape. (At least one TV news cameraman recorded the episode.) As the referee turned right toward the officials' room, Schoenfeld provided the imperfect squelch: "Good, 'cause you fell, you fat pig. Have another donut!" (It would become one of the most quoted lines in NHL annals.)

Witnesses reported that Koharski continued bellowing before making another turn out of sight and into the officials' room. By this time, the corridors leading to both dressing rooms were in an uproar, crowded with print journalists, camera crews, and some NHL officials.

Apparently realizing that Koharski would file a complaint and make sure the coach got the worst of it, Schoenfeld declared, "He slipped, but he said I pushed him. Anyone who was there knows my hands were by my side. I had a point to make, but he obviously didn't want to hear it."

Koharski did officially complain to the league. Although NHL vice president Brian O'Neill normally handled disciplinary problems, many thought that this one appeared severe enough to merit President John Ziegler's personal intervention. Not so. Ziegler was not around. Instead, as was his droning style, O'Neill gathered evidence but pointedly refused to evaluate the tape the Devils offered to send to him. An expected in-person hearing involving Schoenfeld, Koharski, and O'Neill never was held.

By noon on Sunday (Mother's Day), when game four of the series was scheduled to be played, O'Neill had rendered his arbitrary decision. Schoenfeld was suspended for vilifying Koharski. The NHL vice president phoned Devils' general manager Lou Lamoriello with the news. Upon hearing the decision, Lamoriello demanded a hearing, but O'Neill—Ziegler's alter ego, who, inexplicably, still had not left Montreal—refused.

O'Neill then was advised by Lamoriello that the Devils would seek to nullify the suspension through court action. But first, Lamoriello vainly attempted to locate Ziegler. Then he contacted the NHL's top lawyer, Gil Stein, informing him that the Devils would seek a temporary restraining order to nullify Schoenfeld's suspension.

John Conte, a lawyer and Devils season-ticket holder, filed a show-cause order on behalf of Schoenfeld, a portion of which reads as follows:

> The referee, without warning to Plaintiff, Coach JAMES SCHOENFELD, pushed past him, and through use of threats and intimidation, caused a certain concern and anxiety among those in the area, and stumbled through no fault or cause of Plaintiff Coach JAMES SCHOENFELD.
>
> To avoid charges of misconduct due to his threats and harassment, Referee DONALD KOHARSKI deliberately filed a grievance with the National Hockey League, well-knowing the sanctions that could be imposed on Plaintiff Coach JAMES SCHOENFELD.

Events moved swiftly and dramatically: (1) at 6 P.M. O'Neill announced from Montreal that Schoenfeld had been suspended for game four; (2) at 6:30 P.M. NHL officiating supervisor John McCauley was tipped off that the regular game officials would strike if Schoenfeld appeared behind the bench; (3) at 6:40 P.M., under NHL pressure, McCauley approached the New Jersey off-ice officials about the possibility of three of them handling the fourth playoff game in the event that the regular referee, Dave Newell, and linesmen Gord Broseker and Ray Scapinello pulled a walkout.

I had been at the rink since early afternoon preparing for our evening SportsChannel telecast of the game. By 6 P.M. the pressroom was a frenzy of conjecture, as both print and electronic journalists grasped the significance of the impending crisis and awaited bulletins as they arrived.

Although the teams took their regular warmup at 7:10 P.M., there was a sense in the hallways outside the dressing rooms that the game was not likely to start on time. Furthermore, there was a chance that it might not be played at all, despite a capacity crowd of 19,040.

Meanwhile, two egregious omissions were damaging the NHL's reputation. First and foremost, its highest officer, President Ziegler, still was nowhere to be found, although L'Affaire Schoenfeld–Koharski had escalated well into its second day. Then there was the question of O'Neill's probe. New Jersey Superior Court Judge James F. Madden took due note of the latter in his review, stating, "The NHL's investigation consisted of them calling one person [Koharski], then another [Schoenfeld]. In the middle of an important series like this, particularly when they have something like a videotape. What can be more conclusive than a photographic production? Plus the fact that after [O'Neill] made up his mind, the Devils asked for a hearing and everyone runs into the woods and gets lost."

Judge Madden issued a verbal temporary restraining order at 7:20 P.M., which meant that Schoenfeld could coach the Devils in game four. Madden delivered his verdict by phone to McCauley, who was at the rink. He had ordered the NHL to "desist and refrain from suspending Schoenfeld pending a formal hearing and notice of specific charges against him."

At the time I was riding a belt line between my studio opposite the Devils' locker room and the pressroom about 200 feet down the corridor. Once the players had completed their pregame skate, it had become apparent that the game would be delayed. And still no Ziegler, although theories abounded, including one that he was tending to a family emergency.

At game time the Devils called a press conference during which the club's vice president for public relations, Larry Brooks, read a statement from Lamoriello:

> The New Jersey Devils cannot tolerate the injustice that has been done to Jim Schoenfeld and our organization. We are owed the right of a hearing and appeal.

> Two weeks ago, when [our player] Brendan Shanahan became involved with a member of the Washington Capitals, the league conducted a hearing in my office within 36 hours of the altercation. Yet in this case, with the future of the franchise at stake as well as the reputation of our coach, Jim Schoenfeld, Brian O'Neill did not convene an official hearing.

No less potent was Lamoriello's postscript that "a hearing was required because the officials filed reports to the league which were clearly false. We cannot accept this."

The suggestion was that the linesmen and Koharski had trumped up the story that Schoenfeld had actually knocked over the referee. Witnesses insist that no contact was made by the coach and referee. The Devils refused to be intimidated—and they were absolutely correct in taking that stand.

The on-ice officials were dead wrong in their refusal to work the game. By contract they were obliged to take the ice; it was their duty to the league, to the players, and to the fans. It was anarchy, compounded by the absence of President Ziegler.

At 7:45 P.M. the players took the ice as a prelude to the national anthem, but the referee and linesmen were missing. McCauley then informed Coaches Schoenfeld and Terry O'Reilly that the NHL-assigned officials had refused to take the ice. After a confused few moments on the ice, the players gradually returned to their dressing rooms.

The Byrne Meadowlands Arena was filled to capacity with fans awaiting the game's start, although no official notice was provided about the delay. Once the regular officials stated that they would not go on, McCauley rounded up three off-ice officials—Paul McInnis, Jim Sullivan, and Vin Godleski, each of whom had considerable officiating experience on the collegiate and amateur level. McInnis donned the black-and-white striped referee's uniform while Sullivan and Godleski wore yellow scrimmage sweaters. Those sweaters would inspire the term "Yellow Sunday."

NHL Board Chairman Bill Wirtz was contacted. He told the officials that they had a contractual obligation to officiate the game. When they again refused, he ordered Denis Morel—the standby referee—to substitute, but Morel also declined.

Jim Beatty, a Toronto lawyer representing the officials' association and the individual who was counseling Newell et. al., proposed a compromise that would place Schoenfeld in the press box with headphones, orchestrating his club from above. Bruins' general manager Harry Sinden rejected the idea. Notorious for his criticism of officials, Sinden snapped, "We don't need you guys." Thus, Sinden was lining up behind the league—and, in effect, Lamoriello.

I was in and out of the studio, at once trying to obtain the latest information and also working with my colleagues Gary Thorne and Peter McNab in the overhead booth. At one point Devils' owner John McMullen popped his head out of the Devils' trainer's room.

"Will we have a game?" I asked him.

"I'd better not talk to you now," he demurred, "but I think we'll work something out."

They did. McInnis, 52, Godleski, 51, and Sullivan, 50, eventually took the ice and handled the mean-spirited game. Considering the pressure, the importance of the game, and the fact that they were working before a full house, the three imports were both heroic and splendid as the Devils won the game.

All in all it was one of the most intense events I ever had the pleasure of covering. An afterglow of excitement permeated the arena long after the final buzzer had sounded. In the bowels of the arena near the pressroom, an area had been set aside for postgame interviews. Godleski, Sullivan, and McInnis were there mingling with friends and media. I walked over to the trio and shook their hands. "You did a really fine job tonight, guys," I said.

They smiled. "No comment," said Sullivan, a retired New York City cop.

Little did they know it at the time, but their decision to officiate would mark the beginning of a long-running feud between the league officials and the New Jersey off-ice people, not to mention the referees and the Devils.

Godleski would later tell me that linesman Pat Dapuzzo, who had been nurtured through the New Jersey hockey ranks by the likes of Godleski, would pointedly ignore his former mentors in protest against their action.

Once the fallout of the game had ended, attention shifted to the NHL high command and its next move. More particularly, the question on every hockey person's lips was, "What happened to John Ziegler?" The president's extended absence had turned into a huge embarrassment to the league.

On Monday O'Neill still was at the helm in distant Montreal and minus the president. He announced that the NHL would conduct a formal hearing on the Schoenfeld matter on Tuesday in Boston. This pleased the Devils, who firmly believed that the officials' charges were fabricated and that witnesses and videotape would back up Schoenfeld.

Meanwhile, inexplicably, the officials called off their walkout and acknowledged that they would work the remainder of the series. Nevertheless, they had broken a contract while placing the playoffs in jeopardy. All three should have been suspended and fined. Instead, no disciplinary action was taken—a spineless move by the NHL and one that signaled to the officials that walkouts would not result in punishment. It would be a decision that in years to come would have far-reaching effects on the power and independence of referees and linesmen.

By this time Ziegler's absence had become the source of conjecture throughout the league, providing a field day for columnists and television commentators. When the president finally surfaced again publicly on Tuesday, May 10, he ducked questions concerning his whereabouts during the New Jersey crisis.

"Where I was is my personal business," he insisted. "I answer to the board and nobody else." The media were astonished by this arrogant and obdurate comment.

Ziegler's rationale was that he had chosen to take a break between league business and the following round, the Stanley Cup finals. Perhaps it was a reasonable excuse, but under the circumstances the perception that he was ducking his duty became a major issue that his many enemies in the media seized with delight. Not surprisingly, the president—notorious for watching most NHL games at home rather than at the rinks—was asked when he had last been at a game in person. Again Ziegler declined to comment.

At the conclusion of the nearly three-hour hearing, Ziegler required another hour to deliver his ruling. Schoenfeld was suspended one game and fined $1,000. The Devils received a $10,000 fine, and the series resumed.

"It's the kind of thing you wished never happened," said Ziegler. "But the league will survive." (One wag was heard to snipe, "It's a marvelous game, to be sure, to have survived this guy for 11 years!")

The league would survive, but John Ziegler's presidency would not. Yellow Sunday alone would not topple his administration because Ziegler still was propped up by the Wirtz-Eagleson duo, along with several other governors with less power but fully supportive of their chief executive. Other blunders would have to take place to undermine his regime—and they did.

One that was self-inflicted concerned the president's Achilles' heel—public relations. Somewhat diffident in public, Ziegler perceived that he had been unfairly victimized by the media. He tended to downplay the role of his public relations department, leaving it in the care of Steve Ryan, an affable fellow whose primary expertise was in marketing and merchandising. Although Ryan was titular head of the PR bureau, he rarely had others to help him.

The PR role was ably handled by John Halligan, despite unseen "controls" by Ziegler, until 1986, when the veteran pro moved over to Madison Square Garden, where he ran the Rangers' publicity office. Ryan lured author–hockey nut Jack Falla into the PR job, but it turned into an overnight disaster. A writer by trade, Falla couldn't adapt to the Madison Avenue mode and exited the job almost as quickly as he entered.

Next in line was Gerry Helper, a sincere, competent type whose surname befitted his work habits. Helper lasted at the NHL's New York office until 1991, when he opted for a job as publicist for the new Tampa Bay Lightning franchise. In the interim Ziegler made a decision that not only could be considered obtuse, but thoroughly counter to the direction the NHL should have gone.

Incredible as it may seem, Ziegler decided to dismantle the public relations department in his New York (main) office. The publicity function would hereby be handled long-distance from the league's outpost in Rexdale, Ontario, which heretofore had been limited to such functions as officiating, scheduling, and other lesser duties. At best, it was a monumentally unwise move—Ziegler's answer to his media critics.

This was completely counter to the policies of competing major sports such as the National Basketball Association—the NHL's prime challenger—Major League Baseball, and the National Football League. Each correctly reasoned that it was imperative to have a robust, aggressive, and very evident PR department in the world's media capital.

When I directly challenged Ziegler on his decision to eliminate the New York PR office, his rationale was typical of the thinking that had bedeviled the NHL under his administration. "We're streamlining our organization," he said.

"What does that mean?" I asked.

"We're in the age of electronics," he replied. "We can get all the information we want from Toronto in a matter of seconds."

Not having a league public relations presence in New York City was akin to Bill Clinton not having a press aide and media department at the White House. Ziegler ignored the criticism. He signed a pair of expensive Toronto media specialists who had specialized in politics. Bill Wilkerson and Fraser Kelly operated a Toronto PR outfit, and they became Ziegler's consultants.

So quiet was the hiring that for months nobody among the press was aware that Ziegler had employed the pair. But gradually they slipped into the picture and I met them—one-on-two—one morning at the league's New York headquarters.

Two things were immediately clear: (1) they knew virtually nothing about hockey, and (2) they had a mandate from Ziegler to revamp the public relations sector. Their response was to further solidify the Canadian operation, which would be conveniently close to their own Toronto office. Wilkerson in particular had become a much more public figure within the NHL hierarchy, although he never was officially on staff. Gary Meagher, who had been handling NHL publicity out of Toronto, remained the official league spokesman and a competent one at that.

Every so often Wilkerson would prove himself effective as a go-between when Ziegler and his media antagonists would clash. Once, I wrote a column for the *Hockey News* suggesting that Ziegler had not been forceful enough in repudiating carpetbagging owners.

A few days after the column appeared, I received a harsh, handwritten letter from the president, more sharply critical than I thought the column deserved. Apparently, Ziegler had mentioned the letter to Wilkerson because the PR man called me suggesting that we meet for breakfast.

I left that meeting impressed with Wilkerson and wondering whether the president ever would get the hang of public relations.

Some observers believed that he was loosening up; that Wilkerson was having a soothing effect on Ziegler; that the president could still recoup the prestige lost by his disappearance in the 1988 debacle, as well as other leadership transgressions that had occurred over the years.

Ziegler might have cleared the hurdles except for a chain reaction of circumstances, beginning with the decline of Wirtz's power, the eventual ouster of Alan Eagleson as union boss, and a series of harsh journalistic works by such diverse writers as a sports editor for a small New England daily to a Vancouver husband-and-wife team with little previous knowledge of hockey.

The combination of David Cruise and Alison Griffiths' book, *Net Worth*, and Russ Conway's seemingly endless exposé of NHL misdeeds in the *Lawrence Eagle-Tribune* (Massachusetts) helped to irrevocably turn the tide against John Ziegler. It finally reached the point where the combined efforts of Wilkerson and Kelly were ineffective.

But the ultimate coup de grâce was supplied by the players themselves, who called the first leaguewide strike in NHL history. The strike and Ziegler's tepid personal response to it proved to be the chute that slid him right out of the presidency.

This was sad because, when all was said and done, Ziegler seemed like a pleasant, decent man away from the ice.

THE 1992 STRIKE AND
REPLACEMENT OF JOHN ZIEGLER

To the average hockey fan, the idea of a players' strike seemed incomprehensible. During the decade spanning 1982–92, salaries continued to rise despite the fact that the National Hockey League was bereft of a network television contract in the United States. By contrast, Major League Baseball, the National Football League, and the National Basketball Association all were beneficiaries of major "rights" fees from U.S. networks.

Playing in the NHL during most of the Ziegler regime was a decent deal for a skilled performer. Wayne Gretzky, then playing in Los Angeles, was making more money than ever, and the once-tiny list of stickhandling millionaires was growing by the year despite some halfhearted attempts by ownership to curb the inflationary spiral.

Despite his innumerable blunders in the areas of leadership, marketing, and public relations, Ziegler entered the nineties in reasonable control of his organization and gubernatorial constituency. He continued to supervise and to rule by carefully selected committee, isolated his foes, and maintained a strong personal and professional alliance with union boss Alan Eagleson. The president's house, at least superficially, appeared to be resting on reasonably strong piles that had been driven in years earlier. But, as Ziegler soon would learn, major fissures began appearing in the foundations.

The cracks were caused in such diverse precincts as Edmonton, Alberta, and Lawrence, Massachusetts. I learned of the "Edmonton Connection" years earlier. Back in the early seventies when Eagleson was reaching the peak of his powers, I challenged his stewardship of the union and, in return, felt the Eagle's wrath. Through his union's offices, Eagleson attempted to ban me from all the team dressing rooms on the grounds that I was spreading seditious antiunion propaganda.

Rather than accept his ban, I challenged it. At the time, I was New York Bureau Chief for the *Toronto Star* and decided to use the newspaper clout in my Eagleson war. The Ontario Press Council believed that I had a good enough case to order a hearing at which Eagleson was present. They ruled that Eagleson had wrongfully attempted to impose an anti-Fischler ban. He publicly apologized—almost unheard of for Eagleson at the time—then put his arm around me and indicated that we'd now be friends.

I was amazed at the Eagle's absence of rancor and his instant willingness to patch up our feud. Frankly, his hail-fellow-well-met attitude thoroughly won me over. I soon came to regard Eagleson as much a friendly source as I had previously treated him as a foe. Now, in our new relationship he proved a reasonably good provider of information and certainly a ready and easy quote. No matter the topic, the Eagle was ready to chirp with a reply, a newsman's delight.

But as his power grew, so too did concern about his multiple roles. On the one hand, he was czar of the union; on the other, he was a player agent, leader of Canada Cup tournaments, and, of course, a pal of NHL power brokers, especially John Ziegler and Bill Wirtz.

Whenever challenged about his many hats, Eagleson would matter-of-factly dismiss the suggestion of impropriety with a wave of the hand and a chuckle. "I make no secret about what I do," he would say. His contention was that he could adequately serve his player constituency, the NHL Players' Association, as well as the other organizations without damaging his or their credibility.

For considerable time Eagleson was able to maintain his multiple roles. Canada's journalistic establishment didn't challenge him for apparent reasons. It lauded the Eagle's accomplishments and also enjoyed his company, too much to seriously challenge hockey's newest icon.

In the United States, where Eagleson was considerably less known, *Sports Illustrated*'s managing editor Mark Mulvoy went after the Eagle. After what seemed like years of research, the magazine's "exposé"—apparently bedeviled by legal constraints—was lukewarm rather than hot and caused hardly a tremor in the Eagleson empire. The word went out in the journalistic fraternity: if *Sports Illustrated* couldn't bring Eagleson to his knees, nobody could.

Which explains why I paid little attention to a large brown envelope I received in the mail one day, postmarked Edmonton. The name on the return address was Rich Winter, someone I had vaguely remembered as an agent but not one of the stature of Eagleson, Art Kaminsky, and others who dominated the business at the time.

I couldn't imagine what Winter wanted of me until I opened the envelope and began poring through the material. Page after page dealt with Winter's personal indictment of Eagleson and his practices. It detailed alleged abuses, conflicts of interest, and assorted other examples of Eagleson's supposed misdeeds as the union leader.

For sheer bulk alone the package was impressive, but in my case Winter's timing was wrong. It arrived during a week when I was snowed under with writing and television assignments, allowing me virtually no time to study the documents. Nevertheless, my curiosity was piqued, so I phoned Eagleson to obtain his comment on the contents and on Winter.

I got the impression that Eagleson did not consider Winter a threat. "I wouldn't waste my time with him if I was you," he said.

After hanging up, I took another look at the mass of documentation and then put the envelope in a steel drawer, closed it, and conveniently forgot about it and Winter.

Eagleson wasn't so lucky. Whatever his faults—and his critics will waste no time elaborating on them—Winter was smart and not lazy, nor easily deterred. Although other agents such as Kaminsky were willing to assail the Eagle from time to time, Winter had launched an impressive crusade and would not be daunted.

Undiscouraged by journalists like me, who tended to dismiss or ignore him, Winter redoubled his efforts. By the mideighties he had an ally in a California-based agent named Ron Salcer, who was fast becoming a name in the business. Winter and Salcer soon enlisted ex-NFL Players' Association leader Ed Garvey to support their dump-Eagleson movement. By the late eighties it began gaining momentum; Eagleson appeared unaware that a hurricane was about to blow over his carefully crafted tower of hockey cards.

Garvey—an expert—began zeroing in on the Eagle's modus operandi. In 1989 he wrote a report on Eagleson's spending practices. "There are no limits on his travel expenses," Garvey noted, "and he has refused to allow us to examine his expense records. We are not really looking for a dinner here or there, we were trying to find out if you, his employers, are able to review his records. The answer is no."

As the crescendo of criticism finally caught the media's attention, Eagleson had to take note of his tormentors. Those of us who had frequently dealt with the Eagle began realizing that, right or wrong, his scalp was in danger as the decade of the nineties began. As for the media, there was just too much smoke in the Eagle's complicated dealings for there not to be a fire.

Eagleson's treatment of his critics essentially remained the same; they were jealous know-nothings who, more often than not, ignored his contributions to The Game or were outsiders trying to make a name for themselves inside a burgeoning sport.

"I'm sick and tired of worrying about Ed Garvey," said Eagleson. "I am concerned about the players in the National Hockey League, not some of these outsiders who have not contributed anything to the game."

Knowing Eagleson much better than I did Garvey, of whom I knew very little, I accepted Eagleson's critique—again. Yes, the Eagle was flawed, but he had done much to raise the union's standards. He had helped his constituents to steadily rising salaries, whether his critics wanted to accept it or not. I and most of my journalistic colleagues were willing to plod the same route because at least in print, Eagleson remained the Teflon man.

There was, however, one fatal exception. Russ Conway, the determined reporter who had become sports editor of the *Lawrence Eagle-Tribune*, had been a longtime friend of Hall-of-Famer Bobby Orr and other former Boston Bruins, some of whom had felt ethically and financially betrayed by Eagleson.

By national standards, the *Eagle-Tribune* is a newspaper unknown beyond New England. The same could be said for Conway as a reporter, that is, until 1990, when he launched his investigation of Eagleson's performance in office.

However, the Eagle already was heading out the NHLPA's door. The Winter-Salcer-Garvey axis had gained so much support that Eagleson finally was forced to launch a search for a successor with a target date for his ultimate resignation from the union in 1992. Meanwhile, the groundswell of interest in Eagleson's performance grew, thanks to the late night probing at the *Lawrence Eagle-Tribune*.

Despite the newspaper's and Conway's relative obscurity, the two worked to bring down hockey's most powerful figure. Conway already had a track record as an investigative reporter and—no less important—had the support of his editor, Daniel J. Warner, who provided infinite time and sufficient resources for Conway to probe the union boss. This was very unusual for a small, New England newspaper.

"Sometimes duty causes us to go beyond local boundaries," said Warner. "Conway saw such a duty when he detected over the years of covering his beat that something was seriously wrong inside the National Hockey League. So he went inside to take a look."

Over a period of a year Conway interviewed more than 200 people, including retired and active professional players, NHL officials, and others in the hockey world. Many of the interviews were taped and in-depth. According to the reporter, more than 1,600 phone calls were made or received and more than 150 documents, totaling thousands of pages, were reviewed.

In time Eagleson and Ziegler got wind of the investigation. During one telephone conversation with me, the Eagle dismissed Conway in the same manner that he had Rich Winter years earlier. Eagleson understood that Conway was pals with Eagleson's ex-client-turned-adversary Bobby Orr and insisted to me that the entire assault on his honor was Orr-inspired and therefore more a matter of jealousy than substance.

Conway forged ahead. When he attempted to obtain interviews with Eagleson and Ziegler, he was rebuffed. "They answered with letters from lawyers," said Conway. "Ziegler also ordered NHL employees not to talk with me about the investigation."

No matter. Conway persisted, and the more he dug, the more delectable information he discovered. In September 1991 he published the first of many installments in a series titled "Cracking the Ice—Intrigue and Conflict in the World of Big-Time Hockey." Not surprisingly, some of Conway's prime targets were Eagleson and Ziegler.

"Behind the upheaval in the NHL," Conway wrote in the third paragraph of his first installment, "are found charges by players that they have been betrayed not only by the league but also by their own union's executive director, R. Alan Eagleson."

Conway's probe accelerated as Eagleson's protesting momentum decelerated. In the summer of 1990 a Detroit lawyer-agent, Bob Goodenow, had edged out another agent, Steve Bartlett, as NHLPA executive director. It was to emerge as one of the most telling turning points in the history of the NHL. From that moment on, Goodenow began laying the groundwork for new collective bargaining agreement talks that resulted in the strike of April 1, 1992, and a metamorphosis of hockey politics.

Notorious for his hard-nosed style as a player-agent, Goodenow was the beneficiary of a number of events, not the least of which was the Conway series, as well as a book authored by a Canadian husband-and-wife team with no known hockey connections.

I first heard the names Alison Griffiths and David Cruise in 1990 via a phone call from the former who identified herself as a writer from Victoria, British Columbia. "I'm researching a book on hockey," she said, "and was wondering whether you could help?"

An introduction such as that had come across my wire dozens of times, and I readily agreed to provide any useful information she needed. It didn't take long for me to deduce that Griffiths and Cruise were embarking on a powerful bit of journalism, particularly when she began grilling me about Eagleson.

I told her about my experience with Eagleson—the anti-Fischler move within the NHLPA—and its settlement. She asked me for additional contacts, and I provided them on the assumption that Griffiths would have done the same had the positions been reversed.

That marked the first of many conversations with Griffiths. Occasionally I had telephone chats with her husband, who seemed less involved in the project. If I came away with one impression above others, it was that neither was what we in the industry regarded as a "hockey person." I mentioned at least once to Griffiths that this could be a terrific asset to her rather than a liability. Judging by the results, it apparently was more plus than minus.

Cruise and Griffiths had previously won awards for such non-hockey works as *Fleecing the Lamb* and *Lords of the Line* and were now applying their diligence with equal verve to the NHL. Griffiths had mentioned in passing one day that their original purpose was to focus on Eagleson, the character. It was only after significant probing that they widened the scope of their work to an all-encompassing assault on the hockey establishment.

The book was slated for publication in the fall of 1991, and as often is the case with such editions, the authors attempted to obtain as much publicity as possible. One way to do so was to send advance copies to those who might be willing to help the project along.

Because I then was writing a weekly column in the *Hockey News*, I was a prime source of space for Griffiths and Cruise, and because the couple were going to be spending time in New York City, they suggested that we finally meet for an interview.

With the approval of the *Hockey News's* editor Steve Dryden, I told Griffiths and Cruise that I'd read the book before our meeting and then arranged my questions before the interview. We agreed to meet at the Paramount Hotel in Times Square, a hostelry that in another era had been the hotel for visiting NHL teams.

Net Worth, their brand-new book, arrived in the mail a few days before they arrived in Manhattan. I immediately plunged into it with enormous interest. From the start, I sensed that it would be a very special read, and by the time I had read a dozen pages, my attention was riveted to the text.

Net Worth eventually became a bestseller and played right into Bob Goodenow's hands. Here was a book that he could distribute to every one of the union members as a "bible" listing the debits and transgressions of the Eagleson-Ziegler-Wirtz triumvirate and the pluses that would come from the enlightened new NHLPA boss. To no one's surprise, it also solidified the NHL Players' Association's resolve as it entered into negotiations for the 1991 collective bargaining agreement.

Having covered hockey professionally since 1954, I was into my 37th year on the NHL beat when talk of a possible strike began wafting across pressrooms throughout the league. When I heard such talk, I laughed—and argued—with people and players.

Strike! Players were now averaging more than $300,000 a year, and the fiscal skyrocket still was climbing toward the stratosphere. These were athletes who played an average of three times a week and were getting paid vacations for the months of June, July, and August. They were usually catered to, hand and foot; they often operated businesses on the side; they were quartered at the best hotels; they dined at the best restaurants; and they were often asked to actually perform for less than 25 minutes per game. For a deal like that, receiving an average salary of $300,000 in 1991 seemed like a pretty good deal to me.

I didn't think a strike was much in the minds of many players, the media, or the fans, although one of them, a friend of mine from the New York Islanders, was very vehement about it. Ray Ferraro had heard me do an interview on New York's sports-radio station WFAN about a potential strike. "It won't happen," I said, "because hockey players simply are not that stupid to turn down the cushy life they have."

Ferraro phoned and suggested that I had missed the point— that the union was misrepresented by its previous leader and now it was playing catch-up and maybe a strike was a necessity. We talked for more than a half-hour and agreed to disagree. Never did I believe that the players—most still from Canada— would walk out on themselves, the fans, and the ownership.

But I hadn't taken into account the cleverness and ferocity of Bob Goodenow's leadership since he had taken over from Eagleson; nor had the owners. However, Ziegler must have understood that, in labor terms, they were in bed with a crocodile.

My encounters with Goodenow were very pleasant to this point. We shared a table at a *Hockey News* award luncheon and spent considerable time discussing the strike of the Hamilton (Ontario) Tigers' players in 1925 that led to dissolution of the team and its move to New York (Americans). Goodenow proved very helpful in supplying me with lists of agents for the *Fischler Report*, my weekly hockey newsletter, and seemed a most cordial fellow.

Obviously, Goodenow was putting his best face forward. "He's not the same affable guy when you get down to real business," an agent stated a few weeks later. "Bob called the other day and bawled the hell out of me about a contract I had negotiated. He said I wasn't tough enough."

In time I would hear similar complaints from other agents; the prevailing theme was that Goodenow would jump all over them if he felt they weren't fighting hard enough for their clients.

The union boss would become the "hardballer" he wanted his colleagues to be. The proof was in the negotiations. In September 1991, Goodenow broke off collective bargaining agreement talks with the owners. Ziegler warned that if the union got its way, the average NHL salary by 1994 would be $680,000. This time he was close to being prescient. Ziegler, trying to be stern, further cautioned that the teams couldn't absorb it.

By now player skepticism about the NHL operation in general and Eagleson in particular had mushroomed to such an extent that rank-and-file stickhandlers simply couldn't care less about Ziegler's projections. They obviously thought the prexy, to quote the Bard of Avon, "doth protest too much."

It hardly mattered to NHLPA members that they were richer than ever and expansion guaranteed them more job opportunities than big-league hockey players had ever enjoyed. Whenever a critic of runaway inflation—like myself—would complain to a Ray Ferraro, he would answer that nobody was twisting the owners' arms to pay the salaries.

He was right, to an extent. Owners such as Bruce McNall in Los Angeles and Mike Shanahan in St. Louis (the Blues' chairman, but not owner) had been overspending on the likes of Wayne Gretzky and Scott Stevens. "Some owners have opened the floodgates," said Flyers' owner Ed Snider. "We have gone the way of our brothers in baseball and basketball in terms of overspending, but we don't have the TV money to bail us out." (This admission, incidentally, from the owner who would, in 1992, pay $15 million cash, plus players, just for the rights to Eric Lindros.)

The stalemate between owners and players moved into the season's homestretch with no breakthrough. Goodenow was forcing a showdown, and the issue was a better deal for his players.

He was prepared to make the owners blink. In the mind of some critics the players were going too far. One of these critics was Pat Doyle of the *Winnipeg Sun*.

"The players want and want and want," said Doyle. "They fret and frown over free agency. Their wish is to come and go as they please and, under present NHL legislation, it's their belief that harsh compensation limits movement.

"Not true. Mark Messier wanted out of Edmonton; he's in New York. Dale Hawerchuk wanted out of Winnipeg; he's in Buffalo. Adam Oates wanted out of St. Louis; he's in Boston. Doug Gilmour wanted out of Calgary; he's in Toronto.

"So, who needs free agency? If you desire a change of scenery, all you have to do is demand, whine, pout or sulk; or, all of the above. Eventually, you'll get your wish."

What Goodenow and the union really wanted was a fight. They had developed the notion that, no matter how much money they were making, they would be perceived as wimps. "If we back down now," said one player, echoing the prevailing macho thought, "we're stupid. It will be perceived as a sign of weakness."

Notice, there was no mention about how much better the average player's standard of living had become, although there remained a precious few NHLPA members with the courage to put Eagleson and his contributions in a more realistic perspective. One of them was veteran forward Bobby Smith, who had been an NHLPA executive for nine years.

"It has become very popular to dump on the Eagle," said Smith. "People are making a mistake commonly made, judging things that happened in 1983 and 1986 by 1992 standards. No one was paying $50 million for franchises then. A lot of teams weren't making money.

"That's not the reality now. Times have changed. Salaries are higher than anyone thought they would be. Alan has been unfairly slighted."

Unfortunately, Smith's voice was muffled by the union leadership and, particularly, by Goodenow. Those of us who believed that the already well-off players would avoid disrupting the orderly flow of the season were sadly mistaken.

Incredibly, the strike happened. It was early April 1992. I had a firsthand view of it, primarily because most of the major meetings between owners and players were held in Manhattan, close to my home. The elegant Plaza Hotel at the southern tip of Central Park became press headquarters, and it was there that much of the bad guessing among the media took place.

This is not meant so much as a criticism of my colleagues as it is an attempt to portray to the average fan how distant the rank-and-file newsperson standing on the outside actually is from the inside reality.

I recall one meeting that took place in the morning. The owners broke for lunch, and as they paraded down the corridor, we attempted to get some clues as to the direction in which the talks were headed. For a moment someone caught Flyers' President Ed Snider smiling, and, immediately, this was interpreted as a sign that progress was being made. (It wasn't.) Yet this type of misinterpretation was more the rule rather than the exception.

On Saturday, April 4, 1992, day four of the strike, the *Toronto Star*'s Bob McKenzie threateningly suggested that the Monday board of governors' meeting "will ultimately determine" if the strike "is going to be long and destructive."

He went on to quote Minnesota (soon to be in Dallas) North Stars' owner Norman Green: "If we don't reach an agreement on Monday, it won't be done."

Of course, there was no agreement on Monday or Tuesday or Wednesday or Thursday—but it would be done, nonetheless. In the meantime, Goodenow bared his fangs and Ziegler exposed his sensitivity. When the dust of battle had cleared, the union leader's grasp of the jugular and the president's inept and soft defenses would ultimately doom Ziegler and cast Goodenow in the role of the menacing power broker.

Eagleson, for all his bluster and his alliances with ownership, was a true hockey aficionado. Those who dealt regularly with the Eagle sensed that he truly loved the game. Whatever his personal goals, Eagleson wanted the NHL to succeed for hockey's sake nearly as much as his own.

Goodenow was another question and required much more study. But his critics were now being heard from. "Goodenow has transformed the 30-second sound byte to a sleep exercise," said *Toronto Sun* columnist Steve Simmons in what may have been the understatement of the decade.

On this night at the Plaza, as the union boss rejected Ziegler's plaintive offer, I suffered an ache in the pit of my stomach that delivered a message: the NHL as I knew and loved it never would be the same, at least not as long as Goodenow ran the show.

My former intern, Vic Morren, now a hockey producer for ESPN, was with me at the time and shared virtually the same emotion. Not long afterward, we walked out of the hotel and, by accident, happened to meet Kevin Lowe, the then Edmonton Oilers' defenseman with whom I had written a book, *Champions*. I was somewhat astonished as Lowe indicated that the strike might be a long one and even more surprised as he mentioned how difficult the owners' position was for the union to accept.

As Morren and I headed toward the subway station, we turned to each other. "Here's another guy who's making a ton of money and he's still not satisfied," I said.

Another memorable vignette took place on the first Sunday of the strike. That morning word circulated among the media that Mark Messier was calling a special press conference to articulate the union's position. It was an unusually cold spring afternoon when Messier, Andy Moog, Mike Gartner, and other union executives gathered at a posh Park Avenue hotel. The idea was to persuade the media of the union cause and, supposedly, answer questions.

Sounding very much like a high school sophomore reading from the New Testament, Messier tried to articulate the players' position. He sounded more unctuous than sincere, and the question-and-answer period that followed did nothing to convince me that the unionists were a suffering lot.

I spent most of the week in and out of the Plaza as my anxiety quotient became more intense. With each day it seemed more likely that the sides wouldn't come to a compromise. By midweek Ziegler produced a third "final proposal," which was promptly rejected by the union. The president called it a "sad, sad day in NHL history," even suggesting that this could be the end of the NHL.

"I don't know who is more stupid," said Bruins' general manager Harry Sinden, "the owners for proposing the deal or the players for rejecting it."

I appreciated Sinden's hard line, but I also believed Ziegler was sincere vis-à-vis the NHL's overall welfare, although I'm sure that many would say I was duped by the president's style. I was only a few feet from Ziegler as he actually shed a few tears— "Could this be the end of the NHL, forever?"—during his Plaza Hotel press conference.

But the betrayal of the tears did as much harm to the president's image as anything since his "Koharskigate." Rather than empathize with the president's feelings, the media seized upon the sight of a weeping leader and re-created Ziegler as a weak-kneed wimp. The president's statements were a bit too whiny for most of the fourth estate.

Describing his offer on April 7, 1992, Ziegler virtually pleaded, "If it will make the players happy, if it will be the thing that gets them back to what they do best, playing the game, I will call it a surrender. I will call it an unconditional surrender. All they have to do is go back and play hockey."

Ziegler's words cemented Goodenow's resolve. The NHLPA head dug in his heels, and soon two words that would be bruited about

as much as any in the next three years were first uttered in the
NHL: "salary cap."

Aware that the rival NBA had become an immensely profitable (for both owners and players) business, NHL owners began
studying pro basketball's strategy, from marketing to budgeting.
One aspect of NBA planning that caught their attention was the
salary cap, which was crafted under the David Stern regime as a
means of regulating salaries while enabling players to enjoy fair
profits. That it worked to everyone's advantage was evident by
the NBA's overall popularity both at the gate and on television as
well as by the salary figures themselves. Many professional basketball players still were averaging more than $1 million annu-
ally under the new NBA salary cap.

Ziegler warned Goodenow that the NHL would pursue implementation of an NBA-style salary cap. "If they wish to save this
business," said Ziegler, "they'd better be interested [in the concept
of a salary cap]. If they think a partnership is we pay and they
get and take no risk, they've got the wrong idea."

Owners sought a 15 percent cap on salary arbitration raises
and an arrangement whereby leaguewide salary increases would
be limited to 15 percent. Judging by the manner in which the pay
scale was climbing, exploding even, this all made sense.

Chicago's Wirtz, who was familiar with the NBA cap because
of his association with the Bulls, pushed for its implementation.
"That's what all sports need—a salary cap," he said. "The only
thing that's fair is sharing revenue on a 50-50 basis."

Even assuming that Bill Wirtz and John McMullen were talking sense—and I thought they were—it was too late. Goodenow
smelled blood. The strike was now more than a week old, and
playoff monies, which the owners so dearly coveted, would be lost
if a settlement wasn't reached almost immediately.

On Tuesday, April 7, 1992, the owners produced an offer and
set a deadline of 3 P.M., Thursday, April 9, for the players to accept
it or face termination of the season. The players rejected it, but
the owners left it on the table to find ways of breaking the
impasse.

"I thought the season was over then and there," said Blackhawks' owner Bill Wirtz. "I'm usually an 'up' kind of guy, but I
was down then."

Many of us had come to the conclusion that the season would,
in fact, be lost. Goodenow appeared intransigent and impenetrable. The word among some members of the fourth estate was that
Ziegler needed a settlement in order to save his job.

On Wednesday, April 8, New Jersey Devils' President–General
Manager Lou Lamoriello convened a luncheon gathering of

metropolitan area hockey writers. Lamoriello delivered his—and the NHL's—position before throwing the floor open to questions. It was evident from the hostile tones and questioning of the newspeople that they were emphatically on the players' side. Lamoriello remained composed throughout the grilling, but at one point, Frank Brown of the *Daily News* got up and began filibustering about the union's right to strike, among other things. It was an interesting interlude but certainly not on the agenda. Perhaps I should have kept my mouth shut, but under the circumstances it was impossible. When Brown finished, I submitted that the time had come to impede the runaway salaries—that the owners should be doing that right now, whether the players liked it or not. I offered variations on the theme as passionately as possible because I fervently believed the players were demanding too much. When I had finished my peroration, I realized what I knew from the very beginning; I was in the distinct minority. No problem. I had gotten that off my chest and returned home to continue coverage of the strike. From time to time Ziegler and Goodenow would huddle in semisecret locations, including one quick visit to Toronto by the president and several owners.

Pessimism permeated the Plaza's press headquarters until 6 P.M. on Thursday night, April 9, three hours after the NHL's deadline had passed. Goodenow, a practitioner of 11th-hour negotiations, had reconvened with Ziegler.

Some of the old-line conservatives quite correctly were willing to go head-to-head with Goodenow and sacrifice the playoff riches, but the board of governors had divided into factions between liberals such as Norm Green and Howard Baldwin of the Pittsburgh Penguins and right-wingers like Wirtz, McMullen, and Jerry Jacobs of Boston.

"I'm not going to give up the store for one playoff year when the whole future is at stake," said Wirtz.

Had ownership accepted Wirtz's plan of battle and met Goodenow's challenge, the governors might have outlasted the union and beaten the new union boss before he won the respect of his troops. It was not unlike Germany's (illegal) occupation of the Rhineland in 1936. The German high command gambled that neither the stronger French nor English armies would call his bluff. Had either or both moved against the weaker, smaller German occupiers, Hitler would have been defeated, embarrassed, and possibly even prevented from ever occupying Austria and Czechoslovakia.

For an assortment of historical reasons, the Allies flinched and the result was World War II. Likewise, on Friday, April 10, 1992, word filtered throughout the Plaza Hotel pressroom that ownership was about to flinch. The salary cap, which might have imposed some economic sanity with a decelerated payroll sky-rocket, was in no part of the agreement. This was the most egre-gious omission, the one that would become a long-term time bomb that would explode in October 1994.

But ownership had no "book" on Goodenow's modus operandi and underestimated his willingness to play brinkman-ship politics. "Bob says 98 percent of a negotiation gets done the last two days," said Wirtz. "I don't understand that, but every-one's got his own style."

Owners made concessions up and down the line. The clubs agreed to recognize that the players own exclusive rights to their individual personalities, including their likenesses. This would prove to be a major cash cow for the stickhandlers.

The trauma the Canadian owners were suffering, and the pressure from Kings' owner Bruce McNall, agents, and marquee players such as Wayne Gretzky and Mark Messier, accelerated the rapprochement, which crystallized on Friday evening, April 10, at the Plaza. Those of us who had been in and out of the hotel all week sensed that the drama was reaching its climax around 9 P.M., when camera crews began setting up in a pressroom off the main lobby.

Many of us expected the chief protagonists to arrive before 10 P.M., hopeful that they would accommodate those who were on a deadline. But this was not to be. Now the clock was approach-ing midnight and some TV crews had packed up and left. Sud-denly, the room came alive with the buzz that always accompanies the prelude to a peace pact, whether labor or war.

Ziegler and Goodenow finally entered from stage right, adjusted the microphones, and the president declared, "We reached a meeting of the minds and an agreement in principle."

He looked wan, as anyone might after a 10-day marathon. It was difficult to discern whether either of the combatants had a physical edge on the other. I could see no significant differences, even in the smiles, as they indulged photographers with the usual postconference handshakes.

By sheer coincidence, my SportsChannel cameraman had packed up his equipment and loaded his car's trunk just as Goodenow and an aide were leaving the hotel. It was raining, and there were no cabs in the immediate vicinity. Goodenow needed some help.

"You want a ride?" I asked.

"Do you have room for two more?" he replied.

Pat Watters, the cameraman, drove a big Oldsmobile. There was more than enough room. Goodenow and his pal climbed into the back, and we headed west to his hotel. He seemed pumped without saying very much. The talk drifted to innocuous subjects. Goodenow was not giving away any state secrets, but inwardly he must have been savoring an emphatic victory.

My hope, among many, many others, was that something good would come of the conflict. Bruce McNall, who soon would replace Wirtz as chairman of the board of governors, was typically optimistic. "Long-term," McNall opined, "the strike will be very positive. You'll have a movement to where the sport needs to be, to a partnership between players and owners."

It sounded good at the time, but McNall was dreaming. He either underestimated Goodenow's motives or chose to ignore them altogether in a Candide-like imitation. Naturally, Goodenow mimicked the "partnership" theme, and the naive—or hopeful— believed him.

But Ziegler's bosses were less naive. They sensed that they had a bum deal, that the president had capitulated, and that new leadership was necessary. The wheels of change had begun moving against Ziegler, whose litany of problems dating back to 1988, and prior, were weighing against him.

This time the president's allies couldn't help him. Wirtz had been board chairman too long and the young Turks wanted him replaced, and Eagleson's wings had been clipped by the advent of Goodenow. There was talk of a brave, new NHL world on the horizon, but it would be one without John Ziegler at the helm.

FROM ZIEGLER TO STEIN
Punching Up the NHL's Image

You know the gag about the chap who kept hitting himself in the head with a big wooden mallet? When someone asked why he persisted in such apparent madness, the fellow replied, "Because it feels so good when I stop."

When John Ziegler resigned—after a monumental push—as NHL president in June of 1992, the mallet stopped hitting big-league hockey in the head. Not that Ziegler's fade to the wings automatically jump-started the sport to the top of the charts, or even to a U.S. network TV contract, but it at least signaled an end to the league's 16-year migraine. "During Ziegler's reign," TV sports executive Gil Miller mentioned to me one day, "hockey became the fastest growing game in the world; except in the National Hockey League!"

Evidence was available. Consider these doozies:

- Despite having 16 out of 24 teams based in the United States, Ziegler closed the NHL's New York City public relations office in 1991. The league was without a publicity outlet in the United States, which often left the media moguls strapped for data. "I called the New York office for some information about Eric Lindros," said Madison Avenue PR executive Chuck Alexander, "and the woman who answered didn't even know who he was. Eventually they referred me to Toronto."
- When the league's crown jewel, Pittsburgh's Mario Lemieux, was chopped down in the spring of 1992 by New York Rangers' slugger Adam Graves, Ziegler was not immediately heard from. "Ziggy Stardust," as he was known to *New*

York Daily News columnist Bob Raissman, uttered not even one adjective of protest while such august journals as the *Washington Post* and the *New York Times* skewered him.

• Marketing (this is just a euphemism for *sales*) was never a part of Ziegler's lexicon, or his persona. Even in the most obvious moments when the NHL could have reaped immense dividends.

Wayne Gretzky once was invited to be on "The Tonight Show" but found himself stranded in Chicago by a blizzard. The Great One could have reached L.A., but only by private jet. "Wayne offered to pay half out of his own pocket," said then Edmonton Oilers' defenseman Kevin Lowe, who was with Gretzky at the time, "but the league wouldn't foot the other half. Wayne never made it, and the NHL blew the Carson show." Sometimes it was simply flabbergasting.

• "Think small" was Ziggy's philosophy for dealing with everything from promoting marquee players to promoting himself. "I once recommended to John that he have his title upgraded from 'president' to 'commissioner,' but he shot me down," my late pal Harry Ornest, former owner of the Blues, mentioned. "Now that he's gone, the league is doing what Ziegler would never do: have a commissioner . . . and make him available to the media."

That was only one of the many changes as big-league hockey buried its Ziegler past. "What's needed is a total stripping down of the machine and a rebuilding," said TV analyst John Davidson. "Already we can see that the new administration is open to new ideas."

Total them up and you'll find as many cures for the NHL's ills as Eric Lindros has dollar bills. The transition would be painfully slow, but new leaders such as Bruce McNall couldn't wait to turn over a new puck. "We want to get out of the Dark Ages," said McNall, who succeeded Blackhawks' owner Bill Wirtz as chairman of the board of governors, "and already we're beginning to see the light."

One reporter said "Cousin Brucie's" problems were priorities, such as, if you have 100 very important things to do yesterday, which ones come first tomorrow? "Getting us back on U.S. network television is right up there with my primary objectives," said McNall. "We've got the best attraction, but we've got to get it across the country."

However, some Madison Avenue mavens believed Tie Domi had a better chance of winning the Lady Byng Trophy for sportsmanship than the NHL had of signing with NBC, CBS, or ABC. They insisted that the league's negative charisma quotient was directly attributed to players punching one another in the mouth. Fighting, they said, must go. Washington Capitals' general manager David Poile agreed. "We've got a great product," he said, "but we've given ourselves an image problem. We're walking a fine line between a great day and a bad one."

Like wizards crouched over a smoking cauldron, the NHL image changers were searching for the elixir that would transform the toad into a prince and make the game less akin to "Wrestlemania on Ice" and more of a utopian spectacle that combined clean hitting, lyrical skating, and slick stickhandling. They strove for the day when Baryshnikovs of hockey such as Pat LaFontaine could strut their stuff without taking a stick in the mouth. Imagine—may Bob Probert forgive us—an end to fighting as an NHL staple. Some power brokers said it would happen.

"This is a time for change," said then Minnesota North Stars' owner Norm Green. "People used to feel that fighting was an integral part of the game, but the people of the nineties are different from the people of the seventies. It's tough to explain to a mother whose youngster is about to play hockey what the rationale is for fighting."

Ever since *Tyrannosaurus rex* first stickhandled a boulder past a Brontosaurus, the rationales that connected hockey and fighting have been tradition and money. As former Toronto Maple Leafs' owner Conn Smythe proclaimed long ago, "If you can't beat 'em in the alley, you can't beat 'em on the ice." Besides, Smythe noted, fans pay money to see hockey players fight. Over the years, propagandists have endorsed the punch in the mouth as a "safety valve" for otherwise frustrated stickhandlers, and because attendance climbed to around 90 percent of capacity by the start of the nineties, Ziegler reasoned that fighting was not hurting the gate. Some owners believed that was right.

"We've sold every seat for years, and we're not in favor of radical changes in the rules," said Detroit Red Wings' executive vice president Jim Lites. "Aggressiveness is part of our game."

True, but suddenly hockey purists were making a keen distinction between clean aggressive play and gratuitous wood chopping. Exhibit A was Adam Graves' Paul Bunyan act on Lemieux in the 1992 playoffs. His bludgeoning of hockey's most majestic star was so outrageous that it invoked continentwide criticism of goonery. Lemieux unabashedly charged that the Blueshirts had "a contract" out on him and that the game was "too dangerous" in its current state. Penguins' owner Howard Baldwin immediately proposed that the league disinfect itself of

such muggings and filter out the filth while allowing the virtuosos to gain center stage once and for all.

There was only one problem: the officiating. Hockey referees
are a unique breed, a hybrid of zebras crossed with ostriches.
They have eyes and they wear stripes, but they bury their heads
while thugs endlessly perpetrate "restraining fouls" and muck
up what should be a magnificent spectacle. On a given night the
refs will allow at least 50 percent of the obvious fouls to go
unpunished. It happened in 1989 and continued through the
1999 playoffs. But not without reason, some claim.

"Too much goes on for one man to handle," said Scotty
Bowman, who coached the Pittsburgh Penguins to the 1992 Stanley Cup. "We have to have three referees. There's interference,
there's putting hands on the stick. With the one-referee system,
the official only tries to pick out the most flagrant fouls." Davidson agreed, adding, "Eliminating the fouls that hold back the
game's speed should be one of the league's highest priorities."

One of the many problematic aspects of hockey officiating,
according to my late friend Harry Ornest, himself a former
hockey referee, was that the president (meaning Ziegler) of the
NHL himself had known less than nothing about the officiating.
"Ziegler not only knew nothing about the officiating," said
Ornest, "but he made no effort to learn. He was irresponsible in
this, when it should have been a major function of his job. But
John fancied himself an elitist—above these petty concerns. He
was almost childish in this respect."

"Nobody was allowed to speak on anything without some
kind of censure," said *Vancouver Province* columnist Tony
Gallagher. "You talk about the libel chill—in this fiefdom, speech
was never free. It was the Hear-No-Evil League."

Censorship cut right across the NHL board. It even infected the
script prepared for Hollywood's Alan Thicke in June 1992 at the NHL
awards gala, which was carried over Canadian Broadcasting Corporation's TV network.

Thicke was forced to edit out references to the NHL players'
strike. "The people who criticize me for toothless humor should
have been sitting in the damn board room and seen how many
teeth were there before the chickens got their hands on them,"
said Thicke.

Partly because of the gag rule, the players themselves seldom
had anything to say. Or, if they did speak, too many of them
sounded more like Mortimer Snerd than the articulate athletes
they were. Compared to their basketball brethren, stickhandlers
are colossal bores, regurgitating bromides ("We've got to play 60
minutes") as if reciting the "Gettysburg Address."

More frustrating yet for interviewers such as myself, the league had become sprinkled with a new breed of nontalker: the European import. In the 1992 entry draft a record 11 Eastern Europeans were chosen in the first round. The Tampa Bay Lightning's number 1 pick, Czech defenseman Roman Hamrlik, had mastered enough English to report that his favorite food was "ham and eggs." After that the interviewer was in trouble. Ditto for writers who were hopeful of schmoozing with the Ottawa Senators' top pick, Alexei Yashin, a Russian who was great with "da" and "nyet," but otherwise could pass for a silent Gary Cooper. However, the language barrier was something the league, and the media covering the sport, had to accept, as it mined the mother lode of former Iron Curtain players.

This immigration may not have been a joy for journalists, but it did wonders for the league's talent quotient. "One reason why we finished first overall," said Rangers' president Neil Smith in 1994, "is because of the way [Russian] Sergei Nemchinov performed as a rookie. And you can say a good reason why the Penguins won the Stanley Cup was because of the help they got from [Czech] Jaromir Jagr. The Europeans are here to stay."

They had to be, if only to fill the rosters of an ever-expanding league. For a $50 million entrance fee, Ottawa and Tampa Bay obtained minimal talent—Lightning's president Phil Esposito described it as "all the crap thrown our way"—but maximum hope. Despite their impoverished lineups, leaders of both franchises were as optimistic as a newly elected president on Inauguration Day. "We've sold out every one of our [10,500] seats," said Senators' general manager Mel Bridgman, "and some of them are going for $100 a pop."

After a year of fiscal embarrassment, the Lightning appeared to be shaping up, and if the Tampa experiment succeeded, even more NHL seeds would be planted in the Sun Belt. "I can see another team in Florida," said Minnesota's Green (whose team was about to decamp the north and become the Dallas Stars), eyeing the Miami market, "and one in Texas. That would give us a nice spread in the warmer states and open the league's network possibilities."

Perhaps, but all of that was small potatoes compared with the NHL's prime challenges, otherwise known as the "Three Ls": labor, Lindros, and leadership.

Reverberations from the spring of 1992's 10-day players' strike were just being felt at the box office around November of that same year. Losing teams such as the Sabres raised their ticket prices 16 percent to 27 percent above 1991's numbers. Like other clubs that were hiking prices, the Sabres pointed to skyrocketing salaries as the prime reason. In Buffalo's case the payroll had gone up 69 percent in the past three years.

Prime-market clubs such as the Rangers and Kings had been able to feed the fat-cat players, but smaller-market teams such as Winnipeg and Hartford were unable to compete financially with the big-city boys. Under the circumstances, even the rich players were beginning to worry about the NHL's survival.

"We have to come up with a plan that makes it more attractive for players to play for smaller-market teams," said Mark Messier, "so that it doesn't matter what size the city or the market is. If there was a system like [the NBA salary cap], you'd see a lot of players would want to play in the smaller Canadian cities because those are the kinds of cities where they grew up."

Tell that to Lindros. The Ontario-born behemoth made beauteous Quebec City seem like the Black Hole of Calcutta with his unprecedented refusal to play for the Nordiques. The NHL then began to hold its breath, hoping that the "Next One" would be as good as the "Great One" when the Philadelphia Flyers paid Quebec $15 million in American funds (about $20 million Canadian) plus $3 million worth of traded players, as well as $22 million over six years to Lindros.

How good would Lindros be? At six feet four inches tall and 225 pounds, he loomed as an oversized Messier, which would be plenty good indeed. The lad was a steamroller in the slot and could also score. All signs suggested that he would fill seats in the manner of Gretzky. There was one big if, though: "Eric the Large" had yet to play an NHL game. "He may be the greatest thing since sliced bread," said Edmonton Oilers' general manager Glenn Sather, "but he had better be the whole loaf."

While the hockey world awaited "Lindrosmania," the NHL also was casting about for a new leader. Ziegler was dropped through the trapdoor so quickly that even his most rabid executioners were left empty-handed, without an instant replacement. Almost overnight there was a feeding frenzy. The list of potential successors included everyone but Dan Quayle (and even he would have obtained support had he known that hockey was played on ice).

In the interim the league knighted chief counsel Gil Stein as acting president. Stein quickly did one of the most arresting flip-flops since Dr. Jekyll and Mr. Hyde. Known as a quiet, dour legal eagle nesting in the NHL's Manhattan aerie, Stein suddenly flew busily into dozens of interviews like a sporting David Letterman. Every day he seemed to be in another city, making quips and spreading the NHL gospel (more like selling himself) while promising reform. Said one NHL general manager: "Gil visited more NHL cities in one month than Ziegler did in 15 years."

When one listened to Stein, it was possible to believe that a brave new world of hockey was just around the corner. He promised all manner of changes, from better media relations to enhancing the image of hidden stars. Obviously, the man had a grip on things. "The NHL is 75 years old," said Stein, "and hockey is still one of the best-kept secrets in the United States."

Ziggy was directly to blame for that. As Ornest told me, in what has to be one of the best summations of the Ziegler presidency, "John proved that he never failed to miss an opportunity to miss an opportunity."

What fascinated me most about the summer of 1992 was Stein's hell-bent bid for the new commissionership. I had known Stein ever since his days as legal counsel for the Philadelphia Flyers in the early seventies. Any student of NHL politics understood that Flyers' owner Ed Snider was Stein's patron, and when Stein moved to the league's New York office as its legal eagle, Stein became one of the most important aides to Ziegler.

To those of us who dealt with Stein on a one-on-one basis—not very easy, I might add—he oozed an avuncular affability. He was given to quick quips but just as suddenly would turn serious. Under the Ziegler regime, Stein had remained in the background—even further back than Ziggy—rarely granting interviews.

But the moment Ziegler departed, Stein was anointed "interim" president. Stein realized instantly that he had a shot at the top job. How he would obtain the commissionership was another story, because there never had been an NHL commissioner before, nor such an open field for the position.

I phoned Stein one day and suggested a meeting so I could discern his thinking. He told me that he was taking a couple of trips but would be glad to sit down when he returned. In the interim I followed his tour, which many believed was merely a blatant attempt to promote himself for the top job.

"He probably will win the NHL's top job on a permanent basis," said William Houston in the *Globe and Mail*. "But Stein's age (64) is a problem."

On a visit to Toronto, Stein said that fighting was presenting the NHL with an image problem and added that he thought it could be removed from the game completely. He added that a U.S. TV contract was critical to the league's success and said he would be talking to the heads of ABC, NBC, and CBS.

Aware of Ziegler's media phobia, Stein went on to promise a "more open" and less-abrasive relationship with the press. During an 18,000-mile transcontinental "goodwill" junket, Stein reiterated constantly that he was seeking "input" from the newspeople and fans.

"But during his meeting with us," added Houston, "he did not ask one question. Is this a fact-finding mission or a goodwill tour?"

Finally, I got the call; Stein was ready for our interview. Our meeting in his spiffy, well-appointed mid-Manhattan office was pleasant enough although it seemed as if Stein was a bit edgy. I immediately brought up the question of his age being a detriment to his bid, and he laughed it off. Like Houston, I got the distinct impression that Stein was less interested in improving league conditions than he was his own bid for the commissionership. I left his office less impressed than I had hoped I would be but convinced that he would make a powerful run.

Conceivably, he could have led the pack to the finish line, but Stein's heavy-handed campaigning began turning off key influential owners. Moreover, in his new position of power, McNall could influence the decision-making procedure. McNall once said to me, early on in the search, that "since the NBA is so successful, maybe I should try to get [Commissioner] David Stern to come over to our league." And he meant it!

Stern had no intentions of leaving his basketball realm, nor did his first deputy Russ Granik. If McNall still was interested in an NBA guy of note, there was one left, the third banana, Gary Bettman. Sure enough, McNall went after Bettman while the NHL went through the costly motions of hiring a headhunting firm to screen candidates.

As summer turned to fall 1992, Stein remained front and center in all discussions of succession, because he now occupied the throne—the term *interim president* was simply changed to *president*. He made no bones about his interest in staying at the top. Other prominent hockey people also were mentioned, including Washington Capitals' president Richard Patrick and general managers Bill Torrey and Glen Sather.

Stein's preoccupation with the commissionership had one lasting negative effect on the league's economic structure—ownership's desire for implementing a salary cap.

Following the 1992 strike settlement, both sides agreed to form a joint study committee to produce a restructuring of the business and avoid runaway inflation. Written into the collective bargaining agreement was a vital clause that should have been addressed head-on by Stein and his NHLPA counterpart, Bob Goodenow:

> Based on NHL economic studies and projections, the league and its member clubs believe that a continuation of the current system would have a serious negative impact on the business of hockey and hence the parties.
>
> Accordingly, the NHL clubs have expressed an intent to develop and submit to the NHLPA as promptly as possible a proposal for restructuring with a salary cap and a revenue-sharing concept. . . .
>
> The NHLPA commits that, as soon as reasonably practicable after the joint study committee report issues, it will begin bargaining in good faith with the clubs in an effort to reach agreement regarding restructuring by September 15, 1993.

Unfortunately, the joint study committee never was formed. As the *Canadian Press* observed, "Stein was too preoccupied with running for the office of NHL commissioner to worry about the joint study committee."

This would be a tragic omission. When the 1994 lockout took place, the union refused meaningful discussions on restructuring and the salary cap—as their signed agreement demanded—using the alibi that the joint study committee never had been formed.

As for Stein, his energetic bid for the chief executive's role was thwarted in the most unlikely place by the most unlikely opponent.

THE NBA-ING OF THE NHL
Enter Gary Bettman

Once Gil Stein had a full season (1992–93) to preside over the NHL as its president, he appeared to have the inside track for the soon-to-be-created commissioner's position. After all, an incumbent almost always is favored in a political contest, and Stein had been around the league for 15 years, enough time to develop friends in high places—also enough time to collect critics, even enemies, which Stein seemed to do with equal ease.

"Stein's work ethics were almost as inactive as Ziegler's had been," commented former owner Harry Ornest, with his usual dry wit. "In fact, I would have described their jobs as 'half-vacations, with big perks!'"

Bob McKenzie noted in the *Toronto Star*, "His [Stein's] appointment as president was thought to be interim by most everyone except himself." It was a most accurate appraisal of Stein's ego at work.

If nothing else, Stein was creative as he attempted to solidify his presidency. He recognized the importance of public relations and pledged to reopen the NHL's New York PR office. Unlike Ziegler, he showed up in as many arenas as possible, and he recognized the need to clean up the game. With McNall's backing, an edict was issued that called for the limitation of restraining fouls such as holding, interference, and hooking that braked the more artistic performers.

These logical and often-discussed (under Ziegler) moves were enthusiastically received by many critics. Many who had known Stein as the league counsel were astonished by his personality change. It was almost as if Darth Vader had become Dale Carnegie, or vice versa.

But what critics insisted was Stein's dark side also managed to make itself apparent with several shocking moves. Shortly after taking office, he dumped longtime vice president Brian O'Neill. The move caused considerable despair in Montreal. As Clarence Campbell's trusted deputy and heir apparent, O'Neill had relatively little authority.

Except for rare cases, O'Neill had handled all disciplinary matters, acting as Ziegler's stand-in during the infamous Koharski-Schoenfeld affair in 1988. O'Neill had his supporters and his share of detractors, myself among them. But, supported by Ziegler, he enjoyed protection from certain veteran hockey leaders. His abrupt firing by Stein shocked some in the NHL community but not everyone. It was a surprise, surely, although not nearly as much as Stein's new disciplinary moves.

At a time when the public was clamoring for increased punishment for misbehaving players, Stein incredibly went in the other direction. He launched a policy whereby suspended players would only be benched on nongame days. In effect, it was no punishment at all; it was merely silly.

One decision he rendered, which I thought made a lot of sense, was to redo the rules so that players could discard their helmets and play bareheaded. This would have added personality to a depersonalized game and create more identity between fans and players. It made a lot of sense—as long as rules against excessive stickwork and boarding would ensure that helmetless players could enjoy a reasonable measure of safety without the headgear.

Unfortunately, Stein did not sufficiently promote the nonhelmet campaign nor fortify it with the legislation that would have made it practical rather than the subject of ridicule among the media and a large bloc of players. Stein's ultimate downfall developed over his nomination to the Hockey Hall of Fame—a move that inspired an independent probe and, subsequently, a highly critical ruling against the president.

The Hall of Fame episode, however, took place long after Stein's presidential campaign concluded. A few months after the 1992–93 season had begun, the McNall-led board of governors had reduced the competition for commissioner to two individuals. Amazingly, only one of them had a hockey background and that was Stein, but his chances had been flawed by his questionable tactics over the past half-year.

Even more astonishing was the other aspirant for the top job. In a league notorious for its cocoonlike inbreeding, it was rare enough that an American such as Ziegler—and then Stein—would have the presidency, but at least their roots were in hockey turf. It was generally felt that ultimately Ziegler's successor would be a personality connected with The Game, be it Richard Patrick, whose grandfather Lester Patrick was in the Hall of Fame, or Bill Torrey, whose Islanders had won four straight Stanley Cups. Another possibilty was Ken Dryden, the goalie-author who had developed some absurdly Messianic quality after obtaining a law degree and then writing a book—*The Game*—that attained a biblical quality in some areas, although *Sports Illustrated*'s Mark Mulvoy once confessed to me that he found it a bore.

Neither Dryden nor Patrick made the final cuts. It came down to Stein, who in the end never had a genuine chance, and Gary Bettman, who had been a complete unknown outside the hockey industry but was well known in NBA circles as one of David Stern's lieutenants.

As third in command for the enormously successful National Basketball Association, Bettman was credited with stimulating the league's growth in several realms, including marketing and public relations. He was regarded publicly as the "Father of the salary cap" and the man who negotiated a new contract with NBA officials—although some insiders privately whispered that Bettman had simply done the paperwork on these deals and that it had been Stern and the second in command who had actually done all of the spadework.

I called Bettman the day his name appeared in the *New York Times* as Stein's prime competition. He was at his NBA office when I phoned and was as affable as a maitre d', sounding more like a fellow you'd share a beer with at a local pub than a high-priced member of the sports establishment.

"I hear you've got the NHL job," I said, "and I'm doing a [SportsChannel TV pregame] show tonight. Can I run with it?"

Bettman then revealed what would be his style with the media. If he trusted you—and he had no idea which way to go with me because we had never talked before—he'd give you off-the-record information or, as the case may be, even provide some on-the-record material.

"It's not official yet," he said, "so I don't want to say anything. But the minute I can talk, I'll sit down with you for an interview."

That sounded fair enough to me, so I decided to cool it until Bettman was ready to talk. In the meantime, I decided to feel him out. In all the years I had known Clarence Campbell, John Ziegler, or Gil Stein, I never felt comfortable enough to tell them a joke.

But Bettman seemed different. He had what New Yorkers would call a homey, "candy store" quality to him. He instantly signaled that *schmoozing* (Yiddish for idle gabbing) was one of his favorite pastimes. I gambled on a relatively bad joke that I had just heard, and he managed a chuckle while allowing that on a scale of one to ten, this bit of humor ranked about three.

No matter, Bettman was disarming and relaxed enough to indulge in some humor while also bantering about the sports business. A few weeks later he was officially appointed commissioner—Stein would remain "president" until June 1993, whereupon he would become special adviser to the commissioner. True to his word, Bettman called me to set up the interview.

We convened on a leather couch in his NBA office, which soon would be vacated. It was sprinkled with an assortment of promotional items, from autographed basketballs to mugs with team logos. He was, as he always would be (except for one occasion), so vibrant one would have imagined that he had stepped out of the morning shower only minutes earlier.

Before beginning the on-the-record interview, he launched into a number of topics, picking my brain about future decisions. One of his most critical would be the appointment of an aide-de-camp who was well versed in hockey.

"If I were you," I said, "I'd keep Brian Burke in mind. He's at Hartford [as the general manager at the time], but I think he'd make the move."

Bettman knew nothing about Burke so I amplified, pointing out that he had a law degree, had played the game, had been a player-agent for a while, and was hard-nosed yet excellent with the media. I had no idea whether he was seriously considering my thoughts, although I suspected that he had. (Burke got the job months later.) Bettman shot back that he had been very impressed with Glen Sather, president and general manager of the Edmonton Oilers.

"You'll never get him to move to New York," I said. "He likes Western Canada too much and has already rejected a lot of offers to move east."

Nevertheless, Bettman pointed out that he admired Sather enough to try to convince him to come or, that failing, try to get someone like him. I shot back that Burke was as close as he would get to a Sather—maybe even better because Sather had no background in law.

He asked me about the officiating. I told him that the refereeing department required a top-to-bottom overhaul and he had better make it a top priority. I also mentioned that I had just written a book of lists that included "John Ziegler's Eight Biggest Mistakes As NHL President." He wanted to hear them so I obliged.

1. He disappeared during the 1988 Devils-Bruins' playoff crisis, and to this day nobody knows where he was at the time.
2. His media relations were somewhere below minus-the-radical 50.
3. He appeared to spend more time in Europe than he did in North America.
4. He was seen so rarely at NHL games that he could have been put on the endangered species list, there had been so few sightings!
5. He closed the league's New York public relations department, leaving the NHL as the only one of four major sports without a publicity presence in the world's media capital.
6. He fought—rather than listened to—his friends, who became his critics.
7. He couldn't be found in the spring of 1992 when Mario Lemieux was chopped down by Adam Graves and a presidential decision was demanded by the public.
8. He ridiculed his employers—the 24 NHL governors—by saying the league needed a union-management partnership. "We need someone to protect the owners from themselves!"

He was amused and even more interested when I told him I was writing a column for the *Hockey News* in which I would list a few dozen pieces of advice. But it was time for the interview. He was quick to answer and rarely went off the record. The dialogue follows:

Stan Fischler: What are your top priorities as commissioner?
Gary Bettman: Over the next year, I've got to stabilize the franchises that need help, and I've got to stabilize the relationship with the Players' Association. Quite frankly, the two are interdependent upon each other.
Fischler: What do you see as your key to success? What makes Gary tick?
Bettman: Hard work. There's no substitute for applying yourself 199 percent in everything you do. When you have to deal with an issue or a problem or a project, you've got to know more about it than anyone else does. Then you've got to apply yourself to it, and then you've got to make it happen,

dotting every *i* and crossing every *t*. There is no substitute for execution in detail.

Fischler: What are your shortcomings?

Bettman: I may be too hard on myself. I have trouble accepting less than things going 100 percent right. When they don't, I tend to look at myself first in terms of what I could have done to make a difference, to make it perfect. Fortunately, here we haven't had too many missed steps at the NBA, but I believe I may drive myself too hard. But that's what happens when you are a type A personality.

Fischler: The NHL owners gave you a mandate. What are the top items on this mandate? What are they paying you to accomplish?

Bettman: I think what they want is a focus, an agenda, a vision for the future. We are going to try to take this sport to levels that it has never seen before. We need a good labor agreement. We need good marketing. We need good promotion. We need good television. We need to focus internationally. We need to do the things that a major professional sports league in the nineties must do.

There are going to be some issues—collective bargaining and television. There are going to be some new opportunities, new technologies. I think we can improve our marketing, our promotion, especially the promotion of our players. It's going to be my job to set an agenda that deals with all these issues and takes advantage of all the opportunities.

The sum and substance of all this will be to have a healthy sport that has a fan base much broader than it is right now.

Fischler: What's wrong with the game as you see it?

Bettman: I think fundamentally, it's pretty sound. People focus on the issue of fighting. I get asked that in every interview, so you don't have to ask me now. I don't know whether or not that's a problem. But I'm going to form a judgment on it relatively quickly. Some people say it's not a big problem, but it could be better. Some people say it's a terrible problem.

I've had a couple of chats with a couple of former players and some hockey people. I'm going to touch on all bases and try to come to a view that makes the most sense. But basically, I think the game is a wonderful game. There are great athletes doing amazing things on the ice at an incredible speed. Basically, I think we are dealing with a terrific sport.

Fischler: Is it as salable as basketball?

Bettman: I don't like drawing that comparison for a lot of reasons. I think it's much more salable than it has been sold, so whether or not it's compared to something else is not the issue. This is its own sport; it's hockey. I think it can be sold much better and much bigger than it has been.

Fischler: How are you going to deal with Bob Goodenow? What is the solution to this knotty problem? There is a hypothesis that there will be a solution without a strike because the players have never had it so good. How do you see it?

Bettman: I don't know whether or not they've had it so good. I don't know enough about the specifics of this industry. I know the general trends and everything, but I'm going to have to get educated on that.

The way we're going to do it is that Bob Goodenow and I are going to work very hard at it together. I'm going to understand everything he understands and that he thinks, and I hope that I'm going to get him to understand everything that I know and I think. From there—since we both have a big stake in the same thing and that is the success of the NHL—we're going to reason with each other and try to come up with a framework.

I've always had a very good relationship with the National Basketball Players' Association. We haven't always agreed on everything, but we have a relationship. We can talk; we can communicate. I understand where they're coming from on issues. I think they understand where I'm coming from; you need to have that kind of relationship—a strong, businesslike, trusting relationship—to create the type of partnership that is going to be necessary to build that sport.

Goal number one is going to be to start dialogue with Bob Goodenow. We've got a time frame. I would have preferred to have the luxury of a little more time, but I think I have enough of a head start on the issues. I think I have enough understanding of labor relationships in professional sports.

I've been collecting the data. I have mounds of books over here that I have to read, and I'll do that and get myself up to speed very quickly. And Bob will help bring me up to speed.

Fischler: Is revenue sharing a realistic possibility?

Bettman: I don't view revenue sharing as the be-all and end-all. In other words it may not be necessary.

I'll give you an example why. You've got four teams in the league, and the gross for the league is $4 million. One team is grossing $2 million, another team is grossing $1 million, and the other two are grossing $500,000. If they're all spending $4 million or more in expenses, not just players but expenses, and there's no profit, sharing the revenue isn't going to help.

What you need to do, especially when you are dealing with an under-appreciated sport, is grow the revenue pie and create new sources of revenue that can be shared among the teams. That will deal better with the problem than dividing up what may be inadequate revenue anyway.

I think the pie that we're dealing with is too small. I want to make a bigger pie. To get hung up on revenue sharing in an industry that may be in its financial infancy may be putting it backward.

What we need to do is come up with a framework. If we create a structure that should enable all the teams to operate successfully, but then some don't, we have to look at a whole host of things. We have to look at management. We have to look at marketing. We have to look at the markets. Then we have to see how to respond to it from there.

Fischler: How do you plan to give encouragement to fans and ownership in sites such as Hartford, New Jersey, Long Island, and Minnesota, so they can redevelop vibrancy?

Bettman: You've got to look at each market specifically. Hartford's had a particular series of unique problems based on prior ownership. You've got to work through that and get stable ownership in place, and it's being worked on. Richard Gordon has done a terrific job up there, and it takes time to bring it back.

The Long Island market has in the past supported the Islanders in a big way. Then they had some problems, but there's now a new management team in place. I'm hopeful, and I believe that they are on the right track. They used to have 14,000 season ticket holders there. Let's also focus on the fact that Long Island is in the middle of a big-time recession, which may have an impact, and those things are cyclical. I'm not familiar with Jersey, although I know the Nets have had some problems in the NBA.

You've got to look market by market. You've got to do the right things. Then if you've tried everything and you've had good management, you've made the right investments in time, energy, and money, you've tried everything possible and you've got new ownership, then you've got to look at the market.

I get hung up on this. People say big market, small market. I never, even in the NBA context, I never refer to it as big market, small market. I reject the notion. There are plenty of teams in small markets that do great when they are the only game in town. And then there are some teams in big markets that don't do very well because there's either too many professional sports teams or even more in their own league.

Markets that were strong and vibrant 10 years ago aren't necessarily the same markets. Salt Lake City is a great example of a booming market that people at one point thought was too small to sustain an NBA franchise.

These problems are not subject to blanket generalizations in terms of curing them. You have to look at what happened. Have there been problems in ownership? Have there been problems in the market? What is the building like? What are the economic conditions? You've got all those things and you work on them one at a time.

One of the things I'm going to do is work with the owners of franchises that are having problems, look at their problems, look at potential solutions, then stabilize them. I want a stable league office, a well-run office, and I want to push that down to the team level as well.

Fischler: Where do you see the next expansion?

Bettman: I'm more focused now on the two new teams in Anaheim and Miami. I have no doubt that they are going to be successful, but we're going to get them assimilated and we've got to get them competitive.

I want to stabilize the existing teams. We've got three other recent teams. I saw Ottawa play and they need some work, but they play hard. As long as we're on the right track and everything is stabilized, I want that taken care of first before we look at expansion. Expansion in this sport is going to happen down the road if we do everything right because there is going to be more fan interest and we are going to need to expand to satisfy that fan interest.

There are a whole host of cities, especially in the Texas Sun Belt region. I read an article yesterday about the ECHL, which is drawing 5,000 a game in Memphis. They're drawing 3,500 a game in Binghamton. We are talking about real interest across the board in hockey. We're going to help develop that interest and then respond to that interest.

Fischler: What did you learn from David Stern?

Bettman: An awful lot. You don't have enough tapes here for me to tell you. Other than having exposed me to all the aspects of running a professional sports league, he's a wonderful people person, he's incredibly smart, he's incredibly hard working, he's got a great set of values, he's got a great business acumen and savvy, and I hope that he's passed all those things along to me. Some people think he has, in some measure, and that may be the reason why the NHL reached out to me. I owe him a lot.

Fischler: Why did you want the NHL job?

Bettman: The short answer is that I happen to like the sport. I love the sport. I have since I was in college. I think that it's an incredible challenge and an incredible opportunity. I think the ice age is coming.

Fischler: Will ownership give you enough power to do what you have to do?

Bettman: They're going to let me do what I have to do because I'm going to set an agenda that's going to put this league on a course that's consistent with the visions the owners, I believe as a group, have as well.

Coming in I heard a lot about factionalism, disputes, and everything else. I then witnessed two days where they unanimously granted two terrific franchises and they unanimously elected me. I spent two days in Florida meeting with all the owners and talking to them. They were interviewing me, but I was interviewing them as well because I didn't need a job; I had a good one. I was extremely favorably impressed by the ownership group. On an individual level, they were all terrifically nice, and I enjoyed the rapport we developed. I developed a lot of respect for them. I think they're smart businessmen. In the past I think that they have been unfairly maligned because I think it's up to the commissioner to set an agenda and lead. It doesn't mean I think the commissioner sits on a throne and throws lightning bolts and orders subjects around. That's not my view. You set an agenda, you communicate the agenda, you work hand-in-hand with your constituent groups: the owners, the media, the fans. You try to bring everyone together in an agenda that will grow the sport. I think that they are ready for it.

Bruce McNall may have helped to part the seas a little bit. He is viewed as a progressive owner. He has a great deal of respect among the other owners. There's a new era coming. It doesn't matter what the constitution says. I'm going to have the powers on paper consistent with the other professional sports leagues, but that's on the side. I'm going to lead with an agenda. The business aspects of the sport have to be well run so that people can enjoy the sport, and that's my agenda.

Fischler: How important is establishing a network television contract?

Bettman: It's very important. It's interesting. It's a chicken and an egg because you've got to build a fan base to get the network contract, which I'm committed to doing. But with the network contract, I'm going to build a fan base. It's going to snowball once I get it going.

This is such a difficult sports marketplace. It's so fragmented that it's different than it was 10 years ago. Baseball in its regular-season games does a 3 (rating), 3.5, maybe a 4 if it's a really good game. The expectation now isn't as great as it was.

NHL hockey will be able to provide reasonably priced, good network programming for the sports division. As long as I can demonstrate that there is a decent following—it doesn't have to be spectacular numbers—that will give us something to grow on.

We have a relationship that runs out in four years. That's going to give me an opportunity to get the sport on a plane that's going to make the networks and the advertisers and the sponsors come on board. Hopefully, we can generate some more fan interest. We will work very hard with ESPN to make sure that their package is as successful as possible. Maybe along the way we can try some things, more than the handful of games that ABC is prepared to do, since they are related to ESPN. We'll deal with sponsors to do some promotions. We will market the marquee players better and I think increase the fan base. I think that being back on ESPN will help with the exposure, and I'm looking to the point when we're ready for prime time on the network.

Fischler: What's your view on pay-per-view?

Bettman: For a sport that needs more exposure pay-per-view isn't the short-term answer. We need the widest possible exposure that we can get. Pay-per-view might work in the short run for the hard-core fan that can't get, on the usual outlets, the exposure that he wants.

I'll give you an example. You grew up in Boston. All your life you are a die-hard Bruins fan, and you move to Texas. What do you do? Pay-per-view in that context might make some sense. I believe there's a market of people.

Let's assume that you live in St. Louis and you just moved from Winnipeg and you miss the Jets. You get the St. Louis games locally, but you want to buy an additional game that you can't otherwise see. The last thing you need to do is put the Stanley Cup finals on pay-per-view. I want more people to see the Stanley Cup finals, not less.

Fischler: Do you see Europe as a spawning ground for more NHL games?

Bettman: I was responsible for the NBA games played in Europe. Northern Europe is particularly ripe for the NHL interests because a lot of players come from there. But you have to start first with licensing, sponsorship, and television. Then, you move on to the occasional exhibition or regular season games. Then, if the interest is strong enough, you think about whether it's feasible to have franchises on the continent. Right now, it's too far down the road.

Fischler: What's your short-term goal vis-à-vis North America and Europe?

Bettman: To stabilize the sport in North America. Doing TV [for Europe] is easy. I can get a few people. I can get us exposure, use the satellites and all that. We'll do some of that because the opportunities are there and there's interest. Doing expansion in a big [European] way has to take second fiddle to making sure that we are in good shape here in North America.

I'd like to snap my fingers and implement everything that's in my head, but it's not going to happen in 24 hours. I've got to take care of the basics.

Fischler: What's your gut feeling on an NHL Dream Team playing in the Olympics?

Bettman: It would certainly get the sport a lot of exposure, but I have real concerns about the practical and logistical problems in doing it. In the NBA it took years to get it right. I don't want to do it just to do it, because if it's not done perfectly and we can't achieve the benefits that we want, then it's not worth doing. With a four-year lag time to 1998, it may very well be another story.

Fischler: Who are you bringing over to the NHL from the NBA?

Bettman: Nobody except my secretary [Debbie Walsh]. I was under contract to the NBA, and I have been released from my contract on the understanding that I won't take anyone else with me. I'm leaving a big enough hole in this organization that I don't have to create any others.

Fischler: How are you planning to change aspects of the NHL offices?

Bettman: I'm going to put the organization under the microscope, look at the strengths and weaknesses and make the appropriate changes, if any, necessary to make the NHL run as well as any professional sports league in the world. I have a philosophy: if the league—NHL Enterprises—is being well run, and everything is smooth and stable, people aren't going to know we're there; they're just going to focus on the game. When you focus on the game, it's an empty netter. It used to be a slam dunk; now it's an empty netter.

In the early eighties, the NBA was perceived to have a ton of problems. It solved the problems, eliminated the distractions, and the people started to focus on the game. I want people focused on hockey because it's a great game.

Fischler: You dealt with the NBA referees' union, which seemed a little surprising.

Bettman: It's funny. Shortly after I was named commissioner, I was at Byrne Arena watching the Rangers and the Devils. After a second-period interview, I walked over to the officials' locker room, introduced myself, and I said to them, "This is great; I just finished a year of negotiating with the referees in the NBA and I thought I was done for three years. Now I have to do it again!" I was the chief negotiator with the NBA and at the time nobody would have accused me of being a basketball person. But obviously I know the sport well enough that I can sit across the table with the referees. I know what the issues are. I've become an expert because I have to. I'll learn every aspect of the operation including the officials. Officials are important and they always feel underappreciated. They're always the visiting team; it's a tough job.

Fischler: What are you going to do about the NHL's three offices [New York, Montreal, and Toronto]?

Bettman: No question we are going to open a PR office here in New York. I'm going to have to understand the need to have three offices. And they're going to have to operate under my management style.

Fischler: Who will handle discipline under your administration?

Bettman: The hockey operations people. I'm responsible for everything that goes on. But I don't think I should be involved in every disciplinary action that's meted out. But on major incidents, I'll get involved, while the run-of-the-mill stuff will be handled by hockey operations.

Fischler: What about Gil Stein?

Bettman: I like him. He's bright. He's a link with history—what transpired, what's going on. If something comes up, I can go to him and say, "Has this happened before? What did we do? And why?" He can be helpful.

Fischler: Any thoughts about luring more women to the game?

Bettman: I do know that somewhere between 40 and 50 percent of the people attending games are women. It's important to get kids as they are growing up. It's very important to get the next generation of fans. We just need more of everybody. I want full arenas.

Fischler: What about the salary cap?

Bettman: Ask Bob Goodenow. I don't mean that facetiously. There's going to be a system that makes sense, a system that's fair to the owners and the players, a system that's jointly arrived upon by the league and the players' union. Maybe it's an NBA-style salary cap. Maybe it's a new type of salary cap, and maybe it's a system that hasn't been invented yet. I know about this stuff. I know how to create these systems. I know how to invent these things and the owners are counting on me to come up with a system that makes sense to the NHL, and that's a system that I have to come up with, with Bob Goodenow.

Fischler: Which owners did you know best before you got the NHL job?

Bettman: Abe Pollin of the Capitals because he owns the Bullets; and Stanley Jaffe, the president and CEO of Paramount (Rangers); and the Gund brothers from Cleveland Cavaliers' days (the current owners of the San Jose Sharks). Since then, I've met them all.

Fischler: One thing different from the NBA is that you are going to be dealing with the Canadian psyche as well as the Americans.

Bettman: I understand the Canadian love affair with the game. I want to take that love affair and give it to more people. Basketball was always perceived as a U.S. game. It now may be the second—or first—most popular sport in the world. I'm going to be very sensitive to the Canadians and tread very lightly as to the sensitivity that may or may not be there. I want to be viewed as somebody who cares for the game, takes care of the game, and will do good things for the game.

And that ended the interview. At the start, Bettman was saying—and doing—all the right things. Unlike Ziegler, he established a peripatetic relationship with the media. One might have suspected that the commissioner's theme was "Bring on the cameras! Bring on the pencils!"

I got a firsthand view of Bettman at work shortly after he moved to the hockey realm. All executives have styles. Ziegler was reserved, painfully humorous on rare occasions, and extremely loose when with his friends. Bettman displayed a New York neighborly approach. Whenever one addressed him as "commissioner," he instantly injected a "Call me Gary" into the conversation.

He was sensitive enough to the fact that hockey people regarded him as "a basketball man," that Canadians viewed him as an American interloper into their game, and that whomever the bigots were in the NHL crowd, they would take due note of the fact that he is Jewish—in fact, the first leader of bigleague hockey of Hebrew roots.

To his credit, Bettman neither played up nor played down his background. Those who knew him from his pre-NBA and NBA days, however, had reservations about his ability to smoothly orchestrate the executive role. One mutual friend, Marty Blackman, a Madison Avenue consultant who works with athletes and ad agencies on television commercials, expressed some concern to me.

"What I'd be worried about is whether Gary becomes too confrontational in the manner of some New York trial lawyers," said Blackman. "That could turn off people, and I consider it a factor that he should address."

When I mentioned this to Bettman, he pooh-poohed the suggestion as one would to a nervous Nellie. He suggested that Blackman was exaggerating to make a point and, really, this was not a part of his style. The message: not to worry. The question in my mind was how well does the commissioner take to criticism? The answer would be well and not too well in the months to come and badly after five years.

One thing was obvious; I had developed a closer rapport with Bettman in a month than I had with Ziegler in 15 years. That was not so much a knock at the more reserved, deposed president, but more a statement about Bettman the person.

What I liked most about him was his ease of communication and what seemed to be sensible ideas about reorganizing the league. I decided to give him my 22 points of free advice in my *Hockey News* column:

1. When in doubt, do exactly the opposite of what John Ziegler would have done.
2. Prepare yourself this instant for a colossal explosion over the NHL pension scandal. And distance yourself about 3,000 miles from all involved.
3. Do the opposite of your myopic and lazy predecessor. Move the league's public relations center out of an outpost in Rexdale, Ontario, and back where it belongs in New York, the world's media capital.

4. Wear a Teflon suit when dealing with Canadian writers. They will automatically scorn you because (a) you're a New Yorker; (b) you're smaller than Tie Domi (Bob Costas, or Pinky Lee); and (c) you didn't sign a $500 billion contract with CBS yesterday.

5. Never for a minute forget your constituency: 18 American teams and only 8 north of the border. That's more than a two-thirds majority for Uncle Sam.

6. Never underestimate the resentment of some Canadian hockey people for their American counterparts.

7. If you don't think your public relations corps needs trebling, check out the New York papers, where hockey is fourth banana, despite Mark Messier, Brian Leetch, et. al.

8. Make a distinction between phony, premeditative goon fighting and legitimate, spontaneous bouts. Don't abolish legal fisticuffs, but punish the illegitimate goons. Whatever you do, when you finally make a decision on fighting, articulate it loud and clear. And when the critics begin sniping, don't wimp out. Go on the offensive.

9. The referees will try to cow you now that their contract is running out. Don't be fazed. Their inconsistency and ineptitude has degraded the game to the point that a gag rule can't even subdue the critics. If they pull a strike, let 'em walk.

10. The Dream Team idea for the Olympics is for the birds. With creative thinking, the NHL can get as much positive ink on the continent as it would a costly three-week interruption of the schedule. Don't fall for the easy-publicity propaganda.

11. Keep Gil Stein on board. He generated more energy in six months than John Zeigler did in a decade. [So, even Stan Fischler makes mistakes in judgement.]

12. Hockey players can be colorful, distinct personalities, but most come out looking like battleship-gray androids because of the league's public relations program. Open them up to the world or the NHL will remain light-years behind your favorite basketball league.

13. I know you disagree and have used a bunch of buzzwords to say so, but read my lips: revenue sharing is a must (partial, at least).

14. Never stop talking to the fans, even those with a median income under $20,000 a year.

15. It's nice that Disney and Blockbuster are in our midst, but don't let those hockey-come-latelies wag your tail.

16. Listen carefully to Marcel Aubut's idea for shootouts to settle ties in the regular season. Then, approve it for the best reason of all: because the plan will add excitement to the game.
17. Stop expansion at 28 teams.
18. Give expansion teams a break. The protected list should be trimmed to 13 players. While you're at it, institute a National Basketball Association–type lottery.
19. Upgrade linesmen to referee status. Have three referees, the same as in professional basketball.
20. Promote the heck out of street and roller hockey as America's city game alternative to basketball.
21. Don't for a second forget that hockey people are not like basketball people and something that works for hoops doesn't necessarily work for pucks.
22. Don't hang out at Madison Square Garden any more than you do at the Spectrum, Nassau Coliseum, Chicago Stadium, Byrne Arena, or Great Western Forum.

If I do say so myself, I was right on 21 out of the 22 points. The one strike was number 11: my suggestion that he keep Gil Stein aboard. Some NHL insiders believed that Stein could be an effective background man to aid Bettman's transition to the new office. Stein was gifted with the annual Lester Patrick Trophy ("for service to hockey in the United States"), a largely ceremonial-political award. From past experience, I learned that the Patrick winners usually are politically correct personalities who, in effect, are paid off with the prize although it should be noted that there have been several deserving winners such as Brian and Joey Mullen.

Stein accepted the Lester Patrick Trophy before public disclosure of his attempt to rig his own induction into the Hockey Hall of Fame. "As his term as president was coming to a close," said Bob McKenzie in the *Toronto Star*, "Stein found it necessary to hatch the bold but flawed scheme of orchestrating his own induction into the Hall of Fame, using his last-gasp powers of president to influence the outcome of the election."

Although this would be Bettman's first taste of NHL cyanide and although it wasn't fatal to his administration, it was a portent of negative things to come, including a charge that the Ottawa Senators had tanked their end of the schedule to ensure better draft selection.

My information was that the more Bettman analyzed the Ziegler administration, the more he became convinced that the old hockey way was the wrong way. One by one, the "Zieglerites" were cashiered. Joel Nixon, the universally likeable vice president of broadcasting, was put out to pasture, replaced by Glenn Adamo. Steve Ryan hung on a bit longer but eventually gave way to Rick Dudley as head of NHL Enterprises.

After my second face-to-face meeting with Bettman, I had become magnetized enough by his modus operandi—not to mention personality—to consider the unthinkable and actually work for the NHL.

There were a few big-time problems: (1) I was under contract with SportsChannel New York as an Islanders' and Devils' broadcaster; (2) I was writing a regular *Hockey News* column; (3) I had a long list of writing assignments ranging from books to magazine articles; and (4) I loved television too much to forsake it.

First, I had to establish whether Bettman was interested in me. During our third chat, he indicated that he was, but the position remained uncertain. "We need somebody who can write and who can edit," he said. "Eventually, we'll put out a weekly newsletter like the NBA does. We'll need somebody for that."

"I have obligations to SportsChannel and others," I pointed out. "I won't leave TV."

"Maybe you can do work for us as a part-time consultant," he shot back.

Now it was clear that he meant business and I had some serious thinking to do. Did I really want to become part of the establishment? Did I want to enter the corporate world after having spent my lifetime of employment on the other side of the typewriter? Dare I leave the glorified world of television, where my mug was seen on the tube three times a week in season? Dare I forget what happened to others? I was acutely aware of Jack Falla's unfortunate experience after leaving the writing world for NHL PR. He lasted about two months.

These were difficult decisions, accentuated by the fact that Bettman would soon want answers and I was immersed in a delicious regular-season NHL race involving the Devils and Islanders. Both clubs were bound for the playoffs; the Islanders led by a rejuvenated Al Arbour while the Devils were being driven by Herb Brooks.

Before I could even come close to making up my mind, Bettman hired Steve Solomon away from the American Broadcasting Corporation to be his second in command. Solomon's savvy in the TV realm would be essential as the NHL attempted to regain a foothold with one of the major American networks. Although he wasn't a "pure" hockey person, Solomon did have family involvement in the sport. His grandfather had been a major investor in the New York Americans' NHL club when it was a rival with the Rangers at the old Madison Square Garden in the thirties. From our brief meetings, I came away impressed.

Shortly thereafter, the 1993 All-Star Game was held in Montreal. I was covering it for an American radio syndicate and also planned to meet Bruce McNall for a magazine interview. The trip would whet my appetite for the NHL job even more.

We arrived on a Thursday night to prepare for the NHL Old-timers' Game and the skills competition on Friday evening at the Forum. It was during an eight-hour period, from midmorning through early evening, that I got to see Bettman in action. First he was cornered by Canadian Broadcasting Corporation cameras, then it was the print media, and, finally, local radio.

He had time for everybody, and when I asked him for 20 minutes for a magazine piece, the commissioner led me behind closed doors so we wouldn't be interrupted. His manner was extrafriendly, and I got the distinct impression that he soon expected to bring me aboard—presuming that we could work out the details.

Shortly after I returned to New York, Bettman phoned and invited me to a meeting with himself at the NHL offices. He made it clear that an NHL job was available to me. Then, he asked, "What do you know about Arthur Pincus?"

Wow! Pincus had been a Sunday sports editor with the *New York Times* and had since moved to the *Washington Post*. I couldn't figure his hockey background, but Bettman said he was being considered for vice president of public relations. "I know him from his *Times* days," I said in a deliberate, noncommittal way. "That's an interesting choice."

Frankly, I didn't know what to make of it. I could tell that Bettman figured he was aiming high, and there was that "prestige" aspect of the *Times* and *Washington Post* that must have entered the commissioner's thinking. (But so many times corporate heads guess wrong when they think newspeople can simply shed their journalistic clothes and climb into a flack's suit.)

"I'm also going to have a vice president of corporate communications," Bettman added. "We have someone from Reebok in mind for that."

He mentioned the name Bernadette Mansur, which meant absolutely nothing to me, and then cut to the meat. What Bettman planned was a PR hat-trick announcement; Pincus, Mansur, and me.

"But you still haven't told me what I'm going to do," I said.

Bettman talked about me being the league archivist, editor, head of an unborn book sector—a sort of vice president of publishing, for want of a better title. "You write the job description," he concluded with one of the best offers a newsman could expect. "We'll talk next week."

Now the pressure was on me—and mounting. There was no way I could take the NHL job unless I was able to continue my television work, and SportsChannel did not want me to leave. Finally, I told Bettman to go ahead with his announcement about Pincus and Mansur without me. I was locked in by TV—and loved it.

On the one hand, the NHL offer was tantalizingly tempting, particularly the idea of working with a galvanic character such as Bettman. But on the other hand, I enjoyed the television work more than ever.

Meanwhile, I followed the Islanders down the homestretch of the 1992–93 season and observed Bettman handle the first crisis of his administration while I tried to cope with the ultimate crisis of our immediate family.

FACING DEATH AND HOCKEY
About Simon, Mike Keenan,
and a Heart

The 1993 New York Islanders–Pittsburgh Penguins playoff series was one of the most exciting I've ever covered. Although heavily favored, the Stanley Cup champions, led by Mario Lemieux, were being played as equals by Al Arbour's squad.

The series reached its climax Saturday evening, May 8, at Nassau Coliseum. New York won the opener, 3–2, at Pittsburgh, then lost 3–0 on the road, then lost again, 3–1, in Uniondale. This was the fourth game of the series at Nassau.

A Penguins win would virtually seal the series. But if the Islanders could tie the playoff at two games apiece, who knows? They might even pull off a colossal upset.

At the time, my younger son, 15-year-old Simon—his brother Ben was 6 years his senior—was attending Northwood, a boarding (prep) school in Lake Placid, New York. A freshman, Simon chose Northwood principally because of its hockey program and the desire to experience life away from home on his own. *Independence* was the operable word.

Simon was a goaltender but with only limited experience, largely because he had committed himself for four winters to alpine (downhill) ski racing—and even made it to the New York State championships his last year as a Junior IV racer.

However, around the ski season, he enrolled in a hockey program at Sky Rink, a few blocks from Madison Square Garden; participated in Bob Nystrom's Summer Hockey School for a week; and was backup goalie in a Yonkers, New York, house league. This craze for goaltending had come about first because he started out a poor skater (although by now he wasn't bad—he had taken power-skating lessons with Laura Stamm) and because goalies got into rinks for free in local pickup leagues (figuring that the poor parents had already paid a fortune for goalie equipment!).

Then, when Simon was about nine or 10, I was invited to do mock play-by-play at a hockey fantasy camp at the famous old Borscht Belt (Jewish Catskill) resort, the Concord. Simon got to suit up and "play" with the stars, and there were some genuine stars: Dale Hawerchuk, Mario Lemieux, Luc Robitaille, Dan Quinn, Larry Robinson, and Marc Bergeuin. In fact, the first goal scored on him was by Robitaille and the second, by Mario!

That incredible experience, coupled with the fact that he sat at ice level in the Meadowlands parallel to his idol Chico Resch's goal for two periods, during the infamous "Mickey Mouse" game (Wayne Gretzky had called the young Devils a "Mickey Mouse club" shortly before his Edmonton Oilers were to play there), clinched it for Simon: he wanted to be an NHL goaltender.

Having such positive experiences as a goaltender and hungry for more, Simon had done a powerful job of lobbying to go to Northwood, and I, reluctantly, agreed that he could get more ice time at the boarding school.

Unfortunately, he was sixth out of six goalies, obtained limited ice time, and gradually grew to dislike Northwood and the extraordinarily frigid 1992–93 winter in Lake Placid (it snowed the June day my wife picked him up after finals, for instance!). Still, when he did get to play, it was thrilling because the Northwood varsity team played in the 1980 Olympic rink in downtown Lake Placid.

At least once a month Simon and a friend or two would train down to Manhattan on a Friday night and remain with us until Sunday morning, when they completed the Amtrak round trip back to Northwood. On the weekend in question, I arranged for Simon & Company to accompany my wife, Shirley, to the fourth playoff game at Uniondale.

A thoroughly absorbed Islanders' fan (he was five when the Isles won their fourth Cup, in 1983), Simon was tickled to see a playoff game and enamored of the manner in which his heroes conducted themselves. Spearheaded by penalty-killer Tom Fitzgerald's two shorthanded goals, the Isles rallied for a stirring 6–5 victory that permanently impacted on most who viewed the match.

I always enjoyed having Simon at games, but this one was so special and ended so euphorically, I was filled with transports of joy when I got behind the wheel of our Honda and began driving Shirley, Simon, and his friends back to Manhattan. But as I drove, the ecstasy diminished with every mile. From the car's rear, the interior was punctuated by spasmatic coughing that carried right through to my very core.

It was Simon hacking away so intensely that I began asking myself whether I should permit him to return to school the next morning. When we arrived back at our apartment, I mentioned my concern to Shirley and we decided we'd wait until the next morning before deciding. The problem, of course, was that Simon had to be up early and at Pennsylvania Station by 10 A.M. to catch the train.

Shortly after he awakened, I suggested that it might be wiser for him to remain in the city and see a doctor on Monday. With typical teenage bravado, he insisted that he'd be OK, that he'd see a nurse (or doctor) in Lake Placid, and not to worry. Because I wanted not to worry and because my wife figured it was all right for him to head north again, I raised no objections.

Later in the week Simon phoned and seemed completely recovered. I remember admonishing myself for being overprotective. Somehow I managed to forget that he had suffered through "walking pneumonia" during the winter and assorted other ailments that we considered ordinary for a growing boy.

Meanwhile, his Islanders went on to defeat Pittsburgh before being eliminated by the Canadiens. School ended in late spring, and he returned home to prepare for a summer job as a junior counselor at a day camp near our country home in the Catskill Mountains. He appeared to be perfectly normal. One Saturday morning we went to the beach at Riis Park and played a hard game of paddle handball in a broiling sun. I remarked to myself how well Simon held up under adverse conditions. But I also recall that when I encouraged him to take a swim with me later, he said he was tired and just wanted to stretch out. No sweat; teenagers like to nap on Saturdays.

But there were other signs that something was wrong with Simon, physically. First, about a week after returning from Lake Placid, he complained of an earache. Our regular doctor checked him out, found mild signs of an ear infection, and recommended an ear, nose, and throat clinic. The prescription didn't work, so we tried another. There were other symptoms but each taken on its own hinted at only a passing ailment. We thought it might be allergies and took him to see our allergist. He noticed a rapid heartbeat at the time but attributed it to the fact that Simon was taking antihistamines, decongestants, and an antibiotic—all of which could mean an elevated heart rate.

One Friday afternoon in late June, Simon—who had been a competitive mountain-bike racer, too—and I took a leisurely cycle in Riverside Park, adjoining the Hudson River. Our destination was my cousin Gerry's apartment about two and one-half miles away. The sun was bright, the air warm but not overbearing, and the ambience—if you will excuse the expression—swell.

Normally, Simon would speed ahead of me and then circle until his father caught up, then take another sprint and wait. This time, he kept pace with me and, to my astonishment, halted and got off his bike after we had pedaled up a rather modest hill. "I need a rest, Dad," he implored.

That seemed strange to me, but after a brief respite we resumed our ride, and, yet again, after another climb, he requested a rest for a few more minutes. Little did I realize that Simon was just a weekend away from suffering heart failure.

On Monday, June 28, the Devils held a press conference to announce a new coach. Simon had had a difficult weekend. His ear continued to bother him and a lethargy overcame him as well as nausea. Shirley was so frustrated over the doctors' failure to isolate any cause for his problems, she didn't know who to contact next. On Sunday night she obtained a prescription for his nausea, and on Monday she scheduled an appointment at Manhattan's Eye and Ear Hospital for another examination.

At approximately the same time as Devils' president–general manager Lou Lamoriello announced that Jacques Lemaire had been named head coach (to replace Herb Brooks), Simon collapsed in the doctor's office of heart failure. Unfortunately, nobody knew precisely why he had taken ill, but he was rushed (with Shirley) to St. Vincent's Hospital by an emergency medical service ambulance.

When I phoned home to get messages from my office manager, I was told that Simon was in a hospital—mistakenly named Beth Israel—and "probably had an attack of ulcers."

After regaining my composure, I dashed to my car, along with colleague Steve Viuker, who had accompanied me to the press conference. Ulcers? Simon never had a hint of ulcers but, perhaps, the symptoms were there after all. By the time I returned home, word had gotten through that they were at St. Vincent's. I headed for the subway and spent 20 agonizing minutes riding to the hospital.

Upon arriving in the emergency room, I found Shirley and Simon surrounded by doctors and emergency medical service people. All I could think about was the original message, "a bleeding ulcer," and wondered what was going on with the procedure.

I was quickly introduced to the EMS people, one of whom was rather corpulent and perspiring profusely. I was able to give

Simon a hug and kiss and some measure of reassurance although I hadn't a clue as to his true condition.

Neither, as I would soon learn, did the pediatric emergency room people at St. Vincent's. The original guess of "bleeding ulcers" apparently had been discarded almost immediately. They had taken him into the emergency room and immediately decided he was in anaphylactic shock, despite Shirley's attempts to tell them he had been taking the new medications for more than 24 hours and there was no way the kid was in anaphylaxis. Unfortunately, a part of the treatment was pumping him full of liquids, and within moments of my arrival Simon was choking and coughing up pink froth.

At this point the medical crew realized that they were probably killing Simon rather than saving him and they tried to catheterize him (a thin tube inserted up the penis, with no anesthesia) so that they could get the liquid back out of him as rapidly as possible.

It was then that I discovered how brave my son really was under the most excrutiating conditions. Not that he laughed off the pain. Far from it. But he coped with the trauma of it all with a blend of stoicism and fortitude that surely surpassed anything I could match under similar conditions.

Twice they tried the catheterization, which they soon decided was two times too many. I think it began to dawn on everybody in the room that Simon—with no previous history of heart problems; a healthy athlete—was somehow, unaccountably, in heart failure.

Suddenly, I remembered that both Simon and his older brother, Ben, had been diagnosed with heart murmurs. But after careful checking, our pediatrician had determined that both had "systolic" or harmless heart murmurs, which they might well grow out of (Shirley had had a systolic murmur when she was a child). In both cases it was said to have no relation to future ailments as they grew to adulthood.

After considerable examination it was determined that Simon would be removed to an intensive care unit, where he would be further examined and diagnosed. At this point neither Shirley nor I had any indication that his young life was teetering in the balance, nor did we know what to expect in the next 24 hours.

In the relative security of the intensive care unit, Simon was checked regularly and seemed to feel a bit more comfortable. My main task was ferrying cans of seltzer to him from the soda dispenser down the hall to his bedside.

A Dr. Lee, who supervised the Pediatric ICU, indicated that Simon's condition could improve overnight. That would have been comforting had the doctor known precisely the nature of Simon's ailment at the time, which he didn't. He did, however, ask us questions about whether anyone else had mentioned lately that Simon had an enlarged heart. No one had. He told us that the head of Pediatric Cardiology, Dr. Liu, would be performing an echocardiogram on Simon soon. In the meantime, Simon was being given several medications, which we had never heard of, intravenously.

Shirley remained overnight at Simon's bedside. I eventually took the subway home, walked Cleo, the Airedale, flopped in bed, and wondered what was going on.

As promised Dr. Liu performed the echocardiogram and then disappeared for most of the day. Unaware of the details, I returned to St. Vincent's in the afternoon and happened to arrive as Shirley left the ICU for respite.

Instinctively, I sensed bad news when we embraced, although I never imagined the gravity of Simon's condition. After I hugged Simon, Shirley and I were called aside by Dr. Liu. She clearly did not want to converse in front of Simon and led us to an empty children's playroom. "Your son is very ill," she said. "His heart is in poor condition, almost useless."

It was as if a grenade had exploded in my stomach. "Heart. Useless." The words resonated uncontrollably, mystifyingly. We're talking about a 15-year-old who had competed in a world cross-country mountain-biking event, who had played a 21-point game of hard paddleball in a noonday sun only weeks ago.

Four words kept repeating: how could it be?

But it was, and Dr. Liu made it clear that decisions were necessary. St. Vincent's was ill-equipped to deal with acute myocarditis or cardiomyopathy, which were said to be the most likely causes of Simon's heart failure. She insisted that the one place to go was Columbia-Presbyterian Babies' Hospital, then admitted that she had already taken the results of Simon's "echo" and x-rays up to a colleague there. Everyone (whoever that was, and we would find that out very soon) who had looked at the tests agreed that Simon should be moved to Columbia-Presbyterian Babies' Hospital as soon as possible.

Dr. Liu arranged for a bed that night (Tuesday, June 29), and we sent for a private ambulance to take Simon to what would be his "home" for the next two terrifying months.

A pair of pleasant, heavily accented Russian paramedics finally arrived at about 8 P.M. that very hot summer evening and loaded Simon (with Shirley) into the rear patient's compartment. I would again take the subway home.

As I helped them aboard, I experienced a doleful feeling that Simon might not survive the night, that I might never see him again. Yet I tried not to betray my thoughts. I put on an encouraging face. "You'll be OK, guy!" I said as the ambulance door closed and then I turned toward the subway.

Simon had become aware of his deteriorating condition earlier in the day and, somehow, coped with it without any emotional breakdown, although I'm not sure how he managed to do so. He maintained that amazingly strong disposition throughout the ordeal, which began in earnest when he checked into Columbia-Presbyterian and was taken to the Pediatric Intensive Care Unit of its Babies' Hospital building.

At this point you may be wondering what all this has to do with hockey. In fact, throughout the ordeal—from getting the communiqué at the Lemaire press conference to the start of the new season—hockey people were directly involved in the grieving, waiting, and healing process this hideous event was about to become.

Shirley and I had been invited to speak at a USA Hockey symposium in Boston during a weekend early in July. At first we had hoped that Simon's illness would be minor enough for us to head for Massachusetts. But once we began getting results at Columbia-Presbyterian, we realized that we were going nowhere.

Then, there were my dealings with Bettman and the NHL. Now all bets were off. I had phoned Bettman shortly after Simon's hospitalization. "Don't even think about us," he said, sounding very much like the parent he is. "Do what you have to do with Simon."

We learned that sometime in the past—perhaps a month, perhaps several months before—Simon had suffered a virus, and the virus had reached his heart. The destructive process then began and culminated with the collapse on June 28. By the time he reached Columbia-Presbyterian, Simon's heart was functioning at only 13 percent.

Life became an endless nightmare at this point. When Shirley walked into the Pediatric Intensive Care Unit (after sleeping on a chair in a lounge outside the PICU) on the morning after Simon's admission, she found him unable to speak and partially paralyzed on his right side (and this was only moments after he had spoken to his nurse). Simon had had a small stroke, or transischemic accident (TIA), and although he began to recover his speech and movement almost immediately, the episode was terrifying. It turned out that Simon's poor laboring heart was "throwing out" blood clots. They later found one in a lung that was compounding the situation by setting up incipient pneumonia. Now he was on a medication that was keeping his heart pumping and a medication that thinned his blood so that he wouldn't form any more clots; we couldn't keep track of all the medications being pumped through his thin, rapidly weakening body.

The bad news just kept coming. As I look back on it now, I see Shirley and me sitting there, stunned and numb, while the doctors kept rolling out a new litany of horrors. They were wonderful, calm, confident, positive; we were terrified, confused, basically in shock and denial.

After the doctors performed a heart catheterization on Simon, which allowed them to peek into the heart itself, as well as take tissue samples, they had some answers and treatments to try, and some hope (albeit slim, as we could sense by now).

Simon's life was in grave danger. But the doctors told us that they had definitely found inflammation in the heart tissue, signs that a virus had once been present. Cautiously, they said they might be able to treat the virus with medicine and restore his heart to a semblance of normalcy. If that didn't work, only a heart transplant would save the lad.

I can't tell you the profundity of the shock of hearing those words: heart transplant. It was impossible to take in that they were talking about our son—our skiing, skating, biking, soccer-playing son. It was at almost this precise moment in time that basketball star Reggie Lewis dropped dead on the playing court, of what they later confessed was cardiomyopathy. With what Simon was undergoing at the time, it seemed impossible to label him "lucky." But if he hadn't collapsed in a doctor's office, he probably would have died.

For a week Shirley and I hoped and prayed. For one brief period on a late Friday morning, as they began to withdraw Simon from the medication that kept his heart pumping, we all hoped Simon had beaten the virus, beaten the imflammation. But no, almost to the moment they told us the medication would all be out of his bloodstream, Simon's heart rate skyrocketed and simultaneously his blood pressure began to disappear. Simon's heart was irreversibly, irretrievably, irreparably destroyed. Our son was going to need a heart transplant. The unthinkable, the impossible had become our kid's only possible reality.

At first, I had decided to keep Simon's condition from all but family and close friends, but word leaked to *Daily News* columnist Bob Raissman, who wrote an oblique item about the hospitalization. I figured if Raissman had the item, I'd better contact my pal, Phil Mushnick at the *Post*, which I did. The hockey community got wind of it when we had to cancel the trip to Boston. Soon, the outpouring of emotion became a bit overwhelming.

A huge card, signed by the members of the U.S. Olympic team, arrived along with good wishes from Coach John Cunniff and USA Hockey bigwigs.

At this point, I decided to become more proactive. I figured an appearance by a hockey personality or two might be a tonic for a lad who was weakening by the day. I phoned several friends, including Todd Diamond, a former intern who had become an aide to agent Mark Gandler, a good pal.

"How would he like a visit from Alexei Kasatonov?" Diamond asked. Kasatonov had completed his second year on the Devils' defense and was one of my favorite people although he was bashful about being interviewed. Diamond arranged for the Russian to come to the hospital on Friday, July 9, 1993, which turned out to be one of the true bittersweet days of our lives.

That was the morning we were informed that nothing would reverse what had happened to Simon's heart and that measures would have to be taken to keep the destroyed heart working until (hopefully) a transplantable one arrived.

It had been an emotionally draining morning for Simon, who slipped into a nap shortly after lunch. He had been occupying a bed in the far right corner of the intensive care unit. Because of its location, it seemed almost cozy, if such a feeling is possible in the frenzied confines of an ICU.

When Simon napped, I usually busied myself with work that I brought with me, and on this day, I was jotting notes for a hockey book when I felt a tap on the shoulder. It was Diamond, and rubbing shoulders with him was Alexei Kasatonov, his steely eyes softened by his deep, warm grin.

"How are you?" he asked, his English still deeply accented. I was overwhelmed. To this point I had never really expected anyone from hockey to visit, especially a foreigner like Kasatonov who really didn't know me that well. But there was something strong about our bond, and I imagine it was evident from the well-coupled eye contact whenever we would meet.

Damn it! Simon was fast asleep, and considering his condition, there was no way I would awaken him. One of the nurses pointed out that there was another young patient, a few beds down, who was a Devils' fan and wondered if Alexei would mind stopping at his bed.

"Certainly, I will," he said and proceeded down the corridor until he reached the teenager, who was overwhelmed by the sight of the Russian. Diamond mentioned that this was one of Alexei's first trips to Upper Manhattan, and he had left his wife down front in the car.

"Don't worry," Kasatonov insisted, "I will stay."

Simon slept for another half-hour during which Alexei and I schmoozed about the hockey season. Finally, a nurse came around for a checkup and awakened him. A couple of seconds passed before he realized that a New Jersey Devil was at his bedside. He grinned and extended his hand, which disappeared inside the Russian's hamlike grip.

Kasatonov struggled with his English but said volumes with his eyes. He reached into a large, plastic shopping bag with the name "Gerry Cosby Sporting Goods" on the side and said, "I have something for you."

He rustled the plastic and pulled out a large but strange-looking hockey jersey. After doing a doubletake, Simon realized that it was part of the Russian National Team uniform.

"From the Olympics," said Kasatonov. "For you." Simon had already received his share of flowers and cards, but the Russian Olympic hockey jersey was something to which he could relate better than just about anything he had received. He grasped it tightly and profusely thanked Alexei. They talked hockey for a few minutes and then Kasatonov and Diamond begged off; it was time to leave.

It's so difficult to measure how much a morale boost a visit such as that means to a patient like Simon. Kasatonov gave no inspirational speech and communicated very little except his concern for my son, but that was more than enough. The gift of the Olympic jersey—so treasured a momento—was much more than any one of us had expected.

If a visit from someone who lacked English communication skills could be a boost, I imagined that an English-speaking NHL personality would be even better. I phoned the Islanders, Simon's favorite team, and learned that all of the players were out of town. Ditto for the Devils, his second favorite club; they, too, were away. That left me with the Rangers, far from being on my son's hit parade.

When I called the Rangers' public relations man, Barry Watkins, he was very understanding. "Mike Richter might be in town," he said, "and maybe even Mike Keenan."

Keenan. I thought for a moment and without hesitation said, "Sure, if you could get either or both, let me know."

I hung up and then I began hesitating. My relationship with Keenan had taken several strange turns ever since our first encounter nearly two decades ago. I had been broadcasting hockey for several years and was writing a *Hockey News* column, among other things, when I received a phone call out of the blue.

"This is Mike Keenan," said the voice at the other end. He must have sensed that I didn't have a clue as to who Mike Keenan was all about because he quickly added, "I'm coaching the Rochester Americans."

Of course, of course, I said to myself. I should have known that but why would Keenan call me? To my knowledge I had never insulted him.

"I want to coach in the NHL," he elaborated, "and I figured you might help me."

Flattered, I was. Nobody had ever phoned me for an NHL job and here was Mike Keenan wanting a boost from Stan.

"The first thing we have to do," I said, "is figure who might be looking and then make a couple of calls."

At the time there were very few likely openings. As promised, I contacted a couple of people but to no avail. I finally told Keenan I couldn't help him, he thanked me politely, and that was the end of our first encounter. A few years later he got his wish and wound up as head coach of the Philadelphia Flyers. We would meet from time to time in NHL hallways both before and after games and casually gab.

But our next meaningful encounter took place in Toronto at the *Hockey News*'s annual awards luncheon of which Keenan was an honoree. I was seated next to Keenan and his wife, Rita, each of whom was an absolutely delightful tablemate.

Keenan was the antithesis of the ogre who had been portrayed by players as "Adolf" (as in Hitler), and Rita was a pretty, articulate, and sensitive Jewish woman who told me that some of her family were Holocaust victims. On the other side was their daughter, Gayla, about the same age as our Simon; very sweet, very well behaved, and very out-of-place amid the hockey crowd.

My affection for Keenan grew when I learned that he was a biking enthusiast. We exchanged cycle tales and even vaguely talked of pedaling somewhere together sometime in the distant future. Interestingly, the conversation hardly ever dwelled on hockey, which was fine for all of us.

In my eyes, the most noteworthy aspect of the chat was Keenan's remarkable calm, warmth, and insights. He was so totally unlike his image that I wondered whether he needed a new press agent or if he simply pulled a Jekyll-Hyde depending on the season. I also wondered about Rita. She was so totally unlike any "hockey wife" I had ever met. Not that others weren't attractive, intelligent, and witty, but Rita seemed to be two cuts above everybody else.

Keenan and I never bicycled together—although we did talk about it from time to time thereafter—nor did we spend much time in lengthy conversation during the season or after. Eventually, he moved from Philadelphia to Chicago, where he coached the Blackhawks amid the same aura of imminent player-coach warfare that enveloped the Flyers' dressing room.

By this time Keenan had been around the NHL so long that his reputation preceded him wherever he went, and it was not uncommon for the media to allude to him in terms that were more suitable for a Charles Addams cartoon than big-league hockey. Nor was it unusual to hear Blackhawks players complain about Keenan's mania for discipline and the atmosphere of hypertension that characterized his stewardship.

This was not news to me. My close friend the late Munson Campbell had been pals with Blackhawks' owner Bill Wirtz for many years and was operating one of Wirtz's many liquor dealerships. Campbell, therefore, became my best contact vis-à-vis the Blackhawks, because he was in direct communication with Wirtz on a weekly basis.

"Billy is fed up with Keenan," Campbell told me one day. "He can't take him anymore. As soon as he can, Wirtz will fire him."

It didn't happen right away because, as usual, Keenan kept his club competitive and attractive to watch. But the military academy ambience prevailed, and one summer, as I prepared my annual NHL preview for *Inside Sports* magazine, I wrote a squib about the Blackhawks. One of my choice morsels suggested that if the dislike-for-Mike atmosphere had any effect, it would cause a tidal wave in Lake Michigan.

The article hit the stands about a week after training camp began, which is when my office phone rang.

"Jim DeMaria [Blackhawks' PR man], Stan." His voice was unusually austere. "Mister Keenan would like to talk to you."

Uh-oh. It didn't sound good, but I wasn't quite sure what Keenan had on his mind. Before I could think of the *Inside Sports* item, he was on the blower.

His voice was tingling with tension. "That article you wrote in *Inside Sports*."

"Yes."

"Was that line you wrote about me supposed to be humor?"

"It was an attempt to be funny."

"Well, I didn't think it was very funny."

We went back and forth for awhile. At one point I believed he simply was trying to intimidate me, and yet at another, I suspected that he was sensitive enough to actually feel hurt by the barb. Who knows? Maybe it was both.

I was jolted by the call but also pleased that I hadn't bent to his onslaught. After we hung up, I reread the *Inside Sports* item and remained convinced that Keenan had vastly overreacted to the squib, but then again, Keenan has spent his NHL career over-reacting, or overacting, as the case may be.

Wirtz—via Bob Pulford—eventually fired Keenan, and I next met him at the All-Star Game in Montreal when Gary Bettman was taking command of the NHL. Keenan appeared relaxed as we chatted at rinkside, acting as if our clash had never happened. He even offered me his phone number and suggested that I call if I needed any information. Maybe I shouldn't have been sur-prised at his total friendliness, but I was.

Thus, when Keenan was appointed Rangers' coach, I looked forward to a resumption of our relationship—friendship would have been an exaggeration. Now, here I was: Simon was in cri-sis, Keenan was in town, and I was looking to him for help.

Actually, I'm not certain what kind of help I had expected. The hockey community had learned about Simon's plight, and each day we would receive tokens of encouragement, from cards to letters to autographed pictures from Tie Domi, one of my friendly enemies. There was a phone call and autographed stick from Gretzky, another stick from Lemieux. Trevor Linden sent his playoff jersey; in fact, we had received so much hockey equip-ment and gear that we could have opened up a shop! But so far, only Kasatonov had actually lugged himself all the way up here to Morningside Heights.

Keenan's persona offered more strength-giving potential than most of the others, and despite our past differences, I thought it would be beneficial if he visited.

It was another Friday, this time it was July 16, when we got the news that Simon had actually gone on the Columbia-Presbyterian transplant list. This was the actual outward admission that our son couldn't live unless they took out his heart and replaced it with the heart of another. It was still too much to comprehend.

Now it was a matter of waiting—and hoping—for the call that told us a healthy heart was on the way.

Once again, Simon took it with fortitude and with nary a tear in his eye. My wife, Shirley, and I were shaken and attempted to fortify ourselves with the knowledge needed for the next step. The doctors gave us an elaborate handbook that explained all the pitfalls and procedures enroute to the transplant and beyond. To say the least, we were overcome by the challenge.

What we needed now was some kind of a family tonic, and it came on a Saturday morning in the form of the two Mikes, Keenan and Richter. The goalie was the first to arrive; quietly gliding in, looking more like a college sophomore than an NHL goalie. He went right over to Simon and handed him a bag filled with Rangers' goodies that included a T-shirt, pins, and other tidbits. Richter kidded the kid about not being a Ranger fan and got a broad—yet semisheepish—grin in return.

Richter plopped himself in a big leather chair at bedside and began chatting with Simon when, within a minute, another figure appeared in the doorway. I got up to greet the coach, who walked briskly toward the bed, gazing straight at me. Instead of a handshake, he wrapped his arms around me and squeezed the squeeze of a parent who had a special feel for a sick kid. I've been squeezed a few hundred times in my life but none equaled the Keenan hug for a simple message delivery: hang tough, my good friend!

For an hour the two Mikes, myself, Simon, and, later, Shirley, traded stories, exchanged views, and distracted ourselves from the trouble around us. Keenan's demeanor alternated from witty to intensely intellectual as he would carefully explain an aerobic program he thought Simon might try after—we hoped—he obtained his new heart.

Uncannily, we all seemed to realize simultaneously when it was time for the two Mikes to leave, and except for Simon, of course, all stood up as one. As they headed for the elevator, Keenan spun around and grabbed me a second time. I was inwardly hoping that he would. Shirley and I were terribly anxious about the uncertain days ahead and needed outside reassurance. Mike's hug tightened the emotional vise. If he said anything, I couldn't hear, but I was feeling plenty.

The elevator arrived and they both disappeared through the doors. We returned to the room. "It's enough to make you a Ranger fan," I said to Simon.

He thought for a moment. "Well," he said, "I don't know about that." Spoken like a true Islander fan, with a fresh reverence for the two Mikes.

I had been so touched by the two visits, I wondered how I could possibly give the two Mikes fair journalistic treatment. Dare I criticize Keenan who had given me such immense emotional support? Would I ever put the knock on Richter no matter how badly he played goal?

The answers were difficult and, for the moment at least, did not have to be answered. But they would prove perplexing down the line when I returned to the arena, resumed my professional life, and once again began writing and discussing their performances. Believe me, it was not easy.

Shortly after Keenan and Richter had departed, the three of us understood what Simon faced in the next weeks; waiting, hoping, and praying. There was no way of knowing when—or if—the heart would arrive. There was no way of knowing how long Simon's severely wounded heart could last despite the medications. We wanted to think that he could last for months (as it often took months to receive a heart), but we sensed that it could be less—much less.

In the meantime, the hockey community continued an outpouring that was almost overwhelming: a stirring letter from Pat Quinn and another from Devils' owner John McMullen. New Jersey president Lou Lamoriello remembered that Simon had lionized former Devils' goalie Craig Billington—since traded to Ottawa—so he dispatched a Devils' Billington jersey with a funny note about Simon being true to his hero.

As the days passed, we had hoped that the "magic" drug Dibutamine would sustain Simon's heart until the new one arrived, but soon it became clear that he was weakening. Where once he could climb out of bed and walk to the toilet, now he could barely take a step or two, at the most. And still no replacement heart.

Distractions and encouragement were necessary. A steady stream of Simon's friends and some relatives helped immensely. One day, completely unannounced, goalie Sean Burke and forward Jim McKenzie of the Whalers drove all the way from Hartford and showed up in the kid's room. Simon knew and remembered Burke from his 1988 heroics as a Devils' rookie. McKenzie was a complete newcomer but a very gregarious fellow who immediately won over the lad. Burke talked goaltending and McKenzie talked about everything else. It was a key visit.

Even more so was the appearance of Islanders' forwards Mick Vukota and Derek King. As a Long Island fan, Simon had been hoping that one or two of his favorites would show up, but none had been around in the early part of July. Then, old friend Vukota called, said he was coming, and asked if he could bring along his Sega hockey video game. By all means, I said.

Vukota and King said they were coming up on a Friday afternoon but they didn't say when. Simon, in the meantime, was at the whim of doctors and nurses, constantly being wheeled around for tests and x-rays. On this day, he had made several trips and fell asleep exhausted. He awakened at about 4 P.M. and about three minutes later the two Islanders knocked on the door. (Simon was at the moment out of PICU and in a private room on a cardiac care floor in the Babies' Hospital.)

Like Richter, Vukota carried a shopping bag from which he lifted out a set of black wires connected to a video-game console. It was the same system Simon had at home, which somehow none of us had thought to bring.

Just as we had hoped, the visit of the Islanders was extraspecial. King, who always had seemed to be a withdrawn personality, was terribly witty in a low-key way, and Vukota was Vukota: effusive, occasionally brash, and at his best when discussing the art of winning at electronic hockey.

"Kinger beats me up all the time," chuckled Vukota, referring to the video game and not the ice version, where King had been renowned as a soft player.

King was highly amused and went along with the gag, the pair japing back and forth as if they were sitting in the Nassau Coliseum dressing room. This time the hockey talk had more meaning to Simon because it involved the Islanders. We bulled about the 1993 playoffs, the missed chance against Montreal, the craziness of Darius Kasparaitis, and the flubby Rangers. We talked until dinnertime and then the two players had to leave to head downtown. Simon thanked Vukota for the video game and they were out the door.

There was no way for Vukota to know this at the time, but the simple gesture of delivering the Sega had a profound effect on Simon in the days ahead. His condition had deteriorated to a point where he was virtually confined to bed. Somehow, the game became a distraction at critical moments when his attention had to be diverted from the anxiety of waiting for the precious gift of the heart.

It wasn't the only Islander visit, either. Just a few days later Isles' director of publications, Chris Botta, showed up with goalie Mark Fitzpatrick in tow. Fitzpatrick had just been traded to Quebec for Ron Hextall. He was then claimed by Florida from Quebec in the Expansion Draft but was still in the area. Fitzpatrick, too, had been stricken by a mystery ailment a few years earlier—and had sufficiently recovered to resume his NHL career. This was another boost for Simon, and for me as well.

On Thursday, August 5, a doctor on the cardiology team, Dr. Marianne Kichuk, informed me that the Dibutamine was losing its effectiveness, that Simon would have to be returned to intensive care and placed on another, more potent medicine. Without articulating it, Dr. Kichuk intimated that Simon was dying.

I phoned Shirley, who still was at home, and spilled the news, unedited. This was no time to mince words—at least that was what I thought at the time. When I returned to Simon's room, he mentioned that he already had spoken with the doctor.

"Dad," he said, almost matter-of-factly, "things aren't so good, are they?"

I tried to create a verbal cushion. Yes, you would have to return to intensive care, but you'll be all right. The Dibutamine will be replaced by another drug that will sustain you—I knew not how—until the heart arrived. He appeared somewhat reassured and then thoroughly distracted when his friend Doug arrived. That was just the break I needed.

Two hours later, while I tried to relax in the waiting room, Dr. Kichuk walked in and said the precious words: "It looks like a heart is on the way."

It was. When Shirley walked in shortly thereafter, she had obviously been shoring herself up to spend a desolate night with Simon before he went down to PICU for what could be the last time, when she was confronted with a weird scene of what I could only call scared jubilation: a heart was on its way and Simon was being readied for surgery. It would be almost 1 A.M. on Friday, August 6, before he disappeared into the icy operating room.

By 7 A.M. he was in the PICU, tubes and machines all over. But, by God, he was already conscious and trying to speak around the respirator and over the medications they had given him to actually paralyze him. Simon's subsequent recovery bordered on the incredible, until he underwent his first attempt to reject the new heart only a week after the transplant. Other complications would occur, but by August 25, Simon Fischler walked into his own home.

His life never would be the same. He might not ever play goal again, but there was the hope that, despite the many obstacles he would face along the way, he could enjoy a reasonably normal life.

In the meantime, I had hoped to return to a reasonably normal hockey life, although the sense I had was that the ice game never would be the same for me, or for that matter, the NHL.

THE BETTMAN EVOLUTION

W hen Gary Bettman took command of the National Hockey League, I warned him face-to-face that no matter what he did, there would be a residue of Canadian chauvinists who would criticize him no matter how pure his intentions, no matter how sage his decisions, nor how businesslike they were.

And because there never has been a faultless NHL leader, it was inevitable that Bettman would err, which he did. But even before the commissioner committed his first faux pas, he was under the gun north of the 49th parallel.

After all, Canadians realized that their beloved game no longer was the same and never would be in the foreseeable future. It had become Americanized beyond recognition, and the franchise score when Bettman succeeded Stein was 18–8 for Uncle Sam. The rout was on.

On the administration front, where the movers and shakers live, the tilt was even more precipitous. Americans were now running Canada's national sport from top to bottom. For example, the "Big Three" among hockey's power brokers—board chairman Bruce McNall, Bettman, and NHL Players' Association boss Bob Goodenow—were all U.S. born.

At his NHL fortress in Manhattan, Bettman, with precious few exceptions, filled almost every available league command post with non-Canadians. Brian Burke, the new senior vice president, was born in Providence, Rhode Island, and grew up in Minnesota. Almost all the vice presidents, from Steve Solomon to Glenn Adamo to Arthur Pincus to Bernadette Mansur, were New Yorkers or close to Gotham in spirit.

This was a far cry from an earlier era, when Toronto's Conn Smythe and Montreal's Frank Selke Sr. ran the league. The president, Clarence Campbell, and his aide, Brian O'Neill, both were Canadians.

Bettman's Americanization of the NHL did not go unnoticed in Canada, where two major complaints were heard: (1) the league is orchestrated by U.S. attorneys; and (2) they are insensitive to the needs of Canadian markets and would just as soon unload Winnipeg, Edmonton, and Quebec in favor of larger American cities.

"I can sympathize with Canadians whose noses are out of joint," *Toronto Star* columnist Bob McKenzie told me. "How would Americans feel if the baseball commissioner was Japanese?"

Unlike some of his colleagues, McKenzie allowed that quality of performance as well as the new administration's sensitivity toward small Canadian markets remain key bases for judgment. Burke cautioned the nervous Nellies north of the border not to worry.

"We feel the Canadian component is critical," said Burke. "The bulk of players and media interests are north of the 49th parallel. It's important that we promote professional hockey in Canada."

Burke, like others at the NHL office, had become acutely sensitive to criticism. "I resent this 'American attorneys' notion," he told me. "I would be just as offended if someone said, 'Oh, this guy shouldn't be hired because he's black or this guy shouldn't be hired because he's Jewish or Chinese.' It's 1993. Wake up and smell the coffee. The best people should get the jobs."

Not all the critics were in Canada. Vicki Contavespi, a reporter for the prestigious *Forbes* magazine, had been a hockey fan for a number of years and looked forward to writing an upbeat feature about the new administration. *Forbes* had only recently published a positive story on the NBA and featured a sidebar on how Bettman's NHL was poised to be the next NBA.

In researching her article, Contavespi phoned Goodenow and inquired about the union's new "Be A Player" campaign. The NHLPA's director explained that older players do not receive pension money and that all monies from "Be A Player" would go to them. "I began to delve into that and my *Forbes* piece was the end result," Contavespi told me.

The headline over Contavespi's story in the January 31, 1994, issue of *Forbes* was hardly the kind that would be savored by the NHL's relatively new public relations honchos. "Bad Blood on the Ice" was followed by a subheadline, "Can Gary Bettman do for ice hockey what David Stern did for basketball? So far, the outlook is hardly promising."

Hmmmm.

At a time when the press-conscious Bettman was obtaining generally positive publicity, the *Forbes* piece was like a literary land mine for the denizens of NHL headquarters. After lavishly praising Bettman's former boss, David Stern, Contavespi then asserted that "Bettman, by contrast, is alienating hockey's players."

Among other items, she mentioned that players felt they were missing out on revenues for hockey-jersey sales and that retired players were still battling over $40 million in pension money they felt they were owed. Her story concluded with the fact that union members had been skating without a contract since the beginning of the season.

She wondered why Bettman hadn't focused his attention on that issue, an assertion that grated Bettman. "Well, excuse me," he replied to her. "I also have 400 other things that are front-burner items and I have a league to run on a daily basis."

But the woman from *Forbes* had the last word. Contavespi acidly concluded her commentary with two sentences: "A commissioner out of his depth? So it seems." It was awfully—and perhaps unnecessarily—tough stuff.

Because all of the 26 NHL club owners at the time were businessmen, virtually every one of them reads *Forbes*. Many reacted angrily to the feature and some clearly suggested that Goodenow had planted it with Contavespi, a charge that she later vigorously denied. Not surprisingly, Bettman Incorporated was unhappy with her piece.

"The league was very helpful to me until the *Forbes* story came out," said Contavespi. "I actually received a call at my home from [NHL vice president of corporate communications] Bernadette Mansur before my story came out. She accused me of setting out to do a hatchet job on Bettman, which I thought was unprofessional.

"Arthur Pincus [NHL vice president of public relations] tried his best to have any mention of a lawsuit filed by retired players against the league be removed from my story. *Forbes* refused that request because the information was factually correct."

Contavespi, a soft-spoken, unobtrusive reporter who has since become a senior writer for Corning Incorporated, was dismayed over the NHL reaction to the story. "I did not set out to do a hatchet job on Bettman," she insisted in our conversations. "I had nothing against him and had never even met him. But I've come to the conclusion that Bettman has an attitude; of that there is no doubt. He is very arrogant; and coming from the NBA he would be arrogant. The NBA had the world by the basketballs and Bettman came to the NHL thinking he could run it like Stern ran the NBA." Perhaps, but others suggested that Contavespi was unduly harsh too early in Bettman's reign.

Bettman's critics argued that his NBA background precluded him from having a genuine "feel" for hockey. The sacking of Stu Hackel from the TV department was cited by some as a classic example. Hackel was well respected throughout the league for his knowledge and contacts. He had been with the NHL for many years.

"Bettman didn't understand the culture of hockey," Contavespi argued. "He had no idea how the 'boys' thought. In my article, I called Bettman 'pugnacious' and that wasn't a compliment. I think he has a short man's complex."

Then again, Bettman didn't expect everyone to like him. He understood there would be criticism even from critics who liked his performance. Me included. I was terribly unhappy with his handling of the Dale Hunter–Pierre Turgeon affair during the spring of 1993. Late in the final game, Hunter, whose Washington Capitals were about to lose the series, sneaked up on the New York Islanders' center and cross-checked Turgeon from behind into the sideboards.

It was as dastardly an act as any I've seen in a half-century of watching hockey. The result was even worse. Enjoying the best year of his career, Turgeon suffered a shoulder injury that side-lined him for the next series—except for a token appearance in game seven at Pittsburgh—and rendered him ineffective against the Canadiens in the Cup semifinals. Some Turgeon watchers insist he never was the same player after his recovery.

My belief, shared by many journalists, was that Bettman's first major disciplinary case should have set an example for years to come. A year-long suspension would have been justified. Instead, Hunter was suspended for the first 21 games of the following season.

"The Islanders' fans wanted summary execution of Hunter," said Bettman, "and the Capitals have continued to say that I was much, much, much too severe. That tells me we hit it on the mark."

Nevertheless, Bettman was clobbered by some New York media heavyweights, including *Newsday*'s Mike Lupica, but shrugged off the criticism and proceeded to his next crisis, which was the embarrassing Gil Stein affair. As a liaison from the Ziegler regime, Stein might have been a useful aide-de-camp for Bettman based on his long years with the league and his contacts, but when the media got wind of the Hall of Fame shenanigans, Stein got it from all barrels and Bettman had to move swiftly to defuse the incident before it damaged the league.

He made a brilliant move, engaging an independent probe that eventually found Stein culpable. When questions about Ottawa's lack of effort in late season games were raised, the commissioner again went to his investigative consultants and emerged smelling like a rose.

After months of criticism for his failure to hire a right-hand "hockey man," he selected Brian Burke, the one I had recommended to him in the first place just after he had taken office. I wouldn't for a minute suggest that I was responsible for Burke's appointment, but I found it fascinating to see how many NHL personalities Bettman had considered—Glen Sather among them—before making his final decision.

There were those who thought that Burke got the job by default, that many general managers rejected the position because they were dubious about working for Bettman. Some simply didn't want to work in New York City, but Burke, as I had said at the start, fit all the criteria. He's smart, a lawyer, played hockey, has dual citizenship, was an agent and general manager. Moreover, Burke is media friendly, answering any and every question put to him by the press.

He's also notoriously combative, and during his Vancouver stint as Canucks' boss Pat Quinn's senior assistant, Burke singled out *Vancouver Province* columnist Tony Gallagher for criticism in what amounted to a war between the two that still hasn't ended now that Burke is the Canucks' general manager. Its evolution offers an arresting view of team-media relations when a newsman is perceived as overly hostile.

During one exchange in August 1991, the Canucks' Glen Ringdal, vice president and director of marketing and communications, wrote a stinging letter to Gallagher's editor-in-chief, Brian Butters. Ringdal asserted that neither Burke nor Quinn "has any desire or intention to speak to or grant interviews to Tony no matter which media outlet he represents."

Burke-Quinn also ordered that Gallagher "not be accorded the access to club personnel generally given to other reporters."

The reason, according to Ringdal, was that the Canucks' personnel "have been personally offended on numerous occasions by Tony's scurrilous editorial attacks on our company and its people."

Butters responded with a letter on August 6, 1991, rejecting the ban out of hand. "The fact you don't care for Gallagher's reporting on Canuck affairs is beside the point here," wrote

Butters. "Gallagher's job as a contract columnist for the *Province* is to call the shots the way he sees them."

Butters concluded by saying, "The Canucks are attempting to interfere with the ability of a specific individual to make a living."

Gallagher continued making a living as the *Vancouver Province* hockey columnist, where he remains to this day. The feelings between Gallagher and Burke appear to have changed little. The Canucks' attempt at stifling Gallagher was an abject failure.

Although Gallagher might not have seconded Burke's addition to the Bettman cabinet, others did at the very least because he was a "hockey man" in an NHL milieu that was increasingly being dominated by nonhockey people. Meanwhile, the Americanization of the NHL was becoming more and more galling to Canadian chauvinist journalists, the most obvious of whom was the *Toronto Sun's* columnist Al Strachan.

"Once the head [NHL] office was in Montreal," wrote Strachan, "but it's now in New York and staffed by Americans, mostly lawyers. Even the responsibility of overseeing the game itself was given to an American, Brian Burke, a Boston lawyer.

"Burke, who was born in the United States, got his law degree in the United States and always worked in the United States except for a few years as assistant general manager of the Vancouver Canucks. He acquired Canadian citizenship during his tenure on the West Coast and therefore tries to convince people that he's a Canadian. In the new NHL, not one of 25 million real Canadians qualifies to be the chief executive in charge of hockey.

"This fact has not escaped the players, the majority of whom are Canadians."

Bettman and Burke dismissed the criticism out of hand, as well they should. Players, many of whom were either American or foreign born, couldn't care less whether a Ubangi was running the NHL as long as the average salary kept climbing—as it was—and the league remained a stickhandlers' market—which it was, and still is.

But Strachan was right on when he noted that the influx of Bettman technocrats had altered the close feel for the game experienced by NHL workers during the coccoonlike Campbell, Ziegler, and Stein regimes. The NBA-ing of the NHL put the accent on bigness and a more corporate feel than ever before.

"When Canadians ran the game," added Strachan, "even the owners had a hockey sense and the game's roots were in frozen-prairie ponds and cold arenas.

"The roots of today's game are in the boardrooms. Decisions are made not because they may have a good or bad impact on hockey, but because of the manner in which they will be received by large corporations—and all those corporations are American.

"This is the new order and, unfortunately, it's here to stay."

Whether "the new order" would be capable of achieving its goals—primarily to lift the NHL toward the NBA's success level—would depend on its handling of two labor crises, the first of which was a strike by referees and linesmen in the early part of the 1993–94 season.

The zebras' walkout was followed by anguished cries that the use of substitute officials would result in chaos beyond belief and, within days of scab officiating, Bettman's gamble would fail and, conceivably, his regime would crumble.

Opinions differ as to the effectiveness of the replacements. I covered several games that were handled by the nonunion types and, in some cases, they were handled better than games orchestrated by the Don Koharskis, Bill McCrearys, and Andy van-Hellemonds of the world. Granted that Paul Stewart's inevitable showboating was missing, as was Terry Gregson's intensity, but by and large, the newcomers held up throughout the walkout; if they hadn't, Bettman would have been toast.

The commissioner was fortunate. Had there not been enough substitutes, or had they been intimidated by the strikers, games would have been canceled and Bettman would have faced intense criticism.

However, the commissioner and Burke planned well, lined up their replacements well enough in advance, and had them in place when the walkout was called. Although the zebras had plenty of support, they also faced public opposition from those who believed that their on-ice performance hardly merited any raise in salaries.

During the early days of the strike, I had been in close touch with both sides of the dispute. Agent Don Meehan, who represented the zebras, was an old friend through his representation of Pat LaFontaine, while the NHL types, led by Bettman, chatted with me on a regular basis.

I clearly sided with ownership in this dispute but was not averse to giving the other side its voice. One day I received a phone call from referee Kerry Fraser, who had been a pal of mine for years—we once considered writing a book together—and had become a spokesman for the striking officials. Fraser had been exceptionally supportive during my son's crisis and held a special niche in our hearts. Fraser knew that we had given time to the NHL on one of our telecasts from Byrne Meadowlands Arena in New Jersey and asked whether one of the striking officials could get equal time. My SportsChannel producer, Jackie Lyons, unhesitatingly

agreed, and I phoned Meehan to obtain a referee. The most natural would have been vanHellemond, who had been outspoken
from the start of the strike and who was best known among the
zebras.

I considered this an interesting test of personality. As long as
I had known vanHellemond he had refused interviews with me,
presumably on the grounds that he objected to my criticism of
him and his colleagues. Now he was on the blower and I mentioned that I'd like him to be the zebra to articulate his union's
position.

At first he seemed willing, yet there was some hesitation. He
was in Toronto and the interview would be held in East
Rutherford, New Jersey. Yes, he wanted to appear, but no, there
were a few obstacles. I was fervently hoping he would come,
mostly because it would demonstrate that in a contentious issue
such as this, I bore no grudge and left my microphone open to
the other side.

VanHellemond never phoned back. Instead, I received a call
from Fraser explaining that he would be the guest, not Andy. His
explanation sounded reasonable enough—travel, other commit-
ments—but it left me with a sour aftertaste. I had the feeling
that vanHellemond just couldn't get himself to go one-on-one
with me and that was that.

Because the interview with NHL people had been conducted in
our SportsChannel studio adjoining the Devils' dressing room, we
expected to do the Fraser interview there as well. But when word
of the striking referee's impending appearance reached the NHL
high command, we were told that Fraser would not be admitted
into Byrne Arena. Period.

Neither the NHL nor the Devils were pleased that we were giving equal time to the officials, and they certainly would not allow
him into the building—at least not as long as he was striking—
without a ticket. And when Fraser obtained a ducat, he was not
cleared to come down to the dressing-room area without a pass,
which he was emphatically denied.

Faced with these obstacles, SportsChannel had the option of
either scrapping the interview or finding a location where it could
be conducted. Lyons decided that the "best" spot would be in the
Byrne Arena parking lot just outside the vomitory ramp where
the TV trucks are located.

As we set up for the interview, winds were blowing fiercely off
the nearby Hudson River and over the Meadowlands. The cold air
was filtering through my overcoat as Fraser appeared from behind
a row of parked cars. Typically upbeat, he apologized for us having to do the one-on-one in a parking lot, and we insisted that it

was no problem even though we were freezing our tootsies off.

After Fraser had made his points, I asked him if he saw the irony in this situation. Time after time, I had asked referees to be interviewed and time after time they had refused. But now that they had something to gain from going before the cameras, Fraser was suddenly available. There was nothing he could say about that and we parted shaking hands.

Needless to say, the Fraser interview did not sit well with the NHL general staff nor with the Devils' high command. Lou Lamoriello and Dr. John McMullen, president and owner, respectively, with whom I had become quite close, wanted no part of the zebras getting air time on a Devils' telecast, but what was done was done and in 10 days the strike was settled.

Anyone who suggests there was a winner or loser in this dispute is off base. Officials obtained meaningful raises and other benefits—opponents would have preferred that they obtained not a penny more—while Bettman's gamble on using the scabs worked. Had the replacements cracked in the first days, as many had predicted, it would have been bye-bye Bettman. But the replacements performed nobly under adverse conditions.

"We got all the games played and we didn't miss a beat," Bettman glowed when we met in a corridor at Byrne Arena. "We had competent replacement officials who came under the most intense and unfair scrutiny. If this scrutiny was placed on any of our existing officials, I don't know that they could have fared better."

But the settlement did not settle the rancor in the zebra pasture. Many of the officials, speaking anonymously, blurted out their bitterness toward the commissioner, who was viewed as an arrogant outsider. This view was magnified by several Canadian journalists who depicted him as an insensitive dictator.

I pointedly brought up the ill-feeling issue to Bettman after the strike. Typically, he tried to put a positive spin on it while remaining somewhat realistic.

"In terms of the residue of bad feelings," he said, "I don't think it's widespread among all the officials. It was business and people can't confuse that. I was charged to run this place in a credible way. When someone comes in and says, 'I want a hundred percent raise,' and my response is, 'here's 29 percent the first year and 65 percent over four years,' I don't have to apologize for that."

Without question, I agreed with him. If anything, the zebras' work across-the-board would be graded C-minus, at best. With a grade like that, any salary boost should be viewed as a bonus. Bettman need not have apologized for anything.

Public relations was another story. Steve Taub of *Financial World* magazine, and other NHL critics, complained that once the league had identified him as an unfriendly journalist, he was not provided the interview access he desired.

"Their public relations left something to be desired," said Taub. "When I wrote a story, they handled it horrendously. Once when the league had a unified press conference in New York, their PR people wouldn't make anyone available to talk to me. I finally interviewed Bettman at the hotel and he tried to embarrass me in front of the other sportswriters, the 'all-knowing' sportswriters."

A year after Bettman had taken office, *Newsweek* magazine commented that the commissioner had not done enough. Bettman disagreed. "We've put hockey on the right path," he countered. "That includes a reorganization, hiring people like Brian Burke with in-house expertise needed for a businesslike, stable organization."

But ESPN ratings remained mediocre and a spate of stories about "boring" hockey blemished the NHL's image. Aging league icon Wayne Gretzky had lost his drawing power, and Mario Lemieux, Gretzky's successor as pinup star, had become seriously ill. Marketing of the league had stumbled forward without any noticeable gains.

Bettman, of course, had the answers. "It's very nice to say you want to market, but you don't just throw a light switch and reach that market." He was right.

As vital as marketing was to the NHL's progress, it was small potatoes compared with the commissioner's most vexing challenge: a new collective bargaining agreement. The NHL Players' Association contract with the league had expired on September 15, 1993, and under Bob Goodenow's baton, the stickhandlers were singing restless and angry songs.

"Hockey has the most growth potential of all the major sports," said Doug Wilson, the outgoing NHLPA president. "We believe players and owners can share in that growth in a way that is mutually beneficial."

It sounded good but the reality was more complicated and not very good after all. The arguments ahead would surround the issue of how the revenue pie should be divided and who would wield the most power. Meanwhile, Bettman had months to cultivate a relationship with his negotiating adversary, Bob Goodenow, who meanwhile had an opportunity to carefully eye the commissioner's roughing of the referees.

"Sometimes," Bettman ominously mentioned before the CBA talks began, "you have to have a strike because people's expectations are a little out of whack. And they need to be out of work to lower those expectations. Bob and I may not agree with everything, but that's what collective bargaining is all about."

Bettman's future hung on hammering out a CBA that was palatable to his owners. Goodenow, as tough an adversary as the commissioner, would provide the ultimate test. If the commissioner was lucky, he'd have a deal before the 1994 playoffs—without a strike or lockout.

"We'll have to see what the players want to do," he said. "If they want to get aggressive, that will be their call. I'm committed to getting a framework in place that will enable us to stabilize the sport and I'm always optimistic about everything."

Heading toward the conclusion of his first full season, Bettman still was enjoying more kudos than kicks. If he could pull off a new CBA, he would get an A on his report card. But as John Ziegler learned in 1992, a strike or lockout can result in an F, as in Forget it.

"For people to think we were going to duplicate what the NBA did in a year or two years or five years is silly," Bettman concluded. "It took the NBA well in excess of a decade. David Stern was NBA commissioner three years before anyone knew who he was. I don't have apologies for what we've done."

Bettman triumphed in one sense; the 1994 playoffs were played without a hitch. But they came and went without a collective bargaining agreement. Any signs of a quick agreement between Bettman and Goodenow had evaporated in a summer of charges and countercharges. The spark that would explode into hockey's civil war was about to be ignited and there would be hell to pay.

THE FALL OF BRUCE MCNALL

"I'm like a fireman. Wherever the fire is, is where I happen to be."

—BRUCE MCNALL

B ruce McNall's name meant absolutely nothing to me when it was first mentioned during a phone conversation in the early eighties. The fellow on the other end of the wire was Joel Bergman.

"You might want to write this name down," said Bergman, who has been the Fischler Hockey Service's West Coast reporter for almost 20 years. "Bruce McNall. He's a big fan of yours."

He might have been talking about Joe Schlump the Midget for all I knew about Bruce McNall.

"Apart from being a fan of mine," I inquired, "who is this guy?"

Bergman went on to note that the McNall in question was a man of wealth, a devoted hockey follower, and a casual friend of his. Still, it meant absolutely nothing to me until I detected a faint sense of urgency in Bergman's voice. "You really should have his number," Bergman concluded.

I wrote it down on a piece of paper and tacked it on the bulletin board behind the computer. Then, I quickly forgot about Bruce McNall.

In the early eighties there was no reason to think about the roly-poly coin collector. The Kings were being run by Dr. Jerry Buss. Friends of mine on the NHL board of governors admired Buss in one way and chided him in another, but according to one owner, he was rarely seen at governors' meetings.

Buss-watchers hardly were surprised by his casual disdain for the ownership meetings because Dr. Buss's passion was for basketball and his true favorites, the Los Angeles Lakers. This was the official winter glitz team of Tinseltown and was renowned for its ability to lure just about every celebrity from Jack Nicholson to Woody Allen down for a courtside seat at the NBA games. As far as his NHL colleagues were concerned, Buss's Kings were a mere afterthought, a fiscal benchwarmer, so to speak.

This could be a source of annoyance to people like McNall, who lived and died with the Kings. They reveled in the halcyon years when Marcel Dionne, Charlie Simmer, and Dave Taylor dominated the NHL as the Triple Crown Line and petit Rogatien Vachon punted out pucks in the Los Angeles goal.

Although it has become fashionable to declare that Los Angeles was a dead hockey town before Gretzky arrived, this hardly was the case. In 1974–75, the Kings won 42 games, lost only 17, and tied 21. They finished a vibrant second in the Norris Division, a feat they duplicated in 1980–81, when their record was a handsome 43–24–13. The Kings were respected and well covered by the media while attracting a devoted core of followers, McNall among them.

But his name had passed from my consciousness until 1986, when Bergman phoned once more. "Remember that fellow, Bruce McNall, I told you about? Well, he now owns part of the Kings."

It sounded implausible to me until I checked the papers. Sure enough, McNall bought 25 percent of the hockey club from Buss. "I don't think that's the end of it," Bergman added. "Bruce really wants to get involved."

A year later McNall owned 49 percent of the Kings. In September 1987 he was named president, and in March 1988 he became the sole owner. Now I knew why there was a sense of urgency in Bergman's voice three years earlier.

I finally met Bruce McNall during one of the Kings' eastern swings. They had a date with the New York Islanders at Nassau Veterans Memorial Coliseum in Uniondale, where I had broadcast the games for SportsChannel. A few hours before show time, we would hang out in the corridor near the visiting team's dressing room.

One could hardly miss the new owner. He was what my mother would have described as "pleasingly plump." McNall weighed in at about 225 pounds, wore a double-breasted navyblue suit with a silver and white tie. That was the least conspicuous aspect of McNall. His trademark—and that which set him apart from any of the other owners—was his face. It was large and invariably was sealed with a smile.

"I think you'll like him," Bergman mentioned before our meeting.

Disarmingly affable, McNall was hard not to like. His story read like Horatio Alger and his style was right out of Dale Carnegie's *How to Win Friends and Influence People*.

Before he even had complete control of the Kings, the *Los Angeles Times* profiled him with what it tritely called "a success story." "He Has Two Things Going: Luck, Money," noted the headline over Jerry Crowe's profile. Superficially, at least, McNall appeared to be one of the luckiest people in California. In the fall of 1987 he returned from Paris, where Trempolino, a horse he co-owned, won the $1.1 million Arc de Triomphe, Europe's richest race. A full-length film, *The Sicilian*, was about to be released by McNall's production company, Gladden Entertainment Corporation, while his collectible-coin brokerage was discussing a deal with Merrill Lynch.

"I'm like a fireman," said McNall. "Wherever the fire is, is where I happen to be."

I learned that McNall began following hockey while a student at California's Arcadia High School in 1967, when I wrote my first book, a biography of Gordie Howe. A teenage coin collector, McNall learned the numismatic business and soon had Los Angeles shop owners seeking him out to identify and price their coins. McNall's reward was lesser coins, but he soon had the wherewithal to start his own collection and open his own store.

By the time he was 20, McNall had graduated from UCLA with a degree in ancient history and was at work on a doctorate when he decided to concentrate on his coin business. "I decided that maybe I'd make a little money first," he said. At age 24, he paid $420,000 for a 2,000-year-old Greek coin that he later sold for almost $1 million.

When the 37-year-old McNall was named head of the Kings, he claimed that his coin company, Numismatic Fine Arts, Incorporated, was the largest of its kind in the world. In addition Gladden Entertainment had produced a couple of hits, *WarGames* and *Mr. Mom*, and his Summa Stable, Incorporated, was breeding and racing thoroughbreds. McNall asserted that he owned or had interests in about 250 horses.

The *Los Angeles Times* reported his net worth at $34 million, but McNall corrected that to about $100 million. Now he would try to add to it by building the Kings into a respectable organization. "I want to bring the Stanley Cup to Los Angeles within the next three years," he insisted in October 1987.

It was a laudable goal. Also laughable. Nobody expected the Stanley Cup to ever reach Los Angeles. Since the Kings were born, in 1967, the club never got remotely close to attaining big-league

hockey's ultimate goal. Although I admired McNall's enthusiasm, I dismissed his prediction as a function more of vitality
than reality.

What I did appreciate in McNall was his candor and conge-
niality. As rich and famous as he had become, McNall was con-
genitally available, always willing to be interviewed, and quite
willing to state his mind, even if it meant challenging the establishment. More importantly, to his team, McNall was hell-bent on
making the Kings respectable.

"The hockey club needs help," he said. "It's something that
obviously is an ailing thing. It needs something, so I've been trying to develop what the heck that is. I'm not sure what that is yet."

McNall polled his players to determine what they believed
was necessary to improve the club. He became the archetypical
hands-on owner, helping rookies such as Luc Robitaille and Steve
Duchesne find a place to live and showing up at every game.
"He's really somebody special," said Robitaille, who became one
of McNall's favorites. "He really cares about the players."

He became the ultimate jock owner, savoring the liniment-
smelling dressing room, courting the media, and spending money
to get a winner. Unlike original Kings' owner Jack Kent Cooke,
who rarely was seen by the players, McNall became one of the
boys. "He breathed life into the team," said veteran forward Dave
Taylor.

That he did but the Kings remained on a treadmill to oblivion through his first full season as president and sole owner. They
completed the 1987–88 season with a 30–42–8 record, finished
fourth in the Smythe Division, and actually ran through three
coaches, Mike Murphy, Rogie Vachon, and Robbie Ftorek.

While all this was going on, hockey's most arresting star,
Wayne Gretzky, was becoming uncomfortable in his role with
the Edmonton Oilers. I detected this feeling during a meeting
with the Great One in Manhattan. He was accompanied by his
agent, Michael Barnett, to a postseason award ceremony at the
club inside Madison Square Garden. The press timing was poor,
and the press meeting following the ceremony was so lightly
attended that we all were able to sit around a large table.

It was then that Gretzky actually stated that he was contemplating retirement. Mind you, I said contemplating. But even
the mere suggestion that Gretzky was thinking of hanging up his
skates was somewhere between bizarre and stupid. Obviously, he
was angling for something that meant either more money from
Edmonton Oilers' owner Peter Pocklington or a move out of
Alberta.

Gretzky already had won four Stanley Cups and realized that his marketing potential would be better served in a larger American venue. It had become apparent on several visits that he loved New York's nightlife. Playing for the Rangers would have been the ideal, but, then again, nobody ever expected Gretzky to leave Edmonton.

Yet there was something about Gretzky's comment that piqued my curiosity. What I didn't know was that Gretzky and McNall had become friends. "The more I got to know Bruce," said Gretzky, "the more I liked him."

Early in the summer of 1988, I received a phone call from Susan (Sam) Marchiano, then a reporter in the Los Angeles area. "Gretzky and McNall are playing golf," she said, "but I hear that it's more than a golf game. Wayne could be coming to play for the Kings." We argued the pros and cons, concluding that one motivating factor was Gretzky's actress-wife, Janet Jones, who would prefer living near the studios rather than within dogsled distance to the North Pole.

"I'll bet he's coming to California," said Marchiano.

Marchiano had the same kind of urgency in her voice as Joel Bergman did when he originally told me about McNall. Shortly thereafter, there were hints that Gretzky might, in fact, leave the Oilers. They were rapidly and emphatically denied. About a week later, on August 9, 1988, McNall had completed his coup. Gretzky had become a King in an elaborate exchange that also brought Marty McSorley and Mike Krushelnyski to Los Angeles. The cash-short Pocklington also received somewhere between $15 million and $20 million for allowing Canada's icon to pass through the border en route to Los Angeles.

I remember thinking what a monumental gamble McNall was taking because there was absolutely no guarantee that Gretzky would excel in his new surroundings. I also recall that this was a singular blow to Canadian pride and a boost for American hockey.

Until this point in time, sunny Southern California was the last place you'd expect hockey's most popular player to pitch his tent. Canadian chauvinists continued to labor under the misapprehension that hockey was "their" game and had no business being expropriated by Americans.

But the Gretzky move was a benchmark. It signaled what was to be a gradual decline and fall of Canadian cities as focal points on the NHL political spectrum. When Gretzky left Northlands Coliseum, the Edmonton franchise wasn't killed, but it was severely wounded.

Not that we were certain about Gretzky's ability to galvanize hockey interest in California. He no longer had Mark Messier at his side to relieve him of offensive pressure, nor did he have Kevin Lowe and Grant Fuhr to anchor the defense and goaltending when the forwards were beaten. Despite the presence of McSorley the enforcer, it was quite possible that the thin Gretzky would be abused by enemy guerrillas now that he was with the weaker Kings.

I was working with Scotty Bowman on the SportsChannel America telecasts when Gretzky made his debut on October 6, 1988, at the Forum in Inglewood against the Detroit Red Wings. On his very first shot, Gretzky scored and the tone had been set for the season. Gretzky played superbly, scoring 54 goals in 78 games. He also won the Hart Trophy as the league's most valuable player.

McNall exploited Gretzky's presence in a most positive, entrepreneurial manner. He phoned Prime Ticket, ensuring that the cable TV station carrying the Kings' game would provide financial support. Not only did he get Prime Ticket behind him, but also the folks handling the team's concessions and merchandising. In a trice the Kings' value began spiraling upward. A year later the per-game fee for cable rose almost 50 percent and the number of regular-season games carried rose from 37 to 60. The average ticket price jumped from $18.50 to $22 and attendance from 427,721 to 547,952, an increase in average of 3,360 per game. Instead of 5 sellouts, there were 22.

As a hockey journalist, my relationship with McNall became naturally more intense. "Part of McNall's lure," wrote Bryan Burrough in a perceptive *Vanity Fair* profile, "is his almost child-like good humor; he may be the friendliest, most accessible and down-to-earth mogul I've ever met."

Dozens who had dealings with McNall would readily agree. If he had any knockers, they were virtually impossible to find on either side of the border. Canadians were awed by his maneuvering, and Americans were impressed with his swift nurturing of the California hockey soil. If it were possible for there to be a "Mister Nice Guy" in the NHL, McNall was the man. "He's great to everyone he's worked with," said Gretzky, "the secretaries, the players—everyone."

Even cynical nonhockey journalists viewed McNall with a grudging touch of admiration. Jerry Grossman and Kirk Calhoun of Ernst and Young, the leading professional services firm that specializes in sports, noted the meaningful increase in Kings' attendance and TV viewership. "All this was not to watch the Kings win nine more games or even move from fourth to second place in the Smythe Division," said Grossman and Calhoun. "It was to see Gretzky. McNall knew that would happen. Sure, he was out to build a winner, but even if the Kings never won the Stanley Cup, his business deal would prove successful because the focus of it was on the Great One, a man guaranteed to improve revenues."

Gretzky and McNall became close friends and business partners. Their acquisitions ranged from the purchase of collectibles to the acquisition of the Toronto Argonauts professional football team from Harry Ornest. McNall encouraged Hollywood's dazzling personalities to the Forum, and soon Kings games were sprinkled with the likes of Sylvester Stallone, Goldie Hawn, and John Candy. "Bruce loved to bring them into the dressing room after games," said Bergman. "There were some nights when it seemed as if there were more actors in the clubhouse than players."

If McNall made a mistake—vis-à-vis his players—it was in allowing his enthusiasm to get the better of his fiscal sense. Although Gretzky was worth a lot of money, McNall seemed more eager to overpay Gretzky than offer him a less lucrative contract that the Great One would readily have accepted. "Bruce was the ultimate jock owner," said one of his colleagues on the NHL Board of Governors. "He was so tickled to get Wayne that he paid him way more than necessary. In the end he helped drive the market on salaries far, far higher than was necessary."

Peter Pocklington may have best capsulized the McNall personality when he said, "Bruce is America's oldest living teenager."

McNall's power within the league's hierarchy began increasing with the popularity of the team. When McNall annexed the Kings, the NHL was orchestrated by a triumvirate—President John Ziegler, Chairman of the Board of Governors (and owner of the Chicago Blackhawks) Bill Wirtz, and the NHL Players' Association Executive Director Alan Eagleson. But Ziegler's power began fading after his disappearance during the 1988 Devils-Bruins playoff and was eroded to the point of no return during the 1992 players' strike.

Likewise, a spate of legal problems that continued through 1995 undermined Eagleson's leadership and led to his replacement as union boss by Bob Goodenow, a Detroit lawyer with a more hostile attitude toward management than his predecessor. Meanwhile, the political leaning of ownership began to change. Dissatisfaction with the Wirtz regime prompted a change, and the affable McNall was selected board chairman in 1992.

To insiders this was a remarkable achievement. Club owners such as Philadelphia's Ed Snider and Pittsburgh's Howard Baldwin had considerable seniority on McNall, but McNall's apparent warmth and ability to bring disparate sides together cemented his appointment.

No sooner had he taken office than McNall set about to craft a more enlightened brand of big-league hockey. Unlike his secluded predecessors, McNall was open with the media and freely solicited ideas for improving the game. His power was even further enhanced with Ziegler's resignation in 1992 and the subsequent replacement by Gil Stein, who had been the league's chief legal eagle.

The McNall-Stein leadership duet seemed like a public relations dream-come-true for the previously conservative league. Stein, who had been designated interim president, immediately embarked on a leaguewide goodwill tour—also interpreted by some as a barefaced attempt to become the NHL's first commissioner—and received some favorable reviews. Many observers hailed the breath of fresh air that permeated the league's high command. Meanwhile, McNall as chairman kicked off a search for a strong executive who would lead the NHL into the next century.

Although he coexisted well enough with Stein, McNall had his sights elsewhere. He couldn't ignore the NBA's remarkable success under its commissioner, David Stern, and remarked to me that he'd love to get the NBA boss over to the NHL.

Knowing that they could not lure Stern to the hockey front, NHL leaders decided to try his second in command, Russ Granik. The latter had no interest in leaving the basketball domain, so McNall now eyed Gary Bettman, who was third on the NBA totem pole after Stern and Granik.

The race for the commissionership turned into a two-horse sprint between Bettman (who was virtually unknown to the inbred hockey community) and Stein. At first, Stein appeared to have the edge. He had been affiliated with the NHL since the Flyers joined the league in the big expansion of 1967–68 and then moved into a power-broker position as chief NHL counsel under Ziegler.

Stein's cross-continent tour in the spring and summer of 1992 as interim president appealed to the media at large but appeared to many club owners as a blatant attempt at campaigning for the newly minted commissioner's position. It rubbed many the wrong way, but that was only one strike against Stein. Although he valiantly attempted to rebut the twitting, Stein was regarded as too old to assume the new job and not savvy enough in the area of marketing that had become an obsession with the progressive NHL element anxious to exploit areas of development.

As chairman of the league's board of governors, McNall was in an excellent position to influence key hirings. In the end, his nod toward Bettman was critical to the selection of the NHL commissioner.

By the time the 1993 NHL All-Star Game was to be played at the Forum in Montreal, McNall had become hockey's top banana. His acquisition of Gretzky had turned into a gem; his Kings had overtaken the Lakers as the darlings of Los Angeles. He had emerged as the most beloved and accessible hockey leader since Red Dutton was interim NHL president during World War II.

I had an appointment to chat with McNall during his All-Star visit. It was both a heady and yet a heavy time for the man. His man Bettman was now in place, successfully wooing the media in Montreal, while hockey in general seemed on an upswing ready to challenge the NBA for a larger chunk of the sports-marketing dollar.

But McNall—along with his fellow owners—also had concerns. During the latter part of the Ziegler administration, the league had been stung with a series of embarrassments. Former NHL heroes, such as Gordie Howe and Bobby Orr, had filed a lawsuit against the league over the payment of pension funds. In addition, Russ Conway's hypercritical newspaper series running in the *Lawrence Eagle-Tribune* alleged hanky-panky involving NHL Players' Association Executive Director Alan Eagleson.

Conway was a close friend of Orr (a blood enemy of Eagleson). Although it was never confirmed, Orr was believed by the pro-Eagleson bloc to be the direct pipeline of information to Conway. There were reports that Conway was preparing yet another series with still more substantive material damaging to the league. McNall was aware of this when we met late that Saturday morning.

Montreal was immersed in a subzero freeze as McNall played the telephones in his executive duplex suite in the posh Four Seasons Hotel. He was busier than the proverbial one-armed paper hanger with an itch. A day earlier he had been caught in a swirl of rumors that Gretzky wanted out of the fold. In an unprecedented move, "Cousin Brucie," as he was affectionately known to some members of the fourth estate, called a press conference in the bowels of the Forum and denounced reports of a Gretzky-McNall feud.

Whatever McNall said or did became news. Once he appeared on ESPN's "Outside the Lines" series and the subject was "The Sports of Money." An audience member noted that the Kings had once again raised their prices. "I hate to say this," the fan mentioned to McNall, "but the average fan can no longer afford a hockey ticket."

Confronted with this truism, McNall fielded the shot on the first hop and replied, "Basically, you're right. It is a business and the people who can't afford it aren't going to go to games. Unfortunately, that's the nature of the business."

Now he was planning for a high-level conference with his fellow NHL owners. A half-year in the office as board chairman, the 42-year-old clearly was hockey's ultimate power broker. It was McNall who spearheaded the drive to unseat the Bill Wirtz–led old guard so that the NHL could approach the twenty-first century without being braked by a medieval mentality.

As I sat on the couch awaiting the chairman, I couldn't help but notice his sense of urgency. There were two phones in the suite, one on the lower level and the other above. McNall moved smartly between them and finally discovered enough quietude to pluck himself down next to me for a one-on-one. Our dialogue, which is significant in view of episodes that followed, went as follows:

Stan Fischler: The NHL's sudden decision to expand by two teams—Anaheim and South Florida—appears to be precipitous and unplanned.

Bruce McNall: Actually, it has come along very well and I'm thrilled about the two franchises. The best thing about them is the quality of the ownership. When the NHL can have a company like Disney involved in a franchise, that's really something. We're talking about one of the top dozen firms in the world. And they're not in basketball, and they're not in baseball, but they chose hockey! That's a great, incredible statement to hockey in general and to the work that's been done in the past 75 years to make the NHL what it is today. That's why I'm proud of it. Disney is a tremendous marketing company and brings both a breath of fresh air and an air of credibility in certain areas where the NHL lacked it somewhat.

Fischler: But you haven't mentioned the South Florida franchise.

McNall: The same thing is true of Blockbuster Video. Although they're a newer company than Disney, they are probably the most aggressive new company in the world. Again, for them to come in and put the *Good Housekeeping* stamp on the league is, once again, beyond belief. I'm thrilled about them as well.

Fischler: There has been talk that yet another huge corporation, Sony, was considering an NHL involvement.

McNall: What you're hearing and seeing are the various entertainment companies taking a serious look at sports. I know all the people at Sony and Warner Brothers are watching what Paramount did, taking the lead in this entertainment group getting into sports. Paramount did it with the Rangers and Knickerbockers. What's happened is that they are able to merge the software that the sport creates with the hardware that the companies need. It's pretty evident that in the future more and more electronic giants like this are going to get involved with professional sports. It just makes too much sense not to.

Fischler: I have heard from a variety of people, that the way for the NHL to go is complete free agency. And that in the end this would be less harmful to the owners than the current system.

McNall: Most important to me is to have a partnership between players and owners that makes sense in the long run. That would be instead of having a situation where all of a sudden the NHL makes a lot of money and the players get hurt; then the next minute the players are making a fortune and the owners are getting hurt. There has to be some system—if that includes free agency, if that includes a salary cap. Whatever that includes is fine with me as long as both sides understand it's a partnership that can work together moving forward.

Take the marketing areas as an example. I mean, if you can have the NHLPA along with the NHL together attack some of these issues, you're not talking about one and one equaling two. It's one and one equaling three. And it's important that we try to put together and get a true partnership scheme, whether it be free agency or some other system. Gary Bettman is pretty smart about these things. I don't have a formula of my own, but I've been talking to Gary about it. He will handle it.

Fischler: Why did you pick him?

McNall: He's the smartest man that I've ever met, the most qualified man for this particular job. He's young, aggressive, and as bright as they come; a very, very quick study; a very, very smart man. Most of all, he is a tireless worker, which is very important at this stage in our lives. He has a lot to do and he doesn't mind the hard work. He's smart and quick.

Fischler: Perhaps, but the skeptics say that despite all these gifts, he'll have trouble with the old guard—Bill Wirtz and his followers.

McNall: All of the owners have to say, "Look, Gary, you're the CEO now. You're the guy who we hired. Lead us!" For those who feel they still want to run the league in some form and not allow him to do his job, yes, there could be some problems. Most everybody in the league wants to have a good, strong CEO. I don't think the [old guard interference] is going to be a problem.

Fischler: What are your feelings about Bob Goodenow since you've had a year to study him?

McNall: Bob is a very bright guy, a very qualified man, and a very decent man. We've done business together with the out-of-venue games. He's been very honest and forthright. With the new breath of fresh air with Gary, we'll be able to work together and get something done. Bob has a lot of support from his players. He's a man who has command of that.

Fischler: Fine, but what about the concerns among some ownership types that Goodenow will bleed the league white, or, to put it another way, that the smaller markets will be badly hurt by Goodenow's potential aggression?

McNall: That's Gary's most important challenge. We have to let smaller markets—the John McMullens in New Jersey; the Richard Gordons in Hartford—succeed. Even L.A. in its way is a small market, for hockey. But I think there's something we can work out that will be good for everyone concerned. I don't know what it will be or how it will play out, but Bettman and Goodenow are anxious to do something and they'll come up with something good.

Fischler: What about Bill Wirtz?

McNall: Bill and I got along very well for a very long time. I don't think he's real pleased with some of the events that happened recently and I'm sorry about that to be honest with you. Bill probably was my biggest supporter. I've tried to do what I think he would have wanted to happen. And I'll tell you something, I honestly respect the heck out of the man, more so since I got the position than I ever did. I feel a little bad at times. I don't want to lose his support or his friendship.

Fischler: How will having a second team in California affect you?

McNall: I hope it's a positive effect. The hockey awareness issue in California is important. This year the fans have been unbelievable—us selling out even after some terrible play on our part. Hockey has really sold in Los Angeles right now, but we have to make sure that the news and the print, TV, and the fans are talking about hockey all the time. With Disney as a new owner it will be exciting. I hope we can keep up with them, both on and off the ice and hope we don't lose too many fans.

Fischler: Shouldn't you rethink your policy of being good friends with the players?

McNall: No, it doesn't bother me too much. It's become enough of a business that it's changed in the last five years. Ever since the Gretzky trade, there's the feeling that anybody can be traded. Besides, I don't think a rapport with the players is a bad thing to have. It makes negotiations easier. It makes understanding between player and management easier. In some ways I'm not overly tight with them. We go talk business and that type of thing, but we have a decent relationship. It's not like we hang out all the time. That's not the case.

Fischler: Could the 1992 strike have been avoided?

McNall: I thought so and I was wrong. I think Bob Goodenow had to make a statement, but I thought it was a real unfortunate thing. It really hurt some people and particularly some owners—not so much myself—but others like Mike Ilitch. I was not on the [negotiating] committee, but other people like Ron Corey put a lot of time and a huge amount of energy in their incredibly busy schedules. These are important people. Eddie Snider is another example of someone who has been good to his players, has been known to bend over backward for them. The strike hurt them and I feel particularly bad for them.

Fischler: How can hockey be sold better?

McNall: Exposure is an important element in selling anything in the world. We need more exposure. That's why expansion is so important because it leads to more exposure on television. More exposure will lead to more marketing by having companies like Disney and Blockbuster and our own Enterprises company to bolster our marketing aspect. The other thing is stars. The NBA has been very successful marketing its stars. It's a lot more difficult with hockey. For years Wayne was the guy and he made all the money, remarkably, for himself. We have to find a way. We have to look over the back of our stars and help ourselves out.

Fischler: We know the positive side of Gretzky coming to L.A. But the flip side is that you mortgaged your future in getting him.

McNall: I don't think so. There is no future except today. There would be no future of hockey in Los Angeles. We would have been finished. Pack the bus! Support of hockey then, to the tune of $4 million to $5 million in losses a year? If something hadn't happened then—or you had not had a hockey nut like me buy the team—this sport wouldn't have survived in L.A.

From my standpoint there is no future like today. As far as the players are concerned, what we're going to be seeing with additional players from the Eastern Bloc countries is that the talent pool is expanding. It will allow our team as well as others to remain strong.

Fischler: Your relationship with Wayne Gretzky, as a player and a business partner, has been questioned to the point of doubt that it is as strong as it once was.

McNall: It's fine. We have a great relationship in many respects. We have horses together, the Argonauts together, and so forth. He's a bright businessman; very smart and a great asset because he is both knowledgeable, understanding, and also helpful with the business. He helps market the Argos and he does a lot of commercials.

Fischler: What's the most difficult aspect of your relationship with Wayne?

McNall: The tough part is that he feels personally more responsible to me, toward me, than he should. He worries about things. In other words, if he's not playing well, or the team is not playing well, he'll take it all on himself.

The problem with Wayne this winter was that the team wasn't playing well and he blamed himself. He personalized it toward myself. He feels he's letting me down all the time.

Fischler: The media jumped all over the rumor at the All-Star Game that Wayne wanted to play for the Maple Leafs.

McNall: The crazy thing came right out of the blue. First of all, Wayne was going through a lot of pressure with the hockey club. He would never speak for himself and say, "Hey, I've been out with a back injury that I shouldn't even be playing with." And he shouldn't have been playing. But Wayne says, "I know, I love this game." It's going to take him some heat, he had no condition beforehand, he was in a hospital bed, he comes out here, he has no legs, no conditioning, no timing, and he gets out on the ice and wonders, he wonders why he is not playing well at all times. What does he think? That his goal for himself is so high that he, himself, gets frustrated at times. That's tough on him.

Fischler: Los Angelenos view the Kings as a passing fad. Is that correct?

McNall: I don't think so. I was worried about that personally, to be honest with you. When I got Gretzky, I thought, "Are people going to show up with Wayne playing and then the magic is gone, so to speak, he goes away, or the team is not performing well?" What happened, shockingly, was when

Wayne was injured, nobody knew if he would come back or not and they still kept coming. We played poorly, we lost eight or nine home games in a row, and they still kept coming. They are sold on hockey, I believe. The hockey rinks are filled with junior league kids; roller-blade teams are out there going crazy. I think we sold the sport.

And this is where the interview concluded.

It soon was apparent to me that McNall was too busy to sit still any longer, but as always, he was gracious about bidding au revoir. As I left the suite and reentered the frigid Montreal air, I couldn't help but marvel to myself how rapid the McNall conquest of big-league hockey had been and wonder where it would go from here.

The next time I saw McNall it was at the league's annual Lester Patrick Award Luncheon in New York. This year the 1993 Patrick—for distinguished service to hockey in the United States— was going to Gil Stein, of all people. Coincidentally, I had just been notified by Gary Bettman of my nomination to the Hockey Hall of Fame Player Selection Committee. Bettman had phoned me with the news and, in fact, it was as high an honor as I had ever received in my professional years. Nevertheless, I was still somewhat mystified about the machinations that led to my appointment.

Having been a maverick for my entire writing and television career, I certainly numbered few friends among the establishment. I learned this years earlier when my nomination for the Lester Patrick Award—annually submitted by my good friend the late Munson Campbell—was regularly rejected.

While exchanging handshakes with the hockey people, I noticed that McNall had entered the room. I casually made my way to his corner and received the usual enthusiastic greeting. "And by the way," added McNall with noticeable emphasis, "Congratulations. I see you're on the Hall of Fame Selection Committee."

Hmmmm, I wondered. How did he know?

No more than a second was required for the answer. It was a cross between a knowing wink and a smile. Not a word was spoken, but I gathered that McNall had played a part in my nomination and I just left it at that.

The luncheon itself evolved into a retrospective sham. Stein was toasted hither and yon for his service and loyalty to the game. What wasn't mentioned was that the man who aspired to the commissionership had been nominated under questionable circumstances. In time the Stein episode would be one of the first embarrassments confronting Bettman. Eventually, Stein would exit from the league—without being admitted to the Hall.

Although the Stein affair brushed McNall's administration, it was so effectively and quickly disposed of by Bettman's blue-ribbon investigation that McNall escaped virtually unscathed. In fact, he appeared to be as tall as ever in the saddle after the Kings reached the 1993 Stanley Cup finals—the first time a Los Angeles club had advanced so far in the playoffs. McNall's team was "in" in Tinseltown.

The list of celebrities glittering at ice level had now included former President Ronald Reagan, Michelle Pfeiffer, and Goldie Hawn. "Bruce is one of the kindest people I know," said Hawn. "He is loyal and compassionate and as far as I'm concerned, those are the best things you can say about a person."

Others were less enthused about McNall. One, who had had business dealings with McNall, complained to me about what he perceived as McNall's potential financial problems. The businessman suggested that we hadn't heard the end of McNall's fiscal woes.

By the middle of the 1993–94 season, whatever fiscal difficulties McNall may have been encountering were temporarily overshadowed by a literary gaffe that could conservatively be termed as monstrous in terms of its damaging effect on McNall's reputation both in hockey and the business world.

The vehicle was *Vanity Fair*, an upscale American monthly magazine featuring in-depth profiles of the rich and famous. What separates the *Vanity Fair* piece from the traditional McNall article was its astonishing candor and self-inflicting damage.

Instead of accenting McNall's operation of the Kings and his ascent to the NHL hierarchy, author Bryan Burrough zeroed in on the growth of McNall's coin empire. What unfolded on the pages of *Vanity Fair* was a tale of intrigue and hanky-panky coupled with an admission by the man that his empire was about to collapse. (Nothing more prophetic could ever have been written or spoken.) No less arresting was the fact that virtually every damaging quote was spoken by McNall himself.

The piece read as if it had been prepared by McNall's worst enemy; someone determined to sabotage the owner's prestige and reputation. Burrough asserted that during a series of interviews, McNall agreed to speak candidly about art smuggling. To those who know McNall and his savoir faire, it remains baffling why he would even think about revealing secrets of the artifact business, let alone discuss smuggling. But there it was in black and white: pages of remarkably revealing quotes that proved an instant embarrassment to the Kings and the NHL high command.

A couple of the more startling admissions that appeared in *Vanity Fair* were these:

- His coin business: "I'm f——. I will lose millions in this thing. I'm taking a big hit. This business is finished. There may come the point where I go under."
- An 18-year-old experiencing the secret thrill of smuggling: "I committed a crime. But I wasn't thinking then. I was a kid. I was scared at the time. I just hid the stuff and left. I knew it was wrong. But it was the norm in the industry."

Seasoned media types couldn't believe their eyes, reading and rereading McNall's words. "In the article," commented Alan Maki of the *Calgary Herald*, "McNall admitted many of his prized coins had been illegally smuggled out of foreign countries. He painted himself as a sort of Indiana Jones in search of the lost covenant. Others called him a grave robber, a dealer in stolen goods. He denied nothing and it portrayed him in an unflattering light."

Before the *Vanity Fair* article hit the stands, McNall had agreed to sell a percentage of the Kings to IDB Communications in exchange for a stake in a new 20,000-seat home for the hockey club. On May 16, 1994, IDB founder Jeffrey Sudikoff and former Madison Square Garden Network President Joseph Cohen purchased 72 percent of the Kings from McNall.

Meanwhile, whispers began spreading about McNall's deteriorating financial situation, and the tone was emphatically negative. One entrepreneur had mentioned to me more than once that he was owed a considerable sum by McNall but had not received a penny. Because of his immense wealth, the entrepreneur was able to retain his patience and keep his public silence.

The where-there's-smoke-there's-fire bromide proved valid in this case. On April 29, 1994, McNall resigned as chairman of the board of governors after it was revealed that a federal grand jury was investigating his banking practices. Finally, a blaze of headlines swept across newspapers late in the summer. On August 16, 1994, the *Los Angeles Times* reported that McNall was actively negotiating a plea agreement to resolve a criminal investigation into his banking practices.

On August 23, 1994, Joanna Orehek, a vice president and controller of McNall Sports and Entertainment, Incorporated, pleaded guilty to two criminal counts involving a scheme to defraud four lenders of $128 million in loans. Orehek admitted to submitting false tax returns and financial statements to the banks to borrow money, using phony coin inventories and sports memorabilia as collateral for the loans, working through a series of sham companies, and shifting coin inventories among McNall companies to prevent lenders from discovering that promised collateral did not exist.

On August 25, 1994, both the *New York Times* and *Wall Street Journal* zeroed in on McNall and no longer was there any question; McNall was in big trouble. The U.S. attorney's office in Los Angeles was investigating him for purportedly falsifying loan documents to borrow more than $200 million from banks, including the Bank of America. It was suggested that the charges could include bank fraud, mail fraud, and conspiracy and could carry a maximum sentence of at least 20 years in prison.

Almost overnight, the NHL's executive jet was nosediving straight to the ground, leaving the league in a most embarrassing position. After all, what does one do when the board chairman is under investigation? McNall put on a happy face, adding, "I'm OK. You know me. I don't know what will happen, but there's nothing to do but take things as they come."

Unfortunately, they came. On September 20, 1994, Robert J. Houston, an accountant who worked for McNall, was charged with single counts of conspiracy, bank fraud, and wire fraud. He followed Orehek as the second McNall associate to be charged in the U.S. government's probe of bank loans made by McNall.

Still, McNall continued to maintain his titles of president and governor of the Kings, earning $650,000 a year from Sudikoff and Cohen although he was doing little good for the club's image. Then, on November 14, 1994, felony charges that could bring up to 45 years in prison were filed against McNall. Assistant U.S. attorney Peter Spivack said it capped a probe of alleged fraud involving nearly $236 million in loans from six banks.

Not surprisingly, the media jumped all over the story. "There was always suspicion about the flamboyant nature of McNall," said Steve Simmons of the *Toronto Sun*, "but until recently, there were no charges."

By late autumn, McNall's empire was crumbling so rapidly even reporters had trouble keeping up with the breaking stories. Well before Christmas 1994, it had become apparent that he had become a liability to the NHL, if not the Kings. On December 14, 1994, he pleaded guilty to defrauding several banks of more than $236 million and to four criminal counts. McNall's plea agreement was predicated on his admission that he oversaw a decade-long scheme to defraud six lending institutions.

McNall faced maximum penalties of 45 years in prison, at least $1.75 million in fines, five years' supervision by the court, and restitution up to the full amount of the losses caused by his conduct.

"Bruce pleaded guilty because he is guilty," McNall's attorney, Tom Pollack said. "He's accepting full responsibility for everything that took place. There's a lot more to this story than what came out in the charges, and we'll be making that clear to the courts in the coming months."

McNall had pleaded guilty to one count of conspiracy, two counts of bank fraud, and one count of wire fraud. By this time six of his former associates had entered guilty pleas in the matter.

The fallen leader rested his hands on the podium, next to his attorney, and appeared unnerved as he entered guilty pleas to each of the charges leveled against him. Once McNall had entered his pleas, the assistant U.S. attorney, Peter Spivack, required 30 minutes to recount McNall's illegalities over the decade.

"That was a lot that Mr. Spivack had to say," said Judge Richard Paez. "Is everything that Mr. Spivack said about you true and correct?"

"Yes it is," McNall replied.

To that point, the credit McNall had established with the press—me included—had been so substantial over the years that he escaped media criticism virtually unscathed.

My personal feelings were confused. I liked McNall. He had never let me down, be it for an interview or advice. Coming to terms with my feelings about McNall was difficult. He still was a friend but he also was a legitimate journalistic subject. Handling the matter was cerebrally wrenching so I temporarily "solved" the problem by avoidance. For weeks I simply followed the story without comment.

Others reacted differently and I could hardly blame them. One was Helene Elliott, hockey columnist for the *Los Angeles Times* and a woman who once had worked for me during her college years. Elliott had emerged as a significant NHL journalist, first with *Newsday* on Long Island and more recently with the *Times* in California. She takes the game seriously and her writing underlines that view.

On the day following McNall's guilty plea, Elliott eviscerated McNall in no uncertain terms. "We got taken in," she wrote for openers. "Played for suckers. Hoodwinked. All of us. NHL executives, fans, and reporters, too. Bruce McNall fooled us, but we were willing accomplices. . . . We thought he was the best thing to happen to hockey since frozen pucks." A month later, while covering the NHL labor negotiations in Manhattan, I encountered Elliott and the subject of McNall emerged in the conversation. She mentioned that shortly after her column had appeared she received a heated call from McNall's lawyer criticizing her piece. Elliott told me she was unmoved by the conversation.

Other newspeople shared her opinion. Dean Chadwin, a Los Angeles freelancer who authored *Rocking the Pond—The First Season of the Mighty Ducks of Anaheim*, mentioned to me that McNall was still showing up at the Forum rooting for his Kings.

"The fans can't stand Bruce," Chadwin said. "They don't want to see him up at the glass, having a party at every game."

Enough, I decided; it was time that I offered a commentary of my own. I opened the January 30 issue of the *Fischler Report* with a headline, "Tinseltown Troubles," and followed it with the observation, "When Bruce McNall extracted a $25 million territorial indemnity fee from the NHL for permitting Disney's Mighty Ducks to invade his California turf, it was the last, best move made by Cousin Brucie."

I elaborated on the anti-McNall critiques and analyzed the state of the Kings. My conclusion: "The Mighty Ducks will rule Tinseltown on the ice and in the hearts of L.A. fans. The Kings will revert to the Jerry Buss syndrome."

A couple of days later the phone rang. Howard Baldwin was at the other end of the line. Part-owner of the Pittsburgh Penguins, Baldwin had been one of my closest pals among the NHL board members ever since he organized the New England Whalers of the World Hockey Association in 1972 and I began broadcasting their games a year later.

"Bruce was very upset over what you wrote," Baldwin said. "He thought you came down pretty hard on him."

I explained that I had been wrestling with coverage of McNall's situation for a long time and finally decided that something had to be written. Baldwin understood but added that something positive should be noted for all the good McNall had done for the game.

"Bruce is walking the coals," Baldwin added, "but let's not forget that he put Southern California on the hockey map and he cultivated Michael [Walt Disney Company] Eisner, which led to a major coup when the Mighty Ducks joined the league.

"The indemnity Bruce received was chicken feed compared with the benefit to the NHL of having Disney aboard. He gave the club pizzazz and turned a closet market into a great one. His mistakes were unrelated to hockey and he's paying the price, but that doesn't mean we should overlook all the positive Bruce has done."

I agreed and found it heartening that McNall's friends had not all abandoned him. A week later, I wrote six paragraphs in the newsletter pointing out that McNall deserved to be commended for all the good he had done for the NHL as well as individuals like myself.

Shortly thereafter, I phoned Bruce. We had a long, free-flowing conversation during which I explained my position vis-à-vis the McNall coverage. He seemed understanding and at no time sounded as if he was in a self-pitying mode—he certainly could have been under the circumstances—or even bitter.

"Would you be willing to do an interview for my *Hockey News* column?" I asked.

"I'd love to," he shot back as if we had been talking three years earlier without him being choked with legal entanglements. "Call me later in the week and we'll set it up."

A few days later, I phoned his office. McNall said he still was willing to do the interview but added that the legal situation was sticky enough that he had to be more careful than he normally would. "Do me a favor," he went on, "and send your list of questions to my lawyer. After he looks at them, I'm sure I'll be able to talk with you." As requested, the questions were prepared and dispatched.

I waited a week, two weeks, three weeks for a reply, but none was forthcoming. After a month had elapsed, I assumed that McNall was not interested in pursuing the interview and I forgot about it. But a few weeks later, I received a call from Joel Bergman, who informed me that attorney Pollack claimed he had never received the questions.

Hmmm. That didn't seem right, but what the heck. I phoned McNall. "Do you still want to do this thing?" I asked.

"Absolutely," he replied.

We double-checked his lawyer's fax number and, once again, the questions went to Pollack, only this time I made sure that his secretary had received them. She had and, once again, I waited.

My assumption was that McNall was being extremely careful about his statements and interviews, which explains why I was stunned to learn that he would be appearing on a Canadian-produced television special devoted to his problems. Veteran broadcaster Dave Hodge emceed the two-part program called, "The Rise and Fall of Bruce McNall."

The show was noteworthy in several respects, not the least of which was McNall extemporaneously appearing before the camera and microphone. No less fascinating was the supporting cast including Gretzky and O. J. Simpson counsel—and rabid hockey fan—Robert Shapiro.

"I worry for him," said Gretzky, "in the sense that what the future holds as far as what his punishment is going to be."

Shapiro: "I am convinced this is his first and only transgression of the law. He has paid a tremendous debt, suffered great public humiliation. You got to go in there and do it and you'll come out a better person. And he will."

No less arresting was the appearance of Burrough, coauthor of the bestseller *Barbarians at the Gate* and author of the *Vanity Fair* piece. Asked about McNall's admissions to him, Burrough replied, "It just kind of came gushing out of him. And as it came gushing out of him, it became like: can you top this. I'd say, 'Oh, those are smugglers and you didn't really deal with smugglers, did you? That must have been exciting.' He'd say, 'Oh, yeah! It was really exciting. Some of them got killed.' Ya know, it was like that."

Apparently, McNall reacted to the Sports Network interviewing crew the way he did with Burrough. The kick of being on camera was too much to resist and McNall began talking: "One day, sooner or later, I'll be able to say something. Yeah, I'm gonna write a book some time; they're out there negotiating a deal right now. It's gonna take a while. As time goes on a lot of the facts will come out. It'll be a little different from what they say now. But what can you do; you gotta stand up to the plate. In a lot of ways you feel like you let people down. You feel like, you had, you know, like you've tried to accomplish good things. And you try to do the best you can and sometimes you try to do that and you make some mistakes along the way. But basically I hang in there; everything in life is an adventure. You can't sit there and what if and all that kind of stuff. You just gotta go on with things, in my view of life."

And as he went on with things, his Kings franchise continued its nosedive. In late April 1995, coach Barry Melrose and assistant coach Cap Raeder were fired and replaced on an interim basis by Rogie Vachon, who had supplied McNall's bail money, and Dave Taylor, one of McNall's favorite Kings. Some players traced the club's disarray to the day McNall was indicted.

While awaiting the call from McNall and his attorney so we could proceed with the interview, I called someone who was owed money by the entrepreneur. He was unsparingly callous.

"Bruce was broke when he bought the Kings," the insider said. "He had the coins but not the money. Everything he did was for a public persona. Behind his ebullience is a conniving crook;

but I'm not sure that he thinks he is." Through the whole ugly mess, I somehow found myself sympathizing with the indicted. Was I being naive? Perhaps. But when it comes to Bruce McNall, gut feelings run strong and, despite contrary evidence, I still liked the guy. However, when I mentioned this to a hockey acquaintance, he shot back, "Of course, he doesn't owe you any dough!"

True enough, but I still feel kindly to Bruce, who was still serving time in 1999. Frankly, I miss him and once he pays his dues, I believe he should be welcomed back for the good things he had accomplished.

PRELUDE TO CIVIL WAR
The Lockout Looms

The scene was surrealistic, to say the least—a *Waiting for Godot* on ice.

It was the evening of October 1, 1994, supposedly the opening night of the National Hockey League season. All the 19,040 seats at Byrne Meadowlands Arena had been sold for a match between the defending Stanley Cup champion New York Rangers and the hometown New Jersey Devils.

Instead, the seats were empty and rather than a dozen players preparing for the opening face-off, five broadcasters sat on raised chairs in a semicircle at center ice. I was one of them, along with my SportsChannel colleagues Jiggs McDonald and Ed Westfall, who handled the Islanders games, as well as Mike Emrick and Peter McNab, their counterparts in New Jersey.

We were there because there was no hockey game to be played. The unthinkable had been well thought out and was happening. Major league hockey players who were making more money than they ever had in their lives—and considerably more than the average Canadian or American workingperson—would not agree to an owners' offer that would hike their incomes even more.

As a result, the owners refused to launch the season. Instead, they announced a postponement of the campaign, otherwise known as a lockout. The five of us were there to examine the causes and effects of the stoppage in play and also to venture how long it would last.

Assuming that both sides would quickly come to their respective senses, some of my colleagues ventured that the lockout would be over in a week, 10 days at the most.

I wanted to agree with them but a vignette kept reappearing in my brain. It was a scene from the 1992 NHL players' strike. More specifically, a personal interpretation of union boss Bob Goodenow.

Having been a reporter for 40 years, I had developed what I call "a newsman's scent." It's based on nothing more than a feeling about personalities combined with what I see in front of me. There was something about Goodenow in 1992 that remained with me in the years thereafter and it mostly had to do with his style and substance.

He had a toughness that came with playing hockey and then being involved on both sides of the fence in labor law. That would suit his union members just fine.

I believed Goodenow would tough it out. It was just a "feel," so to speak, but that was enough to prompt my prediction from center ice at Byrne Arena during a broadcast. "I'd like to think otherwise but I can see this going on into the new year," I said. "And ultimately it will all be determined by a four-legged animal with three letters in his name—Fox."

I was alluding to the Fox television network, which had concluded a new deal to broadcast NHL games during the 1994–95 season and thereafter. Fox was looked upon as a major stepping stone for the NHL in its quest for TV respectability in the United States.

"Fox doesn't start broadcasting until the All-Star Game months from now," I added, "so it wouldn't surprise me if nothing happened until after Christmas."

As the words blurted out, they sounded totally incongruous. How could the months of October, November, and December evaporate without any major league hockey? Impossible. It had never happened before. How could it happen now?

It was happening for a lot of reasons but mostly because the peace pact of 1992 had failed miserably. It was then that owners and players had last signed their collective bargaining agreement and it was then that both sides agreed to form a joint study committee to restructure the business and avoid the financial plight that owners insisted was confronting them.

Right there in the CBA was a provision that dealt specifically with restructuring the relationship between the league and the union. But the ousting of John Ziegler and Gil Stein's subsequent preoccupation with landing the commissionership distracted NHL leaders from organizing the pivotal joint study committee that would have addressed the critical issues of the salary cap and revenue sharing.

When Gary Bettman took command, he was distracted from the joint study committee by what were perceived as more immediate problems. "Bettman's priorities were to reshape an organization which many felt was being run more like a house league than a professional sports league," commented the *Canadian Press*.

Not that Bettman wasn't trying to hammer out an agreement with Goodenow. But why would the NHLPA leader rush to a new deal? Under the old agreement his charges were luxuriating in fat and fatter contracts as never before. The longer he delayed, the better off the stickhandlers were. Not surprisingly, Bettman found it difficult to bring Goodenow to the bargaining table during the early months of 1994.

By early summer Bettman realized that the kid-glove treatment previously applied by Ziegler wouldn't work with Goodenow so he switched to the mailed fist. In an August 1 letter to players, the league threatened to impose training camp restrictions—including the loss of $2,700 camp allowances for veterans and $55 per-diem payments.

Shortly after seeing the letter, Ray Bourque's agent Steve Freyer phoned me. "This looks like war," said Freyer, alluding to the fact that the restrictions started with the players paying their own way to training camp and got worse after that.

Across the continent, NHLPA members bristled over Bettman's decrees. They ranged from the relatively minor—deducting training camp meal money—to the more significant, such as cutting game rosters, and to the just plain irksome, like rescinding the limit practices can last.

There was a method to what unionists described as Bettman's mean-spirited moves. The commissioner wanted to galvanize the union into action. "The NHLPA refused to meet with us for five months," said Bettman, "using the fictional salary cap demand as an excuse."

Bettman's iron-fisted approach worked to the extent that he pushed Goodenow back to the bargaining table and training camps opened as scheduled at the start of September 1994. The union received a proposal from the league that included a relationship between salaries and revenues. In addition, rumors circulated that there would be a request for a rookie salary cap. Goodenow and company had insisted that they would never accept a salary cap for rookies or others.

The fact that training camps were opened and exhibition games were played was as deceptive as the calm surrounding the

Normandy beachhead in the hours before D-day, 1944. Insiders understood that talks were going nowhere, fast, and nobody knew it better than Bettman.

"I'm a deal maker," the commissioner asserted two days before the scheduled opening night. "But when somebody doesn't want to make a deal, you've got to use all the resources that are available to you. My preference is to go quietly into a room and work things out. But that's not happening."

Then, a pause: "You're as tough as you have to be. And Bob Goodenow isn't a pussycat." That may have been the understatement of the half-century.

Not only wasn't he the purring kind, Goodenow had become a master exploiter of the circumstance. Aware that his predecessor, Alan Eagleson, was under federal indictment in the United States for racketeering and was being sought by American authorities for extradition from Canada, Goodenow was able to position himself with players as the tough but squeaky-clean leader who would never allow his constituency to be intimidated by ownership.

The once mild-mannered unionists had become militant in the two years of Goodenow's stewardship, and the executive director carefully surrounded himself with equally tough-minded negotiating committee members, such as Marty McSorley of the Los Angeles Kings.

"The players don't look at Mr. Goodenow as being the same as Mr. Eagleson," said McSorley, an intense foe of Eagleson during the latter's reign. "They see Mr. Goodenow sitting on our side of the table this time."

It seemed not to matter to McSorley or other NHLPA members that in 1983, Goodenow was on the other—management's—side. "He stared down the teamsters in a 1983 dispute between the union and a firefighting equipment manufacturer," noted the *Los Angeles Times*. "Representing management, Goodenow kept the union out for 11 months before the teamsters gave in."

In 1992 retired teamsters' official Frank Caputo of Pittsburgh told a reporter, "There's no doubt he [Goodenow] was a union buster. He's the most difficult man I ever dealt with."

Bettman would eventually share the same thoughts in different words. Club owners could fill in their new commissioner with horror stories from their 1992 experience. Both Blackhawks' owner Bill Wirtz—he called Goodenow unprofessional—and Flyers' owner Ed Snider were especially critical of the NHLPA executive, but Goodenow couldn't have cared less.

"The level of conflict [in a labor dispute] can get very high," said Goodenow as the September crisis crept closer to opening day. But from the viewpoint of strategy, the NHLPA was in a less desirable position than it had been two years earlier when it struck just prior to the playoffs. At that time ownership's very profitable playoffs had been at risk, and the governors were sharply divided with a less-than-commanding Ziegler totally unable to unify them.

This time ownership was conspicuously together, with Bettman providing a surprising amount of cement to avoid any cracking. Furthermore, the timing of the anticipated lockout meant that the players figured to suffer more than the governors. After all, the stickhandlers had not been paid since spring, and they would miss an October paycheck if they were not playing.

"We're negotiating with a bit of a gun to our head," complained NHLPA President Mike Gartner of the Toronto Maple Leafs.

Perhaps, but then again, perhaps not. Gartner, for one, had become one of the wealthiest players in NHL history—and without ever having been on a Stanley Cup–winning team. Likewise, other players of even lesser abilities were demanding—and receiving—fabulous amounts of money for little value in return.

To underline its case, ownership did not have to look beyond the September 7, 1994, signing of Benoit Hogue by the New York Islanders. A productive performer in his first two seasons on Long Island, Hogue began slipping in 1993–94 and was a total bust in the four-game playoff sweep at the hands of the Rangers. Furthermore, Hogue consistently bedeviled the coaching staff with often indolent play that belied his natural ability. He was, as they say in the dressing rooms, "a floater" who came to play when the spirit moved him.

Yet Hogue, after missing the first three days of training camp after playing out his option the previous season, signed a new contract for an estimated $1.2 million and then proceeded to stink out the joint.

Think about it for a moment: $1.2 million for a performer whose dependability quotient out of a possible 10 was somewhere around 4! "I've been here for three years," said Hogue, "and this is where I want to play." (But before the season was over, Hogue was traded to Toronto after whispers were heard that he couldn't wait to leave Long Island.) Not surprisingly, he was a bust as a Maple Leaf.

It was Hogue, like so many other players, who was figuratively holding a gun to his manager's head over a contract signing. And, as had been the case ever since Wayne Gretzky was wildly overpaid by Bruce McNall in 1988, it was the player who forced management to blink and come up with the big bucks.

Moreover, it was because of such contract inflation that Bettman was determined to impose a system that would firmly put the brakes on runaway salaries. "We need a salary cap," said New Jersey Devils' owner John McMullen, echoing the thoughts of many colleagues.

Which is precisely why Bettman had been hired. The NBA was raking in huge profits and doing so with a salary cap in place. Bettman was the NBA's cap architect. Goodenow knew it all too well and never stopped telling his constituency that the cap was analogous to a noose. And because the joint study committee never was formed, Goodenow figured there was no longer any need to include the salary cap in any discussions and that put Bettman right on the spot.

"Bettman is so determined to get a cap because it's going to mean his job," said Blackhawks' ace Jeremy Roenick. "It's almost like where he promised the owners he was going to get them a salary cap. Now he's under the gun and it seems as though he's pressing. He's very, very proud of quote, end quote authoring the NBA cap—he takes credit for that, which is great for him; it gives him a good name. So now he comes to the NHL owners and says, 'Hey, I got a salary cap for the NBA owners; I can get one for you.' Now it seems if he doesn't get it, he's out the door. That's why he's pushing hard and very, very fast to get this done.

"Bettman also wants to be the guy who wants to turn this league around. And that is great; I hope he turns this game around. But he's not going to do it with a salary cap."

While Roenick was uttering those words, teammate Gary Suter, who had played only 41 games in the previous season, came to terms with the Hawks on a four-year, $6.5 million contract. The fiscal oppression of the players was difficult to discern, yet extraordinarily well paid stickhandlers such as McSorley were behaving as if they were being treated like peons. "If we're put to the wall," said McSorley, whose annual income surpassed $1 million, "you always know that the tiger is most dangerous when it is cornered."

A week before opening night, I refused to believe that cooler heads wouldn't prevail. Then, I spoke with Steve Freyer and the intensity in his voice changed my mind within a half-minute. "I would be close to wagering my firstborn male child on there being a lockout on October 1," Freyer asserted. "I hope I'm wrong, but this time, I'm almost sure I'm right."

Player after player seconded Freyer's motion, although there were some surprising cracks in the NHLPA wall of unity. Kelly Buchberger of the Edmonton Oilers suggested that one way of resolving the argument was to put a cap on first-year players' salaries.

"When I broke into the league," said Buchberger, "I made $60,000; now they [rookies] are making millions. I mean, what do they want?"

Buchberger's sensible observation was exactly what Goodenow didn't want to hear, but the Oilers' tough winger made sense. "There are some guys coming in that are making millions of dollars a year and they haven't even proven themselves. You have to sympathize with the owners that it just might not be fair."

Significantly, Buchberger's orations were no longer heard for the duration. Goodenow was. "A rookie cap is not in the cards," he said putting a period at the end of the thought.

Always, Goodenow had ammunition from previous battles to recycle and use against Bettman. If it wasn't the time-tested Eagleson horror stories, there were fresh tales about the new commissioner. During the officials' strike, NHLPA observers had studied the National Hockey League's techniques for future use. Just days before the lockout, McSorley argued that "Bettman really put it to the refs."

A day or so later in Tampa Bay, the Lightning's player representative Danton Cole met privately with the club's general manager Phil Esposito. When Cole emerged from the conference and walked into the locker room, coach Terry Crisp eyed his forward carefully and said, "No marks on you. That's good!"

They both smiled.

It would be the last time any levity would be shared between management and labor for some time. On Saturday night, October 1, 1994, I walked out of Byrne Arena with Ed Westfall, Mike Emrick, Jiggs McDonald, and Peter McNab.

"Who would have dreamed it would have come to this?" I said to nobody in particular.

"None of us," said Emrick, speaking for the group.

We headed to our automobiles and as I crossed the parking lot, I felt an overwhelming surge of anxiety. The NHL's "civil war" had begun and none of us had any idea when it would end, nor the extent of the destruction it would wreak on professional ice hockey.

THE GUNS OF OCTOBER
War Begins in Earnest

I f ever there was a bittersweet athletic gathering the setting was Lee Mazzilli's Manhattan sports bar in the autumn of 1994. A group of broadcasters and writers had gathered for a luncheon press conference launching a new SportsChannel show called "Game Time."

Normally this would be a time for upbeat chatter about the NHL season; the Rangers' bid for a second Stanley Cup; the Islanders' new coach, Lorne Henning; and New Jersey's tremendous prospects. But the pleasurable talk was counterbalanced by angst over the impending NHL lockout and the fear that a 2 P.M. press conference called by the union in Toronto would merely reaffirm that the players were preparing a long battle with ownership.

As I chatted with colleagues Jiggs McDonald, Ed Westfall, Mike Emrick, and Peter McNab, we wondered whether some miraculous move could be made that would calm the conflict. At precisely 2 P.M. the chatter ceased as all hands gathered in front of the television screen.

NHLPA Executive Director Bob Goodenow was doing what he does so well: wearing a solemn face. He declared that the union was willing to return to the ice and launch the season as scheduled. However, he added that it would do so under terms of the former contract, which expired September 15, 1993, but was renewed for one season by mutual agreement.

Goodenow's air of piety seemed to impact on some of the listeners. "You'd have to say the union is doing everything it can," said Emrick. "Goodenow seems earnest and concerned. Everything would be back to where it was last year, only now the fan interest in hockey is higher."

The union boss went on to criticize his foe, suggesting that "the approach by the NHL has been confrontational."

To which one wag at the bar added, "Well, it takes one to know one!"

Goodenow went on to righteously proclaim that his proposal "would allow the game to go on" with a no-strike pledge through the playoffs in return for an end to Bettman's lockout, which would start the next day.

"He put it back on the commissioner's plate," said McDonald. "How can the owners turn it down?"

Westfall added, "It would be embarrassing if Bettman doesn't accept it."

Everyone seemed caught up in the euphoria of hockey's new boom, which was accelerated by the Rangers' 1994 Stanley Cup triumph. The fact that Major League Baseball was on strike led most onlookers to believe that hockey now had a window of opportunity that it couldn't ignore.

"Now," said Emrick, "it's a question of how much Bettman wants to stick to the principle of not starting the season without an agreement."

I was taken in by Goodenow's performance. His well-studied earnestness and the no-strike offer seemed like a deal that would be hard to refuse. As the group of broadcasters walked out to the sunlight of West 71st Street and Broadway, the rays from above seemed to signal a possible settlement.

Emrick mentioned that this simply was not the right time for a self-imposed NHL drought. "People who might have been won over to hockey for the first time or don't know much about hockey will be turned off," he warned. "The timing is worse than ever because the popularity of hockey is so much greater."

Westfall estimated that we'd have the NHL's answer by nightfall, which, by sheer coincidence, was when we were scheduled to meet again at another sports gathering. During the intervening hours, I felt buoyant, actually believing that the Goodenow offer would be virtually impossible to refuse. Obviously, I wasn't thinking like a realist.

Frank Brown of the *New York Daily News*—and a onetime intern of mine—thought otherwise. We chatted later in the afternoon and he pointed out that Bettman had been hired by the owners to introduce a salary cap. A one-season delay under the status quo was not something the owners would approve. Still, I remained hopeful, as did many others, when we convened for the evening festivities.

Westfall excused himself to make a phone call. He didn't say who he was calling but the feeling among others was that it was either an NHL official or a club owner. When he returned a few minutes later, Westfall turned his thumbs down.

"They won't go for it," was all he would say.

After careful analysis, I found it difficult to see why ownership would accept a return to the status quo. After all, they were attempting a major overhaul of a sick fiscal system. By granting the union a reprieve, they were merely delaying the inevitable.

"The league collectively is losing money," said Boston Bruins' owner Jeremy Jacobs.

Wealthier than ever, the unionists refused to listen to Bettman, who correctly asserted, "This is not about holding salaries down. This is about the mechanism to make this sport stronger so revenues and players' salaries can grow."

The guns blazed as never before: a salvo from one side, a counterattack from the other. Ownership emphasized what it charged was Goodenow's lack of good bargaining faith—that he would not negotiate from the time he received the league's proposals in January 1994 until late summer.

"He didn't come to the table until Mr. Bettman had implemented his 19 points," complained Winnipeg Jets' President Barry Shenkarow. "And Mr. Bettman had notified him of the rollbacks a month earlier and Mr. Goodenow still didn't respond."

This point was reiterated with validity by management types who long ago had become accustomed to Goodenow's negotiating style of frustration at every turn. "The enemy," said Boston Bruins' general manager Harry Sinden, "is the same as it is for the players; as it is for the owners; as it is for the fans; as it is for this great sport of hockey."

He was talking about Bob Goodenow.

The union boss had crafted a simple, workable strategy; turn the salary cap into the bête noire of the NHLPA. This was easily done. By avoiding meaningful negotiations with Bettman from January through August, Goodenow had considerable time to crank up an anticap propaganda program so that the mere mention of the term would cause a negative knee-jerk reaction among his constituency.

When asked why he permitted a five-month delay before reopening negotiations with the league, Goodenow replied that there was no five-month delay at all. "We received the league's system proposals on January 12 [1994]. These proposals contained, in black and white, salary cap proposals relative to an NBA format, an NFL format, or a salary-pyramid format. We told them, repeatedly after that time, that we would not negotiate a cap on salaries.

"I told Gary that as long as this is your initial point to begin with, that I didn't see how fruitful negotiations can be conducted.

Clearly, we've always said, all along, we were not prepared to negotiate a cap."

Yet the union, under Goodenow, had made a moral commitment to work toward a partnership agreement with club owners that would have included a salary cap and revenue sharing. It was in black and white from the memorandum of understanding that settled the April 1992 players' strike.

Under the title "Restructuring," the provision read as follows:

> During the recently concluded Collective Bargaining negotiations, the clubs have stressed, because of their tenuous financial condition, that there is a vital need for a commitment from the NHLPA for cooperative restructuring of their relationship in the direction of partnership sharing. During these negotiations, the parties discussed restructuring. Based on NHL economic studies and projections, the League and its Member Clubs believe that a continuation of the current system would have a serious negative impact on the business of hockey and hence the parties. Accordingly, the NHL clubs have expressed an intent to develop and submit to the NHLPA as promptly as possible a proposal for restructuring with a Salary Cap and revenue sharing concept along the lines of the NBA system. The NHLPA commits that, as soon as reasonably practicable after the Joint Study Committee report issues, it will begin bargaining in good faith with the Clubs in an effort to reach agreement regarding restructuring by September 15, 1993.

Goodenow's sudden claim that discussion of a salary cap was now a taboo upset NHL officials who regarded his position as different from the earlier stance.

Nor was this the only example of Goodenow being challenged on his word. Edmonton Oilers' general manager Glen Sather charged that "Goodenow has told me time and time again, if teams in Canada can't survive, they should move. That has bothered me from the first time he said it. I'm sure he regrets saying it, but I've never forgotten it."

Goodenow: "I did not make that statement."

Sather: "Goodenow also told me that he was the guy who negotiated Brett Hull's first contract in St. Louis and he [boasted] that all he did was keep saying no, and he kept getting better and better offers. Those two situations seem to say a lot about what's going on in hockey now—i.e., players laughing at the owners' stupidity, and the owners continuing to be stupid."

As usual, Sather had an excellent grasp of the core issue. So did Sinden. Goodenow, of course, disagreed. "I think Harry's comments are very slanted," the union head concluded, "and possibly misguided."

Considering such rhetoric, it was difficult to imagine that the sides would come to an agreement in time to start the season on October 15, 1994, as suggested by Bettman. If Goodenow was correct in any of his promises it was that the league and the union were in for "a long, nasty and dirty fight."

The dirt, however, was hurled with unprecedented intensity by the unionists at their commissioner.

THE DIRT FLIES AND
THE IMPASSE HARDENS

Respect for the National Hockey League's office of the president had traditionally been high among players. Through the administrations of Frank Calder, Red Dutton, Clarence Campbell, and John Ziegler, criticism of the NHL leader was muted at worst and inaudible at best. Even when Campbell suspended Montreal hero Maurice "the Rocket" Richard for the final week of the 1954–55 season and the entire Stanley Cup playoffs for pushing linesman Cliff Thompson, Richard's verbal assaults were relatively subdued.

But as hockey players became richer, more independent, and uncontrollable, their deportment vis-à-vis the chief executive began to change. By the autumn of 1994 it had become downright onerous—if not scandalous—and nobody in the union expressed himself more distastefully than Blackhawks' defenseman Chris Chelios.

In some of the most inflammatory language ever directed at a big-league hockey official, Chelios said, "If I was Gary Bettman, I'd be worried about my family, about my well-being right now. Some crazed fan or even a player, who knows, might take it into his own hands . . .

"The main thing is, he doesn't know anything about hockey. That's obvious. He doesn't recognize players like Jeremy Roenick and Brendan Shanahan at the meetings. Maybe it's the little man syndrome. He's the problem."

Chelios had been as respected for his defensive skills as he had been notorious for his short fuse on the ice. But this time the defenseman had trespassed far beyond the line of impropriety and the reaction throughout the continent was negative.

"Open Mouth, Insert Puck" shouted a headline in New York's *Newsday*. Nationally read columnist Mike Lupica observed that Chelios "sounded like the kind of punk who sometimes makes fans hate all athletes. He sounded like someone who had made a career out of stopping pucks with his forehead. He is another athlete who thinks the world will be turned upside down if he misses a paycheck.

"Chelios brought Bettman's wife and children into a dispute between hockey players and owners about money, and acted like just another hockey goon in the process, carelessly using words instead of his stick. It is where an apology from him does not do the job here."

The apology, however, appeared half-baked. It went through union boss Bob Goodenow, who insisted it was the stress of a labor crisis that provoked it. Goodenow said that Chelios called the league office to say he was sorry. Conspicuous by its absence was a vehement denunciation of Chelios by Goodenow. His response was meaningfully tepid and, interestingly, then followed by a continuation of anti-Bettman actions by other players.

Montreal Canadiens' defenseman Mathieu Schneider taped a large piece of white adhesive to his helmet and scrawled the message "Bettman Sucks" so clearly that it became a photo opportunity that could not be refused. The Schneider helmet appeared in newspapers throughout Canada and the United States.

Instead of quiet in the wake of L'Affaire Chelios, players in almost every NHL city seemed choreographed to utter something disparaging about the commissioner. In Quebec City, Nordiques' captain Joe Sakic ridiculed Bettman. In New York, Rangers' goalie Glenn Healy suggested that the commissioner didn't care if the games were played.

In one of the more obtuse utterances of the year, Healy—like Chelios—felt obliged to haul Bettman's family into the dispute. "From what I understand," said the goaltender, "his wife doesn't enjoy the games anyway, at least not Ranger games. Maybe she should take the opportunity to go shopping."

Veteran defenseman Jay Wells, who should have known better, called Bettman a "punk" in an inflammatory statement that almost reached the top of the Chelios scale. "He [Bettman] will get his someday," said Wells. "Some punk [Bettman] comes in who never played the game a day in his life, probably never sweated a day in his life, trying to revamp the league."

Even students of rudimentary propaganda could detect a pattern among the NHLPA attacks: (1) Bettman was foreign to the sport; (2) he never played the game; and (3) there will be retribution somewhere down the line.

Similar anti-Bettman observations were made in the media on both sides of the border, but none were more consistently strident than columns written by Al Strachan, then of the *Toronto Sun*. A persistent critic of John Ziegler, Strachan would become even more virulent in his attacks on Bettman.

Among the columnist's most frequent twists was the reference to Bettman as a "New York lawyer." To some sensitive souls at the NHL's Manhattan office, Strachan was conveniently omitting one word—Jewish—as in "New York Jewish lawyer," and it smelled bad.

Bettman is Jewish but never made an issue of it nor public reference to it, (not that there was any reason to do so) since taking office. However, Jewish journalists including myself, Steve Simmons of the *Toronto Sun*, Jeff Klein of New York's *Village Voice*, and Jason Kay of the *Hockey News* seriously wondered whether the assaults on the commissioner did, in fact, have an anti-Semitic taint to them.

Moreover, there was a pointed suggestion that at least one NHLPA member betrayed the brand of redneck thinking that one associated with skinheads or neo-Nazi groups.

"The reference was made the other day in an off-the-record conversation with an NHL player," Simmons wrote in opening a column on October 19, 1994. "The reference can no longer be ignored. He called league commissioner Gary Bettman a 'Jew.'

"He did so with a sense of malice.

"The matter becomes more important now because of a nasty sequence of events that has surfaced in the backdrop to the labor wars of the National Hockey League.

"Almost predictably, and somewhat dangerously, anti-Semitism has become an issue in a controversy that has nothing to do with either race or religion."

Obviously, it meant something to some writers, one of whom described Bettman as a "nebbish." Leo Rosten, author of *The Joys of Yiddish*, describes a nebbish as (1) a weak sister; (2) a born loser; a very unlucky person; (3) a small, thin unimpressive sort; (4) a nonentity; (5) a namby-pamby.

But why use *nebbish* in the first place unless there was a pointed need to isolate Bettman as a Jew?

The Jewish references continued at both ends of the continent. A Vancouver columnist guessed that the players would not return to the ice until Passover, an important Jewish holiday that takes place around Easter. Why mention Passover in the first place because Vancouver's Jewish population is relatively small? Obviously to introduce Bettman's Jewishness into the issue. (Ignorant of Jewish holidays, the writer actually meant Hanukkah, which takes place in December.)

"He could have easily used Christmas," noted Simmons. "But the inference was both clear and unnecessary. The holiday was Jewish."

Bettman pointedly avoided any entrance into the anti-Semitic arena, but his deputy, Brian Burke, charged that the commissioner was subject to a battering from unnamed members in the Toronto press who Burke felt were anti-Semitic.

"In my mind," said Burke, "a couple of writers are clearly influenced in their coverage by the fact that Gary Bettman and much of the league hierarchy are American and that Gary Bettman and some of the other league higher-ups are Jewish."

The league's vice president and director of hockey operations added, "It's scary in 1994 to think that someone would be that ignorant. For me to state that I feel it's a factor, I have to feel very strongly that it is, but to level that charge against any one writer I'd have to be able to support it."

Boston Herald hockey columnist Joe Gordon wrote on October 23, 1994, that perhaps Chris Chelios's "statements helped foster the anti-Semitism Burke believes exists."

Although Simmons contended that the "New York lawyer" allusion was not equated with being a Jew, others disagreed, me included. So did Will Exton, writing in the October 11, 1994, edition of the *Village Voice*. "To allow anti-Semitic codes to creep in at this critical moment can only poison the game's atmosphere far worse than any economic impasse," commented Exton.

Still, Strachan's repeated "New York lawyer" tweaks throughout the lockout bothered me enough to phone a mutual friend, the late Harry Ornest. The former Blues' owner, then an official of Hollywood Park Race Track, was as intensely proud of his Jewish background as any sportsman I knew. From time to time, Ornest would send me clippings alluding to the Holocaust and similar issues related to our past.

I pointedly asked Ornest whether he thought Strachan was anti-Semitic, and he emphatically rejected the suggestion and offered a few thoughts to reinforce his point. Ornest was very persuasive about the anti-Semitism issue, and it was enough to convince me.

What remained perplexing, however, was Strachan's obsession with New York and his incessant reference to the "New York lawyer" routine. I had hoped at some point to confront him on the issue but, quite frankly, never expected to get the opportunity on television.

As it happened, one day in midwinter I received a phone call from a producer of the "Inside Sports" TV show hosted by Dave

Hodge. Over the years I had done several segments with Hodge, a respected Canadian sportscaster, but most of them had either been one-on-one interviews, whereas this would be different.

The subject was the media and the lockout: how the confrontation was being covered and what to expect. Instead of the one-on-one, Hodge would have a third guest and, what do you know, it would be Strachan.

Never having done a show of this type with him before, I was uncertain what to expect so I decided in advance that I would keep it low-key and reasonably respectful—unless he indicated that he was getting out of hand. Then, I decided, I would let him have it.

The program opened on a fairly calm note and remained that way for a few minutes until Strachan went off on his anti-New York kick. I wouldn't say that my blood boiled, but it certainly did stir and that's when I launched my counterattack. Here's how the dialogue unfolded on the air:

Al Strachan: I think what's happened is that we're in an unusual situation here because most of the people who have covered hockey, and have covered it for many years, we've become fairly comfortable, we know the people in the game, we know who's telling the truth and who isn't. But we're in a situation where the game is being run by a bunch of New York lawyers who are extremely professional in what they do. I don't think anybody really likes them, but they have to give them credit for being very good. They leaked stories when it suited them to leak them; the rest of the time they had a total news blackout. Gary Bettman, the NHL's commissioner or business manager, whichever you prefer, managed to get a bylaw through or rule, whatever, last summer that empowered him to levy six-figure fines to anyone who spoke out of turn, so there were very few leaks and we're used to getting those kind of leaks, so it was an unusual situation for the media and I think that's why we got misled sometimes. My sources say that [unintelligible] situation was a direct leak from the New York NHL office in the hopes of putting pressure on the players, and that's the kind of things they've been doing.

Dave Hodge: Stan, have people been used here?

Stan Fischler: Well, first of all, I disagree with Al completely. First of all, Al likes to use this New York lawyer thing like there's a distinction between a New York lawyer, a Detroit lawyer, and a Toronto lawyer. And I'd like to know the difference between a New York lawyer and a Toronto lawyer.

Strachan: Well, a Toronto lawyer knows hockey, basically.

Fischler: I mean if it leaks, it leaks all over the place. Talk about leaks, I'm sure you could get information on how Bob Goodenow and his henchman have choreographed certain players. I mean you got that whole flak about how Bettman is this and Bettman is that and it all happened at once. You have a series of players who are always the ones they go back to, you always hear a Larry Murphy, this is certainly a choreographed situation coming out of the NHLPA. So I would submit that the amount of propaganda coming out from both sides, whether they're New York lawyers or Toronto lawyers or whoever these guys are, Goodenow has done an excellent job in one respect—he has managed to keep the dissidence quiet, I mean this whole "booshwah" about voting 26 to nothing. I just talked to people who told me several players who dissented—it wasn't 26 to nothing. But that's the way Goodenow presented it, and another thing I haven't read in any of the papers, I don't know if anybody in Canada wrote about it, but how come nobody in the media other than Keith has in the Detroit paper? Why hasn't the union put it to a popular vote? I mean, why is it this Goodenow politburo that decides everything?

Hodge: Let me suggest this, that Al, you probably, if forced to name a villain in this, would say Gary Bettman. Stan, if forced to name a villain, you'd probably say Bob Goodenow.

Fischler: No probably, no probably.

Hodge: You already have.

Fischler: Yes.

Hodge: How easy is it for people to understand this when they get it from polarized sides? We say Al, is it easy to sit on the side you've been painted on and still try to be responsible and still try independently to figure out what's going on?

Strachan: It is at a paper like the *Sun* where we had a number of people who are covering the event. We have four guys at least who write on it on a regular basis, and I'm a columnist, they pay me to take a stance, not sit on a fence. We have our newswriters—Dave Fuller, Lance Hornby—who have done an excellent job of covering the day-to-day negotiations. They give you the nuts and bolts and I try and give you an opinion, I don't think that's a big problem. And referring to what we were talking about earlier, I think the difference between a New York lawyer and a Toronto lawyer is that Toronto lawyers go to hockey games and they understand hockey. And the other thing that is interesting to note, that Stan mentioned certain players whose names keep popping up all the time as sources. Larry Murphy you mentioned, that's true, but who do you ever hear from the league? Because they don't, they just weasel stuff out from under the table that they tell selected players, selected writers. But they don't come out and say, "This is my opinion."

Hodge: Stan, you take a crack about how easy this is to analyze from one side of the post to the other.

Fischler: Well, once again—I disagree again—to say New York lawyers don't go to hockey games is stupid. I mean it's a generalization, it doesn't mean anything. I mean these guys, tons of New York lawyers, subscribe to Ranger games. So that's meaningless. The weaseling it out, I mean there's been so much weaseling on the union side it's ridiculous. Some of the statements are so absurd, I mean you take a guy like Glenn Healy, who played about 25 games tops—the guy's getting $800,000 and the guy's beeping about his deal. I don't see anybody taking shots at guys like Healy. They just accept his quotes and leave it at that. But obviously the average reader is having a tough time and the average fan is having a tough time because it's complicated for the average hockey fan to figure out all these deals, and the various types of free agents, Group I, Group II, Group III, I mean the fans got sick and tired of that stuff a long time ago. I mean, it's very difficult for anyone in the media to keep the fans apprised so the fans don't lose interest. I think a lot of the writing, and I don't mean this as an insult to anyone, but a lot of the writing has gone over the head of the fan. The fan wants it resolved one way or the other.

We had run out of time but not out of venom. The lockout certainly had not run out of time. It lasted through Christmas 1994 and into 1995.

For the first time, I began to question whether we would see NHL hockey again in the 1994–95 season.

GETTING HAIRY
Digging in for the Long Haul

The empty feeling I experienced in the pit of my stomach whenever I glanced at the sports pages was similarly being shared by many friends and acquaintances who made a living out of hockey. People in the publishing business were hurting big-time because fans weren't buying hockey books without hockey on TV. Arena workers, from hot-dog vendors to icemakers, were all laid off, and many teams already began furloughing employees in their public relations and marketing departments.

I was among the lucky ones. Although SportsChannel had lost its usual slate of Islanders and Devils games, the cable television company with which I had been affiliated for almost two decades did not eliminate its broadcasters' salaries. Instead, it made a deal with the American Hockey League Albany River Rats for a slate of games to be broadcast. Because the Rats are the Devils' AHL farm team, the New Jersey broadcast team, including Mike Emrick, Peter McNab, and I, was assigned to the Rats' telecasts.

To say I was tickled would be an understatement. Albany had been a second home to me since I was a kid and I liked New York's state capital. Knickerbocker Arena was a relatively new, handsome building of major league proportions, a good place to work; and the Rats' staff, from President Doug Birch on down to marketing ace Eric Servetah—a former intern of mine—were A1 people with whom to work.

Then there were the players themselves. As hockey players go, the Rats were a journalist's dream come true. They were thoroughly without pretension, eager to do interviews, and cooperative at every turn. "They haven't been affected by the big money yet," said one of the Rats' staffers. "Every one of them is down-to-earth, regular."

Our first televised game of the season was against the Hershey Bears. I arrived at the rink in the late afternoon and drifted down to the dressing-room area. Instinctively, I walked toward the ice and stopped at the visitors' bench. A tall figure had one foot up on the bench with his head tilted upward staring toward the balcony. I decided to share his hockey reverie and rubbed shoulders with Jay Leach, Hershey's coach.

We had known each other from his days as an aide to the Whalers. We pumped hands and then asked each other the inevitable question: how long will this lockout go on?

I mentioned to him that Canucks' assistant general manager George McPhee had assured me that a deal would be cut within 10 days of the season opener. "They'll do a little posturing and then work something out," said McPhee. "Both sides have too much to lose by letting it run long."

But the 10 days had turned into two weeks and there were those, Wayne Gretzky among the most prominent, who ominously predicted that the lockout could extend into (perish the thought!) 1995. When I mentioned that to Leach, he shook his head doubtfully.

"I don't see it going *that* long," he said. "Those players have mouths to feed and mortgages to pay. Once they miss that first paycheck you'll see a lot of pressure being put on the union to make a settlement."

Theoretically it made sense, but practically, no. Hockey players have the "team" philosophy so ingrained in their heads by the time they reach the NHL that they would instinctively back their union leader—even if it became apparent that Bob Goodenow had his own agenda and was engaged in an ego battle with Gary Bettman even more than he was crusading for players' rights. Which, not so incidentally, were at their optimal point in late 1994.

In fact the players seemed totally mesmerized by Goodenow. He had a Svengali effect on their Trilby, and those who earlier had challenged the NHLPA position—Kelly Buchberger and Patrick Roy, among others—were mystifyingly, quickly, and effectively silenced.

I learned this firsthand after appearing on a Minneapolis all-sports radio station to discuss the labor issues. At the conclusion of the interview, I mentioned to the host that it seemed fruitless just to have me on when my anti-Goodenow position was left unchallenged.

"Why don't you get a player or two or Goodenow, himself?" I suggested.

"OK," the host replied. "We'll try for Brett Hull. And if we can't get him perhaps Dennis Vaske or Tommy Kurvers."

"And I say you won't get any of them because Goodenow won't let them appear in a discussion," I insisted.

"We'll try," said the other.

That sounded good. I knew Hull from dozens of interviews and was even friendlier with Vaske and Kurvers from their days on Long Island. I was told that we'd probably have the on-air confrontation in a week and that they would get back to me. But a week went by and no call. Then, two weeks and still no call. Finally, Minneapolis all-sports was on the phone.

"Would you still be willing to discuss the lockout?" he asked.

"Did you get Hull?"

"No."

"Vaske?"

"No."

"Kurvers?"

"No."

"And you didn't get Goodenow either; so who did you get?"

"How would you feel about coming on with Brian Lawton? He's an agent based here and he handles some of those players."

Lawton and I were pals dating back to his season with the Rangers. He was a good guy and we had a frank discussion on the air with plenty of give-and-take. My point was that the players never had it so good; they were offered an even better deal overall; and that by not agreeing to the owners' offer, they were not only jeopardizing small-market teams but their own careers. Lawton countered that owners make more money than they let on; that they were responsible for escalating salaries, not the players; and that abuses of the past had to be rectified.

Lawton was a worthy debating opponent but not the one I had wanted. I still was hoping to go head-to-head with Goodenow and finally thought that moment had come when New York sportscaster Howie Rose invited me to his WFAN studio for a discussion of the lockout. It was now early December 1994, positions on both sides had hardened, and just about everyone had dug in for what appeared to be a lost season.

Rose's producer had told me he expected Goodenow to be on simultaneously with me and the inference was quite clear that fireworks would be the order of the day. Frankly, I wasn't so much looking for fireworks as I was an explanation from Goodenow about how he had agreed to include the salary cap in the discussion with the league as part of the 1992 collective bar-gaining agreement but now would not talk cap, no matter what.

When I arrived at the studio, Rose's producer was at the door. "Are we all set for Goodenow?" I asked.

"I'm afraid not," he replied. "We had him on already about an hour ago."

"But I thought we'd be on together."

"So did we, but he said he had to do the show earlier and there was nothing we could do about it."

These interviews were growing redundantly tiresome and frus-trating because it appeared that neither side would crack. Own-ership maintained a surprisingly united front as did the union, although there were dissenters on both sides. Players seemed will-ing and able to withstand the economic hardship of missed pay-checks, and owners, aware that the International Hockey League might attempt to sign NHL players en masse, talked openly about a non-1994–95 season.

"I learned my lesson from baseball," Devils' owner John McMullen told me one afternoon. Having owned the Houston Astros, McMullen knew whereof he spoke. He had studied the machinations of baseball union boss Donald Fehr and was con-vinced that Fehr was orchestrating Goodenow's moves. (He may have been right!) "We can't let happen to hockey what's hap-pened to baseball," McMullen went on. "And if we have to kill the season, so be it."

It was difficult to find an objective observer when it came to analyzing the lockout, but the individual who appealed to me most for that particular role was Mike Milbury.

When Alan Eagleson was king of the union and hockey's premier power broker, Milbury was the only player to challenge him both face-to-face and in print. I wrote several *Hockey News* columns about Milbury's courageous pro-union stance and knew full well how deeply he felt about improving player conditions. But Milbury also was aware of the management side. He had been an assistant general manager of the Bruins before becom-ing an analyst for ESPN late in 1994. In my estimation, nobody could more objectively articulate the subject than Milbury, espe-cially because he once had been a player representative when he was patrolling the Boston blue line.

Milbury was unequivocal. Goodenow was wrong. He asserted that if he had been a player in 1994, he would have urged his union to go back to work. Remember, this is the man who once charged that Eagleson was too soft with ownership and who nearly was run out of the NHLPA for being too liberal—nay, too radical—in challenging the administration.

"If the players are guaranteed the same money is being spent," said Milbury, "and the benefits are the same, I'm back working. The players seem extremely hung up on the doctrine involved. I spouted the same stuff when the average salary was $60,000, not $600,000. Guys have to realize they are never going to make this money up.

"Some guys are blowing $80,000 checks each month. The owners will pay whatever the total payrolls are, plus a cost of living, and that's the floor. If I were the Bruins in the union, I'd be beating down the door to play. If you're a 32-year-old guy and you give up the money now, you're never going to get it back. You need that for your future."

Players seemed to be oblivious to the fact that there had been a remarkable escalation in salaries, that their average paycheck was soaring through the roof, and that there had to be an end to ownership's ability to continue hiking payrolls.

"The owners are having serious problems," Milbury added. "A majority of teams are losing money, and when that's true, you're in trouble. Based on their actions, the owners are giving a significant signal they need help. They're not trying to fight with the players; they're trying to tell them something."

Milbury acknowledged that Goodenow had wrought gains for his constituency but noted, "Anyone coming after Alan Eagleson would have made progress." Milbury expressed a sensitivity to the issue and an understanding that the players never had it so good.

"If the players have to slow down and suck it up for a couple of years at what they've been getting paid, that's not so bad. Even if they have to take a 5 percent pay cut, no one is saying this is forever. I don't think Gary Bettman is trying to stiff players. How could you say that when you look at where salaries have gone?

"If I was playing and I knew the same general revenues would be going out to pay players, I'd find it damn tough not to go back. When you talk about principles, people get stubborn, but the practicalities of the situation don't merit their stance."

As autumn moved closer to winter, there were suggestions that a deal could be done by early December and, following a brief retraining camp, the players could be back on the ice by Christmas. But no deal was hammered out by the end of November and purveyors of doom and gloom took center stage. One exception was my *Hockey News* editor Steve Dryden, who steadfastly maintained that a deal eventually would be cut. Finally, in mid-December some faint, hopeful signs were heard, and a week before Christmas the *New York Post* boldly announced that the union had capitulated and a deal was in the offing. According to the newspaper, the owners had won the battle, big-time.

This was the most hopeful sign we had since the lockout began on October 1. I vividly recall picking up the *Post* at my corner newsstand that December morning and reading the headline on the back page along with a photo accompanied by a dubbed-in white flag of surrender carried by the players. I said to myself that this was too good to be true, that something would happen to screw up the apparent peace overtures.

But a follow-up story the next day reiterated that only a week or so would be needed to tidy up the loose ends, that the owners had won a clear-cut victory, and that the season would begin after the holiday. If so, this was a major breakthrough, and I arranged to have a SportsChannel camera crew meet me at the NHL office near Rockefeller Center, where I would interview NHL Vice President Brian Burke on the subject.

Armed with the *New York Post* stories proclaiming that the battle was over, I sat down with Burke to discern precisely how the armistice would be handled. To my astonishment, the stories had no relation to what he was about to tell me and, in a sense, the interview was one of the most fascinating and frustrating that I've ever conducted.

It opened with my feeling of elation that a deal was near and followed with the crushing news that I was experiencing a false euphoria. Here's how it went:

Stan Fischler: How close is a deal?
Brian Burke: Not close at all.
Fischler: Can you amplify this?
Burke: We have major differences really in just about every area as far as I'm concerned. We're a long ways away from making a deal.
Fischler: That doesn't jive with stories in the papers. Why would they suggest the end is close?
Burke: Well, I haven't seen the newspaper, but I don't know the answer to the question why there are stories like that. We do not have a deal. We are not close to a deal. We don't have any talks scheduled. So I don't know how anyone could conclude we are close to a deal.

I think the union told the players, given the position they're in, that we have to be close to a deal, that if they move on one or two points we're going to have a deal. That's just not the case.

Fischler: What are the main stumbling blocks right now?

Burke: Well, we've supposedly been discussing a deal with a tax and discussing a deal without a tax; that is not accurate either. We have never proposed a deal which does not include a tax. Players are trying to negotiate a deal. Fine, put enough on the table that a tax would not be part of the deal, would not be necessary whatever. That hasn't happened as far as we're concerned. So that would be the starting point?

I think that the players hope to negotiate a deal that doesn't include a tax. And we can't see that happening at this point. Beyond that we have differences on entry-level systems, we have differences on [the various free agencies] Group I, the old Group I. We have differences on Group II. We have differences on Group III. But other than that we're close.

Fischler: What is the drop-dead date?

Burke: It changes daily. In my mind we're already past the drop-dead date, in terms of the training camp. In order to have the right product on the ice and reduce the risk of injury, we have to have a training camp of a duration that's probably already impossible. So I think if someone is waiting for the clock to stop ticking on the final hour, in my mind, we're already in that time now.

Fischler: What would be the latest start date with 45 games?

Burke: I don't know that date. It changes constantly because we get a date here and there. Like, someone calls today and says Motley Crue canceled and we got the building. Or the circus canceled three performances in Boston, we got the building. The schedule of available dates changes daily. I don't know the answer to the question with the day this date would be and we could play 45 games.

Fischler: Can the league play a 45-game season?

Burke: Not if it's up to me.

Fischler: What's the minimum?

Burke: In my mind the minimum is 50; anything less than that, where you jeopardize the potential for 28 playoff games to determine the Stanley Cup champion, makes no sense.

Fischler: If it was a 50-game season, what is the latest date to start?

Burke: If you're talking about a 14-day training camp, you're into the period now, where I think there should be a training camp. The latest date you would have to start playing subject to dates being made available is somewhere in the first week of January.

Fischler: When will the talks resume?

Burke: Good question. I don't know. We have not heard from the union as far as another meeting, and I don't know when they will resume.

Fischler: How do you explain that you haven't heard from the union at such a critical time?

Burke: There is no question now we should be looking for common ground and not pointing fingers and not throwing grenades. On that one issue, the pace of bargaining, the intensity of bargaining, the frequency of bargaining, what the union has done in my mind is indefensible. It's very frustrating to me personally because we're not playing, in my opinion, in large part because the union has not bargained. They have not made the proper commitment to this. I've said it before, lock the doors; let's make a deal.

We've begged for a quicker timetable. We've said, "Bob, what do you mean you'll call us? Why can't we meet tomorrow?" He'll say, "Well, I'll call you." So why don't we meet the next day? So, on that one issue, the players and union have absolutely no defense to the fans' question: "Why aren't you meeting?" We're not meeting because the union won't meet.

Fischler: What do you think their motive is?

Burke: I have no idea. I assume there is a plan. Bob Goodenow is not a stupid individual. I assume there's a plan, but we can't discern what it is. He's bragged that he is a last-minute negotiator. He's bragged he'll make the best deal at the 11th hour now.

Fischler: If meetings resume next week, could a deal be made before the new year?

Burke: If you're talking possibility, sure. Do I think that it's going to happen? No.

Fischler: Is it safe to say Brian Burke does not think there is going to be a season?

Burke: I'm very pessimistic at this point. I've been optimistic since we began this process. My belief in life generally is if you don't have dreams you have nightmares. I believe you've got to have aspirations of greatness. You've got to have dreams of success to be successful. Based on the last couple of days, I'm no longer optimistic, I'm pessimistic.

Fischler: There has been talk the owners would drop the tax.

Burke: Not from our perspective, and it's certainly not anything we've discussed. The players have said to us they want to put as much on the table as they can, in hopes that that's enough to not have a tax. In my mind, arbitration is clearly inflationary and not necessary. They don't have it in football; they don't have it in basketball. Inflation is one part of the problem that I don't think eliminating arbitration will solve.

The basic problem is: how does the league compete, when you have individual player contract negotiations, but teams with widely dispersed revenue bases? They've solved that in two sports with a cap. Our players don't want a cap. We've proposed a tax. I don't think eliminating arbitration does it. That would be the owners' call if and when we get to them. That has not been proposed, nor do I anticipate it will be proposed by the players.

Fischler: What influence has baseball had on the hockey situation?

Burke: We're fearful of a significant influence. We don't know the extent. The union has denied there is a link, yet the catcher of the Blue Jays allegedly asked a reporter what was going on in hockey and the guy said why do you care? The catcher said, "Well, I know that our guy [union head] and your guy talk all the time."

We're nervous about that. We fear there is an influence. We fear that to a large extent our players are involved in this dispute, indirectly. Maybe they're hostages. Maybe part of the position the NHL Players' Association has taken in large part is to reinforce the baseball players. But we have no concrete evidence of that. It's just a fear on our part.

Fischler: What about Stephane Richer's comment [basically, that there were many players who wanted to play and to bolt the unified union position]?

Burke: I give Stephane Richer great credit for integrity and courage to speak out, speak his mind publicly at this time. We have reason to believe, based on comments made to us by agents and by players to GMs, that he is not alone. That's not an isolated viewpoint. There are many players who believe that Richer spoke the truth for a large group of players. The union makes it difficult, calling guys to a room and having a pep rally and shouting down dissenters. But we have concrete evidence. It's not a belief. It's clear many players share Stephane's sentiments. But at this point there's obviously not enough of them, not enough who are courageous enough to go public.

Fischler: Has the league made its last, best offer?

Burke: No, but we're not far from it. What we'd be prepared to accept to go back to work would not be, from our perspective, far from what we have on the table. We have attempted to negotiate in good faith and get a deal done. We don't have any magic trick to pull at the last minute to make a deal. We're close; we've tried to get to where we have to be.

Fischler: The fans are hurt. What's the message to fans?

Burke: I guess the first thing I'd say to a fan is, be patient. This, too, shall pass, as they say. What we're going through is not unique to hockey. They went through six, seven years of litigation and work stoppages in football before they arrived at a system that made sense. Basketball is going to have its day of reckoning in the future. Baseball is a mess right now. What we're going through here is resolving and defining what the labor relationship's going to be in pro sports in the nineties. We know our fans miss hockey. I miss hockey. But I think it's a fight we have to have if we want the league to survive, if we want the smaller market teams to have a chance. This is a fight we have to have now, unfortunately, but in many ways it comes at the worst possible time.

Fischler: The league and players have taken a financial beating. Can it be defined in numbers?

Burke: I've seen the figures tossed around in terms of the actual monetary losses the owners will sustain, the actual monetary losses the players will sustain by not playing. It's in many millions of dollars. It's certainly an unattractive prospect in terms of the total player payroll, if there's no season at all.

Fischler: If something is worked out, how long will it take the league to regain momentum?

Burke: Well, you've seen great resiliency in other sports after a work stoppage. The fan base, loyal fans recover quickly. They forget quickly. I'm not sure how quickly. We have the best fans in pro sports, in my opinion. The surveys, different statistical bases, indicate that a season ticket holder to an NHL team goes to more games on a percentage basis than a season ticket holder to an NBA team. We have great fans. Very loyal fans.

How quickly they come back, the marginal fan, the fan that has been turned off by this? I don't know. How quickly they forget? I don't know. We think we have the greatest product in the world and the greatest athletes in the world and we think we can get it back on track. What kind of scars you have left? I don't know. We haven't been through a work stoppage of this duration. I think the damage caused by work stoppage is directly proportional to the length of the stoppage and the acrimony of the dispute. This has been a professional dispute for the most part, with the notable exceptions of some nasty personal attacks and a few fairly ignorant comments by a couple of players. Other than that it's been professional.

Fischler: Goodenow said the league has a plan that there will be no hockey 'til January.

Burke: I marvel when I hear a statement that ignorant. I'm mystified by it and I marvel at it. Someone explain to me what percentage we would have to gain by chopping 30-plus games off the schedule, or 40 games off the schedule; hurting the new television deal, hurting the new commercial sponsorship relationship with Busch and Nike to do this.

Sure, that's right; that was our plan all along! That might be the single dumbest comment ever made in the history of labor negotiations in this country.

Fischler: How important is the Fox deal to inspire a settlement?

Burke: In terms of the labor negotiations, I don't think it's a factor. We are very pleased with our relationship with Fox. We think of it as a tremendous, long-term benefit for the league. We think it can make us more of a 50-state sport, in terms of enthusiasm and viewership and everything. We think it's a tremendous partnership. But in terms of getting this deal done it's really not an issue.

Fischler: What about the threat of the players forming their own league?

Burke: This is a case where you're talking about comments your own players make, and you don't want to ever insult your own players. That's our theory. They're a product. We think they're great guys. I see comments by players, "We're going to start our own league. We're going to do this." It's incredibly naive to suggest or to assume that it's a simple undertaking, starting a new league.

Worse, I see journalists egging them on. Saying well, we have 20 corporate sponsors. I mean, you're talking player payrolls of $25 million and they're talking teams' corporate sponsors. What's wrong with this picture? Someone's going to put up millions and I ask, what corporation, looking at our industry, is not going to insist on some type of salary structure, some type of economic system going in. I mean, there's a new baseball league plan that's got a salary cap; that's what the owners are trying to get right now in Major League Baseball. I say to the players, there's a lot more involved in that than you think.

Fischler: Players have been hypnotized by Goodenow to reject a pretty good deal. How can they not see it? Has the league failed in its attempt?

Burke: Well, I don't know if *conned* is a fair word. Hypnotized maybe. I've used this phrase publicly. One agent told me about a month ago that when he heard the reaction to the tax: no tax, no tax, no tax. And, how is it possible to have a philosophical objection to a system without evaluating the merits of that system? It doesn't make sense at this point in time. It's easy to confuse the players, when you distort the facts.

Have we done a good job of getting our message across? I don't know. We have not gotten a deal on that basis; so I'd say no, we haven't done a good job. However, where there are big barriers built up to your message before you get your message there, I'm not sure how you can succeed. I think the players take whatever we say with a grain of salt. I think there's no question this labor negotiation is a legacy of past abuses. I think there is, with a great respect for true rape victims, I think there is a rape-victim mentality here; that our players mistrust the owners, mistrust us. I think there is an historical basis for that. And we're trying unsuccessfully, as of yet, to get the players to realize it's a new day out there. Whatever abuse you feel you've suffered in the past, it's a new day.

Fischler: The essence of the dispute is money. You offered to show them the books. Why haven't they looked?

Burke: I think they're afraid to look. We've offered not only to show them the information we've assembled, but we've offered to submit this to a "Big Six" accounting firm for audit purposes. We are fearless when it comes to the numbers. We're not worried about turning these numbers over to an accounting firm and demonstrating that this is an industry that's in grave danger. Why has the union refused to look at the data? In my opinion, it is because they are afraid of the results. They're afraid the owners are telling the truth. They think if they look at the numbers they're going to see an industry on life support.

Fischler: Is Goodenow the chief problem?

Burke: I have no interest in getting into name-calling. It's not going to help get a deal done now. So I'm not going to answer that question. He's not alone in his position. He's got support with his negotiating committee and with the executive committee in the union.

Fischler: Since October 1, it has been a roller coaster. Can we possibly have one more climb that's the real one?

Burke: After one early meeting, I came out and said to a reporter that I was optimistic, that we had had a real good day, the fact we were in here. And in my opinion, I showed great inexperience. We came out of the meeting and I said to Gary, "You're not as upbeat as I am." Gary Bettman's comment was, "Well, I've been through this before. I'm not going to get sucked in again." I blame myself for being inexperienced in collective bargaining and reading it the wrong way. I was hopeful and then the next day everything ground to a screeching halt.

I'm not getting sucked in again. I'm not going to display any elation or emotion or optimism until I see someone picking up a pen.

Fischler: I've been disappointed in two groups. One is the fact that agents have not helped and two is Wayne Gretzky.

Burke: Well, the agents, what troubles me about the agents as a group is I don't understand the mixed message we're getting from them. Privately, they're telling GMs and they're telling me there's a deal being made there with the tax. They feel the tax we've proposed is not outrageous or restrictive. They're telling me that; then publicly there is no such comment from them. Nor do I discern any pressure on the union from them. And I'm troubled by that; I'm puzzled by that. Either they're not telling me the truth or they're not willing to stand up to the union. They're either not telling me the truth, or our GMs the truth, or for some reason, they're intimidated.

As far as Wayne goes, Wayne's a great player. He's done tremendous things for the game of hockey. Nobody in hockey, myself included, wants a public dispute with Wayne Gretzky because of our respect for him. I'll leave that to the agents and to the journalists, as far as their view of his role, the player tour and everything else. No one in hockey wants to fight with Wayne Gretzky. He's done too much for this game and we prefer to negotiate with the union.

Fischler: Based on our conversation, the realistic chances of a season are 5–1 against.

Burke: I don't know if it's 5–1 against; I'm not a mathematician. But I'm not optimistic. I think there is tremendous doubt whether we will be able to play at all.

Fischler: If no season, where do we go from here?

Burke: I don't know. I mean, there's no plan B. We don't have a plan B. We have one plan, which is to negotiate a deal with our players and take this sport to where it should be in the United States. Grow it. Make it bigger, better. Gary Bettman has demonstrated he has the ability to do that. But we need a partner. You can't dance by yourself. We need someone who wants to dance. We think we can make a deal with the players and grow the sport, start making up ground and catching up to some of the other sports going by, making a better sport for the year 2000 and beyond.

Fischler: Was this lockout, or a strike, inevitable?

Burke: No. Absolutely not. When historians look at this they're going to marvel that we had this work stoppage. They are going to marvel that we had to have it.

Fischler: The biggest sin is that the union didn't start talking in January, February, March 1994.

Burke: We didn't meet for almost five months as you mentioned. We have missed days and hours and weeks. We have had huge breaks in the negotiation. We're not meeting today. We have no scheduled meetings. I'm really frustrated by that. On that one issue alone, as I said before, has no defense, to us, to our fans, to sponsor-members. The lack of pace, intensity, and commitment to this negotiation is shocking. There is no other word for it. There has not been the proper attention paid to this negotiation. From an intensity standpoint, from a time commitment, or preparation, it's bizarre.

Fischler: The union claims it was the NHL who pulled the plug on the season in October.

Burke: I think our fans have seen through that. We have not gotten any backlash about why we're not playing in terms of the no-strike pledge. We think the whole thing was very well done. It was a charade. We got called at 11:00 or 12:00 the day the players announced their no-strike pledge. The press conference was at 1:00. At that point Marty McSorley and Wayne Gretzky had been on a plane all night from L.A. They knew we could not continue under the old system. Now why wouldn't we play five more years with the way revenues are being distributed? The fans have seen through that, although some of the media bought into it.

We truly want to solve the problems facing the industry. Our fans understand that. Hopefully we'll get a deal made and get everyone back to playing and get the fans back in the buildings.

Fischler: Who do you think the fans sided with?

Burke: Oh there is no question about that. There is very little sympathy for the players' position from a fan's standpoint. The mail we're getting, the coverage in Canada. The coverage in the U.S. markets has been very clear. You'll get a different answer, though, from someone in the union.

There is no question in my mind where the support is, and not just in hockey, but in the other sports as well. I think the average fan can't understand why, with an average salary last year of $560,000 or whatever it was, that's not enough. When is it enough? There is no question where the public opinion is on this; it's with the owners.

Fischler: A mediator wouldn't have helped?

Burke: No.

Fischler: Why?

Burke: A mediator is designated to help parties talk. We're talking with the union just fine. When we're together, we communicate well. We understand the issues; we understand their viewpoint. They understand ours. Negotiations are professional. They're amicable. I've been in negotiations before where if you didn't know how to swim when it started you sure as hell knew how to swim when it was over. That's not the case here. I don't think a mediator would be of any value at all at this point.

Fischler: The best-case scenario for settlement.

Burke: I don't know what is next, partly because I haven't done a lot of collective bargaining, partly because I don't understand the union's position on some of the issues, partly because I don't understand the union's timetable. I do think it's very bizarre that we're going into a Christmas holiday with no meetings scheduled. I think it's bizarre that there has been very little contact or communication at all, recently. I don't sense any urgency on the part of the union. Frankly, I'm mystified by the entire process at this point.

Fischler: Anything to fans?

Burke: I'd like to wish our fans a merry Christmas, a happy holiday season, and a happy New Year. It is our intention to get this problem solved and get our boys back on the ice and get playing. We regret the inconvenience and the loss of hockey. Everyone misses it terribly, but we're determined to get this industry back to where it can grow, to where it can be healthy.

As we packed the television equipment following the interview, I looked out of the skyscraper window toward the circular building that was Madison Square Garden. It was a cold and gloomy morning, consonant with hockey's dismal state of affairs. For the first time, I primed myself for a complete season without NHL hockey and wondered when we would ever see an Eric Lindros, Stephane Richer, and Mark Messier again.

A DEAL IS MADE
The 1995 Season Begins

It was a half-hour before midnight, New Year's Eve, December 31, 1994. Rain mixed with sleet coated the New York State Thruway near Albany as SportsChannel's hockey television crew drove toward the Plattekill Rest Stop.

The miserable conditions mirrored the feelings of both the talent and technical staff. Big-league hockey's longest work stoppage had now run through the Christmas holiday without a significant sign of a breakthrough. We had telecast a half-dozen American League River Rats games, but now there was a question in our minds whether the station would continue doing them in 1995.

And if the NHL season was canceled—as many believed likely—what long-term effect would it have on us? Would the International Hockey League move into the vacuum as it had threatened and become a second major league? Could the NHL actually go down the tubes, as some extremists within the media actually had articulated?

Almost abandoned, the rest stop only had one of its six sales areas open. It was a McDonald's and the cocoa was hot and tasty as was the conversation. My colleague, Peter McNab; his father, Max; Roland Dratch, our producer; as well as statisticians Dave Katz and Mark Topaz stretched out. And together we knifed our way through french fries and hamburgers.

"Do you still think there's time for a settlement?" I asked Peter McNab.

"It's getting tight," he shot back. "There's only so many games you can play between the middle of January and the start of summer. And they'll have to factor in a minitraining camp. But the big thing is there's still no settlement."

The clock struck midnight. The new year had arrived and, significantly, not a horn was blown, nor a whistle heard inside the rest stop. It could well have been the middle of July for all the lack of festive evidence. We acknowledged 1995 in the simplest of manners, shaking hands and wishing each other well, but there was a distinct lack of conviction behind the back pats because nobody knew quite what to expect either short term or long term.

"We got a lot of hoping to do," cracked Dratch. "And let's start hoping that Bettman and Goodenow start talking again."

The sides had not held full negotiations since December 6 and were fast approaching the lockout's 100th day. Finally, the talks resumed after the new year with intense pressure on both sides to make a deal. Many agents with whom I had been in constant contact were becoming more antsy. Steve Freyer in Boston had a standard opening when I'd phone: "Suicide Central." None of the agents actually would go on the record as being critical of Bob Goodenow. He had succeeded in keeping the reps in tow, at least superficially. But several confided privately to me that they were unhappy with his performance.

Likewise, owners maintained their united front, but the liberal wing, headed by Howard Baldwin, kept pressing for an end to the lockout. In a conversation with the Islanders' executive Steve Walsh, I was told that it still was possible to cut a deal, but with a January 16 deadline, time was running short.

Nothing in the constitution said that the NHL commissioner and the union boss had to like each other. The more I talked with Gary Bettman, the more I got the feeling that he did not consider Goodenow his favorite person. This had nothing to do with issues and everything to do with style, personality, and any other trait that leads to a turnoff. To me, this meant that the possibility of a settlement was less likely than if the adversaries were fond of each other.

Fortunately for the wheels of progress, there were others on both sides who could add lubricants, namely Bettman's top legal whiz, Jeff Pash; Brian Burke; and union lawyers John McCambridge and Bob Riley. By January 3, the league had agreed to drop its tax proposal, which had been so onerous to the players.

For Bettman to forsake the payroll tax was a major concession on the part of ownership and would require equally significant moves on the other side. Management was seeking concessions such as a virtual wipeout of arbitration and free agency as well as the addition of a rookie salary cap, the likes of which had once seemed out of the question to Goodenow.

Personally, I was torn. As much as I enjoyed broadcasting the Albany River Rats games, I sorely missed the NHL. I was concerned about how a full season without either Devils or Islanders games would affect my employer, SportsChannel, which already had lost considerable baseball coverage because of the Major League Baseball Players' Association strike.

But I also was concerned about the NHL's long-range welfare. Unlike many of my colleagues, I believed that ownership had a very solid case: that the salary cap—payroll tax, call it what you will—was vital to overall league fiscal sanity. It seemed to me especially important to smaller market teams such as the Quebec Nordiques, Winnipeg Jets, Hartford Whalers, Washington Capitals, and Edmonton Oilers.

Then, there was the possible loss of face for Bettman. Had he not been hired by the governors on the premise that he would impose a cap, or payroll tax, on salaries? Goodenow supposedly pledged to his constituency that he would resign rather than accept a cap. But if the NHLPA director accepted a rookie cap, wasn't he losing face as well?

"They'd better make a deal or they'll both be out of work," said one angry general manager. "All this time lost, and one side gets no tax or cap and the other gets no free agency. What a waste."

I had January 16 marked off on my 1995 calendar. Either I'd be preparing for Islanders and Devils telecasts or I'd be rewriting *Uptown, Downtown,* my history of the New York City subway system. Passionately, I hoped that it would not be the latter.

The break came in a phone call—an assignment. The NHL board of governors would be meeting in the offices of the league's Manhattan law firm. This would be followed by a news conference at a Times Square hotel. I was to head for the Marriott Marquis Hotel and meet our SportsChannel camera crew. We then would wait, along with a phalanx of reporters and television journalists, for Bettman to render his decision: hockey or no hockey.

Joe Lapointe, the *New York Times* reporter whose writing throughout the lockout tilted towards labor, predicted that there would be a settlement. Others argued against. Ownership was considering what was purported to be the players' last offer and, if refused, the season was over.

For me it was déjà vu—a repeat of the 1992 strike watch, only this time Goodenow was up against a more formidable foe. How formidable would only be determined by the final outcome.

Ownership's meeting consumed seven hours during which I spent six exchanging ideas with everyone from Lapointe to Frank

Brown of the *Daily News*. Howard Berger, covering for the *Fan* radio station in Toronto, persuaded me to take him for a walk to Eighth Avenue and 49th Street, a block away, for a tour of the old Madison Square Garden site. The wind blowing off the Hudson River pierced our coats as we bent our heads westward toward the corner.

"Hockey sure has changed since you worked the old Garden, hasn't it?" asked Berger, who knew that I began working professionally there in 1954.

"Yeah," I replied, "in those days you didn't have to worry about unions and strikes. Just whether or not the Rangers made the playoffs. Which they usually didn't."

By the time Berger and I had returned to the warmth of the pressroom, it was buzzing with reports that Bettman soon would arrive. Somehow there's always someone among the journalists who gets a tip on such things, and usually, they are correct, as was the case this time.

The commissioner was unusually somber when he took his seat at the podium. He had come from a divided governorship, with some owners warning that if the season were canceled they would face financial ruin. (Both Howard Baldwin and Steve Walsh had independently told me that they felt the season should be resumed.) Others, such as John McMullen, believed that the NHL should not make the same mistake as Major League Baseball.

Owners voted 19–7 to reject the players' offer. That was the bad news. The good news was that negotiations were not dead. Governors had then proposed by a vote of 20–6 to offer a counterproposal.

Instead of resorting to gobbledygook or PR speech, Bettman candidly allowed that the ranks hardly were united. "There was a free, open, candid discussion because of the importance and significance of the issues at stake," said the commissioner, "possibly the cancellation of the season. It was at times emotional. There were some owners who wanted to play regardless of what the offer was, although it was only a handful. They were vocal, they were passionate, and they were adamant. There are two sides to that equation and we debated it."

Once Bettman finished the question-and-answer period, I began lining up interviews for SportsChannel. I was especially interested in Hartford owner Pete Karmanos, who had been relatively new to the NHL, but had a long hockey involvement with his Compuware teams in Detroit. I liked Karmanos as much as McMullen, particularly because Karmanos was virtually unwavering in his demand for a salary cap.

"There are a few people with a lot at stake," said Karmanos, who looked more like a lumberjack in his plaid shirt. "They wanted to make their point that they were not willing to take that risk."

Perhaps most amazing of all were the high number of leaks to the media. One governor insisted to me that an executive for one of the Canadian teams was one of the tipsters and claimed to have caught him in the act of feeding information to Goodenow.

"I'm amazed we have people walking out of the meeting and describing blow-by-blow what happened inside for the media," said Brian Burke.

One of the best day-by-day descriptions was provided by the *Post's* Larry Brooks, who set a new standard for New York–metropolitan area hockey journalism. Brooks's pipeline was far better than any of his competition from start to finish.

Ironically, the finish line still appeared out of sight as late as Tuesday night, January 10, 1995. I had camped out at the press-room early in the day awaiting word from the NHL's propaganda minister, Arthur Pincus. The hope was that the two sides were close enough to an agreement for a pact to be completed by the end of the day.

That night, SportsChannel was hosting its annual Leukemia Society dinner across town near Grand Central Terminal. It was a fete that I never missed, but the 102-day hockey lockout seemed so close to resolution one way or the other there was no way I could afford to leave the now-gloomy pressroom.

The hard-line NHL owners were pushing for still more concessions from Goodenow, and there was a fear that the deal—so near to completion—could blow up in the hawks' faces. With that in mind, I remained with the press gang through the afternoon and into early evening. At about 7 P.M. Pincus walked from the press office into the room, suddenly inspiring hope that something—anything—was about to develop. Instead, he reported that nothing was imminent.

I walked out onto Broadway and then east along 42nd Street to the Grand Hyatt Hotel. It was a 10-minute jaunt but enough for me to mull over the possibilities—mostly that we now genuinely faced the loss of the season. When I arrived at the ballroom, my colleague Jiggs McDonald was chatting with some SportsChannel friends.

"It doesn't look good," I said.

"Nawww," said McDonald, shaking his head. "They'll settle in a day. You wait and see."

Mike Richter, the Rangers' goalie, was the honored guest. Richter had permanently earned his way into our family's hearts with his visit to Simon, my son, in the hospital during our 1993 crisis. Yet when he walked up to the podium for his award, I experienced point-counterpoint emotions. Yes, I was tickled for Richter, a genuinely good guy who proved his sensitivity with the trip to Columbia-Presbyterian Hospital. But I felt no empathy for the goaltender who was earning in the neighborhood of $1 million a year and still was complaining about his lot.

I kept thinking about remarks made by some of the 1970 Stanley Cup champion Bruins, who now owned their own businesses, and frankly couldn't understand what the 1995 players were beefing about. "I feel for the owners now," said Fred Stanfield, "because they aren't making any money. I'm not taking anything away from the players, but I think now it's too much, the salaries are high enough."

Former teammate Don Awrey added, "Hey, I own a business and it's no one's business what I make. [Hockey players know what each earns.] I put up the initial investment, start up the business, and do it. These guys are asking for the world here.

"Okay, so an owner puts up $50 million or $100 million to buy a team. He has to make a percentage on his investment, right? So, what if he makes 30 percent or 40 percent? He's the guy who stuck his neck out in the first place. If he makes money, good for him. He has all the employees, he's the guy paying everybody, and as a player, all you should care about is, 'Am I being paid a fair salary?' Now they want us to understand when they say, 'We have principles, and we aren't going to back down.' Come on, something's wrong."

Awrey was impeccably accurate. The owners were not going to back down anymore. They presented what Harry Sinden described as "the final, final, final, final offer" to Goodenow. I returned to the pressroom at 10 P.M. after subwaying crosstown only to discover that it was practically empty. One straggler mentioned that nothing further would take place that evening.

I then went home still expecting the cancellation of the campaign, but that night Bettman received assurances from both the Devils and Canucks that they would reverse earlier negative votes and would support a new collective bargaining agreement.

When I arrived at the newsstand the next morning, the *New York Post* proclaimed that Bettman had reasserted his control over the governors. Now it was a matter of whether the union would remain obstinate or agree to ownership's "final, final, final, final offer."

The fact that the sides still were in communication was the best news. That we were down to the 11th-and-a-half hour was the negative side of the picture. Except that when I walked into the Marriott Marquis for the umpteenth time, that optimistic buzz was in the air—again. Steve Dryden reminded me that he was about to win the bet (a dinner) he had made with me and that a settlement was about to be announced. Before noon one of the radio people was reporting, unofficially, that the union was accepting the owners' offer. Bit by bit, the news began to filter through; Goodenow had advised Bettman that the players' negotiating committee was recommending to the rank and file that the league's contract proposal be accepted.

I can't say that I felt an ecstatic surge when I learned that the peace pact was official. Rather, it was like the relief—and exhaustion—one feels after completing a marathon. Nor could I feel satisfied that the 103-day lockout really was worth the cost. To me, it was imperative to have a salary cap for everyone, not merely rookies. While other journalists instantly proclaimed ownership the winner, I took the other view. Sure, there were a few fiscal brakes on the union here and there, but essentially, salaries would continue to spiral upward and players would earn more than ever before.

Sure enough, before the ink had dried on the new pact, Mark Messier signed a $6 million a year contract with the Rangers, which was about twice the price I thought he deserved. One by one, other players followed suit with such remarkably good deals that one never would have known ownership had "won" the battle.

However, Steve Walsh, and other NHL governors, assured me that they could operate responsibly within the new CBA parameters. "Sound business practices could make it work," Walsh insisted.

He almost had me convinced; but not quite. Not when the Islanders already had committed a small fortune for completely untried Brett Lindros and were being prodded by Steve Thomas for a contract far in excess of $1 million.

But that would come later.

We had NHL hockey again; I was heading for Hartford for the Devils' season opener with the Whalers and, for the moment at least, all was right with the world.

GAME ON
The Strange Season

D ale Hunter, the irritating Washington Capitals' veteran, is not one to smile very often on the ice, but this day was different.

His club, like the 25 other NHL teams, had ratified the new collective bargaining agreement and had returned to scrimmage at Piney Orchard practice rink in Maryland.

"My nine-year-old is all pumped up," said the Washington captain. "He wants to see some hockey."

My sixteen-year-old, Simon, was equally energized. He had fretted on and off for eight months about his favorite hockey club, the New York Islanders, and their hasty exit from the playoffs in 1994. The lockout baffled him, as it did millions of fans in two countries. He had difficulty understanding why Steve Thomas, who was earning more than $800,000 a year, sounded terribly unhappy about playing another season at his abysmally "low" salary.

But, most of all, Simon couldn't wait for opening night and neither could I, although already some disturbing sounds were assailing my ears. I had heard that members of the Jets had decided to boycott *Winnipeg Free Press* columnist Scott Taylor, who had taken ownership's side during the lockout. Taylor had supported ownership's contention that a salary cap was necessary to preserve clubs like the Jets. When Taylor walked into the club's dressing room following the settlement, the Jets, to a man, refused to talk to him. This set me wondering how members of the Islanders and Devils would react to yours truly because my pro-management stance was as vocal as anyone's.

I'd find out soon enough because I was scheduled to interview New Jersey captain Scott Stevens between the first and second periods of the Devils-Whalers game, not to mention Geoff Sanderson of Hartford and possibly even one other Devil if they won the game.

According to standard operating procedures, my request for the interview had to be made through Devils' Public Relations Director Mike Levine, who then would pass along the information to Stevens. I had never been rejected for an interview by Stevens, which meant that if he turned me down this time, it must be related to the lockout.

Within minutes, Levine returned and said, "No problem," whereupon I quietly sighed with considerable relief. The other cause for concern was the game itself; or to put it more accurately, the games.

The season had been shortened to 48 games spread over 100 days. If you believed the party line, it would be monstrously exciting. "This season won't be as good as a normal season," said Dale Hunter. "It's going to be better."

Perhaps, but just about everyone agreed that the one-week conditioning period was absurdly short and likely would result in injury. "You can't condition yourself in a week," said Capitals' coach Jim Schoenfeld. "If you try, you'll have injuries all over the place."

Nevertheless, the Devils-Whalers game did have a positive spark to it. A healthy crowd almost filled Hartford's Civic Center and they responded enthusiastically to a club that took the body to the favored Jerseyites. I kept expecting the Devils to take over the game, but it was not to be. Their play bordered between interested and lethargic, leaving me to rationalize that the boys still weren't in shape.

Stevens, who appeared with me between the first and second periods, voiced the expected platitudes about wanting to get off to a good start; how every game would be a four-pointer, and the importance of playing within coach Jacques Lemaire's system.

I couldn't tell whether it was me, the strange new season, or something involving the club, but Stevens was conspicuously brief and aloof. I chalked it up to the new season and was quite pleased when Sanderson came aboard for the second period and sparkled in conversation about his trip to Finland during the lockout.

Both owners and players were concerned about fan reaction, particularly in Canada, where there seemed to be more resentment toward the players than in the United States. "I don't think people are bitter," said Capitals' coach Jim Schoenfeld, "but no one really knows how this will play out."

It played out badly in Vancouver, Winnipeg, Quebec City, and Edmonton, where crowds were noticeably weaker than they had been in 1993–94. This was particularly galling to the Canucks' management, whose team had reached the seventh game of the Stanley Cup finals in the spring of 1994. Likewise, the Nordiques' general staff had expected sellouts for an exciting team that featured Wendel Clark, Peter Forsberg, Joe Sakic, and other aces who had catapulted Quebec to the top of the Northeast Division. Instead, the crowds at Le Colisée were conspicuously below capacity and remained that way throughout the season.

I had no difficulty understanding the fans' unhappiness. Vancouverites remembered how superstar Pavel Bure allegedly held the Canucks hostage during the 1994 Stanley Cup finals with the Rangers so that he could obtain a fabulous new contract. Others had watched players' union advocate Ken Baumgartner filibuster throughout the lockout as if he were getting a raw deal. Baumgartner, who on any given night would have been a fourth-stringer on the Anaheim Mighty Ducks, was earning $370,000 (U.S.) before the lockout and received a sizable increase after it had ended. This for a part-time goon with little artistic value.

A few days after the Devils-Whalers game, I was at Nassau Coliseum for the opening night telecast of the Islanders' home season. I was especially interested in the crowd reaction here because of the Isles' dismal finish the previous year and the fact that the hated Rangers now owned the Stanley Cup.

I was pleased to note that the arena was filled just short of capacity and that the audience was as intensely behind the home club as ever before. As was the case with New Jersey, I had suspected that some of the more militant unionists among the Islanders would, perhaps, boycott me the way the Jets did columnist Scott Taylor. But when I ambled down the dressing-room corridor for a chat with coach Lorne Henning prior to the game, every player to a man was as cordial as he had been in the pre-lockout days. (Interestingly, not a single player voiced a word of displeasure from that point on through to the end of the Stanley Cup round in June.)

Way back in the summer of 1994, I had written my annual NHL prediction piece for *Inside Sports* magazine. As always, I ventured a guess as to the Stanley Cup champion in 1995 and decided upon the Devils, who had lost to the Rangers in double overtime of the seventh game of the 1994 semifinals.

After watching New Jersey in the first weeks of the abbreviated campaign, I began suffering second thoughts about my choice. The Devils opened with several road games before returning to Byrne Meadowlands Arena and were depressingly lackluster. Scott Stevens, who now was among the league's highest-paid performers, appeared distracted and nothing like the player who had been runner-up to Raymond Bourque for the Norris Trophy in 1994. Even goalie Martin Brodeur, who won rookie-of-the-year honors, seemed mortal as his club dog-paddled its way around a playoff berth, barely keeping its collective head above water.

There was no end to the explanations.

One had it that the players, as a group, were angry with owner John McMullen, who was among the more militant owners. Another suggested that the Devils had overachieved in 1993–94 and now had slipped to a more realistic level, a theory that I believed may have had some merit. Others lamented the loss of Bernie Nicholls to the Chicago Blackhawks and the fact that his replacement, Jim Dowd, had suffered a recurrence of his shoulder injury.

Ironically, the player who was supposed to be the major problem for New Jersey turned out to be the Devils' major asset. Stephane Richer had been projected to be a physical target of every enemy player who had been angered by his comments made during the lockout.

The way it was written at the time, Richer sounded as if he was criticizing the NHLPA. He supposedly had said that if a secret vote were taken of all the players, the majority would have accepted the owners' proposal and returned to the ice. Richer had become a dirty word to union membership, and talk of retaliatory action led me to think that it would have a terribly negative effect on the Devils' most skilled—and often dominating—forward.

Whether it was because they were a cohesive team or whether they chose to forgive Richer on grounds of free speech, the Devils welcomed their sharpshooter as if he had said nothing. Nor did the opposition appear especially vindictive at any time. For his part, Richer reacted with the verve and self-confidence of one who has courageously spoken his mind and now was, in effect, daring anyone to do something about it.

While other Devils floundered in an attempt to regain their momentum of yesteryear, Richer literally and figuratively moved full speed ahead. His scoring kept the club in the playoff hunt, and his frankness arrested the attention of media types, some of whom had regarded him as a flake.

"What I said," Richer explained one day, "was that I don't see any human being liking to lose money and being in this situation. What I was saying was that if you took a vote of the players, everybody would like to go back on the ice and play the game. But it came out as something else when somebody picked out one quote and it got into the newspapers in New York.

"I wasn't talking about whether the deal was good or not. I was saying that I don't see anybody in the NHL being rich enough to say I have enough money to sit out a full year. On the other side, I said that if some guys have businesses and they know what business is all about, maybe they will understand the owners a little more because I have a business and I know what I'm talking about."

Other players had other reactions and a spate of lockout stories began spreading from locker room to locker room. Although this one may be apocryphal, it did gain considerable circulation.

According to the tale published in the Montreal *Gazette*, union members were on a conference call to consider management's final offer. Line by line, the proposal was considered by Penguins' defenseman Larry Murphy, who had been an NHLPA mainstay.

"Hey, that doesn't sound so bad," said Murphy. "Why don't we take it?"

Marty McSorley, among the hardest of the union hard-liners, took exception to Murphy's position.

"Hey, Murph," snapped McSorley, "where's your balls?"

To which Murphy purportedly shot back, "I don't think with my balls!"

If there was any bitterness engendered by the lockout, it was evident by the smaller crowds in some Canadian cities as well as hostility generated by those whose incomes were directly affected by the work stoppage. In some cases, teams released workers for the duration of the lockout and then rehired them. Some were never rehired.

The NHL furloughed Michael Berger, who had the title of "general manager, publishing." A key public relations and publishing staffer during the Ziegler administration, Berger was among many Zieglerites affected by the lockout. However, he was luckier than most; he was retained as an editorial consultant as well as a consultant to the Fox Network, which began producing the weekly NHL games of the week. John Halligan, who had enormous public relations skills and friendship with every significant sports newsperson, was also given a leave but returned to the league compound after the lockout and has remained into the 1999–2000 season.

Simple wage earners across the spectrum were affected. "The strike put a hurtin' on me," said Jamie Gibson, one of two regular

Zamboni drivers at USAir Arena, home of the Washington Capitals. "We don't get the overtime like we used to before the lockout." He estimated that the lockout had cost him 100 overtime hours.

"And," he added, "it has affected morale more than anything. There was nothing going on there for a long time. It was no fun."

An estimated 250 part-timers—food-service workers, parking attendants, cleaning personnel—were directly affected by the lockout at USAir Arena. "It hurt them a whole lot," said one of the workers. "It was devastating."

Chris Chelios's outrageous suggestion—that commissioner Gary Bettman and members of his family had a good chance of ending up on a hit list if the lockout persisted—could have had a devastating effect on the defenseman's career. However, the NHL boss discreetly but firmly handled the matter. Chelios was flown to New York for a 45-minute conference with the commissioner and then was asked to sign a written apology. Bettman refused some critics' demands that he suspend Chelios.

"But," noted Montreal *Gazette* sports editor Red Fisher, "all is not forgiven. It never will be. The next time Chelly acts up on or off the ice, he can expect the book to be thrown at him. What he shouldn't expect for now, and perhaps forever, are telephone calls from the business arm of the league inviting him to appear in rich commercials."

With the new, abbreviated season, Chelios was on uncharacteristically good behavior although the quality of his play hardly deteriorated. The same could not be said for other superstars. Wayne Gretzky, who orchestrated a questionable European tour during the lockout, supposedly would be in such excellent condition he would lead Los Angeles to the top of the Pacific Division. Instead, the Great One stumbled at the gate, lost his gait, and became a nonfactor—along with his team—throughout the condensed campaign.

Doug Gilmour performed in a similar depressing style for the Toronto Maple Leafs, as did Pavel Bure in Vancouver. But nowhere was lockout fallout more deplorable than on Broadway, where the 1994 Stanley Cup champion Rangers attempted to defend their title under new head coach Colin Campbell.

Although captain Mark Messier played to his capabilities, a number of Rangers—particularly Brian Leetch, winner of the 1994 Conn Smythe Trophy—appeared to treat the season as one long sabbatical. My theory was that the Rangers collectively were suffering from a post-Cup hangover. They were still, figuratively at least, swilling the victory champagne. Among the league's highest-priced clubs, the Rangers disgraced themselves with desultory performances that were alibied away week by week until the Broadway Blueshirts almost missed a playoff berth.

If nothing else, the Rangers' disaster eloquently proved a point that had been made over and over by fiscally prudent owners such as John McMullen in New Jersey and Jeremy Jacobs in Boston: that lavish spending on players' salaries is not necessarily the key to success. McMullen, who was forced to overpay defenseman Scott Stevens, had long maintained that the Rangers had bought the 1994 Stanley Cup. Jacobs insisted over and over again that it was irresponsible to exceed one's reasonable budget.

"Our number one objective with this organization is to win," said Jacobs. "But I am not in business to lose money. I want winning teams and teams that make money. There is absolutely no correlation between spending money and having a consistent winner. None.

"The highest-paid team in the National Hockey League in 1994–95 was the Los Angeles Kings. They were also one of the worst. They didn't even make the playoffs. They stunk on the ice and they lost a ton of money. And they have also put themselves in a hole with those contracts that they won't be able to dig out of for quite a while.

"One of the highest-paid teams in the league was Buffalo. What did they win? They lost a ton of money. A lot of money.

"When you spend enormous amounts of money on a player's contract, you are taking a tremendous risk. Look at Pittsburgh. They have a fine team. They built most of it through the draft. But with the contract they have to pay [Mario] Lemieux and with him not playing, they are really in a bind for the future.

"Our philosophy with the Bruins is this: we will spend whatever it takes to win as long as it makes sense. I don't want Harry Sinden to spend just to spend. That's silly. But we will spend for value. If Harry tells me this is what we need to get the job done on a certain player, then he will get it. But fortunately for me, he doesn't want to do anything stupid, either.

"What you pay doesn't necessarily mean you win. A year ago, the New Jersey Devils had a lower payroll than us and they beat us in the playoffs. This year they had a higher payroll than us and they beat us in the playoffs. The difference was one player's contract from last year to this: Scott Stevens's. He had some things kick into his contract that put their payroll higher than ours. In the NHL, you can move several spots up or down on the payroll scale with just a few player contracts changing each year. For the most part, we have always been about in the middle of the league."

Jacobs was precisely on target.

The "Jacobs Theory" was seriously considered by the New York Islanders' general manager Don Maloney, whose club was torpedoed in 1994–95 by an inordinate spate of injuries that left the club vainly groping for a playoff berth. One of Maloney's most perplexing challenges centered around right wing Steve Thomas.

Earning $877,000 a year, Thomas had been one of the most productive and popular Islanders during the 1993–94 season. When his club ousted Florida from a playoff berth in the final week of that campaign, it was Thomas who provided both goals in a 2–0 clinching triumph over the Lightning at the Thunderdome.

In the eyes of many observers—not to mention lunchpail-carrying fans—Thomas was exceptionally well paid for his efforts, but he didn't think so. Following the 1993–94 season Thomas began telling friends that he expected a significant increase, and the talk continued through training camp, only to be temporarily halted during the lockout.

At least one friend of Thomas with connections to the team complained to me that Thomas's attitude was exceptionally negative and could contaminate the locker room. And when Thomas regrouped with his teammates in mid-January, Islanders' watchers kept a close eye on the forward to evaluate his performance.

What I saw was a well-paid athlete needlessly distracted by contract negotiations—not to mention wild demands—which were having a catastrophic effect on his game. Steve's onetimers that normally would be converted into goals were going off the heel of his stick, checks were missed, and overall Thomas seemed out of synch.

What's more, Thomas was the first to admit it. Throughout what was becoming a keenly disappointing season, Thomas consistently underachieved when the Islanders most needed his contributions. His linemate, Pierre Turgeon, whose annual salary was $2.25 million, was no bargain either. Turgeon, who never seemed to have fully recovered from the behind-the-back clobbering administered by Dale Hunter in the 1993 playoffs, constantly disappointed and added to the club's demise.

As was the case with so many clubs, the salary issue directly and disturbingly impinged on performance. The same was true in New Jersey as it was on Long Island, where Thomas continually disappointed. Across the Hudson River, you could substitute Claude Lemieux's name for Thomas's and get virtually the same result for almost the same reason: money.

Represented by my pal Steve Freyer, Lemieux had emerged from ugly divorce proceedings and, according to the lawyer, was significantly strapped for cash. At $825,000 a year, Lemieux would have seemed to be well paid by an objective outsider, who would point out that Lemieux's salary was far, far above the national average. But Lemieux had seen teammate John MacLean's pact climb above $1.5 million so it was natural for Lemieux—and his agent—to press for a similar deal.

Freyer engaged Devils' president-general manager Lou Lamoriello in talks that got nowhere through the first half of the season. Lemieux's desultory performance was noticeable and troubling although he addressed the problem with only partially successful results. A preseason favorite to reach the Stanley Cup finals, the Devils stumbled through most of the campaign, their performance partially reflecting Lemieux's distraction over his contract.

A theory evolved that the poisonous relationship between the front offices of some teams and their players during the lockout would have a bitter aftereffect. This theory was best tested in Boston, where Harry Sinden was the most visible and vocal member of management in the war against Bob Goodenow.

To a man, the Bruins had good reason to be angry at their boss. During the lockout, Sinden dismissed one NHLPA contract with the observation, "It was like giving a canoe to an Arab."

Shortly after the work stoppage began, Sinden recalled three players from his AHL team in Providence. Although none of them had figured in the Bruins' plans, Sinden now did not have to pay them. "Once the season started," noted David Shoalts in the Globe and Mail of Toronto, "no one would have been overly surprised to see the Bruins implode because of the strained relationships."

Yet the Brian Sutter–coached Bruins immediately secured a position in playoff range and remained competitive thereafter. If friction between Sinden and his employees existed, it was well concealed.

"My players haven't shown me they're angry," said Sinden.

In fact, Sinden's postlockout anger was betrayed on several occasions as he disgustedly observed colleagues overpaying their stickhandlers as if no lessons were learned from the labor crisis. One that Sinden found particularly galling was the Vancouver Canucks' decision to sign defenseman Jeff Brown to a four-year pact worth $7.8 million.

By any stretch of the imagination, the figure made no sense at all. Brown's skills placed him in the average-to-slightly-above-average category. At best, he seemed worth no more than a Curtis Leschyshyn or Sylvain Lefebvre, each of whom was earning $600,000.

"Although the Canucks had a lousy year," said Sinden, "they ended up getting to the Stanley Cup finals [1994]. They didn't make any money doing it, but now they've signed a player for more money than Ray Bourque, who's won 15 All-Star berths. How can I have sympathy anymore? I give up."

Sinden's well-taken exasperation not only was directed at Pat Quinn, his Vancouver fraternity brother, but other free spenders such as the Rangers' Neil Smith and the Blues' chairman Michael Shanahan. "We go through a 105-day lockout and I don't see any signs that we've accomplished anything," said Sinden. "Nothing. And the losing clubs, in terms of money, are the biggest culprits. It's their business. It's none of my business how they run their hockey clubs, but I can't listen to their crying anymore."

The temptation among media critics was to dismiss Sinden as some right-wing kook, when in fact, his points all were perfectly valid. In many ways, the lockout was a waste as agents and players pretended that management had merely been joking about their fiscal dilemma. But they knew that professional hockey had become a player's market. Several cities were clamoring for NHL franchises, and minor league hockey was undergoing an unprecedented boom.

Under the aegis of Bob Ufer, the International Hockey League loomed as a distinct threat to the NHL had the lockout not been settled. Ray Bourque, for one, was negotiating to move to the IHL's Denver Grizzlies a week before the NHL-NHLPA deal was brokered.

But "the I," as it is affectionately known, remained a thorn in the NHL's side. Without asking Gary Bettman's permission, it brazenly opened its own franchises in such NHL strongholds as Detroit, Chicago, Los Angeles, and San Francisco. IHL markets included top-rated cities like Houston, Kansas City, Minneapolis–St. Paul, Cleveland, and Las Vegas. Before the NHL could establish a viable European base, Ufer declared that his outfit would install a division on the continent.

While all this was going on, Bettman, Incorporated, struggled through its makeshift 1995 season. Lockout anger notwithstanding, attendance remained remarkably robust in many areas, especially relatively new territories such as Anaheim, Miami, and San Jose, where sellouts were the norm despite teams of modest talent.

Some critics denigrated the 48-game schedule as insulting to the fans and claimed that it was the cause for erratic play. Nevertheless, with its "Game On" theme, it allowed big-league hockey an opportunity to regenerate itself, and I personally was fascinated by the homestretch, particularly as it affected the Islanders, Devils, and defending champion Rangers.

Despite an unconscionable number of injuries, the Islanders remained within sight of a playoff berth and actually pulled off a monstrous win that could have catapulted them into contention. The aftermath, however, demonstrated to me precisely what was wrong with the game in terms of IQ (as in *intensity quotient*).

The episode began with a typically heated game between the Rangers and Islanders at Nassau Coliseum. Oozing with talent, the visitors appeared capable of demolishing the home team on this night and from the opening face-off penetrated the Isles' defense and tested goalie Tommy Soderstrom. It would be an understatement to report that Soderstrom made a dozen truly difficult saves over two periods, protecting his crease. Having one goal with which to work, he dazzled throughout the third, robbing Rangers such as Mark Messier and Adam Graves through the final 20 minutes.

During my postgame interview with Soderstrom, I mentioned that in all my years of covering the NHL, his performance this night was among the 10 best I had ever seen. Perhaps even among the five best.

The win was an enriching one for the floundering Isles and the kind that should have launched them to a galvanic performance in their next contest, on Saturday afternoon at Hartford, a game we were televising back to New York. Although we broadcasters technically are not supposed to get overly excited about such things, I was looking forward to the Whalers match with considerable enthusiasm.

Hartford was a beatable club running neck and neck with the Islanders for a playoff spot. The victory over the Rangers should have provided the Isles with the tonic to skate the Whalers right off the ice. At least that's what I was thinking. After all, the better the team plays, the more magnetic our broadcast is likely to be.

But my fellow announcers Jiggs McDonald and Ed Westfall opened the show with a cautionary note. Time and again the underdog Isles had beaten a superior Rangers' team and, inevitably, they then would take on a lesser club and play like losers. It was the classic build-up-to-a-letdown and one we hoped would not happen again.

An hour before game time I examined notes in our TV studio, which just happened to adjoin the visitors' dressing room. A few of the Islanders walked in to tape their sticks and shoot the breeze. One of them was Travis Green, a curly haired center whose potential had remained unfulfilled for two years.

I liked Green as a character. He was amiable, occasionally funny, and always available. He was the kind of kid you wanted to make good although management kept whispering that he was a chronic underachiever. But on Thursday night against the Rangers, he was dominating and capped the evening by winning the final face-off from Mark Messier.

"Win this and the club could be on its way," I mentioned.

Green nodded his approval but added little more encouragement. No matter. As long as he worked his tail off on the ice, all would be well. Or, so I hoped.

Soon after the opening face-off, I walked down to my ice-level location near the visitors' dressing room. The Civic Center was nearly packed and its crowd bellowed as the home team immediately bisected the Islanders' defense and forced a face-off in the New York end. Hartford had just obtained Glenn Featherstone from the Rangers in a deal for Pat Verbeek—a deal that evoked Harry Sinden's priceless comment: "Verbeek is made for the Rangers; he's overpaid!"

Featherstone is a rugged defenseman known for his bulk, not his scoring ability. But on this play, as he patrolled the right point, the puck skimmed to him and he took a 60-foot shot at Soderstrom. I watched the puck meander through the air toward an unscreened Soderstrom before it passed the goalie into the net. This same Soderstrom had stopped shots 50 times as difficult in the previous game and now this!

It was excruciating to watch the Islanders from this point on to the conclusion some 58 minutes of play later. They alternately seemed disinterested, distracted, and disillusioned (perhaps by Soderstrom's erratic goaltending), so it was hardly a surprise that the game ended with a Whalers' rout. Green, from whom I had expected more, was virtually invisible all game although he had considerable company.

On the drive home with my producer, Kevin Meininger, I lamented the sorry effort they generated. "You've seen the Islanders' season end with this game," I mentioned.

"I can't argue with that," said Meininger, turning the car into a McDonald's driveway near the Connecticut Turnpike so that we could drown our sorrows in root beer and Big Macs.

For all intents and purposes it was the end. Periodically, Thomas would complain about his salary distractions and Soderstrom would rediscover his magic, but the Islanders never could put enough wins together to make a serious run. Shortly before the trade deadline they shipped Pierre Turgeon and Vladimir Malakhov to the Canadiens for Mathieu Schneider, Kirk Muller, and Chris Darby.

It was a blockbuster deal and big stuff for us, especially because we had a game with the Rangers at Madison Square

Garden on the next night. Although many in the crew were fond of Turgeon as a person and artist, we were just as delighted to see him move on to Montreal. The same could be said for Malakhov. The tall Russian had always been aloof off the ice and thoroughly unpredictable on the pond.

One night he would execute a spectacular foray from end to end, and another night he would mindlessly pass the puck to an obvious opponent, who then would score.

The corridors outside the Islanders' dressing room at Madison Square Garden buzzed with that special excitement of a just-completed trade two hours before the game with the Rangers. Wearing his oversize smile, Schneider arrived with Darby and we exchanged hellos. Schneider's father, Sam, is one of the world's best talkers and he was due to arrive later for the game—and a between-periods interview with me.

However, the TV gang sensed that something was missing when the Islanders' press aides turned their grins to frowns and began pacing the corridor. "Muller isn't here," Jiggs McDonald whispered, "and it doesn't look like he's showing up."

"Any reason?" I wondered.

"Good question," said McDonald.

Muller, supposedly the ultimate team player, was nowhere to be found. Finally, general manager Don Maloney revealed that Muller would not be playing that night. Apparently the trade was sufficiently shocking that he couldn't get himself to jet down to New York and join his new employer.

Cynics among the press corps guessed that Muller's absence had as much to do about money as it did about the trauma of leaving the team he had captained. I grilled Muller about it when he finally did arrive on Long Island a few days later. He insisted that the emotional upheaval was too much to take at the time. Money, according to Muller, was not the object of his brief but unpleasant absence. (The Islanders beat the Rangers without Muller, but with him in the lineup, they faded out of playoff contention.) Even after he had become a regular, Muller dropped hints that he might not remain with the club after the season, that he might demand a trade or whatever.

I found this terribly disconcerting, especially because he had been sought as a potential captain of the hockey club. After the season had ended, an Islanders' official confided that money was the object. Muller had been paid $1.7 million but in Canadian funds. He wanted the sum converted to American currency, which would be substantially more than its Canadian counterpart. Not surprisingly, the general staff agreed to the request. Some observers argued that the Isles had no choice. Others within the NHL high command winced and deplored the run-away inflation.

"Nobody wants to hear it," said Flyers' general manager Bob Clarke, "but we're paying too much for salaries. That's the whole bottom line. If we're smart enough and tough enough to hold the line on salaries until we get our revenues up, we'll be all right, but the big money is not there right now. And it may not be until the next generation of players comes along.

"We don't know when it's going to come, or if it will. We're all hoping that with the Fox TV contract and all the stuff we're doing that things will go well, but you don't know.

"Obviously, the lockout was the start of putting the brakes on salaries. Now we've got to see what the finished product of collective bargaining leads to, see how we all do."

Based on events during the homestretch, ownership was not doing well. Wherever I turned, as the shortened season rushed to a close, money stories took precedence over game stories. Dale Hawerchuk declared that he would leave Buffalo because he was unhappy with a $1.3 million annual salary; Trevor Linden was despairing over his $1 million a year pay in Vancouver; Jeremy Roenick couldn't abide $1.1 million in Chicago; and so it went to the abject disgust of fans, who somehow remained more interested in the hockey than the haggling.

But, as the citizens of Quebec, Winnipeg, and New Jersey would learn—as if they didn't already know—the name of the game was money. Big money. And that's why each venue would undergo a terrible catharsis in the spring of 1995. As it happened, I found myself in the midst of one of them.

FROM QUEBEC TO DENVER
The Americanization and Possible Death of Hockey as We Know It

There never has been a more hockey-minded city than the capital of La Belle Province de Québec.

Quebec City abounds with outdoor rinks, has a rich history with the ice game dating back to an NHL franchise called the Quebec Bulldogs, and has celebrated many local heroes—Jean Beliveau, Camille Henry, and, finally, Joe Sakic—as fervently as any metropolis on the continent.

By any stretch of logic, Quebec City should have been able to support a major league team. For most of the franchise's life, its arena, Le Colisée, was virtually filled to capacity for nearly every home game of the Nordiques, and the team dominated the local media, both print and electronic.

"Hockey talk was the main topic of conversation," said long-time sports columnist Claude Larochelle of *Le Soleil*. "It should have stayed that way."

In 1980, it would have. But this was 1995, the dawning of Bettman, Incorporated, a swing toward Disney-type ownership, the divine right of Fox Network TV, and the NBA-ing of the NHL. For any who expected an easy, hockey-loving ambience of yester-year, all bets were off.

To say the least, I found this somewhat disconcerting as old values—some of which were truly valuable—seemed to be discarded as quickly as Eric Lindros banged bodies. But anyone who studied the evolutionary process at the NHL understood that big money took precedence over anything else on the priority list.

"Gary Bettman's plan was simple to understand," said a former NHL employee who had studied Bettman's transition from the

Gil Stein era. "His agenda calls for him to make the owners as rich as possible."

But to do so, Bettman also has had to be politically correct. He learned early in his administration that Canadians were hypersensitive about their hockey. Beware, Bettman, beware. Any suggestion that small markets such as Winnipeg, Quebec, or Edmonton had no place in the greater NHL only served to invite the wrath of power brokers north of the border. But in terms of the league's future, Winnipeg, Quebec, and Edmonton—or at least one or two of them—had to go. Where, when, and how was another story to be addressed whenever possible.

As the abridged season unfolded in midwinter 1995, I began to sense that a Bettman plan was unfolding. It appeared to be broad in range and pegged to the premise that sooner or later every NHL arena had to be upgraded to whatever he deemed big-league standards through the next century. Replacement of old rinks such as Boston Garden, Buffalo's Aud, and Chicago Stadium became an imperative, not an option.

Corporate boxes became a major revenue source where once they had been an afterthought. On visits to Winnipeg and Quebec City, Bettman began hinting more broadly that new arenas—or vastly refurbished older ones—were an absolute must if the franchises were to remain operative in the NHL. The hint was that these franchises could easily be transferred to eagerly awaiting American cities that coveted big-league hockey.

"I don't view this as blackmail," said the commissioner. "My discussions with the mayors of Quebec and Winnipeg have pointed out that if they want to have a sports franchise in the twenty-first century, they must appropriately house them. If they choose not to, that doesn't make it a bad city. The cities are simply making a business decision on whether it's worth having a sports franchise."

Remember the secret words, "business decision." The two words would underscore the bottom line for virtually every move made by Bettman, Incorporated. As a result, I couldn't help but sense that his NBA orientation was playing a bigger and bigger part in his NHL planning. For one whose roots were deeply planted in hockey, I couldn't help but feel somewhat awed by the increasing numbers of nonhockey people who were added to his staff, some coming over from the National Football League and some from Major League Baseball.

These were big market people with neither cultural nor historic ties to the Winnipegs and Quebecs of the world. When they looked at the league and its future, they could see Canada's decline in many areas or an Americanization of the league. To wit:

- The Vancouver Canucks' team was purchased by a Seattle billionaire, John McCaw, whose controlling interest dwarfed that of the Canadian Griffiths family, which previously ran the club.
- Canadian currency more and more was being regarded by Americans as if it were as valueless as "money" in the game of Monopoly.
- Bettman centralized league operations in New York, leaving Montreal and Toronto NHL offices as distant outposts of no consequence.
- The number of Americans and Europeans in the league was increasing while the number of Canadians was dwindling.
- Formerly run by Canadian-born Alan Eagleson, the NHL Players' Association was now orchestrated by an American, Bob Goodenow, who had no special urge to favor Canada.

Goodenow's players couldn't care less whether they played north or south of the 49th parallel as long as the money was big. "If you had a choice between an ideal situation in Canada and an ideal situation in the States," said Kirk Muller when he still played in Montreal, "90 percent of the guys in this room would be out of here. Just like my friends who have businesses in Kingston, Ontario. A lot of them are trying to move 35 miles over the border because it's cheaper to function in the States."

During the late sixties, I had befriended an aspiring Canadian-born playwright who had moved to Manhattan and lived near our Upper West Side apartment. Rick Salutin was as ardent a hockey fan as any artist I have ever encountered and eventually (1977) wrote a play about his favorite team, Les Canadiens. In his preface he noted that to Canadians hockey was "the sole assurance we have a culture." In conversations with Salutin—and in my encounters in Canada—this was as accurate a representation as one could get.

Nearly two decades after he began writing his play, Salutin could view the Americanization of hockey from a more cynical perspective. "Canadians aren't sure if it's the War of 1812 again or whether it's simply the octopus quality of business, the tentacles clutching the game.

"The lockout hit Canadians more than Americans because the elements of national culture and mythology are more fragile in Canada than in the United States. In the United States they have baseball, but they also have lots of other stuff. In a general sense hockey is one of the few things that makes this place coherent. In the United States there's no worry the country will cease to exist.

"Here, there's a sense the country is falling apart. With free trade, the threat of Quebec separation, issues of national sovereignty, hockey assumes a sense of national loss."

That sense became more evident to me as the Jets were being wooed to Minnesota and the Nordiques to Atlanta or Denver, because both cities were vying for Marcel Aubut's club. Phoenix was not far behind, along with Houston and Portland, to name a few contenders.

I had held the false hope—primarily based on misleading headlines based on misleading quotes—that the so-called ownership victory in the CBA war would have strengthened the smaller markets. And when Bettman hired Bortz and Company, a Denver consulting outfit, to devise a plan to help the have-nots, I actually thought some sort of revenue-sharing program would solve the problem.

Naturally, I should have known better. The "have" teams such as Boston, Chicago, Detroit, New York Rangers, and Toronto wanted no part of anything like a 60–40 home-visitor split used by the NFL. "I thought communism died," barked Harry Sinden of the wealthy Bruins. "You won't see it revived in the NHL."

As I watched the Nordiques inch closer and closer to a transfer and the Jets' high command regularly confer with Minneapolis suitors, I felt a concern. They were, however, distant partners with no direct effect on my well-being; or so I thought.

But then, one day late in the season, I found myself slowly slipping into the fiscal whirlpool. It seemed like the most preposterous of all scenarios, but there it was in black and white. The city of Nashville, Tennessee, was courting *our* New Jersey Devils. My stomach felt as if it had been hit with a pile driver.

McMULLEN AND THE MICKEY MOUSE CLUB
The Devils Strive for Respect

When a huge, white, state-of-the-art arena took shape on swampland in the Meadowlands of New Jersey within view of Manhattan's skyscrapers, it seemed a logical home for a National Hockey League team. Madison Square Garden invariably was sold out for New York Rangers home games, and in the early eighties the SRO sign usually was hung at Nassau Coliseum, where the New York Islanders were in the midst of a four-year Stanley Cup run.

With a seating capacity of 19,040 for hockey, the Meadowlands Arena seemed a natural for an expansion team, a point that was underlined when the Philadelphia Flyers and Rangers played an exhibition game there and filled the place. If two non-Jersey teams could do so splendidly, imagine how much better the state's first major league club in any sport would fare.

I wasn't so sure about the answer to that question and in 1982 I expressed my opinions in an article, "Can the Metropolitan Area Support Three NHL Teams?"

My doubts were rooted in the fact that the NHL never had a situation where there had been three clubs in one greater urban community. I pointed out that Montreal once boasted the Maroons, favored by the English-speaking fans, and the Canadiens, representing the Francophones. Prior to World War II, New York featured both the Americans and Rangers playing out of Madison Square Garden. Both the Maroons and Americans were victims of the Great Depression and disappeared despite a loyal following.

But Dr. John J. McMullen, a shipping tycoon and owner of the Houston Astros baseball team, had been sold a bill of goods by the New Jersey Sports and Exposition Authority, the NHL, and some of his personal friends, including then governor Brendan Byrne.

"The governor came down to training camp with me when I had the Astros," McMullen recalled. "He asked me if I could help bring a sports franchise to the new building and said he'd appreciate if I did so. I've lived in New Jersey all my life and I thought it would be good for the state if it had its own big-league team. Without trying to overglorify it, that was the reason I bought the Colorado Rockies."

The purchase date was June 30, 1982. Having failed to win sufficient fan support in Denver, the Rockies were sold to McMullen and John C. Whitehead, a leading investment banker who would become U.S. Deputy Secretary of State during the Ronald Reagan administration. Byrne was the third man in the triumvirate and even had the Meadowlands Arena named after him.

Soon after he took command of his team—renamed the New Jersey Devils—McMullen read my article questioning the ability of greater New York–New Jersey to successfully embrace three NHL teams. "At the time," he later told me over dinner, "I didn't believe you. Everybody was telling me that I'd sell out every game."

It was the beginning of more than a decade of disillusionment that soon would be compounded by the neighboring Rangers, Flyers, and Islanders, each of whom demanded territorial indemnity. In 1982 McMullen agreed to pay the Rangers $9.2 million, the Islanders $8 million, and the Flyers $2.5 million for invading their protected territory. With league approval, the Devils suspended payments within five seasons, leaving a considerable outstanding balance. But the disappointment, which eventually led McMullen in 1995 to consider an unlikely move to Nashville, was only beginning.

From the start, he mistakenly assumed that the New Jersey Sports and Exposition Authority was both partner and friend, as it should have been in a partnership such as this. Instead, McMullen discovered that authority boss Bob Mulcahy was hardly the pal that he thought he would be and, perhaps, was quite the opposite.

"I brought Mulcahy to every meeting with the NHL prior to the transaction," McMullen elaborated, "fully expecting that the authority would be helpful and cooperative. And from the minute I committed myself, the administration had changed and they brought a new chairman in and I suddenly walked into a very confrontational and difficult management at the New Jersey Sports and Exposition Authority.

"At that point, I should have said, 'Look, let's go back to Denver.' I made a serious mistake and I acknowledge it. But it's a mistake. I think that is understandable. First of all, all the publicity surrounding it. Then I had already committed and paid, I think, $8.5 million to Peter Gilbert [for the Rockies] and had already agreed on things. I should not have completed the transaction."

But he did and thus began a rather rocky relationship between McMullen, the NHL and, of course, the New Jersey Sports and Exposition Authority. Within the league hierarchy, McMullen was part of a small but very thoughtful minority, which included St. Louis Blues' owner Harry Ornest. At one preseason meet-the-press breakfast at the Meadowlands Arena, McMullen mentioned to me how frustrated he was with John Ziegler's administration by select committee and how Blackhawks' owner Bill Wirtz was helping command the league through his league chairmanship.

What impressed me most about McMullen was his brash candor. Also, the fact that he was a navy man meant a lot. My father had served in the U.S. Navy on a minelayer in the North Sea during World War I. A graduate of the United States Naval Academy, McMullen had been an officer during World War II and remained a key figure in the navy for many years thereafter. His pugnacity was evident from the moment he joined the NHL fraternity, especially after the notorious Gretzky affair.

It was bad enough that he had been stuck with an inadequate team and was playing in the shadow of the championship Islanders and fat-cat Rangers, but his club almost instantly became the subject of ridicule and, from the unlikeliest source, hockey's foremost player.

Wayne Gretzky had become king of the NHL by the time McMullen bought the Devils, but he was a benevolent despot in his role as hockey's ultimate performer—an ambassador of goodwill, so to speak. But on November 19, 1983, that all changed. McMullen's Devils limped into Northlands Coliseum with a 2–17–0 record—four points in 19 games.

New Jersey's general manager–coach Billy MacMillan started Ron Low in goal, knowing that Low had tended goal for the Oilers over four seasons. Armed with the hardest shooters in the NHL, the Oilers peppered their old teammate unmercifully and emerged with a 13–4 victory. It was the largest score ever run up against the hapless Devils. Gretzky, who had eight points on three goals and five assists, held court after the game.

It must be remembered that the Great One had been a close friend of the Devils' victimized goaltender and felt for Low's predicament. Also noteworthy is the fact that reporters traditionally bait athletes into answers they might not otherwise want to give. And so it was with Gretzky on this night.

He was asked about the Devils' performance and delivered a peroration that would have reverberations right into McMullen's heart. "It got to a point where it wasn't even funny," said Gretzky. "How long has it been for them? Three years? Five? Seven? Probably closer to nine. Well, it's time they got their act together. They're ruining the whole league.

"They had better stop running a Mickey Mouse operation and put somebody on ice. It's not a question of not working. It's a question of talent. I feel sorry for Ronnie and New Jersey. The 37 shots we took were all good shots. They struggled in Kansas City; they were awful in Colorado, and now look what is happening."

For about eight hours it appeared that Gretzky's comments would be lost in the mountain of weekend sports stories. I had been covering an Islanders game that night and listened to the Edmonton rout on the radio returning from Long Island to Manhattan. But the next day, which was Sunday, the mud hit the fan. Someone phoned and asked whether I'd heard Gretzky's remarks, which then were read to me. On Monday the headlines roared, "Gretzky Takes Slap at Devils' Organization." That was in USA Today. The New York Post put it another way. "Gretzky: Devils Are Mickey Mouse Team."

Naturally, the quotes reached McMullen's office and he reacted with appropriate fury. He dispatched letters of protest, but it was too late to alter the image. The Devils were equated with Mickey Mouse and that was that. What's more, the label stuck for years as McMullen vainly attempted to construct a winner.

McMullen fired MacMillan shortly after the Gretzky affair and hired Max McNab as general manager, and Tom McVie was brought in as head coach. Marshall Johnston was named director of player personnel. McMullen's Devils hardly transformed into playoff contenders, but they showed more life under McVie, and perhaps, they showed too much in the eyes of some cynics.

It was at this point in time when I came to appreciate McMullen's innate sense of honesty. This was early in 1984, the year that Mario Lemieux was the outstanding junior performer on the continent. Every sane hockey person understood that Lemieux would be the first player selected in the next draft and would automatically become a franchise cornerstone for the next decade. The Devils, because of their ineptitude, were in excellent position to finish last and thereby draft Lemieux.

One other team had a crack at Lemieux and that was Pittsburgh, but on the basis of roster quality the Penguins should have finished ahead of New Jersey by at least five or six points and thereby miss Lemieux.

But Pittsburgh wanted Lemieux badly, very badly. Several commentators and insiders held the view that the Penguins were so desperate for Lemieux they would ensure that they finished last. To do so, they would lose hockey games they ordinarily might have won. Naturally, there never has been anyone who would publicly articulate this view, although it has been commonly shared by many journalists and NHL insiders, amid broad hints. Benching regulars and inserting untried rookies, the Penguins continued losing and supporting the cynics' view. When the issue was raised, the Penguins' general staff emphatically denied it.

At this point, McMullen could very well have instructed McVie to do likewise, but as much as the Devils coveted Lemieux, McMullen refused to follow suit. "We're here to win hockey games," said McVie, echoing his owner's philosophy. "It's the honorable thing to do."

McMullen's Devils then won games on March 6th over the Penguins and March 17th against Boston, ensuring a fifth-place finish for themselves and Lemieux for Pittsburgh. McMullen's pick was Kirk Muller, a tenacious, hard-driving center who eventually would become captain of the team.

In the meantime, the Devils' owner continued suffering the embarrassment of nonplayoff teams as coach after coach came and went. I attended just about every announcement always made at the restaurant adjoining the club offices—inappropriately named Winners—for the usual optimistic party line.

McMullen always was there and we began to get chummy as the seasons went along. His general manager, Max McNab, had become a good friend and confidant and it bothered me that McNab couldn't seem to deliver a winner. His coach Doug Carpenter came close a couple of times, but by 1987, the boss decided that a change was in order. Club president Bob Butera was released and McNab was bumped up to a vice presidency. With that decision, McMullen made the most significant move in his franchise's history. He hired Providence College's athletic director, Lou Lamoriello, to run his club.

A former hockey coach, Lamoriello was not your run-of-the-mill manager. The native of Providence was out of the traditional GM loop and a major gamble for McMullen.

To me, Lamoriello was an intriguing choice: an American with no NHL experience but one who I had known through the hockey grapevine. We had spoken a few times when he still was at Providence and had come to know each other through the *Hockey News*.

A few days after he took over the reins, Lamoriello and I had lunch. We exchanged views on the team, its coaching, public relations, just about everything. Being a part of the SportsChannel Devils' broadcasting team—which I was at that time—I wanted to see the club do well. After all, the better the team, the more fun it—usually, but not always—is to broadcast.

Lamoriello retained Carpenter as coach, but after a humiliating 9–3 loss to the Rangers at Madison Square Garden on December 16, 1987, I sensed that Carpenter's goose was cooked. The McMullen-Garden rivalry had been growing by the year with the Devils' boss facing the fact that so many metropolitan area fans rooted for the New York club. "It's like they all have Ranger genes when they're born," McMullen lamented.

On the morning of January 26, 1988, I received a hurried phone call from Dave Freed, one of the Devils' publicists. "Press conference at noon!"

That could mean only one thing; and it was—a new coach. Carpenter had been fired and replaced by Jim Schoenfeld, the ebullient, redheaded, former defenseman. Frankly, I don't get overly excited about press conferences, but this one had a genuinely upbeat air about it.

Carpenter, for his many virtues—and he did have many—betrayed a negative charisma quotient. Part of it may have been a result of the team he coached, but the other part simply had to do with his severe personality. By contrast, Schoenfeld bubbled like a just-opened seltzer bottle and would become the catalyst for one of the NHL's most gripping stretch runs. It all began on a Sunday afternoon at Capital Center in Landover, Maryland.

Apparently out of a playoff berth for the umpteenth time, the Devils scored two shorthanded goals against Washington to defeat the Capitals, 4–2. From that point on, they sprinted forward thanks to the sensational goaltending of Sean Burke. As they approached the final weekend of the season, they still trailed the hated Rangers for the final playoff berth. It came down to a pair of games on Sunday night: Quebec at New York and the Devils at Chicago.

Even if the Rangers won—the game at Madison Square Garden was an hour earlier—New Jersey could clinch with a win against the Blackhawks. That night I was a guest on New York's "Channel 5 News" with Bill Mazer. Prior to the telecast, I watched the Rangers blank the Nordiques, 3–0, and then switched to the Devils game.

As it happened, New Jersey rallied to tie the game late in the third period, forcing overtime. A tie would do them no good; it was win or they were out of it.

Before the overtime began, Mazer had to go up to his set because the show was almost ready to begin. Hockey was going to be the main topic, which is why I was there for commentary. He wanted to make sure we got the Devils' score in, even if it meant doing it in the middle of the news.

What Mazer did was assign a runner to watch the game in the studio. The runner was to come up to tell us if anyone scored and relate the final outcome. I remember being there a long time without hearing a word, and I assumed that was bad news for the Devils. I thought that the game would end in a tie and the whole season would go up in smoke. So, I waited and waited and waited. Finally, the runner walked onto the fringe of Mazer's "Sports Extra" set with a huge piece of cardboard and the writing: "John MacLean—2:21 of Overtime."

I did a doubletake. It was as if I had to see the cardboard over and over to realize that it was for real. After the show, I was still shaking my head. I went to the bar down the block and gulped two Bloody Marys.

So, it was on to the playoffs for me, the Devils, and our SportsChannel broadcasts. In the opening round, the Devils upset the Islanders and then went up against Washington, a heavy favorite to beat the upstarts. But once again, the Devils would not fold. They pushed the Capitals to a seventh game and won it on a late goal by MacLean.

The locker-room scene was straight out of Bedlam with McMullen excitedly pumping the hands of his players. Watching him, I sensed that he felt more like a kid than some of the young fans who were following his hockey club. He walked over to me, grabbed my paw, and said, "This is some hockey team, isn't it?"

That it was, especially after extending Boston to another seven-game set before capitulating. More importantly, in the political sense, was McMullen's bold decision to challenge the NHL—meaning president John Ziegler, chairman of the board Bill Wirtz, and the officials—and go to court.

McMullen's defiance was both unprecedented and infuriating to the establishment; which is why I was so tickled with his brash response. He believed in his cause and simply would not be pushed around, not even by a Wirtz. And if it meant going before a judge to prove his point, so be it.

"Why they wanted me to violate a court order and put the NHL in contempt of court—it's very embarrassing," said Wirtz. "I don't think at the time they [McMullen and Lamoriello] realized what they were doing. That was not a nice thing to do."

But Wirtz, whose hand was forced by McMullen, had to give the order to play the game with backup officials because president Ziegler was nowhere to be found.

After New Jersey lost game seven to Boston, it was freely predicted that McMullen's daring move would have repercussions. In fact, McMullen's own comment proved to be most prophetic: "This is not finished," he exclaimed.

The statement was open to considerable interpretation, including my own. I felt the statement had to do with the extraordinarily tight fraternity comprised of referees and linesmen. Traveling alone from city to city, the zebras lead a life of partial solitude, often feeling paranoid about criticism from players, coaches, managers, and the media. Insult one referee and, in a sense, you insult them all.

With that in mind, it hardly was surprising that, in my opinion, the Devils were subconsciously targeted by the zebras in the 1988–89 season. The officials were going to avenge referee Don Koharski, and McMullen's Devils would pay the price. In game after game, they illogically got the short end of the officiating and—with some help from their own ineptitude and overconfidence—missed the playoffs.

In time Schoenfeld would be fired and replaced by John Cunniff, who in turn was replaced by Tom McVie, who was replaced by Herb Brooks. From time to time the Devils would make headway, but their failure to exploit the 1988 miracle finish with a second straight playoff berth did irreparable damage and severely curtailed their fan growth at a time when the Rangers continued to be a major attraction and competitor.

Meanwhile, McMullen and I gradually were becoming closer friends, as was the case with Lamoriello. My wife, Shirley, and I had dinner with Lamoriello once a year. There was plenty of hockey talk but all off-the-record. By this time Lamoriello had been developing an iron-fisted image, although it wasn't apparent away from the rink. Those who knew him from his Providence days and had dealt with him on hockey matters reiterated that he was one of the most misunderstood characters in the business and that was the feeling that we shared.

Because McMullen continued to be the iconoclast, I found myself constantly in his corner. Although NHL traditionalists scoffed at the idea of Russians playing in the majors, the Devils' owner told his staff as early as 1983 that they should draft Soviet players, presuming good ones became available.

"My feeling was that changes in the European political situation could come about and bring an easing of relations between East and West," said McMullen. "If that happened, we might be able to lure a couple of players to the Devils. At least it was worth a try."

At the June 1983 draft, the Devils' eighth round pick was a defenseman named Viacheslav Fetisov of the Soviet Union. By 1988, Lamoriello was pressing the search and on July 7, 1989, I attended another milestone press conference at the Winners Club. Fetisov and Sergei Starikov, another defenseman, were signed to New Jersey contracts. "It was a long battle," said Dr. McMullen, "but better late than never."

McMullen cornered me after the press conference dissolved. It was obvious he was pleased with himself and he had every right to be. However, it also was evident that he wished that the event had happened six years earlier, when Fetisov was in his prime. "I'm glad I made the move," he said, chuckling in his inimitable way. "You can see he's a quality person."

The good doctor expected quality from his personnel as well as loyalty. The loyalty theme—something that was rooted in his youth and naval days—was among McMullen's most powerful and laudable traits. I noticed this for the first time when Pat Verbeek talked his way into hot water with management.

Verbeek, who had played on a line with Kirk Muller and Aaron Broten, had been a star of the 1988 playoffs but slipped noticeably the following year. He developed a reputation as a whiner and soon lost favor with Lamoriello because of his contract demands. He was dealt to Hartford for Sylvain Turgeon in 1989.

It was a significant deal in more than one respect, but most of all it underlined the point that sedition—or disloyalty as viewed by management—would not be tolerated on a McMullen team. This philosophy would be emphasized even more two years later after the Devils had once again become an attractive playoff team.

By now Muller had become the captain and symbol of the team. Tenacious, effervescent, and productive, Muller epitomized the lunch-pail, hard-working style that appealed to many fans who preferred that brand of hockey over the more artistic kind delivered by the Rangers. Captain Kirk, as he was affectionately known around Byrne Arena, was reaching the prime of his playing career, and the Devils looked better than ever as they led the Penguins, three games to two, in the best-of-seven opening round.

In game six at the Meadowlands, New Jersey scored a quick goal against substitute goalie Frank Pieterangelo, then fell behind only to tie the score on a tip-in by Laurie Boschman. However, the long-running referee's curse struck again. Despite a video replay that clearly indicated otherwise, a goal was waved off by the zebra. Eventually, the Devils lost game six and then game seven in Pittsburgh.

Muller was a monstrous disappointment. He did not score a goal and collected a mere two assists over the seven games. Had he played to his potential, the Devils surely would have beaten Pittsburgh and moved closer to the Stanley Cup. This did not elude McMullen's notice nor did he ignore Muller's walkout during the September training camp. In McMullen's eyes this was a deplorable move for a captain. Before the 1991–92 season began Muller was traded to Montreal for Stephane Richer and Tom Chorske. If ever an owner was directly conveying a message to a player—not to mention his team—about loyalty, this was it.

McMullen's loyalty extended to his general manager, Lou Lamoriello, who was the target of imbalanced reporting. When the Devils did well, he received scant credit, and when they lost, he was overwhelmingly blasted. As one reporter who covered the team mentioned (on condition of anonymity), "The guys on the beat were all Rangers' fans and couldn't wait to rip Lou. They were fans first and reporters second."

What piqued McMullen more than anything was what appeared to be the treatment he received from New Jersey's biggest-selling newspaper, the *Star-Ledger*. Instead of giving the local team an advantage in coverage, the *Ledger* played it even or sometimes favored the rival Rangers from Manhattan. It would be difficult to imagine a tilt toward an out-of-town team by a local newspaper in any other community.

As for McMullen, the more time I spent with him, the more I enjoyed his abrasive yet amusing personality. One day I decided to do something unusual; I phoned him and invited the tycoon and his wife, Jackie, to dinner. I told him it was a payback for a dinner he had invited Shirley and me to at Monmouth College, where he was honored for his contributions to New Jersey education.

We met at the Meadowlands, where I interviewed him for about a half-hour. The focus was on the NHL's future and specifically its labor problems. He made it clear that a basketball-type salary cap was an imperative in the NHL's next collective bargaining agreement. Until that moment, I hadn't even thought about it, but McMullen spelled out the details and how important it was for big-league hockey's fiscal well-being.

Then we drove to an Italian restaurant in Hoboken and he spun yarns about his youth in New Jersey. We talked about the poor contract the NHL had cut with ESPN and the state of the game. His wife, Jackie, met us for dinner on the restaurant's rooftop. A wisp of a breeze put just the right topper on a balmy summer evening as the subject drifted from sports to politics. After telling me how destructive baseball had become and how much happier he was in hockey, McMullen began talking about a New Jersey politician whose name hardly made an impression on me.

"You'll be hearing a lot about Christie Whitman," Mrs. McMullen promised. There was a note of intensity in her voice that caused me to register the name. "She's *very* bright and has terrific ideas. Watch for her." (A few years later, with McMullen's backing, Whitman became the Republican governor of New Jersey.) We also talked about Lamoriello, and Mac—that was what everyone called him in his native Montclair, New Jersey— left absolutely no doubt that he believed implicitly in his general manager and, furthermore, couldn't imagine a harder worker nor one who could better balance a budget.

From time to time beat writers would question Lamoriello's stewardship of the club, particularly after he dismissed Tom McVie, replacing him with Herb Brooks, and then dismissed Brooks after the 1992–93 season. Shirley and I had dinner with Lamoriello early in June 1993 at Borelli's, an Italian restaurant near the Meadowlands. After discussing the season—in which he admitted erring in the selection of Brooks—Lamoriello winked and then said he had a surprise for us.

"I'm not going to tell you," he went on, "until it's certain, but I think you'll like it."

We hadn't a clue and wouldn't know until the morning of June 28, 1993, when the media was summoned to Winners for yet another press conference. Never before had such an effective veil of secrecy been placed on a hockey appointment. There were no hints, not a single forecast in the media.

I was sitting at a table on the aisle with a couple of reporters awaiting the new coach's arrival when I felt a tap on my shoulder. Before I could wheel around to see who it was, the person was past me heading for the dais. He wore a sly smile when he turned back and looked at me. Jacques Lemaire realized that his appointment was a surprise to everyone.

After the introductions, McMullen and I huddled as we had done many times before. "We had to get permission from [Canadiens' general manager] Serge Savard and [president] Ron Corey," said McMullen, "but we think it's well worth it. Jacques is a class act and I guarantee things are going to be different around here."

I wanted to believe Mac, but it was difficult considering the Brooks disappointment. There was no doubt in my mind that

Lemaire and I would hit it off and I had planned to dine with him shortly after he had settled in, but Simon's heart failure and subsequent hospitalization intervened. More than two months passed before we met again, this time at a preseason Devils' breakfast, emceed by publicist Dave Freed.

Curiously, Lamoriello was not present although McMullen, his son Peter, who worked in the club's front office, Lemaire, and new assistant coach Larry Robinson all were there. There was an obvious edge to the questioning, with some of the writers putting Lamoriello on the spot in absentia. The coaching turnover was mentioned as well as the playoff failures. McMullen defended his GM and eventually the hostility was defused by Lemaire's upbeat presence.

But when the media headed for the exits, a few of the journalists ventured that Lemaire was Lamoriello's last hope. If the new Devils' coach didn't deliver, McMullen would clean house top to bottom and send Lamoriello packing. Which set me wondering about Lemaire and his potential.

The *Times'* man covering the press conference quoted Montreal *Gazette* columnist Red Fisher who denigrated Lemaire. (He later learned that Lemaire and Fisher had feuded when Lemaire worked for Les Canadiens. There was no way that Fisher would endorse the new coach.) Others took a wait-and-see attitude and so did I because I would be sharing a "Coaches Corner" segment with Lemaire on the SportsChannel pregame show before every home game.

Having done the same routine the previous year with Brooks, I had cause for concern. Beset with personality problems within the dressing room, Brooks often would be late for interviews—or rush for an early interview—or have one of his assistants do the show himself. I had no problem with that although it unnerved my producer. A coach's job comes first and interviews are secondary, which is why I wondered whether Lemaire would be similarly unpredictable and moody.

Not so. Lemaire was unfailingly on time, regularly amusing, relaxed, amiable, and most of all insightful. The conversations were more like fireside chats than uneasy third degrees, and it was obvious after about a month that we had good chemistry between us.

The same could be said for Lemaire and the Devils. A team that previously had been rent by discord suddenly had united behind an exceptionally down-to-earth, no-frills leader. What you see is what you get with Lemaire, and the Devils liked what they saw, bought into his system, and finished with the best record in the team's history.

Nevertheless, there was something disturbing about the scene. A legacy of disappointments seemed to have dulled the fans' enthusiasm, while a legacy of perceived mistreatment by both the New Jersey Sports and Exposition Authority and the NHL left McMullen wondering whether he should keep his team at Byrne Arena.

These feelings crystallized after his Devils had defeated Buffalo four games to three in the opening round of the 1994 playoffs. It had been a stirring series, topped by a marathon overtime (sixth) game in Buffalo, won by the Sabres, followed by the Devils' clincher at home on a Friday night.

Catering to its U.S. network audience, the NHL scheduled the next round (Devils versus Bruins) to begin less than two days later on Sunday afternoon. This did not allow the Devils to promote the match and do the usual ticket-selling job. Furthermore, it turned out to be the first absolutely magnificent Sunday of spring, the kind of day that any right-thinking New Jerseyite would consider ideal for lawn mowing, barbecuing, golfing, biking, or hiking but certainly not for attending an indoor hockey game whose date was not even touted a day ahead—especially when said game was available on free local television.

The result was appalling to the horde of visiting journalists. Gaps of empty seats pockmarked every level of the arena, suggesting—though incorrectly—that Jerseyites simply didn't care about their Devils. It was difficult to refute, particularly after the home team was defeated and feeling lousy afterward.

Reporters began grilling Devils about the attendance and always-voluble Bernie Nicholls publicly criticized the lack of support while other Devils echoed his thoughts but with less vigor. A much larger crowd nearly filled the arena for game two, but again New Jersey lost and it appeared that the Devils could be eliminated in four straight.

I was worried about the team and its future in East Rutherford, especially because it would impinge on my broadcasting career. Thanks to Lemaire's coaching and Lamoriello's player selection, I had come to really enjoy this club, which was in marked contrast—competitively, at least—to my other assignment on Long Island, where the Isles were wiped out in four straight games by the Rangers.

While waiting for our plane to Boston at Newark Airport, I discussed the Devils' situation with my colleague Peter McNab. Although considerably younger than myself, McNab had an avuncular quality that was very comforting in such stressful times. Living in Maplewood, New Jersey, McNab had developed a keen feel for the state, its fans, and their interest in the Devils.

To my astonishment, he pointed out that the Devils Fan Club was the largest of any such organization in the 26-team league. He told me how the team's fan base was growing and how the first generation of Devils' rooters was attaining maturity. "Fans who normally would have turned to the Rangers," said McNab, "are now growing up pulling for New Jersey. This group is only going to get bigger."

Still, I couldn't shake the thought that a cloud hung over the franchise's future although as Lemaire's club rallied to win four straight over Boston, I began concentrating more on the playoffs than the box office. The strong finish produced robust crowds, which remained strong through the semifinal series with the Rangers, one of the most arresting in memory.

The loss to New York stuck in the craw for several reasons, not the least of which was officiating. The Curse of Koharski still was potent six years after the 1988 series. With the score tied in game six, Esa Tikkanen continually fouled Scott Neidermayer with impunity. When the young Devils' defenseman finally retaliated, he was penalized along with the Ranger.

New York was gifted with a four-on-four situation, which was precisely to the Rangers' liking and they proceeded to score and retain the lead through game's end. In the decisive game seven, two egregious officiating sins cost New Jersey the game and the series.

With seven seconds remaining in the third period, Valeri Zelepukin tied the score at 1–1 for New Jersey with a shot from the lip of the goal crease. Rangers' goalie Mike Richter then charged referee Bill McCreary, bodying the official into the end boards. Such blatant abuse of a zebra should have resulted in a game misconduct or, at the very least, two minutes for unsports-manlike conduct. McCreary called nothing.

The game was incorrectly decided in the second sudden-death period, when Stephane Matteau banked the rubber off goalie Martin Brodeur's pads after an around-the-net excursion. Had McCreary been sharp—or had he cared to check with the video replay official—he would have waved off the goal because Tikkanen clearly was standing in the crease.

Still, the Devils were toasted from coast-to-coast for their invigorating performance and even though New York won the Stanley Cup, McMullen's club had earned a large measure of respect.

It also was clear to those who cared—and especially to the Devils' owner—that there was a wide discrepancy between the Rangers' payroll and that of the Jerseyites. With an unlimited budget, New York plucked players other teams simply would not touch, and once again Mac was on target when he asserted that the Rangers had "the best team money could buy."

Noting that his team's payroll was somewhere in the vicinity of $13 million while the Rangers' was about twice that amount, McMullen added the perfect squelch: "It cost them $13 million for one goal!"

THE NHL IN THE LATE NINETIES
New Jersey Versus Nashville

W hen Gary Bettman became commissioner of the NHL, all bets were off in terms of the power balance among ownership. In conversations I had with Bettman, he kept insisting that he was having no problems with old-guard power-broker Bill Wirtz. "As a matter of fact," Bettman told me, "I haven't had a problem with any of them."

There was an easy explanation; as the new ice boss of bosses, Bettman would not allow rule by committee nor would he permit a group of owners—as in Norris-Wirtz in the Clarence Campbell days, or Wirtz-Green-Jacobs in more recent times—to take over any meaningful committees and thereby gain as much power as the president.

In fact, Bettman quietly allowed the board chairmanship to become powerless. Once a board chairman such as Bill Wirtz exercised as much power as president John Ziegler, but this no longer was the case under the league's first commissioner. Bettman enjoyed unprecedented power and also was open to new ideas and allies. For the first time since he bought the New Jersey Devils in 1982, John McMullen would become a major player in the ownership group and a force working with Bettman in the collective bargaining negotiations during the lockout of 1994–95.

"Gary Bettman is the best-prepared and most-balanced person that I've ever seen to date in my experiences in this league business," McMullen said. "Maybe there's somebody better out there, but I haven't seen one."

His fellow owners had grown to know McMullen as a fiercely opinionated leader and, as one friend put it, "an old-fashioned conservative." He added, "John is the smartest guy I've ever known with an education that rivals anybody's. But unless you know him, he can turn you off with the way he'll say something. He's never been a PR guy, that's for sure."

Bob Goodenow learned this from the start. When talks broke down in October 1994, McMullen withered the union boss with invective, suggesting that he knew nothing about negotiations. At another time during the talks, McMullen was widely quoted after he supposedly alluded to Edmonton, Hartford, Quebec, and Winnipeg, saying, "To hell with the small markets!"

While fellow owners such as Howard Baldwin took a more fraternal approach to their players, McMullen was typically blunt. "Some semblance of common sense has to enter into all this," he snapped when talks reached an impasse. "Every single player on my team has gotten more money from this team than I have. I haven't gotten a dime. I'm not complaining, but for every dollar we make in revenue we spend a dollar-and-a-half.

"I see where the union wants to retain status quo and allow things to go the way they're going. Well, they've hit a wall with all the franchises. All of them. Unless something is done, we may never be able to recover.

"An element of fairness is not being recognized. No one is trying to take anything away from anyone. What we're trying to do is stop the ever-increasing cost of operating the league. We have no intention of limiting the salary of any individual. What we're talking about is a fair distribution of the total gross revenues that go toward player salaries."

McMullen was justifiably furious. His anger with the Blues stemmed from one particular move made by the St. Louis team. An outrageously high $17.05 million four-year offer sheet was tendered to Devils' defenseman Scott Stevens, a player who had yet to win a Stanley Cup or a Norris Trophy. This was far in excess of what Norris Trophy–winner Raymond Bourque was receiving, and it was considered to be totally unrealistic and, more to the point, vindictive on the Blues' part.

McMullen had no choice but to sign Stevens and make the best of it. "From a financial standpoint it was a mistake," McMullen admitted. "But if you're walking down the street and a thug mugs you, what are you going to do? Let him take everything you've got? No, you defend yourself. We defended ourselves the best way we could in the interest of the franchise. But that is why the whole system needs correction. It was a fault of the system and the lack of fiscal responsibility of one team [the Blues]."

McMullen wasn't kidding. During several conversations with me he revealed his displeasure over the Blues' handling of the

Stevens' situation and at being pushed into a corner over the contract. He was absolutely right and would again be proven so in 1998 by a league decision in the Devils' favor over compensation due in the Stevens case.

I had no doubt that McMullen was assessing the lay of the sporting land with 20-20 foresight as well as hindsight. He understood the NHL's problem: the combination of soaring salaries and relatively small television incomes combined with public hostility toward outrageous ticket prices threatened many franchises.

Newark Star-Ledger columnist Sid Dorfman said it best: "The problem is mathematical; a lot of markets got too small only when salaries got too big."

McMullen's fan base in New Jersey was growing, but the club could not sustain the higher and higher salaries on income from tickets alone without decent TV revenue. "It may take a severe scaling down of salaries to correct all this," said Dorfman, "and it will come."

Which explains why McMullen urged Bettman to maintain a hard line during the lockout. As the dispute moved past Christmas, he made it clear to me that he was ready to scuttle the entire season if ownership couldn't get what he regarded as a satisfactory deal with Goodenow.

He wasn't kidding either. McMullen teamed up with Capitals' owner Abe Pollin, Edmonton's Peter Pocklington, and Quebec's Marcel Aubut to overrule Bettman on the night of January 10, 1995, rejecting—by a vote of 14–12—a deal Bettman had negotiated with the NHLPA. In effect, the ownership group forced the commissioner to revise his proposal. Had Goodenow rejected the new offer, the season could very well have been canceled. McMullen believed in his cause and, along with his colleagues, eventually won the day. Goodenow capitulated to the extent that he accepted the new deal, and Bettman, in the end, emerged as strong as he had been when he entered the fray.

Throughout the negotiations, I wondered—and worried—about the health of both the Islanders' and Devils' franchises. How would each hold up if the lockout extended through the entire season? Would McMullen, in disgust, simply decide to chuck it all and get out of hockey? They were legitimate questions and some were answered by the participants.

Steve Walsh, cochairman and chief executive officer of the Islanders, who had maintained a more optimistic air than most through the talks, told me that he was pressing for a deal. He believed that through prudent management his club could live with the deal on the table preceding the final round of negotiations. He wanted the abridged season to be salvaged.

McMullen was farther to the right but told me that the deal was the best the league could get at the time and he, too, believed that it was better to play a 48-game schedule than none at all. When the 15-week lockout finally ended, there was no angry fallout among the Islanders vis-à-vis Walsh, but there was on the other side of the Hudson River.

Before the shortened season began, I had heard whispers that some Devils were furious over their owner's hard-line stance. Furthermore, they didn't appreciate his 11th-hour maneuvering, when he, Pollin, and others demanded a deal that took away two more years of unrestricted free agency for players at age 31.

Devils' defenseman Ken Daneyko, a stand-up individual, had been extremely close to McMullen. He said he felt that the relationship would continue to be positive after the lockout. "Maybe I'm wrong and naive," said Daneyko, "but these guys in management, if they want to win a Stanley Cup, will take care of the guys they need."

McMullen did take care of his players. Slowly but surely, they shaped up and many received significant contract increases right up until playoff time in the spring of 1995. I watched the team lurch forward, stop, fall backward, and lurch forward again during late winter and early spring, wondering whether they would even have enough energy, motivation, and talent to reach a playoff berth.

Despite the disappointing season, attendance was surprisingly high. The Devils were averaging more than 16,000 per game—among the top half in the NHL—and the foundation of fans appeared to be growing. Anyone taking a superficial view of the club's future would have to be optimistic.

But I never got that feeling in my chats with McMullen. He sounded very unhappy about his situation in East Rutherford and would lament his ongoing battles with the New Jersey Sports Authority. One of the most grating episodes occurred during the lockout, when the authority formally suspended the Devils' lease on Byrne Arena.

This development, which occurred on December 22, 1994, was overshadowed by the labor dispute but did not go unnoticed by McMullen. It infuriated him and prompted the team's management to question its relationship with the authority. "This was quite a Christmas present," said a member of the club hierarchy. "It caused the team great concern."

McMullen promptly demanded an audit to find out "how much the Devils may or may not be owed by the authority." Even more infuriating to McMullen was the fact that the Devils were the only NHL club to have its lease suspended because of the lockout. Meanwhile, the team alleged 13 specific breaches of the team's lease by the authority.

I had no idea about these episodes when I chatted with McMullen as his club headed into the homestretch of the 1994–95 season. On one occasion, I was in Philadelphia for a Sports-Channel telecast from the Spectrum. I caught a ride home with *New York Post* hockey writer Larry Brooks, who once had been a vice president of the Devils. He knew as much about the club's inner workings as anyone, and we began the drive with a discussion about the loss to the Flyers.

That done, we switched to other topics, including the fiscal state of the league. Out of left field, Brooks dropped a bomb: "I wouldn't be surprised if McMullen pulls the club out of New Jersey in a couple of years," Brooks declared.

Because of Brooks's knowledge, I found the prediction disturbing, but I listened without comment and said nothing because I wanted this story to go away. After all, over the past six years, I had heard a number of rumors about the Devils' imminent departure—once for Hamilton, Ontario, another time for an American city—but they eventually evaporated and we went on with the business of telecasting and enjoying the team.

Brooks told me he was researching a piece about the move and I wondered about the impact once his story eventually made print.

I didn't have to wait as long as I had expected. Late in the season—once Daneyko returned to the lineup after a long injury—the Devils got their act together and earned themselves a playoff berth. Their opponents in the first Stanley Cup round were the Bruins, which meant that our SportsChannel broadcast would open on the road at Boston Garden.

This was exciting stuff, the playoffs. I could hear the positive tension in my producer Roland Dratch's voice when he phoned and said, "Stan, baby, we're gonna rock 'n' roll!" Sure, I'd been through playoff coverage as a journalist since 1955, but 40 years later the adrenalin still was flowing as briskly as it had when I broke into the business.

I couldn't wait to grab the shuttle for Beantown until the phone rang a few minutes later. It was another SportsChannel colleague, Dave Katz, who once had been my intern. "Did you hear about the story out of Nashville?" he asked.

"What story?"

"Down in Tennessee they're saying that the Devils are going to move to Nashville. It appeared in one of the business papers down there."

Nashville. How could an NHL team move to Nashville? The city was too small, couldn't even support an East Coast League club, and wouldn't have an arena for at least another two years. It didn't make sense and I tried to laugh it off, but Nashville stuck in my craw and wouldn't go away.

For reassurance, I phoned my pal, the late Harry Ornest, who was a longtime pal of McMullen. "I don't think he's moving," said Ornest.

That felt better. When others called, I pointed out the ridiculousness of Nashville until I had given myself a cerebral enema. Then it was off to Boston and the playoffs. The Devils were sharp and easily dispatched the Bruins in game one at The Garden.

Prior to game two, I reported to our SportsChannel TV truck adjacent to the arena. It was time for a staff meeting to lay out the night's show, but instead of production talk, the gang was discussing Nashville. An hour later, after I had walked out of the Garden, I overheard Mark Czerwinski of the *New Jersey Record* telling a colleague that his paper was running a major story on the Nashville situation.

I wanted Nashville to go away, but it was obvious that there was something to the rumors that McMullen and the Nashville-based Gaylord Entertainment outfit actually had been talking about the Devils leaving New Jersey for Tennessee. Like reproducing amoeba, the headlines multiplied. "McMullen Reaching out to Nashville Group. NHL in Dark over Nashville Move."

It reached a point where we at SportsChannel no longer could ignore the story. When we returned to New Jersey for game three on May 10, 1995, Dratch decided that Mike Emrick, Peter McNab, and myself should conduct a roundtable discussion of the Nashville issue.

Both Emrick and McNab were fervently pro–New Jersey and so was I. "The New Jersey Sports Authority was created to keep teams, not lose them," I said. "I certainly think if the authority is trying to woo the Yankees from the Bronx they should spend a lot of effort to keep the Devils at Meadowlands Arena.

"Nashville seems like a ridiculous place to put a hockey team right now because first of all it is a small city of 500,000. It has absolutely no hockey heritage. They have an East Coast League team there and they averaged only 2,200 for the playoffs. So we're not talking about a hockey hotbed."

Now I was angry. The more I thought about Nashville, the more absurd it sounded to me, especially because New Jersey Governor Christie Whitman, her husband, John, and their children were avid hockey fans. Whitman was a regular at home games—a rooter who was there for the opening face-off and remained until the final buzzer. Being at Byrne Arena far transcended politics for her.

I remembered how the McMullens had touted Whitman to me over dinner a few years earlier and I couldn't understand why she wouldn't be more supportive of her friend McMullen. My next move was to get the governor on camera with me during a playoff game. This should not be difficult, I figured, because Whitman had appeared with me several times over the years.

Sure enough, she came down to the studio between periods— flanked by bodyguards and press agents—and did a no-holds-barred interview. She allowed that the issue was emotional as well as fiscal; said she was bringing her husband in as a mediator; emphasized that the Devils had a lease to honor; and pressed home the point that she would do everything possible to keep the club in New Jersey.

We got terrific mileage out of the interview. The *New York Times* built an entire story around it including Whitman's statement to me, "There are a lot of things that would make the deal to move a lot less attractive than it appears on the surface." Bill Pennington's column in the *Record* featured our telecast, as did other dailies.

By now the Nashville story had become as newsworthy as the Devils' irrepressible march through the playoffs. They disposed of Boston in five games and moved on to Pittsburgh for the second round against a team filled with stars such as Jaromir Jagr, Kevin Stevens, Luc Robitaille, and Ron Francis.

Yet, the Devils were growing stronger both individually and collectively. They were buying into coach Jacques Lemaire's game plan, growing more confident by the game. Even though they lost the opening game at Civic Arena, the Devils looked good enough to rebound, which they did in game two.

Enthusiasm for the club was reaching record proportions in the New Jersey–New York metropolitan area, but this fervor was not matched in the NHL office. When I phoned commissioner Bettman, I was inwardly furious and put the question bluntly to him: "Are they leaving?"

"I don't know," he replied matter-of-factly. "That's up to John McMullen."

At this point, I decided that it was important to get Bettman before the camera. He said he would be in Pittsburgh for game two and agreed that he would sit down with me. As always, his word was good and he visited the studio between periods of the game.

Never before had I been so pumped for an interview. My blood was boiling over the possible Nashville move, but I also realized that I had to maintain a reportorial self-control. But if Bettman had expected an amiable and bland interrogation, he was sadly mistaken. Here's exactly how it happened. I opened on camera with the following introduction:

Stan Fischler: The Devils are averaging more than 16,000, they are developing a fan base very rapidly, they have excellent rivalries with the Rangers and the Flyers, and they have a terrific future based on their championship farm team. That's why a lot of Jersey fans are distressed, Commissioner, about the talk of a move to Nashville. And particularly because there is a feeling that the NHL does not care about their move to Nashville.

Gary Bettman: (sarcastically) We're doing the upbeat interview tonight, I see.

Fischler: I'm telling you, there are a lot of people out there who are upset.

Bettman: The fact is, no decision obviously has been made, and until one is, people may be getting prematurely upset based on what may turn out to be, or may not, speculation. The fact is, the Devils have some building problems, have some lease problems, have some disputes with the authority that runs the Meadowlands. And as anyone involved in a very serious enterprise has to do when you're in such a situation, they're obviously exploring their options.

Fischler: One of the points that's been made in print is that the NHL feels that three teams in the metropolitan area is too much. I happen to think not, obviously. I'd like to know what you think about that.

Bettman: I think that if we have to ultimately pass on whether or not a move is advisable, and there's a big *if* there, we're going to have to look at the criteria you use for franchise relocation, but one of the things we're obviously going to be influenced by, or at least have to take into account, is that we've got three franchises in one geographic market, and no other professional sports league has that. Actually, the last time there were three teams in New York, two of them left, meaning the Giants and the Dodgers. And that poses some problems. As much as I'd like us to be the number-one sport, we're still the number-four sport, which means we have the seventh, eighth, and ninth professional teams in New York, and since I think most hockey fans would tell you the

Rangers have the number-one position for hockey, so you're talking about the eighth or ninth team in the market. It's difficult for getting media attention, it's difficult for doing your television contracts, it's difficult for attracting fans to your buildings, so I think that presents some problems.

Fischler: There's also the feeling that the NHL is favoring the Rangers, that the NHL has not done anything to encourage, to help the Devils, and in this particular case, the Devils have nothing to be ashamed of; they make a profit. What I'm saying is, why isn't the NHL doing something positive, like perhaps, as Larry Brooks said in the *Post*, using your considerable influence on the New Jersey Sports and Exposition Authority?

Bettman: Well, first of all you don't know what it is I'm doing, and secondly, one of the problems when you have a team playing as well as this one does, and you take all the attention away from what's going on on the ice, and you do it on speculation on things that haven't transpired yet, I think you do a disservice to the game and to the players.

Fischler: But it is in the news and people want to know and there are NHL bylaws that cover the team, am I not right? One of them says you have to go to the people in that community and see whether they would like to buy it before the club is moved, am I not correct?

Bettman: That's what you do in the course of processing an application to move.

Fischler: Have you received one?

Bettman: No, not yet.

Fischler: Have you spoken with Dr. John McMullen, the owner of the Devils, and has he expressed any opinions to you?

Bettman: Well, actually I sat with him during the second period of this game.

Fischler: So what did he say about Nashville?

Bettman: Well, what he said is, "We've got some game going on here."

Fischler: There's a lot of talk about franchise euthanasia, Winnipeg being one, Quebec being another. Will the Nordiques be moving out of Quebec, and what's the story with Winnipeg?

Bettman: Actually, Winnipeg's a very good example. The Jets are staying. So the hysteria that has mounted, the team's going to be there next year. And Quebec, Marcel Aubut, the president of the Nordiques, is working very hard to see what options he has to stay in Quebec. They've got an old building, one that's inadequate by nineties standards, and there doesn't seem to be much inclination by anybody in the

Quebec market, smallest market in professional sports, lowest per capita income, highest tax rate, fewest number of corporate headquarters, to do anything to help this team be economically viable in Quebec. And if it's not viable, we have to deal with it.

Fischler: Man, I wish I had an hour.

Bettman: Thank goodness you don't.

As the commissioner left the studio, I thanked him for coming on the air and did likewise to his media aide, Arthur Pincus. "Oh, by the way," Bettman said, turning to Pincus, "since you arranged this, you're fired!" (Pincus left the NHL in 1999.)

He was joking, of course, and we all laughed, wondering just how amused Bettman really was or whether this was a convenient way of paving over some pernicious potholes. In any case, the interview inspired the *New York Post*'s Phil Mushnick to open a column about the tête-à-tête. "A Deal with the Devils" shouted the *Post* headline. "Bettman Adds Fuel to the Fire."

The interview infuriated Devils' fans because they interpreted some of Bettman's remarks as suggesting that their favorite team was disposable. Even Governor Whitman picked up on it when I cornered her for another interview a couple of days later in New Jersey.

"I don't think the NHL cares about keeping the Devils here because they don't like three teams here," she said. "I think some of the television networks would just as soon spread the teams around the country, so it's really us fighting for our Devils right now."

Apparently, the league office was feeling the heat and, sure enough, Pincus phoned the next day challenging me on my question to the governor. Meanwhile, SportsChannel printed a precise question-and-answer transcript of the Fischler-Bettman dialogue and distributed it to the media. By far the most pungent response came from the *New Jersey Record*, which led off its editorial page with an open letter to Bettman:

> Dear Mr. Bettman,
>
> We heard with chagrin your comments last week about the Devils, who are threatening to abandon the Meadowlands for the allegedly greener pastures of Nashville. Your remarks were as infuriating as they were off the mark.
>
> Perhaps you were merely providing cover for the Devils as they try to rewrite their lease for the third time in a decade and extract a better deal from New Jersey's

Sports Authority. But don't try to kid anyone. If the Devils move, the reason will be greed, not demographics. Yes, Nashville may be throwing money at the Devils, but they have a loyal following here.

In a recent TV interview, you suggested that the New York metropolitan area may be too small to support the Rangers, the Islanders, *and* the Devils. As proof, you said that major league baseball was the only other professional sport that put three teams in the New York area, and two of them—the Brooklyn Dodgers and New York Giants—left town.

That's a catchy sound byte, but it makes two faulty assumptions: that North Jersey is merely a chunk of the metropolitan area and that you can equate Major League Baseball in the fifties with pro hockey in the nineties. The truth is, northern New Jersey qualifies as a big-league metropolitan area all by itself.

Here's a quick quiz for you.

Of the following areas, which has the most households:

        A. Miami

        B. Pittsburgh

        C. Houston

        D. Minneapolis–St. Paul

        E. Northern New Jersey

Answer: E., northern New Jersey, with 1.7 million households. Houston is second with 1.55 million. Minneapolis–St. Paul is third with 1.4 million. Miami is fourth with 1.31 million. And Pittsburgh is fifth with 1.16 million.

(Incidentally, Nashville—the town that's reportedly throwing so much cash at Devils' owner John McMullen—has 746,000 households. In other words, Music City isn't even a dot on the map.)

Your analogy to Major League Baseball is also a bit strained. Major League Baseball in 1957 had 16 teams, all east of the Mississippi. To have three of those teams in New York City and none in enormous markets like Los Angeles and San Francisco made no sense. That's a far cry from the National Hockey League today, which has 26 teams in 23 North American cities, from Miami to Vancouver.

If you had bothered to check, Mr. Bettman, you'd see that the Devils are doing quite well here in the Garden State. The Devils drew almost 4,000 more fans a game than the Islanders did this season. Does that mean the Islanders should move instead?

The Devils may not fill every seat for most games, but even the Knicks didn't regularly sell every seat in Madison Square Garden until Pat Riley came to town. What's more, Devils' attendance has increased steadily in recent years, from 12,000 a game during the 1991–92 season, to more than 16,000 this year—in spite of your league's little hockey strike.

In fact, it would be in the NHL's best interests to keep the Devils where they are. The last time we checked, the Quebec Nordiques were carpetbagging their way to Denver. The Winnipeg Jets nearly jumped to Minneapolis. The Devils, meanwhile, have already moved twice in their 23-year history. First they were the Kansas City Scouts. Then they were the Colorado Rockies. If the Scouts/Rockies/Devils were to move again, to Nashville, perhaps you might have them call themselves the Ramblers and get Atlas Van Lines for a corporate sponsor.

For the sake of the league's stability, you should keep hockey clubs from picking up stakes whenever they smell a fresh greenback. Otherwise, the Devils and Nordiques might rightly be confused with Barnum & Bailey—just another road show coming to an arena near you, for a little while at least.

Finally, there's a certain irony in your apparent indifference to a relocation by the Devils. The league has done all it can to prevent its best players from becoming free agents and jumping from city to city, but apparently you look the other way when your team owners want to do the exact same thing.

Come on, Commissioner. Greener pastures aren't usually what they're cracked up to be—unless you're a cow. The Devils belong in the Meadowlands. It's time you said so and showed some leadership.

Because of such editorials, the league's hypersensitivity over the Devils-to-Nashville story was growing by the day. When I requested league vice president Brian Burke as a guest for a subsequent game, I was told by Pincus that he could come on the air provided no questions were asked about Nashville.

This didn't wear well with my producer, Roland Dratch, who suggested that I open the interview by stating that Burke would not address the Nashville issue. However, when Burke came to the studio and took his seat, I tipped him off about what we had

planned. He said he preferred we get the question out of the way
at the top and he would respond. Which he did.

It now was early June, the Devils had wiped out Pittsburgh
and moved into the third playoff round against Philadelphia.
Nashville wouldn't go away so I asked Bettman if he would do a
return engagement. This time, he politely refused—although he
would come later—but that wasn't going to get him off the hook.

Journalists who cared about the Devils and who knew that
the NHL had bylaws that prevented the sudden transfer of a team
took aim at the commissioner for his failure to be more obviously
proactive. My position was clear; if Nashville was such a terrific
spot for an NHL team, fine. Put an expansion team there, but
don't rob New Jersey of its maturing franchise. Larry Brooks put
it best in the *Post*:

> Here's what the league seems to miss. That having
> three teams in New York triples the chance of keeping
> the league important in May and June. Triples the
> chance of having the largest market represented in the
> Stanley Cup finals. Instead of discrediting the idea of
> three teams, the league should be exploiting it. It should
> be searching for ways to maximize its impact, rather
> than hoping to find a way to erase it.

Easily the most ironic aspect of the seriocomic tableau was the
Devils' relentless push forward. The more Nashville headlines, the
more Devils' interest snowballed. It had become impossible to buy
playoff tickets at Byrne Arena, and Devils' merchandise became
one of the hottest items among all the major sports teams.

"It has taken more than a decade," noted Brooks, "but there
is now, finally, a generation of young Devils' fans growing in the
Garden State. The next generation of ticket-buying, pay-per-view
purchasing, demographically correct hockey fans in New Jersey
is an overwhelmingly Devils' generation. If the Devils leave, they
have no team to cheer for. And more to the bean-counter's concern, no reason to buy expensive, licensed apparel. Take that to
the bank."

If nothing else, McMullen was banking playoff money. His
club opened the East Conference finals in Philadelphia winning
two straight games against Eric Lindros and the Legion of Doom,
but still Nashville wouldn't go away. Metropolitan area reporters
jetted south to gauge hockey interest there and found that it
ranged from nonexistent to tepid, while McMullen was stung by
a Dave Anderson *New York Times* column that challenged him to
keep his club in the Meadowlands.

Within days of Anderson's column, a spate of McMullen features suddenly blossomed in the local media. The embattled owner emphasized that his dispute was not with Devils' fans, but rather the New Jersey Sports and Exposition Authority, which, as he had told me so many times, had mistreated him.

"I can't design a propeller or a ship anymore," he said. "Time has passed me by. But I don't need anyone to protect me either. Apparently, a decision has been made that the way to settle this dispute we're having is to desecrate me and my reputation. It's not going to work. No decent person is going to submit to this kind of thing, harassment and slurs. I'm sorry we got into this argument, but it wasn't my fault.

"And as for me being greedy, it may be a valid argument that I have plenty of money so who cares if I'm making any off the Devils. . . . But then, shouldn't somebody at least say, 'Thank you'? I think this team has been a great asset to the state."

It certainly has and that's why I expected Bettman to pull all the right strings and keep the Devils in New Jersey. But I was employing a different set of NHL standards than the kind I had learned when I worked for the Rangers as an assistant publicist in 1954–55.

In those days if we had 13,000 fans in the 15,925-seat Garden, it was considered a successful evening. Now attendance was virtually meaningless. Both Winnipeg and Quebec played to more than 90 percent capacity, but that wasn't enough in the Bettman era. The accent was on new arenas, luxury boxes, merchandising, and bigger TV deals.

Nashville might be a disaster at the gate, but who cares? Having cultivated Disney, Bettman sought more corporate ownership. In Nashville, Gaylord Entertainment promised its own network, exclusivity as a major league city, and another spot in the Sun Belt that would please the Fox Network in its quest for more southern exposure.

Businesswise, it might make sense, and Bettman, in his U-turning of a phrase, certainly built an impressive case for Nashville. But it all smelled bad to me and even worse on Tuesday night, June 20, 1995. This was at Byrne Arena, game six of the East Conference finals, New Jersey leading three games to two.

Never had I seen or felt the oversized rink throb with such anticipation. When Jacques Lemaire's Devils overcame a 1–0 deficit on Stephane Richer's power-play goal, I thought the tremors might collapse the ironwork right into the Meadowlands swamp. The noise was even greater when Randy McKay staked the home team to a 3–1 lead in the second period, sending the home club to the dressing room with an oversize cushion.

As Philadelphia desperately attacked midway in the third, Claude Lemieux was catapulted into the clear, one-on-one with Ron Hextall. The Devil faked, lured the goalie to his knees, and then backhanded the puck into an opening at the right. All 19,040 fans knew that this was the clincher and they rocked the arena as never before. I peeked up at McMullen's box in the hopes of seeing his reaction to the mammoth orgasm of joy, but it was impossible to see anything but his shock of white hair.

With five minutes remaining I moved to our television slot between the benches. The Flyers scored a token power-play goal toward the end, but it meant nothing. Soon the fans were counting down the last seconds and finally the Jerseyites delivered their most ardent eruption. They were reacting the way I did as a 10-year-old when my favorite team, the Maple Leafs, won their Stanley Cup in 1942.

I went back to work, interviewing captain Scott Stevens in the aisle leading into the corridor.

Suddenly, Governor Whitman strode by followed by a big brown dog and McMullen; all headed into the dressing room. The dog was McMullen's pet, Hector, who had "watched" the game from the owner's box and now was going to "congratulate" the players. It was a bizarre scene, especially after Ms. Whitman entered the dressing room, catching a couple of seminude players completely by surprise.

"There was a rush for towels," said forward Bill Guerin, one of the more jubilant Devils.

As I went from player to player doing interviews for our postgame show, I couldn't stifle a feeling of exultation for the players, who had emerged from the Rangers' shadow to take center stage as they proceeded to the Stanley Cup finals.

When I interviewed the governor, I sensed that she felt genuinely thrilled by the event, but when I pressed her about a solution to the Nashville dilemma, she replied with the usual clichés. "We're still trying" was her theme.

I spotted McMullen on the other side of the room and he agreed to answer a few questions. After fielding the usual queries about the emotion of the moment, he addressed my pointed inquiry: "What does this victory mean in terms of the negotiations?"

McMullen picked it up on the short hop and shot back, "It means Lou [Lamoriello] is a helluva negotiator!"

Great line. The more his Devils won, the more leverage they had in dealing with the authority and Nashville. But where this tug-of-war would stop, nobody knew; so I phoned Harry Ornest the next morning for a clue.

"I don't know," he said, "but it sure would be tough to move."

My temptation was to believe that they couldn't move after going so far along the playoff trail with the hockey frenzy now at an all-time peak in New Jersey. But then I remembered how keenly McMullen felt about the authority, not to mention the negative media he was receiving.

"Have you ever seen a favorable article?" he asked almost plaintively. "But it doesn't bother me anymore. I'm conditioned to it from experience. I expect it."

What I never expected, however, was to cover the New Jersey Devils in a Stanley Cup final, but it was happening. On the eve of the opener, Gary Bettman attended the annual hockey dinner hosted by the Canadian Society of New York. He was pressed about the Devils' dilemma.

"I can't talk. I can't talk. I can't talk." That was his response to the interview.

Then, someone pointed out that the NBA was about to avoid a lockout by working out a deal with its players' association. He whispered to a reporter: "They [the NBA] have a union that wants to work with you. Their players have a good thing going and they know it. We can't convince our players of that."

So, it was on to Detroit and the finals. As I headed for La Guardia Airport, I wondered whether the Devils as a New Jersey entity would survive July. Even at this late date there was no way of knowing, so I did the best thing I could do under the circumstances; I flipped a silver nickel—heads they stay, tails they go.

It came out heads.

WILL THE DEVILS GET A NEW JERSEY?
The NHL Moves from the Ridiculous to the Bizarre

A s a hockey newsman and historian, I can assure you that nothing—absolutely nothing—is more fun than covering the Stanley Cup finals. But in 1995 it was different, much different. Juxtaposed against the joy of being with a serious championship contender was the abject—and growing—depression over the ubiquitous specter of Nashville, the home of Opryland and country-and-western music.

No matter how many games the Devils won; no matter how many spectacular clutch goals Claude Lemieux scored; no matter how brilliant the goaltending of 23-year-old Martin Brodeur; no matter how crunching and demoralizing the body-checks of Scott Stevens—New Jersey's fast-growing list of accomplishments was diluted by questions about an incomprehensible plan to move the Devils to Tennessee.

"We're trying to concentrate on the games," said Devils' defenseman Ken Daneyko, "but people keep asking us about Nashville."

Although the Devils' general staff pleaded with the media to concentrate on its excellent team, it was impossible not to discuss the possible move simply because it was news—big news. And it kept getting bigger as the Devils enplaned for Detroit and the opening of the 1995 Stanley Cup finals at Joe Louis Arena.

I flew to Detroit on the day before the first game. The series coverage provided by the Detroit newspapers was overwhelming. Both the *Detroit News* and *Detroit Free Press* sports sections ran story after story about the finals in obvious anticipation of the Red Wings' first Stanley Cup victory since 1955.

For me there was a touch of irony in all this. In 1954–55 when the Wings topped the NHL, I worked my first NHL hockey job as assistant publicist for the New York Rangers. Once our club had been eliminated from playoff contention, I was free to cover the playoffs. So I was in Montreal for the Stanley Cup finals between Detroit and the Canadiens. Ken McKenzie, who had been the NHL publicity director, employed me as a *Hockey News* aide in Montreal and allowed me to sleep in the Mount Royal Hotel press suite during the playoff run. This marvelous series ran seven games. It concluded at Detroit's Olympia Stadium. Because I wasn't given the opportunity to go to Detroit, I watched the final game on TV as center Alex Delvecchio led the Red Wings to the title. Now, 40 years later, I was in Detroit for the title games.

Journalists throughout the world had gathered at Joe Louis Arena. After the teams held their first practices, the NHL had scheduled interviews with the players. This was the most relaxed time anyone would enjoy during the finals.

For all the criticism the NHL received over the years, it finally learned something about public relations under Gary Bettman. It was clearly evident that Friday afternoon. Detroit Red Wings' coach Scotty Bowman and his stars, Paul Coffey, Steve Yzerman, and Sergei Federov, were on the dais answering questions face-to-face from the media. This could not have happened under the regime of John Ziegler, who inexplicably feared open discussion.

It was Bowman's métier. If nothing else, Bowman can talk, ramble, digress, and dissect the game. In that setting he is at his affable best. Plus, his team had just reached the finals and had not lost a game to New Jersey. Bowman was as loose as a hockey boss could be on the eve of the series.

The primary subject at hand was what the media had conveniently and simplemindedly labeled "the neutral zone trap." Originally, Roger Neilson was credited with—some would say accused of—devising this forechecking system, which supposedly had created a boring type of hockey. Neilson, who was coach of the Florida Panthers, used the trap as a means of blocking the opposition's scoring potential against his brand-new expansion team.

Now, late in the 1994–95 season, Jacques Lemaire was being targeted as a master-trapper. Interestingly, the accusers among the media had oversimplified the Lemaire strategy and also unfairly criticized it as some sort of hindrance to the game's progress. Actually, *trap* told very little about the intricacies of the New Jersey Devils' strategy nor its successful implementation. But although many beat writers can be shallow when it comes to hockey strategy—just blanketing a scientific defense-offense blueprint with a single word—*trap* made their work that much easier, although far from accurate.

Bowman would not be suckered into any easy rap at the trap. The ultimate strategist, Bowman acknowledged that his former pupil, Lemaire, had devised a very effective checking style that featured a quick counterattack, and rather than being boring—as many erroneously claimed—it could be an exciting aspect of a game.

"Anaheim and Dallas have used it [the trap]," said Bowman. "We did it. There's no sense forechecking so deep because the goalies are so active away from the net, you can't go in [deep in the enemy zone behind the net] now and forecheck foolishly. Now [with the trap], there's selective forechecking. And, remember, the puck is still the fastest player on the ice."

The three Detroit stars and Bowman were patient and gracious, as were the other Red Wings who were sprinkled around various tables in the arena restaurant. I recalled Bowman as a rookie coach with St. Louis just after the first major NHL expansion in 1967. A particular vignette came to mind. Bowman's Blues were visiting New York and Scotty was invited to a hockey writers' luncheon. When it was over, he sat on a table, his legs dangling over the side, gabbing with a few writers until we exhausted our questions.

It was the same 28 years later. Bowman couldn't find enough media with whom to talk. He drifted over to a television interviewer, spent 10 minutes there, then found himself surrounded by Bob McKenzie, Roy Cummings of the *Tampa Tribune*, and me. Most of the talk was analytical and not very printable. But it was certainly appetizing fodder for the hockey minded.

"The trap," Bowman concluded, "is like any other system. It's not unbeatable if you have the players."

After the Red Wings departed, New Jersey's contingent arrived. Jacques Lemaire, whose relationship as a player for Bowman had ranged from frigid to cool, took the podium. Having worked with him all season, I had developed a deep respect for him both as a hockey thinker and as a person. He disdained the limelight but nevertheless felt at ease talking hockey with me. Now he was center stage as never before and facing a large curious assemblage.

"I never thought I'd coach. You see you can never enjoy winning when you're coaching because you're always worried about what's next," said Lemaire, his tanned, bald pate glistening under the television lights. "But here I am. I must tell you that there have been times when I would just sit in the corner, scratching my head, wondering why I'm doing this."

Lemaire's cerebral, yet down-to-earth approach captivated the media as it did his players. "Jacques is successful," said his captain, Scott Stevens, "because whenever he talks, he gets your immediate attention. He's honest. He's open with everyone. He has the believability and credibility to get every player to commit to his system."

His players were obviously pleased to get the attention. They understood that the reporters had an angle to pursue and it came down to an attack directed against the New Jersey–Lemaire style. Although the Devils had become bored with the repetitive theme, they nonetheless parried the questions with uncommon grace.

"When we were in Pittsburgh, people criticized the way we played," said Stephane Richer, one of the NHL's true virtuosos. "But when we finished them off, the same people were saying that's the way Pittsburgh should play. It was the same story in Philadelphia. People said that the way we play isn't good or fancy enough. I can tell you that there are a lot of teams who would like to be in the same situation as we are today."

As a group, the media leaned heavily toward the Red Wings to win the series. In the *Toronto Sun*, for example, four out of five writers picked Detroit. (The exception was Dave Fuller, who selected New Jersey in six games.) The Devils, who opened every one of the four playoff series on the road, laughed the underdog role off. In fact, they enjoyed it.

"Everybody is saying we don't have a chance," said Claude Lemieux, "that we don't have enough offensive players to compete with them. No one believed we could beat Pittsburgh either. Or Philly, or Boston. It doesn't matter to us though. It's time we were accorded some respect for the team we have."

Respect became the buzzword, along with *disrespect*. Respect for New Jersey's hockey team; disrespect for Devils' fans, who found themselves unwanted pawns in the battle for the hockey team between a northern hockey hotbed versus a nondescript southern state.

One New Jersey fan, Herman Zuker, a concert pianist from Manhattan, could not believe what was happening to his favorite team and his favorite game. "This NHL season is transcending The Game itself," Zuker wrote me during the playoffs. "It's overshadowed by off-ice problems—from the vacuum of the lockout to the dizzying drama of the Devils—and could be a script right out of Hollywood. I know there was a movie; what was it? A team has to win a championship to gain respect and not be relocated. But this defies credulity."

Yet that seemed to be precisely the scenario. The more the Devils won and the closer they moved toward the Stanley Cup, the more logical it seemed that the franchise would have to remain in New Jersey. Certainly it would not be moved to Nashville, of all places. Thus, understandably, the Devils' fans became schizophrenic. One part of their personality became obsessed with the off-ice politicking and deal-making while the other part focused on the very important business of winning hockey games. Now the focus shifted to Michigan—where the Jerseyites were regarded as big underdogs—and to win the 1995 NHL championship.

On the eve of the series opener, I was excited by the hockey fever gripping Detroit. At the Hotel Pontchartrain, the media headquarters, an endless line of fans snaked around the sidewalk waiting for a glimpse of the Stanley Cup. It was on display in the lobby 24 hours a day. Red Wings' fans not only expected, but assumed, that Detroit would win the Cup in as few as four games.

This feeling was confidently evident in the bulging 20,000-seat arena during the pregame ceremonies. When the visiting team was introduced, each Devils' player stepped on the ice as his name was broadcast over the loudspeaker. With each name, the sellout crowd bellowed, "Who cares? Who cares?" Disrespect for the East champions carried from the stands to the press box high above the ice, where the majority of the media favored the home club.

The *Toronto Sun*'s Al Strachan had a column headlined, "Wings Have Key to Devils' Trap." Strachan contended that the trap was beatable, that the Red Wings had ample time to prepare for it, and that the "Wings were smart enough to negate the Devils' best defensive weapon."

Strachan and company were correct—for one period. Employing the old Montreal Canadiens' Fire Wagon style of hockey from the fifties, the Red Wings repeatedly assaulted the Devils' defenses but were unable to penetrate goalie Martin Brodeur. The clubs remained scoreless until the second period. Then Stephane Richer beat Detroit goaltender Mike Vernon on a power-play shot from the left side. It was a very telling play because Richer's drive seemed harmless, yet the puck trickled through Vernon's legs for a cheap goal.

Detroit counterattacked with a power-play goal by Dino Ciccarelli, and the second period ended with the teams knotted at one. Despite the tie score, the Red Wings seemed in complete command. New York sportscaster Dave Sims was standing with me during the intermission. He wondered what I thought.

"The Devils had better have steel fingernails," I said, "because they look like they're hanging from the edge of a tall building."

Remarkably, once the third period began, the ice tilted New Jersey's way. Tom Chorske dumped the puck into the Red Wing zone and then headed to the bench on a line change. Meanwhile, John MacLean pursued the rubber against two Detroit players. Somehow, MacLean got the puck and backhanded a shot at Vernon, who made the save. However, Vernon allowed the rebound to come directly out to Claude Lemieux, who promptly fired it past the goalkeeper.

With 10 minutes left in the game, I left my cat-bird perch high above the ice and headed to our studio in the bowels of Joe Louis Arena to prepare for the postgame show. My assignment was to cover the Devils' dressing room while my colleague Matt Loughlin handled the Red Wings. As it happened, our makeshift studio was separated from the working press area by a portable curtain. Consequently, it was easy to watch the print media that gathered there.

The view was extremely meaningful from a comparative perspective. Dozens of writers were gathered in the room with their eyes riveted to the television screen situated in the middle. The people who you would have expected to report the game live— that is, by viewing it from the press box—were actually watching it on TV, as if they were in their home living rooms. Many had begun typing their stories as the third period unfolded on the TV screen.

What this demonstrated to me beyond a shadow of a doubt was the obsolescence of the print media in terms of play-by-play reportage. Technically speaking, any one of these print reporters could just as easily have seen the game at a bar across the street from the arena, dashed to the dressing rooms for postgame quotes, and then written his or her story about the Devils' surprise victory.

The game itself was filled with the tension that comes of two diverse but relatively equal teams. Working the Devils' locker room in the postgame segment of our SportsChannel show, I was surprised at the calm displayed by the winners. Tommy Albelin, the Swedish defenseman, was spread out on the floor while a trainer stretched his legs into a pretzel mold. Long-haired Mike Peluso, one of the most emotional of the Devils, refused to betray any feelings. The goalie, 23-year-old Martin Brodeur, smiled and smiled as he answered questions.

The Devils captivated the media with their total lack of airs. When their stars—usually Brodeur, Lemieux, Broten, Stevens, Richer—appeared at the NHL postgame press conferences, their friendliness was in stark contrast to the well-known obnoxiousness of their Major League Baseball counterparts.

"The image of three or four Devils reminded me of a scene from *The Right Stuff* about the Mercury astronauts," said one observer. "These players were extremely focused on the job at hand. Their mission."

Lemaire put it best in describing his club. "We played very well in our own end. We were trying to contain the puck carrier to keep him to the outside and to also keep an eye on everyone who is moving." Others would have called it effective use of the trap. Whatever, it worked.

The same could not be said for the Devils' attempt to quash the ever-growing Nashville exodus story. Time and again, I tried to get a handle on it. Just when it seemed that I "knew" the answer, another element would intrude to force me to reconsider.

Prior to the second game at Joe Louis Arena, this much was certain: NHL owners would be meeting on June 19, 1995, at the league's New York headquarters. At this time, the governors would be in a position to insist that the Devils' ownership make their position clear.

But the league's new balance of power had so markedly shifted to the commissioner's office and away from the governors that it now had become a matter between Gary Bettman and John McMullen. "A decision like this is left to the guidance of the league office," Pittsburgh chairman Howard Baldwin told me. "It's not like the old days, when John Ziegler and the advisory committee ran the league. Owners no longer immerse themselves in league problems the way many used to do it."

Yet, the league had a clear-cut list of bylaws and other stringencies designed to curb carpetbagging. They were based logically on more than 75 years of existence.

Section 36.5 of the bylaws listed no less than 24 "considerations" requiring detailed review before a franchise can be transferred. For example, item D asks, "Whether the present owner of the club has made a good faith effort to find prospective purchasers who are prepared to continue operating the club in its present location," albeit there is no basis or formula to determine the price.

Or item N: "The extent to which consent to the proposed transfer is likely to damage the image of the League as a major sports league."

Or item O: "The extent to which the proposed transfer would adversely affect traditional rivalries that have been established between the club in its present location and other Member clubs."

Or item T: "The extent to which the proposed transfer, if approved, would affect any contract or agreement in effect between the club and any public or private party."

If the NHL's bylaws had any teeth, there was every reason to believe that a move from New Jersey to Nashville could be and would be opposed by the board of governors.

In terms of item D, Devils' owner John McMullen made it clear that he had no intentions of selling the team. Thus, even if a prospective buyer appeared—two did, but only one was considered serious—he would be rebuffed.

Item N was even more restrictive, if one presumes the NHL was serious about enforcing its bylaws. The league's image—often damaged and buffeted during the John Ziegler regime—would now be severely injured again as would Gary Bettman's role if a potential Stanley Cup winner was allowed to carpetbag out of town before the championship banner even was unfurled the following autumn. The league couldn't conceivably look more foolish if it allowed such a public relations obscenity to occur.

Item O was no less significant. Since 1988, when New Jersey enjoyed its first playoff run, the Devils had developed intense rivalries with the Islanders (1988 playoff), Rangers (1994 playoff), Flyers (1995 playoff), and Bruins (1988, 1994, and 1995 playoffs). Four excellent rivalries would be eliminated. Here, again, a bylaw demanded attention.

But it was item T that packed the most explosive ramifications. After all, the Devils not only had a lease with the New Jersey Sports and Exposition Authority to remain in the Garden State, but it also had a contract with SportsChannel, among others. The Devils, of course, publicly claimed that the authority had breached the agreement in several ways. Now the showdown was fast approaching, with Gary Bettman—unlike the passive and fearful Ziegler of yore—playing a more pivotal, behind-the-scenes role than ever.

The first important question was what would the NHL commissioner do if the Devils attempted to leave the Meadowlands before a court ruled on their breach-of-contract claim or before the lengthy appeal processes were concluded?

As Larry Brooks of the *New York Post* asked, "How can the NHL, which penalized Mike Keenan a year ago for skipping out on a contract, take a position in an ongoing legal process which supports contract-breaking?"

Meanwhile, Bettman told me that he was awaiting the appropriate moment to intervene and that this moment had not yet arrived. But with each game the Devils won, the Stanley Cup moved closer to the Meadowlands. And with each victory came an added negotiating point for McMullen to use.

Brooks, who spoke for the Devils' fans better than any journalist on the beat, summed up the prevailing opinion from Trenton to Teaneck thus:

> Still, though, it is time for Bettman to tell McMullen that the league will not support a franchise relocation if it takes breaking a lease to get the deed done. It is time for Bettman to tell McMullen that contracts apply to owners as well as to coaches and players.
>
> Time for Bettman to inform McMullen that if he attempts to break a lease, he'll face a trap far more distasteful than the one his championship team has already perfected.

But Bettman strategically continued to bide his time as McMullen's bargaining position grew stronger with each game of the finals. His warriors beat Detroit in game two, 4–2, at Joe Louis Arena. The next day NHL ownership convened at a midtown Manhattan hotel. McMullen didn't show up at the conference.

Instead, his president, Lou Lamoriello, attended and merely read an ambiguous statement indicating only that a status quo existed regarding a New Jersey move to Nashville.

"The governors were advised that no decision has been made. The issue wasn't going to be fully addressed, one way or the other, until the Stanley Cup finals are over," said Bettman. "I haven't even given them a date and I don't have one in mind. I'd rather the attention be focused on the games that remain to be played. You see, I understand the Devils' desire to not address this right now.

"Obviously if the Devils came to the league on September 1st and said they'd like to move next season, that isn't going to work. I would expect that very shortly after the finals are concluded, this is going to have to be brought to a head. I'll inject myself when I think it will do some good in terms of bringing about a resolution one way or the other. You have to pick your spots carefully in terms of how you deal with these situations in an effective manner."

I had been reporting this story for SportsChannel since the specter of Nashville appeared over Byrne Arena, so it was imperative that I keep my lines open to each side. My prime focus was on McMullen. Once during a playoff game between the Devils and Flyers at the Spectrum, I tracked him down in a private box. Seeking a scoop, I impolitely requested an interview then and there while his Devils and Flyers were fighting on the ice.

Considering that I had barged into the luxury suite unannounced, McMullen was affable and reasonable. But he insisted that he wouldn't do any television interviews until the Devils' playoffs were over.

Thereafter, we did speak regularly on the telephone. It was during these conversations that I began to fully appreciate the depth of his feelings toward the authority members. He also felt slighted by the media because he didn't think the Devils had gotten their just due for the club's outstanding accomplishments over the past several years. In my liberal-minded family we don't make a point of sympathizing with millionaires, but in this case McMullen was certainly making valid points. He had a right to make a profit; he had to keep up with rival teams such as the Bruins, Flyers, Blues, and Blackhawks, who either had brand-new buildings or soon would get them. As a result he couldn't make do if Byrne Arena was not properly maintained and luxuriously refurbished. Some of these points he had reiterated to me over the years—other comments were new.

I had somehow assumed that the popular election of his friend, Christie Whitman, as New Jersey governor would assure a better deal for him and the Devils at the Meadowlands. But the more McMullen and I talked, the more I realized that, for any number of reasons—some obviously political—Whitman no longer could be counted on as a major supporter.

One night I collared Whitman for an interview between periods at Byrne. I bluntly advised her that she would create public and political disdain if she was governor and New Jersey's favorite hockey team pulled up stakes for Tennessee.

"Actually," she bemoaned, "I'm stuck in a lose-lose situation. If they leave, I lose. But if they stay, my opponents, some of those Democrats, will accuse me of giving away too much in order to keep the team here."

Over the period of a month, from late May to late June, I conducted approximately a half-dozen personal interviews with Whitman. With each discussion, she seemed more frustrated by her pal, McMullen. "We've given him a proposal [more luxury boxes, etc.]," she said at the outset of the finals, "but we're still waiting for a counterproposal from him. We can't do anything more until we hear from John McMullen."

Several friends of mine, who were devoted Devils' fans, were equally frustrated. They knew they were backing a potential champion. They wanted to buy season tickets for 1995–96, but the Devils refused to put them on sale. Normally, next-season tickets were publicized by SportsChannel on the playoff telecasts.

This time they were conspicuous by their total absence from the broadcasts.

"When you have a winning team the way they do, the best time to sell your season packages is while you're doing so well in the playoffs," said an NHL marketing executive. "That they're not sends some form of message to the fans."

There were reasons for withholding ticket sales: (1) Why sell tickets when a Nashville move is potentially imminent? (2) By not selling tickets for next season, the club reinforces its message to the New Jersey Sports and Exposition Authority that it means business about moving. Ostensibly, this is designed to give the hockey club an even better bargaining position with its landlord.

That leveraged position was enhanced at the June 19 owners' meeting in New York City. The board of governors quickly approved the relocation of the Quebec Nordiques to Denver.

Supposedly, a Canadian group had wanted to buy the Nordiques and keep them in Quebec. That group asked the board to delay approval of the move to Denver for 30 days, citing a provision of the NHL's constitution that requires consideration of any good-faith local offer to buy a team seeking to relocate. The board denied the request. Bettman logically claimed the unspecified offer came at "the eleventh-and-a-half hour" from "some unidentified group." In light of the months-long machinations of Quebec's managing partner, Marcel Aubut, nothing would surprise anyone about anything emanating from Quebec City, with or without Aubut. "Remember the Lindros auction?" one governor remarked.

Furthermore, Bettman asserted that there were some two dozen criteria that now must be weighed under the good-faith offer bylaw. What Bettman said was extremely important in terms of bylaw execution vis-à-vis the Devils:

"You look at the whole package and you make a businesslike decision on how you think these specific criteria have or haven't been met. But it's ultimately a decision, frankly, for the board of governors. It is the board that is charged with determining how decisions are made on franchise-ownership changes, and/or franchise relocations."

What if the Devils win the Stanley Cup and then move to Nashville? For the first time Bettman reacted with what appeared to be movement away from a Tennessee possibility and thus a bit closer to a New Jersey solution.

"Of course it presents a problem," he allowed. "Even on something like merchandise for the Stanley Cup champion. My guess is it's more difficult to get retailers to buy Devils' merchandise if there's a concern the team may move and thus change its name and everything else.

"But we are where we are. We're in a difficult position created by many factors. The best thing we can do now, from the game's standpoint, is to put this matter to the side. Let's get through the finals. Then deal with it."

Now the finals were fast becoming a bigger story than even winning and losing. It seemed under Maestro Jacques Lemaire the Devils had thoroughly confounded the Red Wings and all the analysts. At the outset, for example, the *Toronto Sun's* Al Strachan boldly predicted, "Scott Bowman certainly knows what [Lemaire's] trap is. More importantly, he knows how to counter it."

Although Strachan and others were wrong, Bowman was outmaneuvered. The two-game deficit confronting the Detroit commander as he headed to New Jersey for game three under-lined the point. Much of the media refused to see what their New York counterpart, Brooks, clearly understood—the Red Wings had become Dead Wings, destined for a sweep. In fact, Detroit was counted out before game three was half over. The Devils almost toyed with them, delivering four goals in the first 29 minutes, forcing goalie Mike Vernon to the bench. The final score, 5–2, was far too kind to the disorganized visitors, who didn't even bother to hold a workout the next day or the morning of game four.

I was charged with doing morning interviews for our evening pregame show that [Saturday] night. I found the Red Wings at a nearby Meadowlands hotel where the NHL had arranged for Detroit stars and Bowman to meet the press. Under the circumstances, Bowman, Yzerman, and Coffey were remarkably cordial. My only interview problem was with Slava Fetisov, an old friend from New Jersey, who was surrounded by Russian-language interviewers.

Normally, day-of-game interviews are relatively brief, allow-ing each of the reporters an opportunity to get his sound byte. Newspeople respect a colleague's needs for the most part. Rarely will anyone dominate above and beyond the call of duty. But this was different. The Russians went on interminably without any concern about others. So finally an NHL honcho intervened and I was able to pop a question at Fetisov.

Instead of giving me a normal reply in English, he answered in Russian—with a healthy touch of sarcasm. When he finally said a few words in English, they were banal to the point of insult-ing. I thanked him and moved on to Coffey, who was typically eloquent and patient—nor did he speak any Russian.

Our crew left the Red Wings at their hotel and drove to a nearby restaurant for our pregame meal. Here we were just hours before game four and what could be a previously unlikely series sweep. The prime question being asked was not whether Bowman would start Mike Vernon or Chris Osgood in goal, but whether the Devils would move to Nashville a few days after they won the Stanley Cup.

In a matter of but two weeks the Devils had become *the* compelling story in the ravenous New York media market. This is where the Yankees fight the Mets for space; the Mets battle the Knicks, Rangers, Nets, Giants, Jets, and so on. New Jersey rooters simply couldn't maintain their focus on the Stanley Cup. At least not as long as they knew that Gaylord Entertainment had offered their favorite club a $20 million relocation bonus, a generous share of all arena revenue, and other financial sweeteners.

"The relocation situation made this so much more urgent, complex, dramatic, and poignant," said pianist-fan Herman Zuker. "No player was terminally ill. There was no 'Win one for the Gipper.' But when a franchise is so wounded and yet its players are able to pull this off [with a great coach], it is a heroic story—full of daily drama."

The denouement would come not in the evening, but early in the afternoon. When I arrived back at Byrne, the parking lots were already alive with thousands of people. Tailgaters had set up their barbecues; teenagers were wheeling around on in-line roller skates, whacking hockey balls with their sticks; and miniature Stanley Cups were being fabricated out of pieces of tinfoil by some creative fans.

At our pregame TV production meeting, I slyly mentioned that Rangers' fans had similarly been carried away with such emotionalism after New York had taken a three-games-to-one lead against Vancouver a year earlier. The Rangers then proceeded to lose the next two games. Nevertheless, we prepared with confidence for the possibility of victory and a gala postgame dressing-room show. Two hours before game time I went out to the parking area with a cameraman to do some fan interviews.

Bedlam had nothing on New Jersey at this moment. I could have used a phalanx of New Jersey State Troopers just to guide me through the overflowing, joyfully expectant throng. We did manage to reach a van whose roof was adorned with a mammoth replica of the Statue of Liberty and a Stanley Cup. I actually couldn't hear myself speak as the fans repeatedly chanted, "Let's go Devils! Let's go Devils!"

As I made my way back to the arena, I wondered whether this tremendous emotional surge and pride in the home club would have any effect on the hardbitten negotiations, which had screeched to a temporary halt. I realized, nevertheless, that it was the height of naïveté to even consider for a moment that the business side of The Game would ever take a full backseat to the emotional part.

But once the players skated out on the ice for the beginning of game four, the raw pulsating emotion carried the evening. The roar from 19,040 mouths was the loudest, most intense I had ever heard at Byrne. It was accompanied by an assortment of placards reminiscent of the Mets' 1969 World Series triumph at Shea. One cleverly read, "Nashville already has enough people without teeth." Another simply proclaimed, "This is hell."

Those of us who had spent time with the Red Wings that morning wondered what effect Bowman's verbal spanking (in public) would have on his charges. Hockey's winningest coach had indicted his players after the game three loss. He described the game—in pretty incisive adjectives—as "embarrassing," "humiliating," and "unacceptable."

Based on the first 15 minutes of the opening period, the rebuke had a palliative effect on Detroit. The Red Wings moved ahead, 2–1, and were more composed than the home club. But late in the period, New Jersey defenseman Shawn Chambers took a pass at the left point, glided into better position, and then drilled an obscured shot into the upper right corner of the net. The Devils never trailed again. Neal Broten diligently worked the crease in front of goalie Mike Vernon, eventually lifting his own rebound over the goalie's pads for the go-ahead goal.

The goal was scored at 7:56 of the second period. Time was running out on the Detroit Red Wings. What 19,040 fans were still wondering was whether time was also running out on Byrne Arena as the home of their beloved Devils.

CHAMPAGNE VERSUS THE COURTROOM
Climax of the Nashville–
New Jersey NHL War

Between the second and third periods of game four of the 1995 Stanley Cup finals, New Jersey Devils' coach Jacques Lemaire was confronted with one of his most difficult assignments. His club owned a three-game cushion, was nursing a one-goal lead and, after having been outshot five minutes into the second period, 13–8, had skated off the ice with a 16–15 lead in shots on goal.

"I didn't want them to get overconfident," said Lemaire. "I wanted them to keep their focus."

His Devils could have been forgiven for allowing their attention to falter. Game after game, they had taken the favored Red Wings' best shots, counterpunched, and then destroyed Detroit in every aspect of the game. They outshot the Red Wings, outhit them, outscored them, and, seemingly, outcoached the Motor City skaters.

"Ten minutes into the first game I knew we were going to win this series," said Devils' center Bobby Carpenter. "We hadn't played them. We saw they had the best record. We heard how good they were. We didn't know what to expect. But in those first 10 minutes we saw we could play with them and outcheck them. I knew then we were going to win."

But Lemaire knew that this fourth game wasn't over. A one-goal lead against a desperate team like Detroit is but as firm as a gossamer string. He encouraged his troops to maintain their diligence, and as they trooped out of the dressing-room door and through the vomitory to the ice, they were greeted with a roar that might have been heard in Cape May on the distant Jersey shore.

Observing the coach's dictum, the Devils became atrocious hosts, refusing to allow the visitors to handle the puck. The final shots-on-goal totals for the third period were 10–1 for the Devils. If there ever was a barometer of one-sided play, that was it. Yet, for more than seven-and-a-half minutes of the third period, Lemaire remained uneasy behind his bench. The score remained 3–2 in the Devils' favor. The Red Wings still had the great forward Sergei Fedorov, who had tied the game in the first period, taking his regular turn.

As the overhead clock ticked toward the eight-minute mark, the youthful line of Bill Guerin, Brian Rolston, and Sergei Brylin controlled the puck in the Detroit end. Back in November, a still-green Brylin skated for the Albany River Rats of the American League and appeared too inexperienced for NHL play. "What he needed," said Rats' coach Robbie Ftorek, "was lots and lots of ice time. That's what I gave him. We knew he was a comer."

Rolston had also been with the Rats, but because of a contractual technicality involving the NHL and the NHL Players' Association, he was forbidden to play in the AHL during the lockout. Instead, he practiced with Albany and worked as a radio analyst for the River Rats games. "I worked as hard as I could in practices in case the lockout was settled and then I'd get a chance to play," said Rolston. "What I didn't want to happen was getting depressed about the whole thing. I stayed as positive as I could."

Guerin, who had been somewhat of a disappointment during the regular season, already had fashioned Broten's go-ahead goal. Now he and Rolston combined to pierce the Detroit defense. Then the puck skimmed to Brylin, who had yet to score a playoff goal. The miniscule Russian pivoted from about 20 feet in front of Detroit goalie Mike Vernon and cleanly rifled the puck into the corner of the net for the third Devils goal.

A majority of those in the house fully understood that a two-goal lead with 12 minutes remaining simply would not be overcome by Detroit. But if the game had to be irrevocably stamped, it was done so by the ubiquitous Chambers. Taking a perfect feed from Guerin, which originally came from Brylin, the smiling veteran defenseman, who dresses faster in the postgame than anyone in the NHL, uncorked a missile from virtually the same spot he had shot late in the first period. Now it was 5–2. The game and series, for all intents and purposes, was over.

Already hoarse, Elaine Groh of Emerson, New Jersey, continued to cheer. A designer by trade, Groh epitomized the Devils' fan who felt emotionally torn as her team was about to annex the long-sought championship. "Being a Devils' fan," she would say later, "was like a roller-coaster ride: plenty of ups, mainly downs.

But definitely a lot of laughter and many tears. It was hard to keep all of my emotions in check those last few weeks through what should have been one of the best times for long-suffering Devils' fans. We haven't had respect all this year, but the media treatment we received during the playoffs was the most despicable."

But Groh, like her seatmates in the corner of Byrne Arena—and, for that matter, everyone—put aside personal feelings of anger at the New Jersey Sports and Exposition Authority, Governor Whitman, and even Dino Ciccarelli. They simply cheered lustily as their heroes suffocated the Red Wings until the final buzzer had sounded.

Preparing for the postgame festivities, I had moved into the corridor between the two benches during the last half-minute of play. The vomitory already was jammed with NHL security, who protectively surrounded Gary Bettman. The commissioner had appeared as a Fox Network guest between periods in a visibly exposed area of the arena and thus had been roundly vilified by the fans. Now he would have to face them again—all of them—at center ice—a prospect that was unmistakably daunting.

For a brief moment, my mind flashed back to that game 12 years ago between Edmonton and New Jersey immediately after Wayne Gretzky had delivered the now famous "Mickey Mouse" insult. My wife and I had taken our son, Simon, to that game. He sat close to the protective glass, almost suddenly becoming infatuated with a short goalie named Chico Resch, his goaltending, and hockey. On this night Simon was again sitting in the stands roaring with the rest of them. My reverie was disturbed when a security guard pushed through carrying the Conn Smythe Trophy. He handed it to Bettman, who stepped onto the rubber matting, quickly grabbed the microphone, and presented the award to Claude Lemieux. The boos turned to cheers the moment Lemieux's name was heard.

Bettman retreated to the alleyway once more. This time he was handed the Stanley Cup. Momentarily, he again was showered with catcalls. His brief but cogent speech about the Devils epitomizing "teamwork in the best sense" was on target. He handed sport's most-cherished team trophy to captain Scott Stevens, whereupon cacophony was the order of the day.

Just then, I noticed a white-maned figure step off the ice and onto the carpet next to the Devils' bench. It was McMullen. He noticed me, we shook hands, and he said, "Whenever you want to do that interview, I'm ready."

I was surprised that he would think of such a seemingly unimportant matter such as that right in the midst of this monumental event in his ownership career. "I'll phone you

Monday," I said. Then I retreated back to my cameraman, who was preparing for the postgame show in the dressing room.

At this point it was difficult separating the professional part from the emotional. Having covered the Devils since their opening days, I had remained intrinsically close to the hockey club although this new Nashville business had begun mining some deep-seated cynicism within me. I was happy for many of the skaters I had come to know, especially Ken Daneyko, John MacLean, and Bruce Driver, who had been with the club almost from its inception in New Jersey.

Then, there was my pal, Mike Peluso, always the first one in the dressing room on game days. In the midst of shaking hands, Peluso made a strange beeline off the ice to his locker. I later learned that Peluso was so overcome with emotion he had to compose himself in the room before returning to the ice minutes later.

When Scott Stevens, the Devils' captain, hoisted the glistening, silver Stanley Cup over his head in front of the vast, cheering throng, I was reminded of our first interview of the season at Hartford's Civic Center in mid-January. At the time the Devils' captain sounded so uncertain about the club. I thought of our trip to Philadelphia late in the season when Stevens lashed out at Larry Brooks of the *Post* for challenging his leadership and suggesting that he be traded—an idea that I considered sensible at the time. Now, it was totally impossible to imagine New Jersey winning the championship without Stevens' presence and leadership on the blue line.

Finally, after the handshakes and traditional Cup skate-around ended, the Devils trooped back to their quarters. This was the first time a SportsChannel-covered team had won the Stanley Cup since the Islanders captured their fourth straight championship in 1983. By that time, the Isles had become ever so slightly jaded about Cup wins—but not this Devils club.

The tableau in the winners' quarters was right out of the Marx Brothers' chaotically funny stateroom scene from *A Night at the Opera*. Side by side with my cameraman, John Ackerina, I elbowed my way to whichever Devil might be available. The first was Bruce Driver, with whom I had feuded years earlier. Driver had become much friendlier in recent seasons.

Driver had been team captain prior to Stevens's arrival from St. Louis four years ago, but he remained the club's union representative and a symbol of the beat-up Devil who got up off the canvas to triumph. "We're going to have a lot of fun the next couple of days," said the veteran defenseman. "A lot of people cracked jokes about where our victory parade would be if we won the Stanley Cup. It doesn't matter now."

Driver's wife, Tracy, was sobbing while her husband and I did the interview. Their cute eight-year-old daughter, Whitney, stood by smiling. "My wife was with me all the way," said Driver, who grabbed Tracy and hugged her to his chest.

The "pop" of champagne bottles echoed through the room. Peluso opened one and generously poured the bubbly over my head. It was the first time I had been doused with Korbel Brüt. When my glasses became blurred, I stashed them in my pocket and plowed forward. Directly ahead was one of my favorite Devils, Bill Guerin, whose hair was being ruffled by his father, William Guerin Sr., a stockbroker from Hartford. I began interviewing them when, unexpectedly, Bill Guerin's mother, Ligia, an arresting, dark-haired professor of Spanish, appeared in the background.

I had met and chatted with the Guerins several times since their son had come to New Jersey and knew that Bill Guerin's mother was a terrific talker. While chatting with her son and husband, I waved her over to our side. Bill Guerin had not seen her until that moment. When Ligia Guerin came into view, the two—mother and son—collapsed in an uncontrollable, weeping embrace.

For a split second, I wasn't certain whether I should turn away and allow them a private moment or offer an on-air commentary as they tried to regain their emotional equilibrium. I chose the latter, which turned out to be the right thing because our camera caught the touching familial scene, easily one of the most poignant of the entire evening.

Typically, coach Jacques Lemaire ducked the limelight after the Cup presentation. I had been tipped off that he was hidden in the coach's cubicle, across from the dressing room. Roland Dratch, my producer, told me to try to persuade Lemaire to come on-camera for an interview.

I hustled through the crowd, across the corridor, and banged on the door. Without waiting for an answer, I opened it to find the tiny room filled with Lemaire's family and assistant coach Larry Robinson. Lemaire unhesitatingly agreed to come back to the locker room. Lemaire had been burned by some who had criticized his trap, and he hammered his point home during our chat.

"I thought the guys deserved a little more respect from their opponents," said Lemaire. "That's one reason our guys were aggressive. Because they got no credit."

Conn Smythe Trophy–winner Claude Lemieux was no less passionate in rebutting the critics. When one of them challenged the champions' style, Lemieux shot back, "Too bad you didn't like the show. You can go watch something else."

Despite the media critics a significantly high number of fans chose to watch Lemaire's intellectual brand of hockey, even after his team had amassed an unbeatable three-game lead. The proof was in the numbers most coveted by Bettman, Incorporated—U.S. television ratings. The Fox Network drew a 3.6 A. C. Nielsen rating, the highest-rated NHL broadcast on Fox in its first NHL TV season. It also tied the 1990 NHL All-Star Game on NBC for highest-rated NHL telecast since 1990. It represented some 954,000 U.S. households who watched the game.

Once our postgame telecast was over, the dressing room had opened to all sorts of visitors, from family members to girlfriends. The Devils' Gallic trio—Claude Lemieux, Martin Brodeur, and Stephane Richer—mounted a special platform that had been erected for TV interviews and lustily chanted victory songs in French.

A few minutes later my wife, Shirley, and son, Simon, drifted into the room and soaked up the joy if not the champagne. Throughout the Devils' Cup run, Simon had remained devoted to his Islanders but admitted that he got a special charge out of watching long-haired Mike Peluso. Because Peluso was still sitting in front of his dressing area, I walked Simon over to him whereupon the lad said, "You made me a Devils' fan!" Peluso got a kick out of that, ruffled Simon's hair, and assured us that after all the celebrations were over, we all would go to Brooklyn's fishing village at Sheepshead Bay and down cherrystone clams together.

It was an hour later when we traipsed through the parking lot, still filled with disbelieving fans. The Devils were Stanley Cup champions. It still was hard to digest. It was almost as difficult as accepting the transient potential of the new Cup winners. During their finest hour, the Devils were still bombarded with questions about a distant city they had not known. Nashville was on everyone's mind and especially that of John McMullen.

During the afternoon after the championship night, McMullen startled me with a phone call. He repeated his willingness to do the television interview. I mentioned that I had planned to make the appointment on Monday. McMullen told me about his recent visit—he reluctantly and unavoidably missed game three of the finals because of it—to Annapolis for a class reunion at the United States Naval Academy. With a very audible quiver in his voice, this multimillionaire, who had too often been unfairly mischaracterized for his insensitivity, choked up as he told me how many of his World War II classmates had been lost. I told him about my father's stint on the minelayer U.S.S. *San Francisco* during World War I. I promised him that I would bring a copy of my father's minelaying squadron's yearbook when we would next meet.

We arranged the interview for Monday afternoon at McMullen's business offices in Secaucus, New Jersey. It loomed as a big one for SportsChannel so I arrived early and carefully prepared my questions. When I arrived at the headquarters of Norton Lilly (McMullen's firm), my cameraman already was setting up and McMullen invited us to partake of an enormous cake shaped in the form of a Stanley Cup.

That done, we began the interview, which covered what I thought was every aspect of McMullen's dispute with the New Jersey Sports and Exhibition Authority. He was sharp, incisive, unwavering, and articulate in his claim that his hockey club had been getting the short end of the fiscal stick from day one as a Byrne Arena tenant.

"The governor told me that she still was awaiting a counter-proposal from you," I mentioned at one point. "What about the privatization plan?"

"What we'd like to do," McMullen asserted, "is lease the building."

Here was a concrete response that—as far as I knew—had never been articulated before by McMullen. This would be the core of the interview, which, according to early plans, might run in its entirety. That meant as much as an hour of air time. Despite the playoff run that consumed four rounds and nine sold-out home Stanley Cup dates, McMullen insisted that he was operating at a financial loss for the season. "I can't continue to do so any longer," he emphasized.

At one point, I seriously offered, "You don't strike me as a Nashville kind of guy."

He smiled but then responded, "I'd rather make a profit in Tennessee than be debt-ridden in New Jersey." By the time we had concluded the session, I was convinced that (1) we had a meaty interview; (2) the positive side of McMullen would be better revealed than ever before on television; and (3) he was dead serious about leaving unless he could strike a significantly better deal with the authority.

After thanking him for the time, I got in my car and proceeded to buck the rush-hour traffic snaking its way to the Lincoln Tunnel toward Manhattan. Instinctively, I turned on the radio, tuning in to the all-news station WINS. Having heard most of it on the trip out to Jersey, I listened with only half an ear until 5:45 P.M., when the sportscast was delivered.

It was then that I suffered a temporary case of lockjaw. The newscaster blurted, "And the Stanley Cup champion Devils have announced that they will break their lease with the New Jersey Sports Authority next year."

Break lease. Next year. Devils announced.

Wait a minute! I had just spent an hour with John McMullen and never did the lease ending come up in conversation. What was this all about?

My head was swimming as I drove up Broadway to our house. Try as I might, I couldn't explain why the saga was playing out this way. Naturally, when I walked into the apartment the phone was ringing off the hook. On one line I had Pete Silverman, my new boss at SportsChannel and a hard-nosed newsman if ever there was one. On the other was the network's publicist Paul Schneider, who only hours ago had notified all the sports-TV columnists that we were going to run a hot McMullen interview.

"We just heard on WFAN that the Devils are ending their lease in 1996," said Silverman. "Did McMullen tell that to you?"

"Not a word," I shot back. "But I'm going to call him right now to find out."

The Devils' owner had just left his office so I knew it would take a while before he reached his home in Montclair. About an hour later he picked up the phone and I explained my amazement at hearing about the lease termination on the radio.

"It's just a legal technicality," he said. "When we sent it to the New Jersey Sports and Exposition Authority, it was with the understanding that it remain a private matter. Then, they went public with it despite our agreement."

This was a key point. The original broadcast I had heard erroneously made it seem as if the Devils had made the announcement about the lease breaking. Actually, it had come from the New Jersey Sports and Exposition Authority without McMullen's knowledge and that is what angered him.

I phoned the authority spokesman John Samurjan and asked why the authority had gone public with the lease story when McMullen specifically had wanted it to remain private. "We had a document [the letter from the Devils] and apparently some members of the media learned about it," Samurjan explained. "They began asking questions so we decided we had to make a decision—to tell the truth or not. We chose to release the document that they sent us."

The one-paragraph announcement, which was enough to scuttle our grand plans for the "McMullen Interview Show with Stan Fischler," was released by the authority while I had been closeted with the Devils' boss. Which meant that it was impossible for McMullen to know that New Jersey Sports and Exposition Authority Chairman Michael D. Francis and President Robert E. Mulcahy III had gone public.

Their statement went as follows: "The New Jersey Sports and Exposition Authority today received a notice from the New Jersey Devils terminating their Franchise Agreement as of the 1996–97 season, based on their position that the 1991 Amendment to the Franchise Agreement is not valid. For the past four years, the Authority and the Devils have abided by the terms of that amendment which the Authority maintains is valid. The Authority's General Counsel is currently reviewing the termination letter."

Why did the authority go against its agreement with McMullen to keep the matter under wraps?

In so many words, the authority was saying that it broke its word simply because reporters were asking questions. No wonder McMullen was furious. From my viewpoint, his anger was completely justifiable but that didn't help us in terms of the validity of our interview. The late-breaking, lease-busting story preempted whatever good stuff I had from McMullen. Silverman told me he couldn't use the interview as we had originally planned.

Instead, he had me come to the studio to do a one-on-one with the *Game Time* news show host, Matt Laughlin. The point of my being there was to explain why the original interview was killed while at the same time I would provide as much insight into the fast-breaking story as I could.

During the program, we showed a couple of segments of the actual one-on-one I had with McMullen. Once it was over, I repaired to our offices to field the phone calls. One was from Nat Gottlieb, sports-TV columnist of the *Newark Star-Ledger*, who asked a number of questions about the sequence of events leading to the killed interview. Another was from Howie Rose, a probing newsman from WFAN and a friend.

I explained to both that I was very disappointed that the lease-breaking story hadn't come up in the interview but I reiterated that I believed McMullen was as much surprised by the authority's breaking of the agreed-upon news blackout as I was by the announcement on the radio.

Gottlieb ran with the story, giving it considerable space in the next day's (Tuesday, June 27) edition. The popular "Mike and the Mad Dog" (Mike Francesa and Chris Russo), jumped on it the next day, phoning me for yet another interview.

Needless to say, McMullen was less than thrilled that the interview was killed, but everyone at SportsChannel agreed that Silverman had done the right thing under the circumstances. Meanwhile, we sprinted ahead, keeping pace with a story that was exploding like an atomic chain reaction.

A day after announcing that it was terminating its franchise agreement after the 1996–97 season, the Devils pulled off another shocker. This time they said that as of July 6, 1995—just 10 days away—they would terminate their lease with the Meadowlands!

Counterpunching as quickly as McMullen's attorneys could, the authority's lawyers filed a complaint in Bergen County Superior Court. Francis and Mulcahy were seeking a preliminary injunction that, among other things, would prevent the Devils from moving to Nashville.

The July 6 target date made it appear that McMullen was dead serious about Tennessee. But several elements mitigated against the move: (1) the New Jersey Sports and Exposition Authority had the backing of Governor Whitman in seeking an injunction. A courtroom battle could prove embarrassing to the NHL; (2) in the hockey club's June 27 press release—titled "Devils Describe Actions Taken to Preserve Legal Rights"—a meaningful paragraph left room for compromise. "The Devils' organization does not intend to foreclose the possibility that an acceptable proposal may yet be forthcoming from the Authority"; and (3) Gary Bettman had entered the negotiations.

During a phone conversation with Bettman, he told me that there was little to nothing that he could say publicly. However, others told me privately that the commissioner had become an influential and, no less importantly, a calming influence on the negotiations. In our discussions, Bettman repeatedly used the term "leveraging" to describe the give-and-take.

An NHL owner put it another way: "When McMullen set the July 6 date, it was a case of 'ultimate hardball.' This was his best way of getting these authority people to do some real negotiating and for him to get some meaningful concessions."

No doubt, but the July 6 D-day announcement came on the eve of the gala pep rally to celebrate the Devils' Stanley Cup championship. Some fans regarded it as an ironic and crushing point-counterpoint. At the time when they should be sharing their most joyous moments, they were now faced with a very real prospect that their favorite team would be departing

Making it even more personally confusing was the fact that SportsChannel had planned complete coverage of the celebration at the Meadowlands. Our broadcast team—Mike Emrick, Peter McNab, Matt Loughlin, and myself—were scheduled to arrive at the arena at 3 P.M. for our production meeting and then prepare for the evening festivities, which were set to kick off four hours later.

When I arrived at the sun-drenched parking lot that afternoon, I didn't know what to expect. Some fans were so furious about what seemed like a guaranteed Nashville move that they said they simply wouldn't show up for the party. There also were hints of violence to protest the July 6 ultimatum, yet what I saw throughout the concrete expanse were happy faces. Despite the early hour fans already were gathered around barbecues, enjoying their tailgate parties. True to the theme, they had come to celebrate, not denigrate.

But no sooner had I arrived at the TV truck, Pete Silverman was on the phone. A story was circulating that (1) McMullen already had received a $25 million check from the Gaylord people in Nashville; and (2) some Devils, purportedly led by Mike Peluso and Stephane Richer, knew about it and planned to boycott the event. Silverman wanted us to break the story, if we could have it verified.

The Devils had just finished their official team picture taking in Byrne Arena and the dressing room now was open for interviews. Richer was nowhere to be found, but Peluso was sitting in front of his locker and soon was surrounded by newshounds. I waited about 10 minutes until they cleared away and then whispered the report I had heard. Puluso calmly denied it and I left the room convinced that he had leveled with me.

By the time I reached the pressroom down the hall, clusters of reporters were gathered around discussing a rumor that WFAN planned to run with virtually the same story that we were trying to unravel. Silverman had just arrived and phoned a contact at the radio station. "They're going with it as an unconfirmed report," he told me. "But we have to keep on it."

Unable to find Richer, I decided a call to Dick Evans at Gaylord headquarters in Nashville was in order. Evans and I had had a very distant relationship when he had been head honcho at Madison Square Garden several years earlier. When he got the call, Evans seemed surprised at the WFAN report and thoroughly ridiculed it as nonsense. I then phoned the commissioner and with typical Bettmanesque sardonic humor, he asserted, "And that's why they should ban sports-talk radio!" Both persuaded me that the move-to-Nashville rumor was fiction.

With his sharp news sense, Silverman knew we had to deal with the story on the show so he recommended that I open it with Emrick on the upraised SportsChannel platform amidst the crowd. The plan was for Emrick to immediately reveal the unconfirmed reports being circulated about the alleged transfer of a $25 million check and then for me to offer my analysis and any late update.

By 6:30 P.M., as we prepared to ascend the platform, a sea of humanity filled the vast parking lot. (The unofficial estimate later varied from 25,000 to 75,000, but most settled on the former. In either case it was more than anyone had expected under the circumstances.) As Emrick and I made our way through the crowd, fan after fan pleaded with us for information about the threatened move. At one point, when a youngster approached me, I was suddenly reminded of the classic episode involving Shoeless Joe Jackson of the White Sox, who was accused, along with teammates, of dumping the 1919 World Series to Cincinnati. As Jackson ascended the courthouse steps in Chicago, the lad pleaded, "Say it ain't so, Joe!" In effect, the Devils' legion was urging, "Say it ain't so, John!"

But the unconfirmed reports heard on WFAN were scary. We all were thinking the same "Where there's smoke, there's fire" bromide, hoping against hope that no Nashville money had been deposited but also cynical enough to realize that it could have happened.

I asked one of our interns to place another call to Evans just in case he had anything further to add before airtime. Meanwhile, Emrick and I moved into our positions on the platform. We were in full view of the throng and, believe me, if they had taken a sudden disliking to us, we would have been in big trouble. Fortunately, many of the spectators had either seen or heard about my Bettman interview and my pro-Devils stance.

In 20 years of broadcasting—make that 40 years as a reporter-columnist—I had never been overwhelmed with such emotion. Frenzied over the celebration and furious over the threatened Devils' exodus, the fans began chanting "Stan, Stan, Stan," in deep-throated unison.

What could I do? I gave them the thumbs-up sign and that merely aroused them even more. Our stage manager, John McComb, suggested that instead of a thumbs-up, I give them a Papal wave instead. "Even better," he said, "just do what they do in the TV studios. Give them a 'c'mere wave,' for even more applause."

I settled for the thumbs-up because that seemed most appropriate and left it at that. Now it was 6:59 P.M. and we were ready to go on the air. As the final 10 seconds were being counted down, I noticed the intern, Rick DaCruz, rapidly climbing the platform steps, waving a piece of paper in his hand.

"Ten, nine, eight, seven, six . . ." the countdown continued.

DaCruz reached the top of the steps and, unaware that we were about to go on the air, pushed the paper toward Emrick. "Five, four, three, two, one."

Just as we went on, Emrick took the notes and quickly glanced at them. It was an update from Nashville. This time Evans was even more vehement in his denial that a check had been sent to McMullen. So forceful was the statement that I could only conclude that the story was false and I said as much in our precelebration discussion although there always was the concern that Evans was making a false denial.

That done, I left the platform and moved among the spectators for interviews until the players arrived for the Stanley Cup deliverance. On center stage an upbeat band worked the crowd, which sang along, "Go, Devils, go! Go, Devils, go!" Makeshift Stanley Cup replicas and banners were everywhere, including one proclaiming, "NJ Devils Forever."

Finally, the player-carrying motorcade snaked around the arena toward the stage. I was particularly interested in two personalities, McMullen and Lamoriello—how they handled the crowd and vice versa. The Devils' high command occupied the front-row seat in one of the open convertibles and seemed at ease as the motorcade moved to the stage entrance. I was there with Governor Whitman and interviewed her before she made her way up the steps. She was more intense than usual but emphasized that she remained hopeful because the warring parties were still talking.

McMullen alighted from his car, accompanied by his pet dog, Hector. Suddenly, he was surrounded by New Jersey State troopers who formed a flying wedge as he made his way to a special celebrity grandstand. It was a rather courageous move by McMullen who easily could have ducked the audience if he had so desired.

A circling helicopter then made a landing on a strip adjoining the stage whereupon captain Scott Stevens reached in and was handed the Stanley Cup. He carried it on stage, transporting the crowd into an even higher form of ecstasy. One by one, each player danced with the silver mug to the accompaniment of techno music. An even greater ovation overcame the throng when Bobby Holik stepped forward with the Cup and was accompanied by his linemates, Mike Peluso and Randy McKay.

It seemed as if there was even more energy being generated than one might have anticipated but it was only because a majority of the fans were seriously doubtful whether they would see this team play again at the rink in the background. Thus, they were determined to clear their lungs with unusual vigor.

However, when Whitman stepped forward, the cheers turned to jeers. With considerable aplomb, she easily hushed the dissenters and shouted, "They can play the trap and they can do things other teams are just finding out about. And I look forward the same way every other fan does to watch them defend that Cup and bring it right back home here next year."

I was desperately trying not to get engulfed in the emotional whirlpool. To that end, I kept telling myself that hockey is a business and the Nashville threat is Exhibit A. Yet when Jacques Lemaire stepped forward, it was difficult to contain the goose-bumps. Here was a mensch, a gentleman, a man's man, a regular guy.

"I heard a lot of things during the season," he began as the lights brilliantly reflected off his bald pate, "but I never thought I'd ever hear about the trap from the governor; I had enough of that all year."

Following the laughter, a fan raised a sign, "Whatever Bo knows, Jacques knows better."

Lamoriello was an even more interesting study. How would he handle himself amid the tidal wave of doubt? What would he say to the growing legion of skeptics?

The club president grabbed the lectern as a coach would when he wants to shake some sense into a player. With a remarkable sense of conviction, he emphasized how much management wanted to remain in New Jersey. Then, he turned to goalie Chris Terreri and implored him to walk to center stage and unfurl his makeshift sign. It read: "Nashville. No way!" The crowd went wild.

It ended after 10 P.M. on what had been an exquisitely clear, magnificently cool night. As we headed for our cars, we walked through minefields of beer cans and soda bottles, any of which could have been armament for an ugly crowd. Instead, decorum was the order of the day and now we wondered whether decorum would be the order of the courtroom.

Barring a sudden turnabout, the Devils and the New Jersey Sports and Exhibition Authority were due to face-off in court only five days after the last beer bottle was swept away from outside Byrne Arena.

AND THE FINAL VERDICT IS . . .

On the morning after the deliriously joyful Meadowlands celebration, two extremely significant events took place in two different states involving the New Jersey Devils.

At a press conference held in Nashville, Dick Evans, the man who ran Gaylord Enterprises, made it clear that he had no deal— as *Star-Ledger* columnist Jerry Izenberg put it, "with the Devil or the Devils." More than that, Evans uncharacteristically blasphemed the New York–New Jersey metropolitan area. When a reporter from the *Record* of Hackensack interviewed him, Evans snapped, "Why don't you go back to New Jersey? Why the hell would anyone want to go to New Jersey? It's a hellhole. I lived in New York for 10 years and I fought to keep from going through the tunnel to that hellhole." *New York Post* columnist Phil Mushnick, a New Jersey resident, retorted: "Dick Evans hates New Jersey? Good for New Jersey!"

Obviously, Evans was rapidly becoming disenchanted with negotiations. More than that, he apparently sensed that the New Jersey Sports and Exposition Authority (NJSEA) might very well launch a lawsuit against his firm for tampering with a major league team that had a major league lease with it. In fact the NJSEA had planned to sue both Gaylord and the National Hockey League, an event that must have been understood by lawyer Gary Bettman.

The second event was taking place behind closed doors in New Jersey, where members of the authority, John McMullen, Lou Lamoriello, and Bettman were attempting to strike a deal. Only 24 hours after the Meadowlands celebration, the parties reportedly were extraordinarily close to forging a pact, but they adjourned for the evening without dotting any *i*'s or crossing any *t*'s.

Looming ominously ahead, like a detour sign on a road, was Judge Peter Ciolino in Hackensack, New Jersey Superior Court. On Monday, July 3, 1995, Judge Ciolino was to hear the New Jersey Sports and Exposition Authority's lawsuit to bind the Devils to their contract. The word in legal circles was that there was a "shark-feeding frenzy" among judges who wanted to hear the case. "Every one of them wants to be *the* judge who keeps the Devils secure in his home state," was the way one New Jersey attorney put it.

Neither side relished the idea of going to court especially because the prospects for a long battle could have badly bruised both parties. In the meantime, the Devils were legally obligated to file their own papers rebutting the authority's charges. As talks continued, the Devils asserted in court papers filed on Friday, June 30, 1995, "The authority has continually and repeatedly represented that the authority would deliver a base of 19,000 fans at the arena." The Devils have "lost millions of dollars" because of that unfulfilled albeit unwritten promise. "I was promised 19,000 fans and they never gave us a chance to produce them," McMullen said.

If there was to be an agreement, the authority would have to concede to McMullen's basic demands. For example, just a few weeks earlier, he reminded me of a second trip he had made to see the new Boston NHL arena, which still was under construction. He marveled at the 104 suites that were included in the design. Byrne Arena sported 29.

"They don't give a damn about us," McMullen insisted. "Aren't I entitled to break even?"

McMullen knew whereof he spoke. In the NHL of the late nineties, a club needs not only gate receipts and a good television deal, but monies from stadium ads, concessions, and suites, of which the Devils had far too few.

"Luxury boxes are critical," said Craig Simon, director of sports marketing for the Chicago consulting firm of Frankel and Company. "A stadium that doesn't have them is in danger of losing its team."

Which explains why the Nordiques abandoned Quebec for Denver. The antiquated Colisée couldn't compete with a brand-new arena in the Colorado metropolis that would be oozing with luxury boxes. At the United Center in Chicago, opened in 1994, owner Bill Wirtz boasts 216 suites selling for between $55,000 and $175,000 a year.

"The luxury suites are the financial engine that offsets the cost [$175 million] the Blackhawks and Bulls incurred in constructing the facility," said Steve Schanwald, vice president of marketing for the Bulls.

The authority was working out a plan to provide considerably more suites for Byrne Arena, but first there was a court date on Monday, July 3, 1995, at which time there would be either war or armistice.

I arrived in the sleepy and neatly trimmed city of Hackensack about 20 minutes before the 9 A.M. court date accompanied by a cameraman. At least a dozen other media types were there for the event, including my pal Larry Brooks of the *Post* and several local reporters.

Our advance tip was that the authority would ask the court for a postponement and the Devils would agree. This would be done only on the assumption that Judge Ciolino would receive assurances that both sides felt a negotiated settlement was near.

"The judge will not ask this lightly," noted Jerry Izenberg of the *Star-Ledger*. "In this game, he is goalie, referee, head linesman, and the only licenced Zamboni driver in the rink. If they say peace is just a couple of days away—and they will—they had better mean it."

Sure enough, Joel Kobert, the authority's general counsel, did just as predicted and Judge Ciolino postponed a hearing until Tuesday, July 11, 1995. When I interviewed Kobert, one-on-one outside the courtroom, he made it clear that progress was being made. "Everyone is encouraged," he said, "and they'll keep talking this week."

The handsome old courthouse was bathed in pleasant sunlight when we stepped outside to do the on-camera opening for the TV segment. "Not so fast, Nashville," was my opener. "The Devils are still in New Jersey and appear to be here to stay."

Naturally, the operative word was "appear" because there still was a possibility of the talks erupting with the rancor that had pockmarked the earlier negotiations. And, as Izenberg so wittily noted, "The negotiations move forward with all the speed of a pair of herniated ants trying to drag a large potato chip back to their communal pantry."

I spent the rest of the week awaiting a resolution that never came. On Friday, the Devils' contingent, led by Lamoriello, was scheduled to leave for Edmonton and the annual Entry Draft on Saturday, July 8. On Thursday, Lamoriello hosted a media conference call ostensibly to discuss the upcoming draft, but he also gave an unequivocally positive response when asked about the negotiations.

"We are making progress," said Lamoriello, who normally is cautious about such matters.

A day later, Izenberg wrote, "Logic dictates that the authority and the Devils will settle this thing over the weekend before the Honorable Peter Ciolino settles it for them, starting Tuesday in Superior Court."

The weekend began with the NHL draft and no further news. On Sunday, McMullen was profiled in the *Star-Ledger*, a newspaper that he had continually claimed was in the authority's corner. He sounded more optimistic than usual about a settlement.

Not wanting to be caught unawares, I urged my bosses to have a cameraman on hold just in case an announcement was made on Sunday. Early in the afternoon I received a call from the authority's spokesman, John Samerjan. "They're still talking," he said.

I mentioned that the Devils were scheduled to meet President Bill Clinton at the White House on Monday afternoon. Might there be an announcement before then? "I'll let you know if there is," he politely replied.

By 9 P.M. on Sunday, I had not heard any further word so I assumed that the armistice would not be proclaimed until Monday, perhaps even by Governor Whitman at the White House. Now wouldn't that be a beauty.

I made an Amtrak reservation for 9 A.M. on Monday, still perplexed as to how this passion play was going to unfold in its final act. It now seemed obvious that Nashville was out of the picture and a deal would be made. But how and when would it be announced and what would the Devils get out of it?

While mulling over the possibilities, I could not help thinking about the effect these months of agonizing threats and counterthreats were having on the people who were directly involved or even tangentially affected. One of them was my colleague Jiggs McDonald, with whom I had worked as part of the Islanders' SportsChannel broadcasts for 14 years.

McDonald's contract had expired with the network, but its other hockey play-by-play man, Mike Emrick, had a pact that extended through the 1995–96 season. If Nashville claimed the Devils, SportsChannel would lose a team and have no need for two play-by-play broadcasters. From a purely business sense, the network would opt for Emrick because he already was under contract.

When McDonald was advised that his pact was put on hold pending resolution of the Devils' dispute, he decided to part with SportsChannel. He phoned me and we discussed his disagreement, but naturally, there was little I could do other than make mention of his availability in our weekly newsletter, the *Fischler Report*. On a personal level, I knew that I'd miss working with McDonald. Over the years, McDonald and I had a number of disagreements—about hockey ideas, not broadcasting—but they never adversely affected our on-air relationship. Quite the contrary; we bristled through a number of arguments, particularly Mario Lemieux versus Wayne Gretzky, and were all the better for them.

As the Metroliner rolled out of Pennsylvania Station for Washington on Monday, July 12, 1995, I thought about McDonald and the many big games we had covered together, especially the Stanley Cup winner in 1983 at Nassau Coliseum, when the Islanders won their fourth straight championship. I felt more than a twinge of sadness at the breakup of our team and then was suddenly reminded of a remark made by old friend Marty Blackman.

The Madison Avenue marketing executive had closely followed the Nashville-Devils odyssey. One day I mentioned to Marty how emotional the New Jersey fans had become about the possible loss of their favorite team and how that emotional factor should be considered by owner John McMullen.

"Remember," said Blackman, "sports is big business. A hockey team in New Jersey is no different than a wire-cutting company. If the wire-cutting company got a fabulous offer to relocate to Tennessee the way the Devils did, the owner wouldn't think twice about moving south."

The Metroliner click-clacked over Newark Bay and braked to a stop in the grand art-deco station of New Jersey's largest city. Here I was en route to a presidential ceremony honoring that state's first championship team and still there were broad hints that the Devils might leave.

In the *New York Post*, Larry Brooks hinted at the possibility of a conspiracy between the NHL commissioner and Nashville. "Maybe," wrote Brooks, "Bettman, no advocate of the current metropolitan three-team market, is using his considerable influence to negotiate an out for the Devils they could not win through litigation.

"Maybe the Sports Authority, which will make every attempt to steal the Islanders if the Devils get away, can be bought off at this point. Maybe there are promises of which we know nothing, being traded in the modern version of the smoke-filled room."

If the Brooks' theory—and it was based only on maybes—held water, no NHL community would be immune from lease busting. Each club would be open to the highest bid. Or, as Blackman kept saying, "It's a major business in a capitalist society."

But it was—and is—personal to all the fans involved, be they in Winnipeg, where the Jets were hanging by a thread, or Tampa Bay, Miami, and Hartford. All these communities had supporters that passionately followed their big-league club but who could easily wake up one day and learn that the Lightning, Panthers, or Whalers were victims of a buyout, takeover, or move-out.

In no time at all our train had rolled across the New Jersey countryside and pulled into Philadelphia's grand 30th Street Station. I watched passengers strolling along the platform and wondered something I never had thought about before; was there ever a championship hockey team that picked up and left its city after winning a title?

Sure enough, it happened in the Paul Newman movie, *Slapshot*. If the Devils left Jersey for Nashville, it would be the most exquisite example of life imitating art.

But Paul Newman's club never enjoyed the honor of being greeted by the president of the United States and this was about to happen to Captain Scott Stevens and his Devils. Accompanied by teammates Bill Guerin, Jim Dowd, Bruce Driver, Kevin Dean, Ken Daneyko, Martin Brodeur, Brian Rolston, and Neal Broten, Stevens arrived in the East Room well before Bill Clinton.

The place was filled with familiar faces, and people-watching was the order of the day. I noticed the venerable Helen Thomas, queen mother of the White House press corps, who still was covering for *United Press International*, and Wolf Blitzer of Cable News Network. I found it amusing that Thomas was inconspicuously crammed behind a rope barrier with the New Jersey–New York hockey beat writers.

Seated in the high-powered guest section was Governor Christine Todd Whitman, looking attractive in a beige suit and accompanied by her husband, John, who supposedly had been brokering peace talks between McMullen and the New Jersey Sports and Exposition Authority. McMullen was sitting next to his handsome son, Peter, on the other side of the aisle. Because I had been tipped off that McMullen and Governor Whitman had been at odds recently, I watched carefully to see if there was any social byplay between the owner and the governor.

Sure enough, she graciously walked past six chairs to McMullen, who rose, hugged her, and posed for a photo with his arm in a palsy-walsy grip around her shoulder. The authority's Michael Francis and Bob Mulcahy wore appropriate smiles but kept their distance from McMullen.

Suddenly, a hush fell over the room and a voice blared, "The President of the United States."

A door opened to the left of the lectern and in walked the chief executive. He was wearing a dark suit with an intriguing red, yellow, and blue tie adorned with little human figures that I assumed were all Democrats. I had never seen Clinton up close and was instantly impressed with two aspects of his carriage: (1) he was bigger than I had imagined; and (2) his nose was sunburned red.

Clinton's humor surfaced immediately, and it was obvious that he had done his hockey homework. He knew that the Stanley Cup had once been left on a Montreal sidewalk after the Canadiens had stopped to fix a flat tire en route to a celebration. And he told about the time a member of the Ottawa Senators had drop-kicked the Stanley Cup into the frozen Rideau Canal. He made only one faux pas, calling the Conn Smythe Trophy (won by the absent Claude Lemieux) the Conn "Smith" Trophy.

When Devils' captain Scott Stevens thanked Clinton for inviting his team, Stevens added, "Like you, we've had a long, tough year."

Fielding the line on the short hop, Clinton immediately responded, "Hope mine comes out the way yours did."

Stevens presented the president with a Devils' jersey adorned with Clinton's name and the number one on the back.

"I identify with you because you were cast as classic underdogs, but your determination and teamwork paid off," Clinton added with telling sincerity.

Then, he compared hockey to the rough and tumble world of politics: "The difference is here we don't have a penalty box and sometimes the referees back there pile on, too!"

The ceremony was as pungent and tasty as sweet-and-sour soup. When it was over the president hung around shaking hands, mine included. (He has an engagingly firm handshake.)

But almost as quickly as he had appeared, the president disappeared behind the big doors of the East Room while the Devils moved out on the lawn for interviews and picture taking.

All things considered, it was a rather euphoric occasion. You could tell by rookie Brian Rolston's beam that this was one of the best days of his young life. Even a seasoned veteran like Stevens was visibly moved.

"I'm still on cloud nine," said Stevens. "It'll take a while before I come down. I think it will last until the start of the season."

McMullen had moved among his players and I seized the opportunity to interview him. I wasn't sure how he would react because of the problem we had after the post-Cup tête-à-tête in his office, but he was cordial, even to some of his adversaries such as Rich Chere of the *Star-Ledger*.

"It was a very nice ceremony," said McMullen. "This doesn't happen every year, although we'd certainly like it to."

Some of us wondered whether there would be an armistice announcement made before his Devils left the White House. McMullen made it clear that we would be covering the dispute in Hackensack court the next morning. "It won't get resolved until then," he added, but he steadfastly refused to admit that he would keep his club in New Jersey.

Then, he betrayed a rare emotional reaction; McMullen allowed that the rally and parade for the Devils outside Byrne Arena four days after they had won the Stanley Cup affected the negotiations to keep the team in his home state. "It was one of the greatest emotional outcries I've ever encountered," McMullen went on. "I was personally very affected by the rally and it definitely had an effect on the negotiations. It made it obvious to everyone how important it is to try and resolve this. A lot of people care."

Filtering through his comments, I tried to discern a pattern but it was difficult because McMullen uttered both positive— "We're holding out hope"—and negative—"What difference does it make [where we play next season]?"—remarks.

While we were gabbing on the White House lawn, word came down that the Devils' charter jet back to New Jersey was waiting at National Airport. "Do you want a ride?" McMullen asked.

I hesitated. My plans had been to return by train, but Amtrak wouldn't be leaving for another two hours. Besides, this was a chance to spend a last hour or so with some of the players, so I accepted. Before I knew it I was sitting in the charter, watching Daneyko chomp into an apple. Two of Daneyko's false teeth remained embedded in the core. He turned to me and grinned a semitoothless smile. "All I was hoping for was that the teeth hung in there through the White House—and they did."

McMullen sat in an aisle seat across from Bettman at the front of the airplane. About a half-hour after takeoff McMullen walked to the rear, chatting with just about every passenger. Dr. Barry Fisher, the team orthopedist, along with trainer Ted Schuch were orchestrating a game of blackjack and motioned to the owner, "Doc, lemme relieve you of some of your millions," said Fisher. McMullen grinned and simply said, "No thanks."

McMullen and I chatted for a few more minutes after which he asked if I needed a car to take me to the city. It was a terrific offer but I figured I would just as soon take the bus. We agreed that it was a neat White House ceremony and then he repaired to his seat for more conversation with Bettman.

I had no doubt that they were discussing the ongoing negotiations, which would continue later that evening and last until two in the morning. That meant another date for me in court, and promptly, when the doors to the superior court opened, I was there along with the usual corps of print and electronic media.

Once again Joel Kobert, the authority's counsel, and Frederick Lacey, who represented the Devils, agreed that the parties were closer than ever. Sources said the two sides were discussing the possibility of selling a corporation the right to put its name and symbol on the 14-year-old arena as a means to pay for renovations sought by the team. The authority already had agreed to install more luxury suites and new, high-priced club seating in the arena, and negotiators had been considering strategies to raise private-sector money to help pay for them.

"The deal is just about at the handshake stage," said one insider. "There's still some volatility, but the details are being worked out."

Some of the volatility was being generated by McMullen. He railed to the *New York Times* about what he called a "demeaning" negotiating process. Asked if he was feeling close to a deal, he shot back, "How can I be confident? It's a very undignified procedure."

Then, he elaborated: "It's demeaning to go over every little point for them to offer me anything. They should give me concessions without breaking my back. To lock myself into a 12-year deal with these people is difficult. We have a vast difference of opinion about the quality of the arena. It's tough to get them to understand what it takes for me to run the team profitably."

McMullen said he deserved givebacks that would produce profits for a team that he said lost $2 million while winning the Stanley Cup and $20 million since he acquired the team in 1982.

"I'm generating the hockey revenues, the money that can help me break even," he said. "Without the money, they can't generate those revenues." He also brought up Nashville again.

"There's no comparison, particularly as far as the future. Nashville creates a pleasant environment and we'd operate the arena and be our own landlord. No way this can approach Nashville. It's secondary."

I was due back in court on Thursday, July 12, 1995, unless a deal was hammered out before then, as most expected. On Wednesday morning I made my usual call to the authority's public relations man, John Samerjan, and he cordially mentioned that "the wheels grind slowly." But he also indicated that there might be a break in the afternoon. At 3 P.M. I phoned him again.

"Does this mean I should be in Hackensack court tomorrow?" I asked.

"Not necessarily," he replied. "Sit tight and call me a bit later."

Meanwhile, I alerted SportsChannel to have a crew waiting should we have to move quickly to a press conference.

This was almost as exciting as the Stanley Cup finals.

D (AS IN DEVILS) DAY
The Final "No" to Nashville

One more phone call to the New Jersey Sports and Exposition Authority offices wouldn't hurt, I figured, so late on Wednesday afternoon, July 12, 1995, I dialed John Samerjan.

"Has a deal been done?" I inquired. "Are the Devils saved for New Jersey?"

Ever courteous and thoughtful, Samerjan insisted that there was no new news, and furthermore, he assured me that there would be nothing further to report today. This time he was emphatic so I took his word and phoned Gary Bettman at the National Hockey League.

The commissioner had been holed up all day trying to figure out ways and means of reviving the fiscally comatose Los Angeles Kings. Nevertheless, Bettman was amiable and patient as I prodded him for information. He had told me a few days earlier that he planned a trip on Thursday. I had assumed he was heading for the West Coast.

"When are you leaving?" I asked. "You are leaving for L.A., aren't you?"

"I'm not going to the coast and I'm not sure when I'm leaving," he cryptically answered.

"Does that mean you'll be around long enough for a [Devils-NJSEA] press conference?" I asked.

There was a lilt in his voice. It was telltale without actually telling me anything specific. "I might," he said. "If there's a press conference and you have a camera there, I'll be happy to do an interview."

Without actually spelling it out, Bettman had told me that, yes, I had better be ready for the big announcement tomorrow, Thursday, and that the end of the saga was near.

In the meantime, SportsChannel arranged to have a mobile truck ready early the next morning (Thursday). I would meet it in front of Byrne Arena in East Rutherford, New Jersey, precisely where the Devils' victory party had taken place. If a deal had been cut, we would head for the press conference, wherever it might be, and if one had not been hammered out, we would drive to superior court in Hackensack, where Judge Peter Ciolino was prepared to hear the authority's request for a temporary restraining order to keep the team from terminating its lease at Byrne Arena.

But Samerjan had told me days earlier that when the pact had been signed, word would immediately leak to some well-connected media type. And, sure enough, at 6:05 P.M. on Wednesday, I received a call from a friend, Steve Viuker.

"Channel 13 is running with a story that a deal has been cut," said Viuker.

Sure enough, the station's political expert, Pat Scanlon, was saying it was a $25 million pact that would ensure the Devils stayed at Byrne Arena. Scanlon was well connected enough to be trusted on this, but to be sure, I phoned Steve Hirsch, a political reporter at the *Record*. He checked with Samerjan, who checked with his boss, Bob Mulcahy. The latter offered a flat denial. Samerjan added that there was a one-in-a-hundred chance that an announcement would come later in the evening.

It was the classic scenario. Progress had been reported in court on Tuesday; the judge ordered everyone back on Thursday; if a deal had not been cut by then, a messy legal battle would carry on through the next hockey season, embarrassing the authority, the Devils, and the NHL. There *had* to be an armistice and it was inevitable that word of the truce would leak before the actual, formal announcement was made.

From 6:15 P.M. to 7:15 P.M. the phone nearly rang off the hook with the usual follow-up calls from various sources. Scanlon, based at Trenton, the capital of New Jersey, had phoned Lou Lamoriello, but the Devils' president had not yet returned the call. Scanlon was staying with his story despite the NJSEA denial and even offered some details—the Devils would get considerable club seating; the authority would provide more ad awareness; and there would be a sizable chunk of cash for selling the arena name to a corporation such as Continental Airlines. Because Scanlon was based in Trenton, the assumption was that someone in the governor's office had provided the leak. It made sense.

All signs suggested that a formal press conference would be announced before the parties were due in court. Hockey's latest version of the Treaty of Versailles was rapidly reminding me of the famed Gary Bettman–Bob Goodenow peace parlay that I had witnessed across the Hudson River in the winter of 1995. But when I finally went to bed on Wednesday night, I still had no confirmation from any source and had no idea what would transpire the next morning.

David Kolb, a young man from Queens College (New York), who had worked with me through the season on Devils' telecasts, drove up at 8 A.M. and we were off to our meeting with the SportsChannel truck in the Meadowlands parking lot outside the main entrance. Traffic flowed smoothly and we arrived at least a half-hour early, but to my surprise, the television truck already was there with several crew members. Obviously, our outfit was not fooling around today.

When my producer-director, Stu Wiener, and another aide, intern Anna Horton, pulled up a few minutes later, we laid out a battle plan. First, we had to establish whether there was going to be a press conference or a meeting at the Hackensack courthouse. Then, we had to move all our equipment and trucks to the site for what would be a live telecast. Ironically, all of this breaking news was happening on the day when SportsChannel premiered its new logo and new image. For us, it was a big deal.

My prime contact was Samerjan at the New Jersey Sports and Exposition Authority, whose offices were at the Meadowlands Racetrack about a half-mile from our site at the Byrne Arena. Samerjan had suggested I phone him at 9:30 A.M., but Keith Fernbach from my office already had checked with Samerjan, who insisted he had nothing yet to report. The secret word was *yet*.

Instead of waiting around, Wiener, Horton, Kolb, and I drove over to the New Jersey Sports and Exposition Authority, where we were stopped at the gate. A Samerjan aide came down to accept a book I had promised the authority spokesman, but he would not give us any further information about whether we should be in court or somewhere else in the next hour. "Call me at 10" was the message, so we headed back to our trucks and the crew in front of Byrne.

By this time the temperature was climbing toward 95 degrees. The parking lot was broiling, but this did not stop visitors who had come for a religious festival that night at the arena. Suddenly, one of our crewmen got a bright idea and walked over to the Winner's Restaurant inside Byrne, where most of the major press conferences are held. A few minutes later he rushed back and breathlessly said, "They're setting up for something big. A couple of guys already are working on microphones. That's gotta be it!"

We dispatched another team of spies to double-check. One of them met a restaurant employee who confirmed that a press conference would be held there at noon. An Einstein wasn't required to deduce that it *was* the Devils–New Jersey Sports and Exposition Authority event, but still Samerjan didn't confirm it. This time Horton trekked to the Devils' office and, finally, got the official word; it was going to happen after all, at noon, in Winners, not the Hackensack courthouse.

Great! We had the jump on everyone and immediately moved the television trucks and equipment to a location right outside the restaurant. Wiener immediately developed a plan of attack with the little information we had at hand. Our cameraman would hustle up to the podium and install our microphone and then he'd place the camera in the best position. That was considered a key strategic advantage and gave us enormous leverage in terms of our opposition.

According to Wiener, I would open the show live the moment it appeared that the press conference was close to starting. For however many minutes necessary, I'd elaborate on the events leading up to the armistice and then we'd turn it over to the speaker at the lectern.

Despite all the planning I was extremely nervous. So far, we had no official notice that the press conference was, in fact, happening and I had neglected to phone back Samerjan. Adding to my concern was the absence of any other media types. I returned to the Winner's Restaurant and immediately came upon a woman who I only know as Sue, who managed the Devils' pressroom and now was involved in preparations here. She confirmed that it was indeed the authority-Devils armistice event for which they were preparing. That done, I exhaled deeply and prepared my opening for our live show.

By 11:30 A.M. a sprinkling of newspeople had drifted in and TV cameras were being mounted. Our SportsChannel people had planned to open the show as soon as any of the principals arrived, but that wouldn't happen for a while. In the meantime a crisis developed. Having been first on the scene, we planted our microphone in the middle of the lectern, but subsequent technicians had dislodged it and a minute before noon—the scheduled starting time for the event—we had no sound from the main microphone.

My right ear was nearly peeled off by decibels as Wiener demanded that we stall the start of proceedings until the mike was fixed and get the damn mike fixed before anything begins!

While this was being accomplished a camera suddenly appeared five feet behind me—closer to the dais—that blocked the view of our cameraman. My stage manager set a record for expletives while the intruding cameraman beat a hasty retreat to another portion of the room. Just then a Madison Square Garden Network cameraman blithely moved into the empty spot whereupon more expletives served to hasten his exit.

Our two gofers, Kolb and Horton, were then given explicit instructions: get guests! We didn't expect to do interviews as they were coming in, but it was imperative that they grab whomever they could once the formal part of the press conference had ended.

About a minute later, Kolb, who was scouting the perimeter of the room, tipped us off that the entourage was making its way to the door. We gave the signal to Wiener who counted me down from the truck—"four, three, two, one. Go, Stan!"

Off to the right of the podium, I began my spiel: "D day has arrived. That is, *D* as in Devils day; the Stanley Cup champions are staying in New Jersey . . ." I continued until the principals were being introduced by Mike Levine, the Devils' PR man. Then, we cut to the dais microphone for the live conference.

Gary Bettman led off the speakers, confirming that he knew a day earlier, when I had spoken to him, that he would be in New Jersey. "The Devils are staying," said Bettman, appearing characteristically jaunty, "at least for the next 12 years. This marks the beginning of a new era in New Jersey."

The commissioner then spelled out how the hockey club would have new revenue streams, how the Byrne Arena would be renovated, and how other goodies would provide John McMullen the fiscal wherewithal to compete with the Rangers, Red Wings, and other big-money clubs.

McMullen was next and, typically, his theme was the recently crowned Stanley Cup champions. "We beat the Bruins, Penguins, Flyers, and Red Wings to win the Stanley Cup," said McMullen, "and the payrolls of every one of those teams was higher than ours!"

It was a wonderful line, but also profound in its simplicity. The buy-a-championship theory was refuted by McMullen's club, and he wanted to underline that point. It was a lesson that the Blues, Rangers, Maple Leafs, Canadiens, and other big spenders simply could not or would not acknowledge.

Eventually, the white-haired leader moved on to the traumatic topic at hand: the peace treaty. "We do need much more cooperation," said McMullen, "and I believe it will happen."

As the speakers came and went, a particularly fascinating aspect of the armistice was revealed. A condition of the Devils' declaration of intent to stay was that the New York Yankees, whose owner, George Steinbrenner, had for years been threatening to leave his Bronx turf for New Jersey, could not move into the Meadowlands until the year 2003, at the earliest.

"There can't be another major league team here," asserted Lou Lamoriello. "Not another pro football team, another pro basketball team, another NHL team, or a baseball team."

The feud between McMullen and Steinbrenner was like a roller coaster, but the Yankees' boss never forgave McMullen for a remark the Devils' owner had made after being a "limited partner" of the Bronx Bombers. To wit: "There is nothing more limited than being a limited partner of George Steinbrenner."

It was not that the Yankees were barred from New Jersey forever but rather until the Bombers' lease with New York City runs out in 2002. What the anti-Yankees' clause did was buy time for Team McMullen to sell its new suites and take advantage of its new signage and other revenue deals before a fifth team of any kind could set up serious housekeeping in the neighbourhood.

"We are not about to do the whole Nashville thing," said Mike Francis, the New Jersey Sports and Exposition Authority chairman. "We are not going to try to get any major league team to break its lease. We respect leases."

There was, however, an "if" involved, and in the view of some observers it was a big "if." The agreement to keep the Devils in New Jersey for a dozen years was contingent on the renegotiated lease being approved on September 15, 1995. If the deal was not completed by then, the authority would reactivate its request in state superior court for a temporary restraining order to keep the team from terminating its current lease. Thus, if the lease was not approved, the warriors would return to the legal battlefield.

A major aspect of the agreement stipulated that if the authority did not help the team secure a $25 million loan by September 15, 1995, the Devils could cancel the deal. "The pressure on the authority is not a negative," added Lamoriello. "I believe pressure can be a positive. We put pressure on ourselves every day.

"But I'm very comfortable that the relationship is going to be better than ever before. And one of the major reasons for that is the way [Authority Arena and Stadium executive vice president] Michael Rowe was involved in the talks, the manner with which he made us feel as though our needs were important. The communication and feedback we had with him was absolutely outstanding.

"The reality is that if the Sports Authority delivers what has been promised, the Devils have a 12-year lease and commitment to remain in New Jersey. This is not a 1-year agreement with an 11-year option."

Bettman, who had inspired the ogre image in New Jersey after his appearance with me on television during the Penguins' playoff, suddenly had become a hero of sorts. Virtually every one of my sources credited him with persuading the authority members of the need for compromise.

"On balance, each side left the table believing the commissioner was an advocate of their particular position," said Rowe. "If he were billing for his time, I'm sure we'd each be pleased to pay the bill."

Throughout the press conference, we anxiously awaited the moment that it would break into the one-on-ones that are so precious to television interviewers. In this case—because we were live—it was imperative that one of our gofers latch on to a chief protagonist in this passion play. Suddenly, Bettman stepped forward and stopped further questions, signaling the end of the general give-and-take.

That was my cue to ad-lib on camera until someone was fetched for a live interview. Enough had taken place for me to cruise through the fiscal waters without capsizing, and about 90 seconds after I had begun my peroration, out of the corner of my eye, I noticed that Horton had Lamoriello in hand. He moved right into camera formation and proved to be a solid opening interview.

Bettman followed, maintaining his upbeat style of the day. When I asked him to pinpoint the turning point in keeping the Devils in New Jersey, he wasted no time replying, "You may have accelerated the process when you interviewed me in Pittsburgh!" (I actually believed that he meant every word of it.)

It was evident that Bettman would not drop Nashville as a prospective NHL site and underlined it by saying, "I think it's a good market." Later in the day, Nashville Mayor Phil Bredeson said, "We want an NHL or NBA team in Nashville and I think when our arena opens next year, we'll have a team."

I was most interested in McMullen's reaction. This had been an extraordinarily trying few months for a man his age, and he had been vilified beyond the call of duty, considering the losses he suffered along the way. When he had begun addressing the audience, he was upbeat and remained that way until the question-and-answer period began.

For the most part, he maintained a temperate flow of replies until someone mentioned the hostile reaction toward him expressed by some fans during the Stanley Cup celebration in front of Byrne Arena. What had been a positive mood began turning sour as reporters hammered away at this issue.

Exasperated, McMullen remarked, "Most of the negative impression comes from the press not the fans." By the time the leaders had broken up into separate groups, McMullen was in a foul mood and balked when one of his less-charitable critics, Bob Page of Madison Square Garden Network, attempted to get him one-on-one. It was then that Horton intercepted him and mentioned that I was standing by hoping he would come over for a chat. He obliged while we waited out a station break. In a matter of seconds we were on camera and I began the interview.

"We're not guaranteed to break even," he declared. "That depends on salaries in the NHL. But I will say this: the NHL has the most constructive labor agreement in all of pro sports."

He was lavish in praising Bettman, insisting that the deal could not have been brokered without the commissioner's insights. "He has a knowledge about leases throughout the league that surpasses anyone's and that was a big help to us."

When McMullen was finished, I concluded the interviews with authority members Mulcahy, Francis, and Rowe. Having been tipped off about the infighting between Francis and McMullen—not to mention the fact that they hadn't talked for almost a year before the intense negotiating began—my attention was caught by his accent on peace in our time. "It's critical that we be able to work together," said Francis, "and we're genuinely looking to work jointly with the Devils."

I signed off the air about an hour after we had opened and, for the most part, I was satisfied with our show. It was live TV and we had covered it from the start, obtaining all the key individuals for interviews.

On the drive back to Manhattan over the George Washington Bridge, I began reflecting on the similarity in the two major off-ice hockey stories I had covered within a year—first the lockout and then the Nashville caper. They had a lot in common, beginning with the acrimony shared by both sides and the same 11th-hour drama that kept newspeople in suspense. The owner-union war certainly was more bitter than sweet, whereas the Devils' Stanley Cup triumph was the honey that softened the unpleasant taste of Nashville.

Both wars were closely intertwined. The NHL Players' Association—with the encouragement of agents—had driven salaries to record levels. To keep pace with the salary spiral an owner such as John McMullen had to find additional sources of revenue. Nashville was such a terrific enticement that McMullen, the businessman, had to consider the offer and then demand a better deal from the New Jersey Sports and Exposition Authority. Surely, if salaries had been at a lower, more reasonable level, the battle would not have been fought.

It always has been terribly easy for sportswriters and sportscasters to criticize owners for being cheap, frugal, or whatever. The knocks come from hockey writers who wouldn't spend a dime for a ticket. Had McMullen not invested a considerable fortune in the Devils through the years of fiscal abuse, New Jersey never would have had a big-league hockey club and surely never a Stanley Cup winner.

"He from day one has taken the hit, personally and financially," said Lamoriello. "He went through every lean year and no one helped him, not one dime. He sustained all of this. In past years no one wanted us. Now people want us. There's not any greed involved, but we're just trying to get back a little. He's never going to get whole."

By the time I had arrived home, there was a phone call from a reporter with the *Asbury Park Press*. She had been listening to radio station WFAN and was surprised at the vituperation of hosts Chris Russo and Mike Francesa. "They're saying that the Devil thing is all a joke," she said, "because they could be out of New Jersey in a year. What do you think?"

I was taken aback by their vehemence and when she asked me for a comment, I suggested that the Russo-Francesa shtick was cynicism and I didn't for a second believe them. It seemed to me that the New Jersey Sports and Exposition Authority had too much at stake to allow the Devils to leave now and that it would only require a few months to iron out the bumps in the agreement.

In any event their negativism, followed by some dubious comments made by *New York Times* columnist Dave Anderson, had me wondering again. Just when it appeared that there was cause for celebration, another reason for doubt intruded.

There was only one thing to do: contact the journalist I considered the most tuned in to this story from the start. I called Jerry Izenberg from the *Star-Ledger* and he immediately dismissed Russo and Francesa out of hand. He pointed out that there was too much for either party to lose—including a serious trip to superior court in Hackensack—by reneging on the pact.

"This is a deal where everyone can make money," said Izenberg, "and that's why everyone was involved in the first place. You cannot fault the New Jersey Devils for that."

I certainly couldn't, not when the bottom line in the NHL clearly had switched from pucks to bucks.

A ROLLER-COASTER FRANCHISE
Ups and Downs with the New York Islanders

Once considered the jewel of the National Hockey League, the New York Islanders described a descent during the 1990s that was remarkable in its intensity, swiftness, and turbulence.

The tailspin, which actually can be traced to the drafting of Dave Chyzowski in 1989, went out of control in the summer of 1993 and concluded with a deafening crash following the 1997 playoffs that reverberated through 1998 and 1999 as well.

During that time, a club that (under Bill Torrey's leadership) had once won four consecutive Stanley Cups—between 1980 and 1983—was riddled with blunders, bad luck, and deceit to such an extent that its long-term survival on Long Island remained in doubt through 1999.

When Chyzowski was drafted, during the ownership of John Pickett and the general managership of Bill Torrey, there was every reason to believe that the Islanders were embarking on a new era of success. They had finished first in 1987–88 and, despite the retirement of Hall-of-Famer Denis Potvin, had a young nucleus—led by center Pat LaFontaine—around which to build.

Armed with the second overall pick in the 1989 Entry Draft, the Isles selected Chyzowski, a six-foot-one-inch, 190-pound left wing out of Edmonton. That Torrey would opt for a Western Canadian hardly was a surprise. Guided by top scout Gerry "Tex" Ehman, the Isles favored prairie prospects.

In the 1987 Entry Draft, Torrey's first pick (13th overall) was defenseman Dean Chynoweth, son of the former Western Hockey

League president, Ed Chynoweth. A husky, eager defender, Chynoweth never rose above the mediocre level. A year later the Isles' top pick (16th overall) was another Western Canadian (Saskatoon) junior defenseman, Kevin Cheveldayoff.

Playing junior hockey in Brandon, Manitoba, Cheveldayoff suffered a devastating knee injury and although he eventually did turn pro, he never played a game in the NHL. Had Cheveldayoff not been so seriously injured, there was every reason to believe that the intelligent, hard-hitting blue liner might well have been an Islanders captain. But bad luck is bad luck.

The Chyzowski blunder, which followed Cheveldayoff by a year, was not bad luck but rather a judgement that was difficult to fault at the time. The Chizzer, as he became known in Nassau, had been a scoring machine as a junior in Kamloops, British Columbia, and no slouch in the penalty department either. He starred on Canada's National Junior Team, but unlike many of the earlier prospects, Chyzowski did not have the luxury of learning his trade for a long stretch of time in the minors.

The Chizzer was promoted to the big club in 1989–90, then demoted, promoted, demoted, and promoted as the high command desperately attempted to turn a minor leaguer into something that he wasn't—an NHL ace. The persistent attempts at reincarnating Chyzowski symbolized the Islanders' problems as they entered the nineties. Buffalo Sabres general manager Darcy Regier, who was with the Isles staff at the time, perceived the problem. "After no later than two years," said Regier, "people at the organization's 'factory floor' level [those involved in development of players] were convinced that we didn't have a player. Upper management and the scouting department went into denial. Hell or high water, we were going to make this guy into a player.

"But there was something missing at the pro level that wasn't evident at the junior level. We had made the decision and we couldn't bring ourselves as an organization to move beyond it. What happened was that we had an asset that, if we had talked to the 'factory workers' and involved them a bit more, it would have been very evident that we had to move quickly to get something back in a trade or we would end up with nothing at all before the other teams picked up on what we knew."

It was too late. Chyzowski didn't have it, and his abject history as a big leaguer since then proves the point. But the chain reaction of horrific decisions would continue. In 1990 the Islanders owned the sixth selection overall. Yet again, they selected a Western Canadian (Saskatoon) and, typically, it was a disaster.

While Ehman and Company could have plucked Keith Tkachuk, Derian Hatcher, Darryl Sydor, or Martin Brodeur, they bypassed these future stars for center Scott Scissons, who was quietly being low-rated even as he was being picked. Scissons's NHL career was even more abbreviated than Chyzowski's.

Torrey was able to survive the staggering draft setbacks and actually had crafted a nucleus of a contending team with some artful moves. But the veteran general manager's time ran out when absentee owner Pickett designated a quartet of Long Island businessmen to manage the team for him.

The quartet, Bob Rosenthal, Ralph Palleschi, Steve Walsh, and Paul Greenwood—each a successful local entrepreneur—became minority investors along with owner Pickett. Right or wrong, the foursome concluded that Torrey had become jaded and named Don Maloney as the new general manager. It would prove to be a disastrous move.

Groomed by Torrey, the bright, galvanic Maloney had one strike against him. He made his playing reputation as a New York Ranger, and if there was one type of individual an Islanders' fan did not want running his team, it was an ex-Ranger.

For Maloney, the unraveling of the franchise began during the summer of 1993. The Islanders had come off a brilliant playoff in which they had upset the Stanley Cup champion Pittsburgh Penguins in seven games and reached the third round of the postseason. Three of their players—goalie Glenn Healy, defenseman Darius Kasparaitis, and center Pierre Turgeon—numbered among the most popular players in Islanders' history.

During the summer of 1993 a contract dispute between Maloney and Healy's agent, Larry Rauch, inspired the general manager to seek another netminder. He opted for Ron Hextall, a former Philadelphia Flyer who arguably was one of the most hated non-Rangers ever to skate at Nassau Coliseum. For Hextall to follow Healy was roughly equivalent to the Wicked Witch of the West following Madonna as the headliner at Caesar's Palace stage show.

Erratic through most of the campaign, Hextall completely disintegrated during the 1994 opening playoff round in which the Rangers swept the Isles in four straight games. It was the most humiliating experience in the club's playoff history

Even worse, the Broadway Blueshirts then proceeded to win the Stanley Cup. This event produced profound fiscal and psychological setbacks for the Islanders. Until then, the Nassau loyalists would regularly chide the Rangers with chants of "1940, 1940" as a reminder that the Manhattanites had not won a Stanley Cup since before Uncle Sam entered World War II. The

Rangers' 1994 Cup triumph and subsequent victory march up Broadway produced incalculable damage to Islanders' season ticket sales as well as morale.

Desperate to get his team back on track as they staggered away from a playoff berth in April 1995, Maloney engineered a major trade that momentarily invigorated the fans, as most blockbuster trades do, whether they are positive or negative. Convinced that Pierre Turgeon had lost his touch, Maloney dealt the French-Canadian center and gifted-yet-undependable defenseman Vladimir Malakhov to the Montreal Canadiens for defenseman Mathieu Schneider, center Kirk Muller, and minor-leaguer Craig Darby.

Ironically, the deal was completed on the morning of an Islanders-Rangers match at Madison Square Garden and, superficially, it looked good. Schneider was a feisty backliner and the first Jewish player ever to skate for the Isles, who were based in a community with a large Jewish population. Muller supposedly would provide leadership as well as scoring punch.

Covering the game for SportsChannel, I was at the Garden that evening eagerly awaiting the new players. When Schneider arrived two hours before game time, grinning broadly, every one in the Islanders contingent felt invigorated, hopeful that a Muller-orchestrated homestretch run might even result in a play-off berth.

A few minutes later, Islanders publicist Ginger Killian walked out of the elevator and down the corridor toward the visiting dressing room. She appeared unusually somber for the supposedly festive occasion.

"Where's Muller?" I asked, already fearing the worst.

"He isn't here," she replied. "And he won't be here tonight." Maloney had failed to determine in advance whether Muller actually *wanted* to play on Long Island. Kirk had captained Les Canadiens to the 1993 Stanley Cup and had been promised by general manager Serge Savard that he would not be traded. To say that Muller was unenthused about being moved out of Montreal would be the understatement of the half-century.

More than a week was required before Kirk could be persuaded to visit Long Island. I attended the hastily called press conference on a Sunday afternoon at Nassau Coliseum. Interviewing Muller on camera, I asked him whether he could dedicate himself to the Islanders' cause. Armed with his patented infectious grin, he insisted that he could.

Naively, I believed him. Like others who covered the Isles, I wanted to see the club turn itself around with Captain Kirk at the helm. But it wasn't to be. Alternating between average and mediocre, Muller proved a major-league disaster from which the franchise would require years to recover.

Meanwhile, the management quartet sought ways and means of resurrecting their investment. Investor Ralph Palleschi told me that he urged his comrades to import former Islanders' hero Butch Goring as head coach to replace the dismissed Lorne Henning. But the others favored erstwhile Boston Bruins defenseman, then coach, then assistant GM Mike Milbury.

The local media correctly speculated that it would only be a matter of time before Milbury displaced Maloney as general manager. Milbury was named head coach on July 5, 1995 and early in December of that same year, Maloney was fired. But his legacy, Muller, continued to disturb the team's equilibrium with his ineffective play. Milbury, now in charge, dealt Muller to Toronto in a multiplayer deal that cleared the dressing room air but failed to generate a playoff berth.

Through the whole ugly mess, I had maintained an amiable, off-the-record relationship with Steve Walsh, one of the four minority investors. Engaging, humorous, and candid, Walsh blended the enthusiasm of a fan with the hard-nosed earnestness of a businessman. A conversation with him never was dull and usually was fun.

The impression I had received over a period of two years was that he and his partners would like to buy a larger portion of the team from Pickett if not the entire franchise. Early in the summer of 1996, I heard whispers from other sources that Pickett would like to divest himself of the team.

Then, it happened.

An old friend, author–sociologist–motivational specialist Allan Turowetz, flew down from Toronto to visit family in the New York area. I had known Turowetz since the mid-seventies, when I worked for Home Box Office and we telecast a Buffalo Sabres game from the Aud. Allan had been working for Sabres general manager Punch Imlach as the team shrink and made a fascinating subject for an interview.

We hit it off immediately and became lifetime friends. Turowetz's passion for hockey was translated to print several times. His most famous work was the bestselling *Lions of Winter*, a chronicle of the fifties Canadiens dynasty and one of the finest hockey books ever written.

As we strolled along Broadway on Manhattan's Upper West Side, Turowetz dropped his bombshell. "What would you say if I told you I wanted to buy a National Hockey League team?"

I knew that Allan had saved some money but not that kind of money. "This is a joke, right?" I replied.

His smile turned down to a frown and now I knew that he was not kidding. "I should point out to you that it's not my money; there is a sugar daddy; and, furthermore, there's a third party, whom you know, who would run the team along with me."

"Which team?"

"We want to buy the Islanders," Turowetz went on, "and I want you to find out from your friend Walsh whether they are available."

Convinced that he was sincere and that he had Mister Moneybags—whomever he might be—in his corner, I phoned Walsh.

"Does Pickett really want to sell the Islanders?" I asked.

"What do you mean?" he replied.

"I have a friend who's interested in buying."

There was a pregnant pause. "What's the matter?" I inquired. "You're a little late," Walsh shot back, "and I'm sorry to tell you this. But tell me what you have in mind."

I explained the Turowetz connection and how much Allan wanted to talk with Walsh, but he stopped me in my adverbs. "The problem is that someone has come along who Pickett likes and who appears to have a lock on buying the team."

"So, why are you sorry?" I wondered.

"Because I don't like the guy," he said firmly.

That was the first time I heard the name John Spano mentioned in conversation. Walsh asserted that this fellow, Spano, had made an offer to Pickett that was favorably received. "I would love for your guy to be involved," Walsh went on, "but we have to see what happens."

When I asked Walsh what it was about Spano that left him cold, he suggested that it was more a gut feeling than anything else. It wasn't a question of finances—that would be handled by Pickett and the NHL—but rather one of personality.

Spano. Spano. The name intrigued me until, finally, I checked through some old clippings and then recalled that he was the same John Spano who headed a Dallas-based outfit called the Bison Group and who had failed in a bid to buy the Dallas Stars.

I reported back to Turowetz and suggested he call Walsh just for the hell of it, which he did. They hit it off well but Walsh made it clear that unless Pickett somehow rejected Spano, a letter of agreement stood in the way of any deal between Turowetz's entry and Pickett.

Walsh and I exchanged many phone calls through the summer of 1996 and well into the fall. By the start of the

1996–97 NHL season, it had become clear that Spano was the man. "I'm sorry," Walsh concluded in one of our last conversations on the subject.

Neither he nor Pickett nor Gary Bettman realized how sorry they would be.

The hockey term is *deke*. It means "faking out" an opponent with a head swerve; a quick, wide lateral dribble of the stick and puck; or similar mode of deception. Spano's deke of the NHL would prove to be Promethean in its proportions.

His first and most obvious victim was Pickett, one of the smartest operators ever to become a big-league hockey owner. In the late seventies, when the Islanders appeared to be foundering on the shoals of insolvency, Pickett not only rescued the team, but steered it in the direction of profit making and four Stanley Cups. It was Pickett who concluded the ultraluscious deal with SportsChannel that ensured the Islanders' fiscal viability.

But when he decided to emigrate from Long Island to the South, his hands-on approach to the team disappeared and the distance would create problems that were only evident after the years of neglect. Now, at last, Pickett would exit stage left and Spano would enter on the right.

It all seemed very neat and very right on Tuesday afternoon, November 26, 1996. A press conference had been called by Pat Calabria, the excellent, former *Newsday* hockey writer, who had become the team's VP of Communications.

Walsh had kept me informed of the developments. He had been accurate in his appraisal of Spano's chances and Pickett's infatuation with the deal. The Turowetz group never had a hope, and now we were in the Nassau Coliseum, awaiting the club's savior, or so we hoped.

The press packet distributed to the media included a biography of Spano. He was described as Chairman and Chief Executive Officer of the Bison Group, an equipment-leasing firm based in Dallas. It added that he founded the Bison Group after working in New York, where he learned the financing and leasing business.

"The Bison Group," the release added, "originally began as one company with four employees, including himself, specializing in financing leases for the equipment, aircraft, and automotive industries. In just six years, Spano has grown the business in ten separate companies with over 6,000 employees worldwide."

It sounded good, especially when adding that Spano's company also includes leasing for food services, convenience-store equipment, commercial real estate, municipal leasing, medical equipment, computer systems, and office furniture.

"I chose the Bison as my company logo because it is recognized internationally as an American icon symbolizing strength," said Spano. "That kind of strength and longevity is what I hope to deliver to Islanders fans, who are hungry for the next generation of champions."

Yet, standing at the podium, he appeared anything but a symbol of strength. At age 32 and balding, he looked like a much older man. He spoke nervously with little assurance, but what he did say was in tune with what Islanders followers wanted to hear. "People keep asking me about my style of ownership," he said. "The real questions concern the amount of time I will spend here. This is an important investment for us, an investment for the future. My style is hands-on and I demand results. You will see me here." Although the slight, balding leader was hardly imposing, he did offer another morsel of hope. Unlike Pickett, Spano said that he had kept his home on the East End of Long Island and that he was leasing an apartment in Manhattan. Clearly, this would not be an absentee owner, and as everyone present believed, this man was on the up-and-up.

Certainly, John Pickett—who rarely made a business mistake, if he made any—thought so. "The Islanders are in good hands with John Spano," said Pickett, who would be paid $165 million for the franchise.

What followed was as bizarre a set of circumstances as professional hockey ever has witnessed and one of the most embarrassing moments in Gary Bettman's commissionership of the NHL.

For starters, the gala November 26, 1996 press conference was less than it had appeared. The Islanders had not actually been sold to Spano but rather the media event actually was a declaration of his intent to buy the club.

"We look forward to working with the Islanders and Mr. Spano on moving the approval process toward completion," said Bettman.

The movement was slow and agonizing. From time to time, I would ask Bettman about the delays. "These things take time," he would say.

At first, the response was credible. But when delay piles on delay, it causes concern and makes one wonder. Meanwhile, Spano became a ubiquitous figure at Nassau Coliseum. One afternoon of an evening game, he even took a spin on the ice and then invited members of the print media to lunch.

"One of my best friends is Mario Lemieux," said Spano. "When he heard that I had bought the Islanders, he said, 'What in the world are you doing?'"

What he did during the winter of 1996–97 was play the part of club owner. He would breakfast with former Islanders' coach Al Arbour, take in a practice, and have cocktails with advertisers and luxury box tenants.

One such luxury box tenant was a Long Island publisher of educational books. Michael Rudman and family represent the quintessential hockey nuts. Rudman's wife and children not only follow the game but play it assiduously. When Rudman discovered that his luxury box at Nassau Coliseum rubbed shoulders with Spano's, he immediately struck up a friendship with the new owner.

"Spano was like someone who had been given a new toy and was having fun with it," said Rudman. "He was on a big high. He was flying his private jet back and forth from Dallas, and he talked about how much he was spending on fuel."

Perhaps Spano's ebullience had something to do with the fact that no money was yet needed to pay Pickett and that the sale would not be official until the NHL approved it at the owners meeting scheduled for December 1996.

Like so many who had intimately followed the Islanders' fortunes over two decades, I viewed the December approval date with more than the usual enthusiasm. This, I felt, would put a stamp on the new era, certifying the end of Pickett's regime.

But the December meeting came and went without the approval. At precisely this time I began to hear the first of a disturbing series of rumors about Spano. Taken alone, each whisper could have been dismissed as idle gossip. Collectively, they were disturbing because the whispers came from a range of sources, beginning with NHL ownership and ending with the comment of a Manhattan Honda dealer.

Apart from my interviewing him at the initial press conference, I had few encounters with Spano in the next month. On one occasion, I had been informed that soap opera star Susan Lucci—a Long Island native—was the owner's guest in his luxury box. I made my way to the suite and chatted briefly with Spano before interviewing Lucci. He seemed more at ease than at his opening press conference, but what I found interesting about the Lucci interlude was that nobody in the Spano box seemed to be watching the hockey game below. Drinking and eating were the priorities.

Shortly thereafter, Spano attended a SportsChannel charity auction. My broadcasting colleague, Sam Marchiano, cornered him for a while and later told me that he vowed to take a close look at the broadcasting situation.

During a meeting with leaders of the Save the Islanders Coalition (STIC), a fan club that had been intensely critical of the Isles' operation, Spano listened to complaints about the Pickett ownership and how management had not been friendly toward the fans. One who attended that conference was Tom Croke of Huntington.

A computer consultant, Croke was a cofounder of STIC, whose aim, among others, was to restore the Islanders' traditional logo, which had been abandoned by Walsh's quartet. STIC was regarded as a bunch of crazies (by some in the Islanders' hierarchy) but Spano gave them recognition, and the group replied by changing its name to Support the Islanders.

"We no longer felt like an adversary of ownership," said Croke.

During December 1996, while he awaited the NHL green light of ownership, Spano invited Croke to sit with him in his box at a home game. Among matters discussed were customer relations and the club's computer system, which Croke suggested was less than up-to-date. Spano seemed so interested in the feedback, he asked Croke to provide more information.

Just before the holidays ended, Croke delivered a comprehensive analysis of the Islanders, encompassing fan relations, management, and the computer operations. Croke, who also viewed Spano as a savior, believed that he was approaching the owner's inner circle.

So did Hall of Fame defenseman Denis Potvin, who had failed in an earlier attempt to become Ottawa Senators' general manager but who continued to have designs on an executive's position. A hockey television analyst for the Florida Panthers, Potvin had known Spano well enough to introduce him to the Panthers and at one point believed that Spano had the wherewithal to buy out Florida owner Wayne Huizenga.

"When that didn't happen," said Potvin, "I mentioned to him that there might be an interest in Long Island with Pickett. I was introducing him to someone who by all accounts—by the NHL, by Pickett himself, by Fleet Bank, and everybody else—always checked out pretty well. Who was I to question if he could do it or not do it?"

Potvin, never enamored of Mike Milbury—and vice versa—appeared to be a candidate for the Islanders club presidency under Spano. Milbury, now general manager and coach of a team on a treadmill to oblivion, could never coexist on a general staff with Potvin. If Spano did hire Potvin, Milbury would be out of Nassau by early summer.

"The presidency is what we talked about all along," said Potvin. "Spano lived in Dallas and would have needed someone in Long Island to take care of his business interests."

One of those interests was construction of a new arena for the Isles. Constructed in 1970, Nassau Coliseum had become obsolete by late-nineties NHL standards. Nassau county executive, Thomas Gulotta, wanted new ownership to redevelop the 70-acre Coliseum property, but Spano would have to line up co-investors and reach agreement with the county, which owned the land and the Coliseum.

"If I don't get this new building," warned Spano, "as a businessperson, I have to make an ugly decision. Is it move the team? Is it sell the team? Is it do something else? I don't want that to ever be the case."

Nor did Islanders fans, who shuddered at the mere mention of moving the franchise. Like it or not, that threat remained as long as teams like the Flyers, Bruins, Sabres, and Canadiens were opening new cash-cow arenas while the Islanders remained stuck with a 27-year-old rink.

Meanwhile, January 1997 came and went without any sign of NHL approval for Spano, just growing—albeit quiet—concern. The prevailing critique that I heard, vis-à-vis the new owner, regarded his personality. During a visit to a Manhattan Honda dealership, I engaged in a hockey conversation with one of the salespeople.

"I met that Spano fellow," the auto manager mentioned. "It had nothing to do with hockey; we had a business dinner over another project. He's a very strange fellow. Very strange."

Naturally, I was curious and pressed him for details. "Just the way he interacted across the dinner table. But I sure hope he works out for the hockey club."

The description was hauntingly similar to the one I had heard from Steve Walsh when I had originally phoned him about the Turowetz offer. And it was underlined during a face-to-face meeting I had with Spano at the Coliseum.

This was a Sunday afternoon game, not televised by SportsChannel. Wives and children of the broadcasters and production crew were invited to view the game—as Spano's guests—in one of the Islanders' luxury boxes. It was an Islanders-Canadiens game to which I brought my son, Simon.

Between the second and third periods, Islanders press agent Ginger Killian accompanied Spano to the luxury suite. He was introduced to all the visitors and then Spano pulled me aside and we chatted for a few minutes about superficial hockey matters.

Unlike Walsh, with whom I could converse for hours without any tension, Spano seemed somewhat edgy, and after the first few moments, the conversation went over the cliff. The pause became endless until I finally suggested that my son was interested in me watching the game with him. "Why don't we get together for lunch someday?" I offered. "Good idea," Spano replied and then left.

I felt rather good about ending it that way. Perhaps over a sandwich we could loosen up and discuss matters of mutual interest concerning the team. I suspected that Spano already was considering a shake-up in the front office and wanted to be sure to put in a plug for my pal Chris Botta, who was a member of the PR staff.

Botta and other staffers had been concerned about Spano's liaison with Croke—and for good reason. Early in February 1997, Spano invited the 45-year-old computer consultant to the Garden City Hotel, where he offered him a job with the team.

According to Croke, his title would be Special Advisor and his role would be to provide input into non-hockey areas to improve efficiency and productivity. It would be a six-figure salary and Croke would begin working on March 17, 1997. This would give the new staffer enough time to split from his personal clients and drop another job offer he had been considering.

"I had zero suspicions about Spano at the time," Croke insisted.

This was not the case with at least one NHL owner. John McMullen, who usually is about two miles ahead of his fellow governors when it comes to divining hockey's future, viewed Spano with concern and told me so. He was unsure about his ability to purchase the team and must have made those feelings known because Spano later told me, face-to-face, that the one league owner he liked the least was John McMullen.

Yet on February 24, 1997, the NHL's Board of Governors unanimously approved the sale to Spano. Shortly thereafter, season box holder Michael Rudman noticed a change in the new owner's demeanor.

"He had been very friendly," Rudman noted, "but now he was a little less friendly."

On March 17, 1997, as suggested by Spano, Croke showed up at the Coliseum to begin his new job as Special Advisor. When he entered the offices, Croke was startled to learn that nobody had been told about his job, nor that he was coming to work for Spano.

As Croke later told *New York Post* columnist Phil Mushnick: "I thought I was being lied to; that they were just fighting the new management team that eventually would take their places. They had no idea why I was there. Special Advisor? They must have thought I was some nut. It was humiliating."

A call was put through to Spano. "He said he was a little hasty," Croke continued, "and that I should start next week but that he'd pay me starting on the 17th. He told me to go across the street to the Marriott and call him for an explanation. So I did. But then he wouldn't take my call. That was my first inkling that he has a screw loose."

My first inkling came in a conversation with McMullen after the NHL had put its official stamp on the Pickett-Spano sale. Despite all the whispers, I was enthused that the deal had finally gone through. I chatted with Spano now on a more frequent basis and looked forward to our lunch. During a phone chat with McMullen, I revealed my delight with the sale.

McMullen, who made no bones about his dislike for Pickett, surprised me with his skepticism. The Devils' owner told me that he wasn't sure how much money Spano had to his name and questioned how much of Spano's own dollars were being used to buy the team.

Frankly, I was taken aback by McMullen's intensity on the subject but I preferred to be positive. Hey, if the supposedly efficient and sage Gary Bettman gave Spano the green light, how bad could Spano be?

Another who asked that same question was Bob Gutkowski, a former president of Madison Square Garden who had become a sports marketing executive with the New York–based Marquee Group. At Spano's request, Marquee had done consulting work for the Islanders at a tab of $20,000. Gutkowski's analysis was strikingly similar to McMullen's: "Spano would talk a good game. I would ask him, 'John, are you sure you have the money to do this?' He would become indignant and say something like, 'I have a private plane. Of course I have the money. Why would I be having this conversation if I didn't?'"

Certainly, Spano's passion for the team continued unabated despite their failure to gain a playoff berth in the 1996–97 season under Milbury. The poor finish naturally fueled speculation about Milbury's future, particularly because the general manager–coach had not been a Spano appointee in the first place, and the specter of Potvin hung over the Coliseum. According to the former Islanders' captain, Spano had offered him the Islanders' presidency before the season had ended.

Croke, who also had been offered a job by Spano, still couldn't get himself past the reception desk and now it was April. Should Croke have worried? It would not have appeared to be the right response, not if the commissioner's office was to be believed.

Commenting on Spano in April 1997, Bettman described Spano as "the type of person we want as an owner." It was a quote that would come to haunt him.

Certainly, Nassau County officials retained a similar faith in Islanders' ownership. Morton Certilman, an East Meadow attorney who had become Nassau County Executive Gulotta's point man on the Coliseum redevelopment project, had arranged a meeting with Spano to redevelop the arena property. What's more, Spano had commissioned the Kansas City–based HOK Sports Facilities Group to produce four concepts for the arena development.

"I want a place where you can come and walk," said Spano. "That's my vision."

The playoff-less hockey season had ended for the Islanders, and the only one who seemed to quietly doubt Spano's vision was Denis Potvin. The defenseman-turned-broadcaster later told Peter Botte of the *New York Post* that his last conversation with the owner was in April 1997.

"It's very simple," Potvin told Botte. "Spano basically told me he couldn't pay me. And that put an end to that. What he told me was—and this was the last conversation we had in April—he told me he was running out of money. I took that, at that point, as giving me a clear message that he couldn't deliver what he had promised in terms of my role and a contract."

Likewise, the turning point for Croke came in April but in different circumstances. After waiting for weeks, Spano finally called the job aspirant, inviting him to start work the following Monday. By this time Croke was leery enough to at least demand to know his salary. Spano said it would be $135,000. The owner called again the night before Croke was to begin work and added that he would be there to make the introductions.

Croke showed up but Spano did not and the supposed Special Advisor again was rebuffed at the reception desk. As Croke told Mushnick, he contacted Spano on April 29, 1997, and gave a play-by-play of his game of rejection. According to Croke, the owner replied, "I told you it would be difficult."

Who could fault Croke for asking, "If the NHL considered him credible, why wouldn't I?"

Precisely. And as the 1997 playoffs began, not a soul in the print or electronic media even remotely suggested that Spano was anything but what he purported to be—legitimate owner of the New York Islanders. Although I may have been fueled with suspicions, I remained on the positive side and finally worked out a meeting with Spano in early spring.

The episode was typically curious. He phoned me on the morning of the Rangers' opening home playoff game against Philadelphia at Madison Square Garden. We were to meet at 3 P.M. in the bar at what had become one of his favorite Manhattan haunts, the St. Regis Hotel.

No problem with that, but then Spano added, "By the way, Stan, do you know how I can get a pair of tickets for tonight's Rangers game?" "John," I replied, "you own the New York Islanders. Why don't you just pick up the phone and call [Rangers' general manager] Neil Smith. I'm sure he'll accommodate you."

Spano asking me about playoff tickets? Bizarre. Still, I asked no questions and walked into the St. Regis Hotel bar promptly at 3 P.M. The room had a darker-than-usual, mysterious air about it. As I passed the first table, I noticed the balding gentleman sitting on a stool with a phone pressed to his ear. The bartender, apparently alerted to my arrival, waved me over. When I finally had come to within two feet of Spano, he looked up and acknowledged me with a "hello" wave of the hand and continued his conversation. I ordered a Perrier with lime and waited.

After about a minute Spano folded up his portable phone. "Did you get those Rangers tickets?" I asked. "Not yet," he answered.

I didn't think that conversation was worth pursuing because I already had given my advice. We began chatting about the team. I knew that Milbury wanted "president" added to his GM-coach title and asked about it. Spano answered that it was too soon to give Milbury that much work. Maybe sometime down the line.

We discussed other aspects of the team without going into any detail, other than my plug for Botta. Spano seemed more and more distracted as we spoke. When his phone rang, I suggested that we call it a meeting and I wished him a good afternoon. As I walked away, I felt the same reaction as Rudman had the last time he had been with Spano in April. "He didn't seem to be as relaxed as he had been. He seemed to be far away, in another world."

Perhaps. Others wondered why he did not sit at the Islanders' table during the NHL Entry Draft. After all, it was his first draft as the club's owner. But he did show up at the Garden City Hotel on June 14, 1997, for coffee with Newsday hockey writer John Valenti.

The story that followed also seemed rather curious to me because it reflected the feelings of a man who didn't realize what a challenge he faced owning a hockey club. I remember reading the piece and feeling concerned.

"It's a tremendous amount of work," Spano told Valenti. "If I only knew," he added with a laugh.

A day later *Newsday,* the Long Island daily that most closely scrutinized the Islanders, splashed another story, on page A7. This time the owner was upbeat again, as was the article, proclaiming Spano as the man who would not only rejuvenate the franchise, but 70 precious acres in Nassau as well. Following a meeting between Spano and Morton Certilman, regional planning board chairman, *Newsday's* banner headline boasted, "Spano's Arena Vision—Islanders' Owner Unveils Scenarios for Nassau Complex."

At the meeting Spano offered blueprints for a mini-countdown-town with boutiques and second-story apartments as well as a Las Vegas–style entertainment complex. Certilman, who is highly regarded by Long Island politicians and business-people, also had doubts about Spano.

In retrospect, Certilman asserted that Spano didn't seem right from the start. "He would come to meetings," said Certilman, "and there would always be someone with him. The other guy would always do the speaking and Spano would hold his head down. That didn't feel right."

Certilman's comments sounded strangely similar to those I had heard from the Honda dealer, not to mention the observations of McMullen and Walsh. According to *Newsday* columnist James Bernstein, Certilman even related his feelings about Spano to Gulotta, yet after the mid-June meeting the Nassau county executive declared, "It's a clear signal that we are one step closer to reality. We now have serious parties at the bargaining table."

If Gulotta had only known.

The house of cards that Spano had erected at the corner of Hempstead Turnpike and Charles Lindbergh Boulevard was beginning to crumble, although the cracks were concealed temporarily by putty-hype. On June 18 Spano applied the putty in the form of a full-page ad in *Newsday*. It was billed as "An Open Letter from John Spano, Owner of the Islanders."

Thanking the fans for their support, Spano went on to push for a new facility and promised that he would work toward that end. He concluded:

> Although I'm in business to make money, that's not my only goal. I have taken on this great task of turning around a fallen franchise because my heart is part of the investment. As Jerry Maguire would say, "This is my mission statement," and it's a very personal one from

> me to you. It's the fans that drive me, and it's the fans
> who support us. I consider myself one of the fans.

It was signed, "Sincerely, John A. Spano."

The full-page ad cost $26,000 and was billed to the Islanders. It looked good, except for one thing. If John Spano was, in fact, owner of the Islanders, how come he wasn't representing them at the NHL's Board of Governors meeting, which was held a few days later at the league offices?

Instead of Spano, the Isles were represented by Jack Krumpe and Bill Skehan, both representatives of the Pickett regime. Something was fishy. And sure enough, before the week was up, Spano had taken his first, devastating media hit. Led by *Newsday*, New York's dailies revealed that Spano's hold on the Islanders was considerably more tenuous than imagined.

Spano had previously told Pickett that his lawyers had instructed Lloyds Bank in London to wire a major portion of the money owed the seller. It was to be $16.8 million—the first installment for the cable TV rights—but the money never arrived on its due date, April 7, 1997, and almost three months had elapsed without Pickett getting his cash. This significant development had been kept secret until June 28, 1997, when it was leaked to the press.

Newsday also excerpted a letter that a lawyer for Pickett had written to Bettman that added that Spano had made five false starts on the payment. Once, he stopped payment on a check and another time his check was returned because of insufficient funds. According to the letter, Spano had paid Pickett only $26,200. The letter asked Bettman to arbitrate the dispute. *Newsday*, which covered the Spano saga more intensively than any of the other papers, also reported that Bettman had "ordered" Spano not to touch team assets until the situation between himself and Pickett had been resolved.

Spano wasted no time responding to the allegations. He denied that access to the Islanders had been restricted by the commissioner. "It's true there are some outstanding issues between John Pickett and myself," said Spano. "And it will be settled between John and John."

But it wasn't as easy as all that. Like the sharks who swim off the coast of Long Island, the reporters smelled blood and headed directly to the prey. I was one of them and phoned Spano. It was to be our last conversation. He began by insisting that the brouhaha would be settled and that he would continue owning the team. Then, he added, "By the way, what are the people at SportsChannel saying about this?"

It seemed like an odd question at the time. "Do you mean the broadcasters?" I asked. "Those are the only people I've been talking to."

"No," he said. "The people upstairs."

I told him I didn't know but I added that one insider had told me the FBI would be entering the case. Incredible as the words sounded at the time, I felt obliged to mention this to him.

Spano reacted angrily, charging that rumors were flying all over the place and that this was as absurd as any of the others. I left it at that and said good-bye. But Spano wasn't through talking. On July 6, he issued a statement accusing Pickett of "political maneuvering and attempted character assassination as a way to regain control of the Islanders hockey team."

Pickett was astounded when the statement was read to him. He said he had just been on the phone with Spano but Spano never said he had issued the statement. "I had a nice conversation with him," Pickett revealed. "He said he was down in the dumps. He said, 'I want to get this thing resolved.' He told me, 'I want to be your friend. I don't want to hurt anybody.' All that and he had already sent this [anti-Pickett] statement? That takes a lot of nerve. Good God. This is just sick. This is the most bizarre thing of all. Releasing that statement, then calling me and crying on my shoulder. That is just the most unbelievable thing."

That is precisely what reporters such as yours truly and Peter Botte of the *New York Post* were thinking as more startling developments kept crackling like an Independence Day fireworks display. "If this indeed is the most well-orchestrated scam in sports history," wrote Botte, "at least give John Spano points for persistence."

In what was his last meaningful public utterance before the NHL stepped in to settle the war, Spano insisted that he did have "the resources to fund the deal." He added, "What John Pickett and his lawyers are not telling you is that last Wednesday [July 2, 1997], I was prepared to finalize our agreement and write the conclusion of the Pickett ownership era."

Meanwhile, Spano faced trouble at home. According to court documents, he was late on a $62,743.10 property tax bill on his University Park (Dallas) home, valued at about $2.5 million. *Newsday* further reported that Spano bounced a $1.6 million check to South African business partners.

Of all the conversations I had with Spano, the one that bothered me the most related to the tip I had received that the FBI was on his case. And, of course, Spano's heated reaction. But on July 9, 1997, I picked up a copy of *Newsday* and there was the blurb on the front page: "Feds Eye Spano." The story on page four carried the subhead, "Seek Documents on Allegations of Fraud."

As my friend, the late Harry Ornest liked to say, this story was straining credulity. Yet federal authorities would soon charge Spano with bank and wire fraud. *Sports Illustrated* would later compare him to "Forrest Gump and Ferris Bueller rolled into one."

Meanwhile, Bettman had issued a gag order as the dispute headed to arbitration. The commissioner had three options: (1) award ownership to Spano; (2) award ownership back to Pickett; or (3) award ownership to Fleet Bank of Boston, which lent Spano $80 million to purchase the team.

On Friday afternoon, July 11, 1997, Bettman convened a press conference at the NHL's Rockefeller Center office. I attended with a camera crew and wondered how the commissioner would handle this debacle. Already, his critics, such as David Shoalts of the Toronto *Globe and Mail*, were pointing a finger at Bettman.

"This is embarrassing to Bettman," wrote Shoalts, "because he is the person who brought Spano to the negotiating table with Pickett despite the fact a respected Dallas businessman, who knew Spano from his attempt to buy the Dallas Stars, had warned the commissioner to be cautious about him."

Bettman was unusually somber as he entered the crowded conference room. He was accompanied by Mike Milbury and NHL flack Arthur Pincus. Remembering what McMullen had told me, I asked Bettman if he recalled being warned by an owner about Spano. The commissioner said he couldn't recall it.

As the questions heated up, Bettman remained composed until Jason Diamos of the *New York Times* suggested that L'Affaire Spano gave the league a black eye.

Angrily, Bettman turned to Diamos and snapped, "I don't think it's a black eye for the league. It think it's a black eye for the owner."

How, he was quickly asked, could the league have given Spano its stamp of approval?

"That's an excellent question," Bettman shot back, "and one I have spent many hours of the night contemplating. Our sports league, like all others, has procedures. We all basically use the same ones in terms of investigating prospective owners from a personal, professional, and financial standpoint.

"We are not the CIA, but we have tools available to us. And the proper processes were complied with on more than one occasion. From a financial standpoint, at least six banks checked out Mr. Spano. If you ask me exactly what the true story is with respect to John, only John can answer that."

What Bettman did not say—but what was revealed two weeks later by Bloomberg News Service—related to the NHL's Spano probe.

BNS revealed that the NHL had paid a private detective about $525 to investigate Spano, adding that it was "much less than other major sports spend on background checks." The National Football League and Major League Baseball estimate that they spend more than $30,000 and as much as $50,000 to check the backgrounds of potential owners. Speaking for the NHL, Pincus countered that the league spent "much more" than $500 and used its staff as well as outside attorneys and investigators.

If anything good would come of the mess for Bettman, it was his assertion that the league would learn and move on. "It's unfortunate it happened," the commissioner concluded in a much more composed manner. "But it did. Maybe we'll never learn how or why it happened. But we're going to clean it up. And we're going to go forward. That's the best I can do."

Apart from his outburst at Diamos, Bettman orchestrated the disaster relief better than the captain of the *Titanic*. Reminded that he, Bettman, helped broker the Pickett-Spano marriage, the commissioner even managed to humor his way out of that irritating question.

"There's no doubt that I confirmed to John Pickett that John Spano was interested in the club," said Bettman, with the candor appreciated by the media. "When a married couple gets divorced, I'm not sure you blame the person who introduced them. I'm not the one who didn't make the payment. It happened. It's unfortunate it happened. I wish it didn't happen."

He also may have wished that the Spano story would go away but it continued to pockmark the sports pages through the summer of 1997. On July 17, federal authorities did, in fact, charge Spano with bank and wire fraud. Among other things, the Feds noted a letter from Lloyds, which was signed by a senior vice president. The name used was Clive Jones, of the trust department, who supposedly confirmed the existence of a $107 million trust set up for Spano. Lloyds replied that it did not employ a Clive Jones in such a job.

On July 23 Spano showed up in Uniondale, home of Nassau Coliseum, but not to visit his offices. He sat in federal court as a prosecutor described him as a fiscal fraud who lied, forged, and faked his way into buying the Islanders.

Assistant United States Attorney Joseph Conway described Spano's machinations as "a tangled web of lies and promises." If convicted, he was told, the erstwhile sports magnate would serve a minimum of three to five years in prison. Leaving the courthouse, a half-mile from the Coliseum, Spano said nothing to the media.

If anyone could smile, it was Pickett. Not only did ownership of the Islanders revert to him but, despite the convoluted Spano melodrama, the value of the franchise was escalating. "It won't be a fire sale," Pickett asserted. "The team value has increased substantially over the past year."

Not so coincidentally, Spano's value was decreasing by the week. Soon another devastating piece—this one by *Sports Illustrated*—hit the stands. Authored by Alexander Wolff, abetted by a quartet of reporters, the article was simply titled, "Busted."

Spano insisted in the SI exposé that his purchase was torpedoed in the spring of 1997 by a "significant" capital call and a note that came due. "I had to step up and pay," he insisted. "Timing wasn't good. I had hoped to then regroup and resolve my issue with Pickett. It had the ability to get resolved. I want to make that clear."

In fact, one NHL owner told me that Spano came "this close" to concluding the deal. But, Spano added, his "ability" to smooth out the rough fiscal edges disappeared when the angry-that-he-had-not-been-paid Pickett demanded NHL intervention and the media was leaked the news. "That made it impossible to settle because my reputation went from savior to devil," Spano said.

To which SI noted, "Listening to Spano and reviewing his actions, one wonders if there is any financial pickle he'd admit to having no 'ability to resolve.' If he had deluded the bank, Pickett, and the NHL, why wouldn't he delude himself?"

It was a good question. *Newsday*, in a brilliantly researched series collectively put together by Valenti, Steve Zipay, Ford Fessenden, John Riley, Ken Moritsugu, and Eden Laikin, among others, provided considerable light on Spano's murky waters.

"How did he do it?" *Newsday*'s team asked. "It is a tale of a remarkable and sometimes impenetrable mixture of fact and fiction that spanned Spano's lifetime. It is a tale of a career spent in the leasing business, which taught him how to turn bad credit risks into hard cash and put him in touch with a man who had a criminal record for fraud, and of lapses by a wide array of professionals—bankers, lawyers, accounting firms, and investigators—that allowed him nearly to succeed."

The confounding saga seemed to reach a denouement on October 7, 1997, when Spano appeared again in the Federal courthouse in Uniondale. Wearing dark glasses, he admitted that he had lied about his wealth so that he could buy the hockey club.

Spano pleaded guilty to four counts of fraud, which could have resulted in more than five years in jail and $2.75 million in fines. He allowed that he had used false documents to put his net worth at more than $200 million to fortify his ploys.

"I provided these false statements in order to commission the purchase of the Islanders and made it seem as if my net worth was $230 million," Spano declared.

U.S. District Judge Thomas C. Platt questioned Spano face-to-face and the would-be owner answered quietly:

"Did you participate in this scheme?"

"Yes."

"Knowingly?"

"Yes."

"Willfully?"

"Yes."

"Voluntarily?"

"Yes."

But by December 1997 Spano was not in jail. Instead, he backed out of plea agreements in three federal fraud indictments. Those agreements had protected Spano from a prison term of more than 63 months. However, if he was convicted at trial, the charges would carry prison terms ranging to more than 50 years.

Bloomberg News Service quoted Dallas attorney Bob Fink saying that the plea agreements were canceled because "it was John Spano's belief that he was getting a raw deal. We're pleading not guilty."

Fink added, "He doesn't think he defrauded banks, the Islanders, or anyone. His admission was very narrowly defined, and it's his position that he is not guilty of the essential elements. He's ready to fight this."

When Assistant U.S. Attorney Gary Brown was advised of the comments in New York, he responded in the manner of many who had followed the Spano serial from the beginning: "You've got to be kidding."

It was no joke. Nor was an example of gallows humor when, in mid-July 1998, it was revealed that Spano still was not in jail. Bloomberg News Service reported that he was cooperating in a widening probe of a Comerica, Incorporated, executive who helped him buy the Islanders.

Spano's motive, apparently, was to convince the Feds to trim his prison terms down. Agreeing that the several month delay was a long time for one who had pleaded guilty to await sentencing, Nicholas Gravante Jr. added that the case was complicated because it involved three jurisdictions.

There was nothing complicated at Nassau Coliseum. Pickett sold the Islanders for $195 million to a group headed by Phoenix Coyotes co-owner Steven Gluckstern and including New York real estate developers Howard Milstein and Stephen Ross.

I attended the press conference hailing the new ownership. Sure enough, Tom Gulotta was there once again wearing an Islanders jersey and vowing, with the ownership, that Nassau needed a new arena. By March 1998 David Seldin, formerly of the NFL's Jacksonville Jaguars, had taken over as president of the team.

"People want to feel good about the team they root for," said Seldin. "I don't think that feeling exists now."

Nobody could argue with him. The Spano disaster had torpedoed an already foundering franchise. In Gluckstern, Milstein, Seldin, and Company, the club seemed to have the fiscal wherewithal to compete with its rivals. How well the new leaders would fare remained a moot question.

As *Newsday* columnist Steve Jacobson so aptly noted, "Seldin will be judged like Red Adair, who puts out fires in oil wells. He doesn't have to stay forever to have done a job."

But between March 1998 and the start of the 1998–99 season, the Islanders franchise would suffer tremors that in some ways were even more disturbing than L'Affaire Spano.

The problems involved three major areas which were diverse yet inextricably linked to one another: Construction of a new arena, development of 70 acres around the proposed new arena, and the relationship between the Islanders and the SMG Corporation, which managed the Coliseum and many other arenas.

Having been burned by the Spano fiasco, Bettman had tightened requirements for clearing new owners but few doubted that Milstein's unit would pass muster. Milstein was a billionaire whose family operated a well-known real estate empire. Gluckstern, although not as wealthy, was highly regarded for his work with the Coyotes.

The suggestion at early press conferences was that the new owners had what Spano did not: the wherewithal to once and for all rejuvenate the ailing franchise. Unfortunately, there was a hitch before the team formally was signed over to them.

SMG—formerly Spectacor Management Group—had emerged as one of the nation's foremost arena operators and included Nassau Coliseum among its clients. At the time of the sale SMG requested that Pickett certify that SMG was a capable operator of the arena.

When certification was not granted, SMG asserted that it would block the sale, which it did. The impasse threatened sale of the team and once again Nassau County Executive Tom Gulotta took over. At a press conference which I attended at the county seat in Mineola, Gulotta criticized SMG and urged that the two parties huddle and hammer out an agreement.

SMG, headed by a pleasant Chief Executive Officer named Harold (Wes) Westley, was reluctant to consent to the sale without the missing approval stamp from Pickett.

A few days later, my producers, Joe Whelan and Kevin Meininger, tipped me off that a crucial meeting was being held at NHL headquarers in Manhattan. I phoned a publicist for Milstein-Gluckstern—they were being handled by the big-time Howard Rubenstein Associates—and the press agent, Gary Lewi, confirmed that the meeting would likely continue through the afternoon.

I hustled over to the NHL office where I met my cameraman and headed up to the 47th floor reception area. My hope was to hang out there until the conference ended and then confront the principals. But soon after I checked in with Lola, the affable NHL receptionist, Arthur Pincus, then Bettman's top public relations man, threw us out.

His attitude—hostile would be an understatement—surprised me, but I chalked it up to the secret negotiations which, I assumed, neither Bettman nor Pincus had wanted covered by any media types.

That put us in a pickle. My strategy was to camp out in the lobby and periodically take the elevator up to the 47th floor in the hopes of getting some information. Meanwhile, I had to hope that one of the many Rockefeller Center security guards wouldn't decide to toss my cameraman out of the lobby.

Our vigil proved fruitless for the first couple of hours. Pincus, when I did encounter him on one visit to the NHL waiting room, offered no clues. But I inadvertently stumbled on one bit of insight.

Prior to the assignment, I had no idea who Westley was or what he looked like. But on one of my trips to the 47th floor, I noticed several lawyerly types huddling in the waiting room. Ducking Pincus, I loitered as long as possible and finally heard one of the gentlemen say, "And by the way, Wes . . ."

That had to be Westley. I quickly introduced myself to him and asked if he would grant me an interview in the lobby once the meeting had ended. Cordially, he said that he would.

I returned to the lobby and continued the interminable wait, studying the faces of everyone who stepped out of the elevators.

Finally, at about 4:45 P.M. Pincus bolted from one of the elevators. As he headed for the exit, I asked him about the proceedings. He said they were continuing but offered little other information. "And don't bother going upstairs," he concluded before going through the revolving door.

We eventually intercepted Westley and got the story: a deal had been cut and everyone seemed happy. Milstein later confirmed it to me, as did Bettman. SMG, the new management, and Nassau County all seemed to be on the same page.

They were—for about three months. By late summer war had been declared again. This time ownership was claiming that Nassau Coliseum was "unsafe," putting the blame on SMG for the problem.

If that wasn't bad enough, Islanders' fans were shocked to learn that management had packed and left the Coliseum offices, moving to Manhattan, home of the hated Rangers, of all places.

Gulotta then summoned team and SMG representatives to his office in an attempt to hammer out a peace pact. Instead, the war escalated. Gulotta accused the Isles' owners of being "pigs at the trough" and at least temporarily allied himself with Westley and SMG.

Nassau County's first move was to challenge the club's shocking attempt to move home games out of the Coliseum to such proposed sites as Continental Airlines Arena in New Jersey and even Madison Square Garden.

In retaliation, Gulotta, after heated sessions in the county courthouse in Mineola, obtained an injunction against any move.

The defeat hardened management's position and when Gulotta invited Seldin to join the county in negotiations for a new arena, the club declined.

Meanwhile, the crisis-beaten Islanders fans were punch-drunk from the spate of crises. The season's opener drew a sparse crowd, while at least one bloc of fans began protesting against management.

Their protests were based in part on reports that Howard Milstein was bidding for the Cleveland Browns NFL franchise. Milstein's indication that he was willing to sell his interest in the hockey club further infuriated the fans. No less disconcerting was management's inability to sign the team's lone superstar, Zigmund Palffy, to a new contract.

By early winter, Milstein had lost his bid for the Browns, but turned his attention to the NFL's Washington Redskins.

Spano had not yet been sentenced by Christmas 1998, while the Islanders' fate remained as clouded as ever.

Bettman, who continued to meet regularly with Certilman through the autumn and early winter, finally brought Seldin back into the peace process.

On December 22, 1998, Islanders' followers received their Christmas present. A new $4 million scoreboard was unveiled and Palffy, signed to a long-term contract, returned to the lineup.

At this point in time, it would have been reasonable to assume that the Law of Averages would take over; that the endless chain reaction of Islanders ill-fortune would, once and for all, end. It was not unreasonable to assume that some semblance of sanity would prevail and that in 1999 the Islanders would emerge from their franchise funk.

The events that greeted the new year hardly supported this hope. Instead of getting better, things got worse with the franchise. On January 9,1999, Milbury made another trade that not only raised eyebrows but turned stomachs from Massapequa to Montauk. Bryan Berard, who had been touted as the "franchise" defenseman and who had been obtained at the expense of Wade Redden, already a star with Ottawa, was dealt to Toronto in exchange for goalie Felix Potvin. Understating the case, prize-winning *Newsday* columnist Johnette Howard described it as a "lousy trade." Others were more profane in their assessment of Milbury's move.

And why not?

A rookie-of-the-year only two years earlier, Berard had struggled through a sophomore slump in 1997–98 and now was finding himself. Besides, he was only 21 years old. Every hockey person knows that defensemen take longer to mature than others. Surely, Milbury—himself once a defenseman—must have known that.

And why would he want Felix Potvin?

The Maple Leafs, run by a Hall of Fame goalie named Ken Dryden, had given up on Potvin and signed Curtis Joseph as a free agent to replace him. If Potvin couldn't impress Dryden, why would he impress Milbury? It was a question that puzzled hockey people throughout the league.

"The surprise in a lot of people's minds," said Florida Panthers' president Bill Torrey, "was that whatever problems the Islanders were having, the opinion was that goal was not a major one."

Of course, Torrey was right. Tommy Salo was enjoying a solid season in the pipes for the Isles despite the fact that he resented

Milbury's persistent criticism. But Milbury's sin was more egregious than that. He had obtained Potvin as an obvious replacement for Salo yet he had failed to find a buyer for Tommy. Thus, the general manager was stuck with a pair of first-string goaltenders as well as second-stringer Wade Flaherty.

"Mike should have traded me before he had two of us," said Salo. "He pointed the finger at me for the team failings."

Meanwhile, Potvin had been AWOL from the Leafs for nearly six weeks because he was pushing for a trade. The goalie had not faced NHL pucks for nearly two months before he joined the Islanders. He needed at least two weeks to get himself back into game shape. Instead, Milbury had him start within forty-eight hours, insisting that Felix "said he wanted to play." *Newsday's* Howard called Milbury's rationale "a rather weak explanation." To put it kindly, Potvin was a disaster. After eight games, Felix had one win, six losses and a tie. He often looked like a sieve and his 3.86 goals against average reflected his ineffectiveness. Then, a strained groin sidelined him.

Surprisingly, the return of Palffy did little to improve the Isles' fortunes and the team in general seemed as if they had tuned out Milbury. On January 21st, Mike fired himself as coach. It had been expected in many quarters that he would insert Lorne Henning into his vacated position. Henning had NHL head coaching experience, was respected by the players and, of course, was a former Islander, a claim that could not be made by any other member of the coaching staff.

Despite the impressive credentials, Henning was bypassed in favor of Bill Stewart, one of the many assistants whose hard-nosed approach appealed to Milbury. Stewart wasted no time being his own man while embarassing his boss. He benched Potvin and restored Salo to the starting rotation. Tommy immediately responded with wins that were impressive enough to cause the media to wonder why Potvin was there in the first place. Forthright and tireless, Stewart proved to be a pleasant surprise. "With Milbury gone from the dressing room," said Salo, "it's more relaxed. Players are more confident. They're less afraid of screwing up anymore."

But there was no end to management screwing up, whether it was the previous one or the present. Incredibly, on February 18, 1999, John Spano re-emerged. A *Newsday* headline—EX-ISLES OWNER SPANO ARRESTED AGAIN—said it all. According to the Long Island daily, federal agents had arrested Spano on charges that he "may have violated conditions of his bail." The former Islanders' owner had posted a $3 million bond to avoid jail when he was arrested in July 1997. He had remained free in 1999 pending sentencing on six fraud counts.

Newsday: "Sources said Spano allegedly violated conditions of his bail by recently writing at least $10,000 in worthless checks in Philadelphia, where he has been living."

If Yogi Berra had been there, he might have uttered his deathless line, "It's *déja-vu* all over again."

As for the existing Milstein-Gluckstern ownership, there was no end to the turmoil. Howard Milstein, who had once vowed "to fill that empty place in every fan's heart with another Stanley Cup," seemed to be rapidly losing interest in his team. This was evident in January when Milstein made a second attempt to obtain a National Football League franchise. Along with a Bethesda, Maryland business partner, Daniel M. Snyder, Milstein had offered to purchase the Washington Redskins for $800 million.

It was a disturbing turn of events for those who had hoped that Milstein would pour his millions into the hockey club. "Palffy was a guy who was the team's bread-and-butter," said Islanders icon Clark Gillies, "and you don't want to give him an extra million dollars to play? Then Milstein turns around and tries to buy the Redskins for $800 million. There's something I'm missing in that whole thing." Had Milstein's Redskins bid been accepted, he would have been compelled to unload the Islanders because NFL owners are not allowed to own competing professional teams in NFL cities.

"There was a perception that Howard was not committed," said Mort Certilman, Nassau County's top negotiator. "The facts certainly make it look that way, don't they?"

It was difficult to obtain an assessment from the man himself. Milstein had three sets of public relations people on his payroll. But one of them, Chris Botta, tended strictly to Islanders team business and did that well. When it came to Milstein and the hockey club, the contact was Gary Lewi, working out of the Howard Rubenstein PR office.

Acting on orders from Milstein, Lewi repeatedly rebuffed interview requests for the owner. Once, the Islanders' beat-writers were preparing for a road game in Washington when they got wind of Milstein's plan to be in the capital on NFL business. They contacted the Milstein PR office and were told that Howard had changed his mind and was not coming.

But Milstein was there, holding court with the Washington media, unbeknownst to the New York press. "They totally lied to us," said *Newsday's* John Valenti, who had been covering the team for three seasons. "We were staying at a hotel only six blocks from where he was meeting the Redskins' press. They easily could have told us about it. But one of our guys (Marc Berman of the *New York Post*) was staying at a different hotel and he discovered the Milstein press conference, so he went over there. But they wouldn't let him (Berman) ask any questions." But Fox Sports New York's Mike Crispino also spotted Milstein and ambushed him with a cameraman. Virtually trapped, Milstein granted an impromptu interview that was aired that night during the broadcast.

Valenti said that the New York media corps later received an apology for the deception but the damage had been done and it would not be easily repaired. That night—at the Islanders–Capitals game—reporters from the *Associated Press*, *Washington Post*, and *Washington Star* gathered with the New York writers and were told about the day's events. Previously, they had welcomed Milstein's potential involvement in the Redskins and wrote glowing stories about his ownership possibilities.

"After what we told them that night," said Valenti, "they began looking at him in a different light."

It is difficult to assess precisely what effect the negative press had on Milstein's Redskins' bid. But this much is certain: In early February, it appeared as if his $800 million offer could not be refused. Once the media bad-mouthing began, stories started to appear suggesting that his ownership approval was not a sure thing at all. Eventually, it was reduced to an even money proposition as February gave way to March 1999.

Meanwhile, Milbury, once gregarious, sharp and witty, had become a turn-off for a couple of beat writers. After turning the coaching reins over to Stewart, Mike was rarely seen around the Coliseum. "He has become the Greta Garbo of the NHL," said Johnette Howard, alluding to the 1930s film star who proclaimed, "I vant to be alone!"

However, Milbury was sighted during an Islanders–Bruins game in Boston and was approached by a reporter who asked if he had a moment to talk.

Milbury: "Not even a second."

Finally, on March 3, 1999, after the team practice at Nassau Coliseum, Milbury emerged from media seclusion and met with reporters in an informal session. To the decade-long riddle: When are the Islanders ever going to snap out of it, Milbury supplied no answers. He couldn't because he remained trapped in a Catch-22 managerial position. Milstein still had not received approval for his Redskins' purchase and the GM had no idea whether he would be given a budget that would enable him to make significant deals before the March 23rd trade deadline.

But he did make a statement which, like others in the past, would come to haunt him. This time it was about his self-appointed coaching heir, Stewart. Milbury stated that he liked the job Stewart had been doing as a rookie coach with limited resources.

Then, a pause: "I don't think there's any question about his future here. I expect Stewart to be doing what he's doing right now (in March) in September (1999)."

As for Milbury's future, it amazed some that he had survived for so long with limited results. "Mike Must Go!" chants had been resounding through the Coliseum both before and after the coaching change. "His approval ratings have plummeted after trading Berard," said *Newsday*'s Mark Herrmann, who had been an Islanders' observer-reporter for more than a decade. "Milbury runs the risk of becoming known for one deal."

"I'm not happy with the results of our work here," Milbury acknowledged. "It's been under difficult circumstances, yes. But we've got to make it work somehow."

Even some of the press corps, who had been so negative towards him, managed a sympathetic response. "Rag on Milbury for the Berard trade," said the *Post*'s Marc Berman, "and skewer him for being a horrible coach earlier this season. But do understand the embattled GM never had a chance to work under an ownership situation that was not in flux."

As bad as it was, the ownership mess did not filter through and contaminate the dressing room. Players worked hard for Stewart and over a seventeen-game stretch compiled a 6–7–4 record. Captain Trevor Linden, who was sought by Ottawa in a pre-deadline trade, said "It's nice to be wanted but I don't want to leave Long Island."

Some wags questioned his sanity.

Other more serious types began pursuing a purchase of the team. If Howard Milstein was approved for his Redskins' bid, the Islanders would have to be sold. On March 2, 1999, it was reported that SFX Entertainment, a group which, among other things, was in the concert business, had made an offer for the Islanders.

April 7, 1999 was declared "D-Day For The Islanders" by Berman. Reflecting the feelings of team supporters and media, the reporter asserted that if Milstein's purchase of the Redskins was approved by the NFL at its meeting in Atlanta it would "hopefully be a day of celebration for all Isles' fans".

That morning I flew down to Georgia to cover the meeting for Madison Square Garden Network and Fox Sports New York. I had been advised by Gary Lewi that Milstein might not be there but my producer, Paula McHale, believed otherwise—and she was right. "Ambush him if you have to, but get him to talk," Paula advised.

For seven months, Milstein had been avoiding our interview requests and, except for the Crispino ambush in Washington, Howard had succeeded in avoiding us. This time I camped out with my cameraman outside the NFL meeting room on the second floor of the Westin Hotel at the Airport at 9 AM. The strategy was to bivouac at the top of the escalator which led to the meeting room. And if Milstein chose to take the elevator instead, we were in position to intercept him on the walk from elevator to the meeting.

After a two-hour wait, Milstein arrived. His limousine pulled up in front of the hotel and he strode in with an entourage that included Lewi and an attorney. But they fooled us. Instead of taking the escalator—as I had hoped—or the elevator to the second floor, they went all the way to the tenth floor where the group waited until summoned by the NFL.

Fortunately for us, Milstein emerged two hours later from the elevator and we were directly in his line. I grabbed the microphone from the cameraman and planted myself right in his path. Howard would have to run over me to get to the meeting room.

He spotted me and smiled.

"What's going to happen to the Islanders?" I shouted.

He smiled again. "Bill Stewart is doing a good job as coach," he replied. "We looked good last night." (The Islanders had won at home.)

Clearly, he would duck every question about his hockey club right up to the door. Oh, yes, we got him on camera but, no, he said nothing of substance.

An hour or so later, Milstein walked out of the meeting flanked by his aides. He headed directly to the escalator and rode down to the lobby. With the cameraman at my side, we dashed down and cornered him once more. I hurled questions, along with the other newsmen, but got no meat at all other than that Howard had lost his bid for the Redskins.

By this time the team was out of playoff contention and the rumblings of discontent became a roar. Even out-of-town papers such as the *Newark Star-Ledger* took note of the team's state of disarray. Respected reporter Rich Chere interviewed several Islanders icons and obtained many views, including dismay that Milbury had refused to use "consultant to the GM," Al Arbour, the team's most revered coach.

"Al has really been asked to stay out of the way," said Clark Gillies. "I think that's one of the stupidest things in the world. Here is one of the smartest hockey guys in the world, one of the most successful coaches ever, and you don't ask for any feedback from this guy?"

There was, however, feedback from an unusual source but in a different manner. As coach Bill Stewart gained confidence behind the bench, he became bolder with the New York media. At one point he suggested that he might not return to the club in 1999–2000 were he not satisfied with the direction management was heading.

On the Islanders' last visit to Manhattan, March 29, 1999, Stewart huddled with a couple of media friends—myself included—in the corridor outside his dressing room. He voiced concern that management's cost-cutting was hurting the team. I assumed that Stewart was speaking off-the-record. My colleague from Fox Sports New York, Joe Michelleti, was alongside me and I knew that he and Stewart were friends. Although neither of us discussed the comments, I decided they were meant as not-to-be-used on the air and I avoided any mention of them.

The game itself was another crusher for the Isles—and Stewart. Their arch-rival Rangers still were battling for a playoff berth and an Islander win would just about torpedo the Blueshirts. Through most of the game, Stewart's skaters battled hard and played even until late in the third period when Wayne Gretzky scored and won the game.

Frustrated, Stewart unloaded in his post-game press conference but this time it was not off-the-record. He told the gathering that management's budget cuts had hurt the team and, in so many words, charged that it could not compete on an even field with the other NHL clubs.

It was a direct indictment of his bosses and Stewart would pay. He was privately roasted by Milbury and Stewart responded with a public apology. The coach allowed that he had made a rookie mistake and asserted that he still wanted to coach the team next season.

A month later he was replaced by Butch Goring. That same day it was revealed, with a lower decibel level, that David Seldin had given up the presidency to John Sanders, a less confrontational type. Skeptics viewed the Goring hire as mere window dressing. "Now All They Need Is Players" was the post–press conference headline in *Newsday*.

But players were exiting rather than arriving. A few weeks after Goring landed on the Island, Trevor Linden departed. It was now clear that those who earlier had warned of a drastic payroll-cutting strategy were right. The 29-year-old captain was dispatched to Montreal for the tenth pick in the 1999 Draft.

One former owner who still had a small piece of the team told me that the objective was to pare the payroll down to a barebones $14 million from what had been a $24 million roster budget. And it was happening before our very eyes. The Islanders dropped the Lowell American League farm club—taken over by Los Angeles—in May and then zeroed in on the most sensitive cut of all, Zigmund Palffy.

There was no doubt that Palffy would go. Having claimed losses of $20 million for the 1998–99 season, management fingered him for the next deal. Despite his attractive scoring numbers, Palffy disappointed the team when his offense was most needed in each of the past two campaigns. Privately, some in management complained about his attitude not to mention his fat contract.

"We're commited to building a team around prospects," said Sanders as Palffy was shopped throughout the league.

The dismantling of the roster finally got the attention of the commissioner's office. During his annual state of the league address, Gary Bettman warned that he was carefully studying the Islanders' moves.

"We will monitor all trades and make sure that we are comfortable from a hockey standpoint that the team simply isn't being stripped down."

Bettman added that he wanted to ensure the fans were not being faced with a team only concerned about a "fire sale" and not the quality of its product. "We have got to go through a balancing act of making sure that the losses aren't so severe that the ownership doesn't give up."

No sooner had Bettman uttered those words, it seemed that Milbury was about to give up Palffy. On June 12, 1999 the New York papers reported that a Palffy-to-the-Rangers deal was in the works. On June 13, it was virtually confirmed: Palffy to Broadway, along with defenseman Rich Pilon for Todd Harvey, Niklas Sundstrom, the Rangers' first-round draft pick, $2.5 million cash and a collegiate prospect.

"Armageddon has struck the sinking Islanders," noted a saddened Marc Berman in the *Post*. "The unthinkable has occurred— the tragic trade of Palffy to the Rangers."

When I phoned Rangers GM Neil Smith that Sunday afternoon, he confirmed he had completed the deal with Milbury. I mentioned that I was going to discuss it on the MSG Network's Sports Desk show that night.

"Might Bettman hold it up?" I asked.

Smith said he doubted that the commissioner would reject it. He added that an announcement should be forthcoming within forty-eight hours. The newspapers had treated it as a *fait-accompli* and some reporters already had fully analyzed the pros and cons of the exchange in print.

Newsday columnist Joe Gergen was among several who deplored the deal. "The Islanders are not only giving comfort to the enemy," said Gergen, "but supplying the Rangers with a successor to the retired Wayne Gretzky."

The Isles public relations department already had a release prepared announcing the Rangers' trade but it never was released. Somehow, the deal was finally pulled off the table. Instead, the Islanders turned to Los Angeles for an exchange that would not include NHL caliber players.

Meanwhile, criticism mounted. "Isles' Owners Deserve an Empty Coliseum" shouted a *Post* headline. "Season-ticket packages have been mailed out," wrote Berman. "The owners should recall them and slash the prices to make up the nearly $10 million worth of salary the Isles dumped."

But through the whole ugly mess, there always seemed a flicker of hope. On June 22, 1999, negotiations for funding a new arena to replace Nassau Coliseum resumed. It included the NHL commish.

"I would characterize the meeting as constructive and cordial," Bettman said, "but there's still some work to be done and the parties are going to get together in the near future. We're trying to get everybody on the same page so we can move forward. I'm not going to get into the specifics."

Even *Newsday* got into the act with a lead editorial urging the county to do everything possible to keep the team.

Just days later the Islanders did extraordinarily well at the entry draft, picking three top-rated prospects, Tim Connolly, Taylor Pyatt and Branislave Mezei. For the moment, at least, the future looked wonderfully bright, particularly with the young nucleus.

"If the organization gets a new building and gets sorted out at the top, it could be a great team to play for," said Trevor Linden.

To which, *Sports Illustrated*'s Kostya Kennedy replied, "Yes, and with balmy breezes and fruit-bearing trees, the Arctic could be a great place to live."

Anyone who has studied the Islanders over the past five years will attest that stranger things have happened.

The Byzantine twists and turns continued through the summer of 1999. Suddenly, in July, the Islanders indicated that ownership was willing to completely finance a new arena in exchange for the right to manage it for all events. But before such approval would be granted, the team wanted Nassau county's help in buying out its lease with the SMG management group.

FROM ALAN EAGLESON TO BOB GOODENOW
How the Players' Association
Became an NHL Power Broker

One would be hard-pressed to find a more powerful figure in any realm of sport than Alan Eagleson, which is why his jailing early in 1998 remains to this day a stunning event in hockey annals.

Consider his career, one in which he has constantly defied his critics.

When others argued that it was impossible, the hyperamiable Toronto lawyer organized the first National Hockey League Players' Association in 1967.

Although NHL owners insisted that they would have no dealings whatsoever with agents, Eagleson became a virtual one-man cartel in the representation of stickhandlers in the late sixties and into the seventies.

The peripatetic—and indefatigable—Eagleson orchestrated the first international tournaments between NHL stars and the Soviet National Team. He organized other similar events in North America before his downfall. The Eagle was beloved and admired by many until his plunge from favor.

Who was most responsible for exposing Eagleson is, at the very least, debatable, but there were several protagonists. Bobby Orr, who had been the Eagle's top client until the Hall-of-Famer got the idea he was being bilked, certainly is the marquee name.

Agents Rich Winter and Ron Salcer began the pursuit of Eagleson before any of their colleagues. From a journalistic viewpoint, only one name really matters and that is Russ Conway, sports editor of the *Lawrence Eagle-Tribune*, a suburban daily outside Boston. Conway ventured where others feared to tread and it won him a nomination to the Hockey Hall of Fame.

"Eagleson," Salcer recalled, "was a man who was more powerful than the prime minister of Canada. He dealt by intimidation and fear."

Like myself, Salcer felt the heat of Eagleson's wrath in the early eighties after Salcer had become a players' agent. Ron met and befriended a few Los Angeles Kings players and was amazed at how shabbily the Eagleson-run NHL Players' Association treated its clients.

"He started with good intentions," said Salcer. "He launched the NHLPA and he united the players, but he just got too powerful and too greedy." Salcer decided to pursue the issue and jetted to an NHLPA meeting in Las Vegas. When he attempted to sit in as a concerned agent, Salcer was asked to leave by Sam Simpson, Eagleson's aide-de-camp.

Pressed to learn why he was being evicted, Salcer was told that agents were verboten at the NHLPA conference.

"Isn't Alan Eagleson an agent?" Salcer inquired.

He was told that the Eagle was a special case. Which was true to a certain extent. At the time Eagleson was the most special hockey man in the world, and if you didn't believe it, any one of a dozen club owners could confirm the point.

"That's when the seed was planted," Salcer revealed. "Over the next six or seven years, I realized I wasn't getting the support I needed to do the best job I could for my players. I'd call Eagleson and ask to speak to him and the answer was, 'He's in Europe doing something for international hockey.'

"I was hearing horror story after horror story. I watched players' salaries go up maybe five percent every year, and we never knew who was making what. They'd say eight guys were making X amount and 72 were making the median. But nobody knew who was making what.

"Eagleson said to players, 'You're making more money than your parents. Don't rock the boat.' I felt if I was going to continue as an agent, there would have to be dramatic changes."

Others felt likewise. Suspicions rose about profits that Eagleson allegedly was pulling in from the Canada Cup tournament and other arrangements whose details somehow eluded the players.

"Year after year," said Hall of Fame defenseman Brad Park, "we played all those Canada Cup games for nothing because Al told us the money was all going to our pensions. It was a lie."

Undaunted, Salcer became a ferret on the spoor of a hot story.

Convinced of Eagleson's double-dealing, Salcer visited teams across the country. When he came to Boston, the agent was threatened with eviction from Boston Garden by Bruins general manager Harry Sinden.

By 1989, Salcer and Winter believed they had enough evidence to make a case before the NHL Players' Association. The NHLPA was meeting in West Palm Beach, Florida, and Salcer asked to address the stickhandlers.

When Eagleson objected, defenseman Marty McSorley intervened, and the players heard a damning appraisal of their union's operation. Charges against Eagleson included diversion of money from dasher-board advertising and improperly lending NHLPA pension money to friends, among other accusations.

"Sometimes," said New York Rangers player representative David Shaw, "we don't know whether Eagleson is representing us or the management."

The Eagle was able to temporarily retain his nest because the union's executive committee was top-heavy with Big Al's pals. "Sure, he rubs some people the wrong way," said defenseman Brad Marsh. "But he always had the best interest of hockey at heart."

In January 1993 the Royal Canadian Mounted Police (RCMP) began its own investigation, which surprised many who believed that north of the 49th parallel, Eagleson would remain immune from authorities.

Early in 1993, Conway's *Eagle-Tribune* revealed that Eagleson had been reimbursed more than $62,000 for personal expenses from 1987 to 1989 in a story based on NHLPA documents. "We never knew any of that information," said goalie Andy Moog, an NHLPA vice president.

Citing advice from his attorneys, Eagleson rebutted U.S. authorities who sought him for extradition. "We're not going to have a trial by ambush," insisted his lawyer, Brian Greenspan. In December 1995, U.S. prosecutor Paul Kelly filed a three-volume extradition request with the justice department in Ottawa. In the document Kelly noted that Canada and the United States normally extradite criminals back and forth and he expected delivery of Eagleson. But it never happened. The anti-Eagle claque soon discovered that Alan's connections in Canada—not to mention the NHL—ran deep.

"For two years," said Kelly, "the extradition request remained in limbo. It never left the minister of justice to be publicly filed. We urged the Canadian side to act on it, but we heard nothing from them. Nothing. There was no more the United States could do in terms of getting Mr. Eagleson back to the United States, short of coming into Canada and kidnapping him."

Meanwhile, the Eagle's wings kept getting clipped. He lost a lawsuit filed by former Bruin Mike Gillis over a disability-insurance claim. This put Eagleson on the hook for almost $750,000. Steadfast, Eagleson confessed nothing.

On a visit to Toronto, I asked a friend, Robert Johnstone, who had been a crime reporter for the *Toronto Star*, how he explained the Eagleson legal strategy. Johnstone said he believed that the Eagle's Canadian attorneys were exploring every conceivable loophole to simply delay and delay and delay until the former power broker simply had lived out a long life.

But not long after I had returned to New York, Eagleson's security wall began betraying fissures. On December 3, 1996, the RCMP charged Eagleson with eight counts of fraud and theft.

What amazed many Eagleson watchers was that the Eagle remained very public and seemingly reassured about his status. "In many ways," commented *Maclean's* magazine of Canada, "it seemed that right up until he was taken to jail, Eagleson was still acting as though he was above the law."

Certainly, the Eagle was encouraged by his many cronies, some of whom unabashedly remained loyal to the discredited union leader. For example, former Canadian prime minister John Turner noted, "I have known Alan Eagleson for 20 years personally and professionally and I hold him in high regard. All my experience with him attests to his good character."

Many NHL executives stood shoulder to shoulder with the Eagle. "I am very proud to be a friend of Alan Eagleson," said Philadelphia Flyers general manager Bob Clarke. "This man has been the best leader hockey ever had. He has done more for hockey players and their families than anyone else has ever done."

Clarke would have had a hard time convincing Orr, Park, or Glen Sharpley of that. Not to mention the likes of Ed Westfall and other former NHL players who showed up at Courtroom 8 in Boston's Federal Court on January 6, 1998, for an event that they had waited years to finally happen.

The FBI had taken its mug shot and fingerprinted him as part of the booking process. According to one agent, the Eagle examined the fingerprinting equipment as if it were some exhibit. "He just didn't get it," the FBI man observed. "He doesn't realize he's a criminal."

When the 48-year-old reporter, Conway, entered the courtroom, the entourage of NHL players hailed him with a round of applause. "It was like being applauded in church," said Eagleson's most persistent literary nemesis. "It was embarrassing."

Embarrassing or not, the kudos came from the heart. Conway, who deserved a Pulitzer Prize for his work but was only a runner-up, had become the hero to both the hockey media and the NHLPA alike. The results would soon prove why.

Eagleson pleaded guilty to three counts encompassing a wide range of fraud and paid $1 million restitution. He wore a green blazer, and carried a raincoat over his right arm as he was escorted by two FBI agents to the courthouse. The grey raincoat succeeded in concealing the handcuffs underneath.

"There's the sonofabitch now," snapped Orr, as the Eagle entered the courtroom.

Other players felt the same feeling of revulsion. Westfall, with whom I had broadcast Islanders games for 18 years, had told me he couldn't wait to attend the proceedings. His enmity for Eagleson—if possible—matched that of Orr and Park.

Westfall, like the others, stared intently as Judge Nathaniel Gorton asked Eagleson how he pleaded to the first felony count of stealing thousands of dollars from international hockey that was headed for the players' pension fund.

Quickly, the Eagle muttered, "Guilty."

This was small solace to Park, who once escorted Eagleson across the Luzhniki Palace rink during the 1972 Canada-Russia series. This was after the Eagle had been apprehended by Russian guards after charging a goal judge.

Thinking of that pension fund, Park knew that his return was $13,000 (Canadian) while Eagleson's pension was $50,000 (United States). "It sickens my stomach to think of it now," said Park.

Hall-of-Famer Frank Mahovlich had jetted down from Toronto and listened as Eagleson continued pleading guilty to the second and third charges. "I would not have been surprised if he had turned around and laughed at us," said Mahovlich.

Actually, Eagleson did oblige. In the courtroom, former Maple Leaf Carl Brewer stood tall and observed, "Thank God for America, because this never would have happened in Canada." The Eagle responded with a laugh.

By the time Eagleson had uttered his third "Guilty" plea, Brewer had tears in his eyes while ex-Bruin Terry O'Reilly wore a grin on his face. Orr, who, ironically, had become a major players' agent, displayed little emotion. Park claimed it was because the Bruins' hero felt bad about the entire episode.

"Bobby was the guy who brought Al in," said Park, "and Bobby is the guy who personally lost the most."

John Bucyk, a teammate of Orr and more recently a Bruins broadcaster, also was in the courtroom. "The FBI wasn't wrong," said Bucyk, "and neither was anybody else who checked into his past. He abused our trust as players and he abused the very game itself."

Salcer, who had been so instrumental in the development of the case, put it simply: "I didn't do it because of any personal animosity. Eagleson damaged a lot of people's lives. For me, the satisfaction is, the story is out and he's on the front page of every newspaper in Canada as a criminal."

The scene at U.S. Federal Court was a major news event but nothing compared to what happened the next day in a Toronto courtroom when the onetime Canadian icon pleaded guilty to another three charges of fraud. This time the 64-year-old Eagleson's wife, Nancy, attended in the second row of the public gallery.

Wearing his Order of Canada pin in his left lapel, Eagleson endured the two-hour episode. It concluded with an 18-month sentence at Ontario's Mimico Correctional Centre. Before leaving, Eagleson, standing at the defense table, offered an apology for his crimes to several players.

One of them was Glen Sharpley, whose career ended abruptly in 1981 after a serious eye injury. After the Eagle's guilty plea in Boston, the judge ordered that $15,000 of Eagleson's $697,810 fine in U.S. dollars be handed over to Sharpley.

"Even though he pleaded guilty," said Sharpley, "I don't know if he really thinks he's guilty. I'm not sure he gets it."

Eagleson was incarcerated in a jail that was designed for white-collar and other nonviolent criminals and, by Canadian standards, is a medium-security penitentiary.

"In a move that astonished veteran courtroom observers," wrote Jane O'Hara of *Maclean's*, "he was not handcuffed as he was led away from his Toronto court appearance."

One such observer was Toronto *Sun* columnist Christie Blatchford, who asserted that the most galling aspect of the sentencing was his escaping the handcuffs:

> An accused is handcuffed after he has been convicted; it is the signal to the public at large that he is now a guilty person, and that his punishment by state has begun. It is an integral part of sentencing, and an important one, because it is a public rebuke. Eagleson wasn't handcuffed; to the bitter end, he received the special treatment he has sought and expected all his working life.
>
> He also wore, in both courtrooms, the Order of Canada pin of which he was so proud and of which he has subsequently been stripped. It was a gesture of monumental egoism, I thought, as sure an indication as his

> mumbled, clearly insecure one-line "apology" for any
> harm he might have caused or his breezy grin that
> while he may have pleaded guilty, he sure as hell didn't
> feel it.
>
> In my view he was never sorry. I don't think to this
> day he feels he did anything wrong or remotely out of
> line, let alone criminal.

The Edmonton-based agent, Winter, who had been so vilified by Eagleson in the early eighties, said he would not be satisfied with the legal process until players who were bilked of money were compensated. "This guy destroyed the lives of a lot of people," said Winter. "Until they get their money, I won't be happy."

Eagleson shared a one-story dormitory with 27 other convicts. He was assigned to office-cleaning duties and was allowed two visits a week. While he served his term, he remained as much a focus of controversy as he had when he was an ordinary civilian.

No sooner was he put behind bars, there were accusations that he was getting celebrity treatment. "He jumped to the front of the line," one officer said. "He got preferential treatment."

Another guard claimed that the processing for Eagleson was done in record time. "It was the fastest classification in the history of classifications," said another officer.

Corrections Ministry spokesman Ross Virgo countered that the jail, which had a capacity for 525, was overflowing with 561 inmates, and new arrivals such as Eagleson had to be dealt with quickly.

Once that issue faded away, yet another erupted that caused endless debate among hockey people across Canada and parts of the United States. Because Eagleson had been jailed for committing frauds against the game that once made him rich, should he now be removed from the Hockey Hall of Fame?

Since the jailing he had been stripped of his Order of Canada and drop-kicked out of the Canadian Sports Hall of Fame. Overtures to Eagleson suggesting that he voluntarily leave the Hockey Hall of Fame did not work.

Under pressure, leaders of the hall decided to hold a vote on March 31, 1998, on whether to expel Eagleson.

The date was significant because it also was Gordie Howe's 70th birthday. On March 6, 1998, Howe had notified Hall of Fame Chairman Scotty Morrison by letter that he would dissolve his membership in the shrine unless Eagleson was removed. Once Howe's decision was made public, it seemed to inspire a groundswell of support from other legends.

Bernie Geoffrion, Andy Bathgate, Mike Bossy, Johnny Bower, and Dickie Moore were among 18 NHL aces who declared that they would leave the Hall of Fame as well if Eagleson won approval from the 18-member board of directors. Even the normally apolitical Jean Beliveau took an anti-Eagleson stance.

"He's a self-admitted felon," said Beliveau. "He's guilty. He admitted it himself. Why should he be there now? I don't want to be associated with a liar. He lied and now he has to pay for it."

Morrison allowed that losing so many players would devastate the hall. "I suppose the hall could survive," said Morrison, "but there are some great, great names on that list. We would hate to see them leave."

One Hall-of-Famer remained steadfast at Eagleson's side. Bob Clarke, who had been NHLPA president under Eagleson from 1976 to 1979, insisted that the disgraced NHLPA head not be pushed out. Five other prominent ex-players—Ken Dryden, Bob Gainey, Jacques Laperriere, Serge Savard, and Darryl Sittler—rode the fence.

Savard: "He's a friend, he's in jail. I'll respect the decision of the committee that is voting whether or not to keep him in the hall."

More typical was the reaction of Hall-of-Famer Alex Delvecchio: "He pleaded guilty. If he's an embezzler, a criminal, the way he's treated people and abused their trust, he doesn't deserve to be in the Hall of Fame. Common sense says he should be removed."

Or Gerry Cheevers: "He's got to be out; that's all there is to it!"

Or Carl Brewer: "Alan Eagleson never had friends. All he had were dupes and stooges."

The 18 board members were expected to wrestle hard with the demands as well as some 30 letters that were submitted testifying to Eagleson's good character. Brian Greenspan, Eagleson's lawyer, wrote Morrison indicating that his client would not resign.

"It's going to be a bloodbath in there," predicted Eagleson's NHLPA successor, Bob Goodenow. "This is a sensitive issue. Al Eagleson still has a lot of friends."

That he did, but there weren't enough to persuade him to take the Hall of Fame fight to the limit. Just six days before the climactic vote was to be taken, Eagleson sent a letter of resignation to Morrison, resigning his place as a builder of the sport.

"It is with great personal sadness and regret that I advise you of my decision to resign," Eagleson wrote.

He added that he was "deeply aware of those voices that have been raised against my continuing presence in the Hockey Hall of Fame. I have always had the greatest personal respect for the career achievements of all the players whose contributions have been recognized by election to the Hall of Fame."

Many were surprised that a battler such as Eagleson would cave in as he did. "We certainly weren't expecting this," said Morrison, "but it is in the best interest of hockey and the Hall of Fame."

Eagleson's plaque was removed from the honored members wall amid applause from the hockey community. "It was the only thing he could do," said hockey broadcaster and former NHL coach Don Cherry. "He saw the handwriting on the wall and he did the right thing."

Sharpley: "They've stripped him of all of his honors. He's less than a common man. He's a common criminal."

Sensitive to the needs of unknown players as well as superstars, Conway was quick to recall Eagleson's insensitivity to a second-line defenseman named Ed Kea, whose career was destroyed by a 1983 injury.

"The man [Kea] was badly injured," Conway said. "He had brain surgery and he came out of it not only unable to play hockey again, but unable to work. In fact, he'll never work again. Eddie had a family with four kids. It's not like hockey players have brain surgery every year but Eagleson didn't have the common decency to go visit the family. He wouldn't help them in the insurance process. He was gone. Crush the cigarette pack. Throw it out. Next!"

While Eagleson served his sentence, his enemies continued to question his dealings. A vexing question was whether the Eagle had somehow hidden a large sum of money although he was claiming that his fortune had been wiped out. Carl Brewer, for one, maintained that Eagleson's assets still went as high as $50 million. *Maclean's* magazine theorized that only the tip of the financial iceberg had been grazed.

"This is a labyrinth," said one investigator. "It's like one of those video games in which the doors open, and you go through, and then they slam the door shut, and you don't know where you are. You cannot tell where real money is changing hands or what is only paper. I don't think there's any question that the assets are there. It's a question of who's going to be sharp enough to find them and under what name."

In his continuing probe, Conway asserted that Eagleson "still may be a millionaire." He added, "There has never been a full accounting of all the money earned by the international competition [Canada Cup] that Eagleson ran as his personal fiefdom with the blessing of his friends in the NHL and the Canadian government."

Greenspan countered that Eagleson was broke. "He needs a job to support his old age pension," the attorney claimed.

On July 7, 1998, Eagleson was paroled after serving only six months of his eighteen-month sentence for fraud. He smiled as he left Mimico Correctional Centre but made no comment to reporters as he strode briskly from the jail and entered a waiting vehicle.

Not surprisingly, another hue and cry was heard over the seemingly brief incarceration. "There's no justice," said Hall-of-Famer Bobby Hull. "That guy should have been pitched in the cell and the key thrown away. I don't know who allowed him to walk but all he got was a slap on the wrist."

Through the summer of 1998, Conway continued to be the journalistic machine that kept the Eagleson watch going. Russ, whom I had interviewed on television several times during the 1997–98 NHL season, seemed satisfied when we chatted in July 1998 about Eagleson's walk out of jail.

"Was my eight years work worth it?" he asked me rhetorically. "I'm pleased that three important things were accomplished through all this business.

"First of all, the players were able to get back their pension money. Secondly, we helped expose the cancer of the sport. And, finally, Eagleson ejected himself from the Hall of Fame.

"I could also add that he was dropped from the Order of Canada, that he was disbarred as a lawyer, that he pleaded guilty to theft, that he still will have to report to a probation officer for a year, and that he's forbidden to leave Ontario for a year . . . If we were keeping score, it would be 14-to-nothing!"

One thing is certain, Eagleson's departure was a sweet use of adversity for the NHLPA. Bob Goodenow studied the Eagleson Era and revamped the NHL Players' Association into a formidable operation.

"Everything with Bob is disclosure-disclosure and information-information," said goalie Andy Moog, a prominent member of the NHL Players' Association. An obvious result is the average player's salary. In December 1998 it had reached an all-time high of $1.2 million.

The endlessly orbiting salary average seemed unreal in terms of the business facts of life. Team income simply was not keeping pace with salaries and even winning teams suffered with losing bottom lines.

According to *Forbes* magazine, the 1997 and 1998 Stanley Cup champion Detroit Red Wings were $19 million in the red. And this a team that sold out every one of its home games. Which prompted the question: How could such a successful team lose money? Sports industry expert Dean Bonham found the answer as easy as others: "Even if you garner revenues from post-season (playoffs) you're still in jeopardy of losing money because of small TV revenues and escalating salaries."

Through 1998, Bettman kept insisting that the collective bargaining agreement which he had crafted in 1995 would work. Most observers—not to mention his bosses, the owners—believed him for the first three years of the CBA's existence. But by the end of the Olympics in Nagano, more and more critics came out of the woodwork. Average salaries had climbed 59 percent since 1995. Smaller market clubs were in greater jeopardy than ever.

"It's an issue the league has to deal with quickly or teams like Buffalo and Pittsburgh won't survive," said Bonham. "The NHL needs to get a collective bargaining agreement similar to the NBA's."

The problem was that Bettman and Goodenow had worked out an extension of the CBA through 2004 to allow NHLers to participate in the 1998 Olympics. By the middle of 1999 many league executives were whispering that the league couldn't wait until 2004 and a win-at-all-costs lockout would be necessary much sooner.

Not even the much ballyhooed NHL television deal with Disney-owned ESPN and ABC, which kicks in during the 1999–2000 season, will alleviate the fiscal problems. Compared to huge fees obtained by baseball, football and basketball, the ESPN-ABC deal, which pays $600 million over five years, compared to Fox's five-year, $155 million pact, is a drop in the bucket.

No less depressing were the NHL's TV ratings in the United States. Fox Sports and ESPN displayed mediocre numbers in the 1999 playoffs although Fox had spent several years and millions of dollars trying to make the game more TV-friendly. After a hopeful start in its first year when the ratings peaked at 2.1 in 1996, it slipped to 1.4 Nielsen during the regular 1998–99 season. ESPN and ESPN2's regular season ratings fell to a 0.6 and 0.3 rating.

To Fox's credit, it upped its regular season coverage from six weeks in 1996 and 1997 to eleven weeks of coverage leading into the playoffs in 1998. This expansion of coverage was considered a bonanza for NHL exposure. Unfortunately, the Fox coverage ended in June 1999. At that point ABC shocked the hockey world with an announcement that it would only televise four weeks of the regular 1999–2000 season; a reduction of seven weeks from the Fox slate. That is the absolute minimum required by the contract.

"Regardless of what our ratings were, we were the best platform the NHL has ever had," said Ed Goren, co-executive producer of Fox Sports. "With ABC doing four weeks, it will reduce hockey's exposure to the country. I'm not sure four games on ABC serve hockey. There just aren't enough hockey fans or national personalities to drive the sport."

In its attempt to rationalize low ratings and a general perception that hockey is a relentlessly regional sport, the NHL put on a happy face. Steve Solomon, the league's chief operating officer and official who dealt most closely with the networks, argued that viewership was still recovering from not seeing hockey on network television until Fox arrived to telecast the games.

"If you watch your team only on local television, you get accustomed to not watching hockey as a national sport," Solomon insisted. "People are less interested in the sport nationally if their team is out of the playoffs."

As the Fox pact wound down, NHL officials began taking subtle potshots at the network, claiming that it failed to promote hockey in the manner that was anticipated. Solomon claimed that an ABC-ESPN cross-promotion will be a big boost starting in 1999–2000.

"We were never fully satisfied with the amount of support the sport has received and part of that was the reluctance of Fox to cross-promote with ESPN," Solomon added.

Perhaps, but the fact is Fox pushed hockey with $25 million in promotion before ABC-ESPN came along and it didn't work.

"Furthermore," said *Boston Herald* sports-television critic Jim Baker, "all the cross-promotion that ESPN and ABC can muster won't make hockey healthy on TV."

Other respected sports-TV critics echoed Baker's theme; that no matter what ESPN-ABC may do, it won't change the ratings.

"Why doesn't hockey present well on TV?" asked Bob Wolfley of the *Milwaukee Journal Sentinel*. "For me, it's the same reason we talk about the camera 'liking' certain actors. Either the camera likes you or it doesn't. The camera just doesn't like hockey."

At least Fox tried to get its cameras to like hockey. It went so far as to put a computer-generated trail on the puck for easier viewing and it put NHL games on prime time. It helped create the single highest rating for an NHL game in the life of the deal: 4.1 for the 1996 All-Star Game.

"A 4.1 rating in the world of prime time," said Wolfley, "is pathetic." Or, half of what the World Wrestling Federation draws on Monday night.

Bettman's positive spin on the CBA finally ended during the 1999 Stanley Cup Finals. As more and more owners began to criticize the NHL's sorry economic state, the commissioner finally acknowledged that the inflation could not continue at its run-away rate, particularly since the average salary had climbed now to $1.4 million.

"Players' salaries for the last two years have grown faster than our growth in revenues," Bettman said in his annual state of the game message. "In the final analysis that is not going to continue forever.

"When the time comes and we need a new CBA we will have a system that is sensible and enable all our clubs to be competitive."

As always, Bettman's words sounded good but they didn't jibe with the real world. His opposite, Goodenow, was playing it cool. With agents reaping record profits, Goodenow remained firmly in control of the NHLPA with only an occasional challenge from maverick representative Rich Winter. When the latter requested a rump gathering of reps before the annual NHLPA agents' meeting in June 1999, only a handful attended.

Meanwhile, some owners finally were willing to stand up and be counted on the issue of budget balancing. Their theme essentially was this: We have a right to break even in this business just as players have a right to earn a substantial living. Devils' owner John McMullen and his Bruins' counterpart Jeremy Jacobs were the most vocal on the issue.

Jacobs shrugged off criticism that challenged his refusal to pay crazy money in the manner of teams such as Dallas and Detroit. "As long as I own this team," said Jacobs, "it will make money. We are a business. I'm not going to go out and do what some of these owners have done in this league, spend so foolishly that they have put the league in terrible shape."

In a face-to-face encounter, McMullen told Goodenow that the NHLPA leader was doing too good a job for his players. Killing the goose that laid the golden egg was not the best policy to pursue, McMullen insisted.

McMullen and Jacobs both were well aware that the NHL would lose about $225 million in 1999. Their position was as plain as a hockey puck; overspending will destroy the league.

"Colorado was sold because the owner spent so much money he couldn't afford it anymore," Jacobs concluded. "Abe Pollin sold in Washington because he lost so much money. If I do what those owners have done, in five years I would have to sell this team myself. I couldn't afford to be able to keep it."

As salaries rose, so did ticket prices. In some arenas, the tickets were so expensive that longtime fans in the lower-middle and lower-class categories were priced right out of the building. As more and more tickets went to the corporate clientele, fan ambience changed from blue collar to grey suit.

Likewise, the league ambience continued changing from north to south. In the fall of 1999 Atlanta's Thrashers would make their debut while the Carolina Hurricanes would move into a brand, new Raleigh arena. Nashville's 1998–99 debut was a huge success and the league expected expansion franchises yet to come—in Columbus, Ohio and St.Paul, Minnesota—to be equally well-received.

But these additions have to be contrasted with the grim situation north of the border where four of Canada's six teams are in particular jeopardy and the Maple Leafs' player budget is an insane $52 million in Canadian currency. Exorbitant taxes, unfavorable exchange rates, and unheeded calls for community help threaten the Flames, Oilers, Senators and, yes, even the once mighty Montreal Canadiens.

"Hockey has an uncertain future in Montreal," said *Sun Media* reporter Yvon Pedneault, a long-time Canadiens commentator. "The Canadiens are badly scarred. The infatuation of old has vanished. The fans' interest is dwindling from year to year. The Canadiens, formerly a model team, now has to live at the pace of small market teams."

Hall-of-Famer Serge Savard, a former Canadiens general manager and now a successful Montreal businessman, echoed the pessimism.

"The hockey situation in Montreal is precarious," said Savard. "I don't think small markets will be able to resist very long to soaring salaries. It's unthinkable. Who wants to buy a team and a sports center when teams need to operate with a $40 million payroll to stay competitive? It's madness."

It is a madness created by the 1995 collective bargaining agreement which was designed by Bettman and thought to be workable by the commissioner and most of his owners. But apart from a McMullen or Jacobs, most owners capitulated to pressures around them.

"Yes, salaries are out of line," conceded Maple Leafs' alternate governor Brian Bellmore, "but it's a reality of trying to compete."

The Avalanche succumbed to that reality by paying $10 million a season to Peter Forsberg while the Red Wings spent more than $15 million at the 1999 trade deadline just to get ready for the playoff war.

Unless drastic improvements are wrought other Canadian franchises are expected to follow the Winnipeg Jets and Quebec Nordiques south to locales such as Houston and Portland. Ottawa

Senators' owner Rod Bryden asserted that he will not continue suffering annual losses of $7 million and will move or sell the team if outside financial help is not forthcoming.

What made the rampant player overpayment so incongruous—not to mention illogical—was the absence of marquee talent. When Mario Lemieux and Wayne Gretzky retired, the NHL lacked a superstar who could fill a rink.

Underlining that point was a 1999 ESPN Chilton Sports Poll which asked people who their favorite athlete was now that Michael Jordan retired. No hockey player made the top 15.

And at a time when player availability to the media was more needed than ever, stickhandlers have become more and more removed from the press. It has become commonplace for players to avoid post-game interviews. Typical were Toronto players who, *Montreal Gazette* columnist Jack Todd decried as "The Maple Leaf players and their habit of hiding in the showers until an hour or more after the game."

During the 1999 Pittsburgh–Devils series, when Bettman was encouraging his players to be more accessible to the media, Martin Straka of the Penguins had become a big story. With captain Jaromir Jagr sidelined with an injury, Straka had become the Penguins' ace-in-the-hole and the logical subject for between-games interviews. Yet, when print and electronic reporters requested interviews following an off-day morning skate, Straka—who speaks fluent English—refused. He said he was superstitious!

One can only wonder how much better the entire hockey scene might have been had Alan Eagleson not screwed up. The Eagle, for all his flaws, had a special sensitivity to ownership needs as well as the players. Surely, salaries would have climbed—they had been climbing already—and continued to grow, but at a more sensible rate. Owner-NHLPA relations would have been better and the Armageddon that had been freely predicted throughout the 1998–99 season would not likely frighten NHL people on every level.

But Eagleson is gone and Goodenow continues to rule. Whether or not he and Bettman can broker a more realistic peace is anybody's guess. General William Sherman once described war as hell.

If there's another hockey war, Sherman would be guilty of understatement.

PUTTING TAMPA BAY AND PITTSBURGH BACK ON TRACK

The fact that a National Hockey League team called the Lightning continues to play in Tampa Bay through the 1999–2000 season ranks among the largest feathers in Gary Bettman's hat.

From the very first, Florida's first big-league hockey team was an anomaly if not a skating vaudeville show. Consider the following:

- Its first rink was nothing more than an oversized barn.
- Its second rink was a baseball park without a baseball team but with artificial ice machinery.
- Its third—and present—rink, called the Ice Palace, remained unfinished two years after its official opening in 1996.
- Its owner through the late 1990s, Takashi Okubo, never saw a Lightning game and almost never spoke to a member of the Florida media.
- Its scouting system, for some time, consisted of no pro scout but several satellite dishes.
- Its two most visible personalities, general manager Phil Esposito and coach Terry Crisp, appeared more interested in dumping on each other than uniting behind the franchise.

In April 1997 the *Tampa Tribune* ran a headline over Martin Fennelly's column that accurately summed up the situation: "Poison Runs Deep Within Lightning."

Despite the sideshow, the Lightning proved that grade-*A* hockey could sell in Florida.

There was, however, a major problem. Okubo, whom not even NHL Commissioner Gary Bettman had met until April 1998, badly wanted out of the hockey business.

The team was put on sale in the autumn of 1996 but nobody would buy it. The reason was obvious: Kokusai Green, Okubo's Tokyo resorts company, wanted an outrageous $230 million for the team and its 40-year lease with the Ice Palace. Throughout 1997 reports of a sale were as frequent as whitecaps on Tampa Bay. But those in the know never believed the reports. Among the more insightful skeptics was John F. Sugg, senior editor of the Tampa Bay *Weekly Planet*.

A muckraking tabloid from the *Village Voice* genre of irreverent journalism, the *Planet* dug beneath the superficial and fingered the Lightning no-sale folly in August 1997.

"Here's the bottom line: the Tampa Bay Lightning—under legal and financial assault—may not be sellable," said Sugg. "One buyer, with cash to do the deal, left the table. Other suitors remain, but they aren't talking the astronomical prices sought by the Lightning's mysterious shogun, Takashi Okubo."

When one suitor group, the Maloof family, backed out of a supposed $160 million purchase, it was suggested that the family was to blame because they continually changed contract details.

"Don't believe it," said Sugg. "The worst that could be said of the Maloofs is that they're prudent. The offer from the family was between $123 million and $147.5 million, according to sources familiar with the team's affairs.

"The big problem is that Okubo probably needs $160 million to pay his debt on the team and the arena. But both are losing money and cash flow justifies only the lower numbers."

Although the Lightning had attracted what appeared to be a loyal following at the new Ice Palace, sports economists did not share a similar enthusiasm. *Financial World* magazine placed the team fourth from the bottom among National Basketball Association, National Football League, National Hockey League, and Major League Baseball teams.

Financial World added that the Lightning represented a "high risk" and suggested that the club "may not be able to sustain historic growth in value, or generate sufficient operating income to compete with other teams."

Even Tampa Bay's mayor warned that the new arena posed a problem. "Do you think the arena is making money? I don't see how that could be," said Mayor Dick Greco.

While Lightning officials buried their heads under the sand, Sugg fingered further problems: "No major company would risk putting its name on the building. AT&T was close to a deal, but wouldn't sign up for more than three years, indicating a lack of faith in either the team or Tampa, or both.

"Such a deal was worth $1 million a year, more or less, to a team, and the Lightning undoubtedly have already borrowed against such anticipated revenue."

As potential suitor after suitor disappeared and the 1997–98 season began, insiders warned that the problem facing the Lightning was that the Japanese had borrowed so much that the franchise and the arena weren't worth what was owed. It was suggested that the club file for bankruptcy on its subsidiary that controlled the Ice Palace

By this time it was virtually impossible to cover up the growing mess. *Forbes* magazine called the Lightning pro sports' most leveraged team. Other wealthy clubs, such as the Philadelphia Flyers, circled the Tampa Bay carcass like vultures. The Lightning's best young forward, Chris Gratton, received an offer sheet from the wealthy Flyers and started the new season in the City of Brotherly Love. Ironically, Gratton returned to Tampa in December 1998 in yet another bizarre Lightning deal.

Desperate to keep the club afloat, general manager Phil Esposito wheeled and dealed. But Espo's problem was internal. Neither he nor his coach, Terry Crisp, saw eye-to-eye, and rumors persisted that Crisp had the ear of the Japanese owners and would soon displace the general manager.

The adversarial nature of manager Esposito versus coach Crisp became a hot topic among the Lightning media as early as the 1996–97 season. "One JFK theory had the Espositos [Phil and brother Tony] planting stories about Crisp being deserted by his players," said *Tampa Tribune* columnist Fennelly. "That such a notion doesn't immediately sink like an Oliver Stone in water, that it could seem plausible, even for a second, shows that the top of this team is close to touching bottom. Winning isn't even an antidote anymore, and that's hard to swallow. Like poison."

Partly because the Lightning could not be sold and partly because Crisp was locked into a lucrative contract, he managed to survive through the start of the 1997–98 season. But Crisp's dilemma off the ice couldn't match the Lightning's problems on the ice. They couldn't win hockey games and became an embarrassment to Chief Executive Officer Steve Oto, who was deputized to run the club for the mysterious owner Takashi Okubo.

Oto's easiest fall guy was Esposito. In December 1997 he hinted that Espo's job was in jeopardy and warned him against making "Band Aid" or "Mickey Mouse" trades. Esposito countered, "I'd like to make the final decision, but I can't, and that's the truth."

But he was able to fire Crisp and temporarily replaced him with an assistant coach. Meanwhile, Esposito searched for yet another successor and this, too, became a typical Tampa Bay charade.

Terry Murray, who had been fired by the Flyers after leading Philadelphia to the 1997 Stanley Cup Finals, seemed to be a lock for the job until, somehow, Jacques Demers emerged at the 11th-and-a-half hour and took over as head coach.

With a 16–43–9 record in late March 1998, the Lightning was labeled "the worst franchise in sports" by *Sports Illustrated*.

Few would dispute the claim but the NHL's concern had less to do with the win–loss record and more to do with profit and loss. Not to mention those responsible for the losses, because there were no profits. As the 1997–98 season reached the homestretch, reports surfaced that the Lightning's fiscal situation was so bad that the league was considering a takeover of the franchise in the summer of 1998 if new owners had not been found.

By that time the franchise was said to be $100 million in debt and sinking rapidly. Fans, who once filled the Ice Palace, were staying away by the thousands, and even the arrival of so-called miracle worker Jacques Demers did little to encourage the potential ticket buyers.

Meanwhile, more and more of the focus turned to the phantom owner, Okubo.

Nobody paid much heed when he originally bought a limited stake in the team in 1990 through his company, Kokusai Green. Okubo later explained that he decided to invest in the Lightning because he was "informed American sports franchises are sound investments." But as losses mounted and lawsuits were filed, the distant Okubo and his firm came under more scrutiny.

The Internal Revenue Service entered the picture in 1994, prepared to file liens on the Lightning for $750,000 in past-due taxes. Concessionaire Sportservice Corporation was owed a sizeable sum, and others were screaming for unpaid bills.

Also haunting the franchise was Marc Ganis, who originally had hoped to build an arena for the Lightning prior to its NHL debut in 1992. Ganis filed a suit in Tampa federal court in 1997 against the Lightning ownership and management. Pivotal to the litigation was Okubo, who was described by one potential Japanese source of financing as a "gangster."

On April 16, 1998, Okubo showed up at the NHL's Rockefeller Center headquarters with his wife, Keiko. That night the Lightning played the Islanders at nearby Nassau Coliseum. However, Okubo ducked the game, the club's final road contest of the season.

Although Okubo steadfastly refused to enter a face-to-face question-and-answer session, the mystery man agreed to answer written questions submitted by the *Tampa Tribune* by fax.

Okubo, who answered the questions from his headquarters in Japan, rationalized his absentee ownership and vowed to find a "qualified" buyer for the team. And as far as his endless absence from Florida was concerned, Okubo vaguely concluded, "I hope to someday visit Tampa, although I cannot tell you exactly when that might be."

Nobody was holding his or her breath, especially after the devastating *Sports Illustrated* piece ("Team Turmoil") and an equally damning article by Richard Sandomir that followed in the *New York Times*.

Lightning management was so offended by the *Sports Illustrated* article, it counterattacked with a powerful verbal barrage distributed to the media:

> The management of the Lightning was both bewildered and dismayed to discover that their persistent nemesis, Marc Ganis, was again apparently successful in planting a slanted story littered with factual errors, incomplete information, and unfounded innuendos.
>
> In a published report in 1997, it was reported that Marc Ganis had promised he would be willing to sink $1 million into destroying his nemesis, the Lightning and former Lightning Governor David LeFevre.
>
> This is one of the few promises made by Marc Ganis over the past several years that he has shown any inclination to keep, but we have no intention of allowing him to do so.
>
> Ganis's plan to hurt the Lightning has taken two fronts. The first was to file a suit in March 1997 in federal district court, in which Ganis misrepresents the content of documents among potential Lightning investors and the NHL. Lightning attorney Paul Davis stated that "a simple examination of the documents referred to in the Ganis complaint clearly contradicts key allegations and seriously undermines the basis of the lawsuit."
>
> That Ganis's lawsuit was filed in March 1997, years after the event took place but within public announcement of a possible sale of the franchise to the Maloof

family of Albuquerque, New Mexico, suggests to the Lightning that his motivation was to interfere with that possible sale.

Ganis has now adopted new tactics. His new strategy apparently involves "planting" stories in the national press which are both highly critical of the Lightning and based on misinformation spoon-fed by Ganis. Lester Munson, the Chicago-based coauthor of the *Sports Illustrated* article, admitted to Lightning representatives that the article was published at the request of fellow Chicagoan Marc Ganis.

The article is replete with factual errors and relies heavily on information provided by former Lightning executive Mel Lowell and Ganis. Munson fails to mention in the article that Lowell previously and unsuccessfully sued the Lightning after the team failed to renew his contract.

Ganis had apparently engineered the placement of an article published last December in *Forbes* magazine which suggested that the Lightning were the most leveraged team in professional sports. His company, Sportscorp, Limited, is cited as authority for the assertions in the article.

Although the many significant mistakes in the *Forbes* article were detailed in a multitude of documents provided to *Sports Illustrated* by the Lightning, the *Sports Illustrated* piece cites the misinformed *Forbes* piece as one of its sources. Although both *Forbes* and *Sports Illustrated* rely heavily on information and quotes from Marc Ganis, neither publication informed its readers that the Lightning had asserted and subsequently sued Ganis, alleging that he had in effect taken hundreds of thousands of dollars of suite and seat deposits made by Lightning fans and had used them to pay down debt owed to Barnett Bank.

Although the team remains for sale, Lightning ownership has shown it is committed to the franchise with the recent signings of Rob Zamuner and Stephane Richer to lucrative contract extensions. And while 28 percent of the team's payroll has spent a great deal of time on the injured reserve list this season, the Lightning have started to head in the right direction after the addition of several new players and under the leadership of head coach Jacques Demers.

The local press digested the propaganda and took bets on when the next fiasco would unfold. It wouldn't be long. Shortly after the Lightning had finished dead last in the NHL, a new suitor surfaced in the buy-the-Lightning sweepstakes.

At last it appeared that Tampa Bay had a live one. William Davidson, who had owned the NBA's Detroit Pistons since 1974, had dispatched an advance team to the Ice Palace early in May 1998. Davidson, one of the most respected—not to mention wealthy—sports team owners, was serious about purchasing the Lightning.

Davidson also owned the Detroit Vipers of the International Hockey League and was well known to NHL executives. "He knows how a sports franchise should be run," said Detroit Red Wings vice president Jimmy Devellano. "He has always operated on a first-class basis." Unlike Okubo, Davidson was ubiquitous, press friendly, and a pal of Commissioner Bettman, whom he had known through Bettman's long NBA association. Davidson assigned his aide, Pistons' president Tom Wilson, to conclude the deal. He set a June 1, 1998, deadline to complete negotiations.

Okubo had dropped his asking price to $130 million, and on May 17, 1998, the package appeared to be sealed and ready for delivery. The *Tampa Tribune* thought so, running a "Davidson Expects Okay from Japanese" headline. The *St. Petersburg Times* countered with "Lightning Expected to Accept Buy Offer."

Apparently Davidson thought he had a deal, too; except he should have remembered more distinctly that he was dealing with the Lightning and not a normal sports organization. This was on Saturday, May 16, 1998. "My understanding," said Wilson, "is that we'll wrap this up on Monday."

On Monday the deal was wrapped up—except that William Davidson was not the new owner.

It was, however, Arthur L. Williams Jr., a 56-year-old insurance tycoon, who unexpectedly surfaced as the owner-to-be. Ironically—or should we say *typically,* because it was the Lightning—Williams wasn't even in continental North America when the shocking news broke on Monday. He was vacationing somewhere in Europe and had deputized his son-in-law, Mark DeMoss, to deal with the media.

Why would Williams want a team that was more than $102 million in debt and finished with the worst record in the league?

"He's been itching to pour himself into something other than his golf game," DeMoss explained, "and he's an avid sports enthusiast who is ready for the challenge of taking over this team."

It turned out that Williams's sports itch had been evident before. In 1995—supposedly bored in retirement—he bought the Birmingham Barracuda, of all things—a Canadian Football League franchise. Vowing that the team was "here to stay," he paid $3 million for the expansion CFL club. The Barracudas proceeded to lose $10 million, whereupon the bald Williams folded the team after one season.

"Williams," said Birmingham newspaper columnist and sports-radio host Paul Finebaum, "was a carnival act."

The NHL didn't think so. It approved the sale of the team, and Williams then did something his predecessor, Okubo, never did. The Lightning's owner showed up at the NHL Entry Draft in Buffalo to observe the club's first overall selection.

As expected, it was what most experts considered a prize pick: Vincent Lecavalier, who had starred for the Rimouski Oceanics of the Quebec Junior Hockey League. Sounding more like a high school sophomore, Williams bubbled exuberantly after the draft that Lecavalier was a cross between Michael Jordan and Mario Lemieux.

"I told Vincent he has a chance to build a legacy with the Lightning," said Williams, "or he could blow it all and be a dud."

Many media types ridiculed Williams much in the manner of *Pittsburgh Post-Gazette* sports writer Dejan Kovacevic. "The ridiculous comment," said Kovacevic, "came from the mouth of Art Williams."

Based on the franchise's history, one might say that Williams was merely maintaining its cockeyed tradition.

Before the first month of 1998–99 was over, Williams had fired both Phil and Tony Esposito. Jacques Demers was made GM and coach, and—guess what—the Lightning plummeted to the NHL's basement.

By December 1998, Williams was calling his players unpleasant names and the skating vaudeville show that characterized this curious franchise threatened to continue on into the next century unless positive changes were made.

The turnabout took place early in the new year when Detroit Pistons' owner Bill Davidson renewed the interest he had previously expressed in the franchise before it was annexed by Williams.

Davidson, who successfully operated the International Hockey League's Detroit Vipers, surfaced early in February 1999. By March 1999, Williams was conducting an orderly retreat. In this deal Williams sold the Davidson group the NHL team, its lease to the Ice Palace, and a small parcel of undeveloped land next to the downtown Tampa arena. The price was $115 million.

At age 76, the avuncular Davidson had less of Williams's bombast but more sports savvy, having successfully run both the NBA and IHL franchises, as well as a WNBA club, the Detroit Shock. But why would Davidson buy a club that was losing an estimated $20 million a year and had such a star-crossed history?

Quite simple; the hockey club was merely an adjunct to better money-making possibilities. "Our main attraction," said Davidson, "was the arena, probably even more than the hockey team. I've been a long-time hockey fan. The hockey we like . . . I won't say we love it yet, but that remains for the future."

Davidson's right-hand man was Tom Wilson, who had been president of the Vipers. "Hockey is a tough business now," said Wilson. "Almost no one makes money in the NHL but we hope within two years to make it profitable." To achieve this goal, Davidson and Wilson imported lieutenants who had made things work in Detroit. This change in personnel, in turn, brought about more conflict which had begun to embarass the team. After all, it was Williams who had dumped the Esposito Brothers and thrust Jacques Demers into the saviour role as general manager and coach. But Demers was not a Davidson man and by June 1999 the embarassments were piling up.

Rick Dudley had been Davidson's major domo in Detroit, spearheading the Vipers' march to the IHL's championship Turner Cup with Steve Ludzik as coach. But Dudley had moved on to become the general manager of the Ottawa Senators. He was loved in Canada's capital as the Sens enjoyed their best campaign in 1998–99. But as soon as Ottawa's playoff had ended, Dudley was completing plans to leave the Senators for Tampa Bay. The move did not sit well with the Sens' ownership but a deal was cut and Dudley was imported to oversee the entire Lightning hockey operation.

By mid-summer 1999, Demers had been fired and Ludzig brought in as his replacement behind the bench.

"It is going to be a whole new day," said Wilson.

For a change, a statement uttered by someone in the Lightning hierarchy was believed.

The same could not be said in another precinct that was causing Bettman, Inc. considerable discomfiture; and that was Pittsburgh. A cradle of hockey in the United States, Pittsburgh's roots as a stickhandling site dated back to the 19th century when a former trolley car barn in the Oakland section of the city was converted into an arena.

Duquesne Gardens, with a state of the art ice rink, became a hockey hotbed. When the NHL expanded to the United States in the mid-1920s, Pittsburgh was one of the first three American franchises granted entry. Following Boston (1924–25), Pittsburgh and the New York Americans entered into the 1925–26 campaign. Unfortunately, the undersized Duquesne Gardens proved to be too small for a growing league that would feature such large rinks as Madison Square Garden, Chicago Stadium, and Detroit's Olympia. Pittsburgh would lose its big-time franchise in 1930 and not regain one until the grand expansion of 1967–68.

The Steel City welcomed the Penguins but ownership problems plagued the team. In 1975 owners Tad Potter and Peter Block couldn't pay off roughly $6.5 million in debt, including more than $500,000 to the Internal Revenue Service. The IRS imposed a lien on the club and seized its assets, prompting it to file for protection under Chapter 11. Eventually, the league took over the franchise and sold it to Ohio businessman Al Savill.

Ownership problems surfaced in one form or another until the Penguins were purchased by The DeBartolo Corporation, headed by Edward J. DeBartolo. Some believe that DeBartolo saved hockey in Pittsburgh, stepping forward at a time when it needed solid leadership. He hired Craig Patrick to run the team and Patrick ultimately brought in Bob Johnson and Scott Bowman, two of the foremost hockey minds of all time. They guided the Penguins to their first Stanley Cup in the Spring of 1991.

In November 1991 DeBartolo sold the franchise to a group headed by Howard Baldwin (former president of the World Hockey Association), Morris Belzberg (director of Budget Rent A Car), and Thomas V. Ruta (one of the founding partners of the respected New York certified public accounting firm of Behan, Ling and Ruta). The new owners immediately solidified the franchise by approving long-term contracts to stars of the championship team, including Kevin Stevens, Ron Francis and Ulf Samuelsson. Patrick also was signed to a multi-year deal. The future seemed rosy for a team whose nucleus included superstar Mario Lemieux and budding ace Jaromir Jagr.

Baldwin's goal was to maintain the nucleus and build from there. His challenge was to retain the marquee players during an era when salaries were beginning to skyrocket. "We have some exciting young players, a quality farm system and an experienced and respected hockey operations staff that will continue to produce a successful hockey team," said Baldwin.

The team sold the rights to the Civic Arena lease to the SMG arena management company in 1991 in exchange for $24 million Baldwin needed to buy the franchise. SMG thus held operating rights for the Civic Arena and the team had to pay SMG between $6 million and $7 million a year to play there.

But if the team was to be kept in Pittsburgh—one of the smallest NHL markets—a price had to be paid and Baldwin was determined to keep the Penguins in the Steel City. His philosophy was supported by both the fans and media, neither of whom complained about the restructured deals nor the big salaries he was required to pay his stars. Everyone agreed that these moves were necessary to retain the team and its high caliber of play.

Baldwin's moves paid off. Pittsburgh won its second consecutive Stanley Cup in 1992 beating Chicago in four straight games. Howard was regarded as a sports owner hero in Pennsylvania—and rightly so. The championships proved it and the fact that he was able to retain his nucleus of aces underlined the point. However, a drive for a third Cup was torpedoed the following year by the New York Islanders who upset the Penguins in a seven-game series. It was a devastating defeat which was compounded when Kevin Stevens was seriously injured in the final game. The sharpshooter would never be the same threatening scorer he had previously been. For the Penguins, it was a portent of trouble ahead.

The Great Lemieux would be stricken with Hodgkin's Disease in 1993 and played only twenty-two games in the 1993–94 before undergoing treatment. He would also miss the whole 1994–95 season as well before making a heroic comeback in 1995–96. Prior to his illness Lemieux had signed a longterm contract with extensive deferred payments. Baldwin correctly deduced that it was imperative to keep both Lemieux and Jagr in the fold if the Penguins were to retain their drawing power at Civic Arena. Lemieux was the all-time hockey hero in Pittsburgh while Jagr was fast becoming his heir apparent.

On March 8, 1997 a major restructuring of ownership took place. Roger Marino, co-founder of the EMC Corporation in Hopkinton, Massachussets—a leading supplier of intelligent data storage solutions—became co-owner of the Penguins. Marino began overseeing the day-to-day operation of the franchise in February 1998.

But in March 1998 Lemieux filed a grievance against the team through the NHL Players' Association and then sued Marino in June. Lemieux was seeking $33 million from a contract he had signed with the Penguins in 1992. The love affair was beginning to fall apart and the word "bankruptcy" was being whispered around downtown Pittsburgh for the first time. It actually surfaced in a tangible way on July 31, 1998 when Marino hired J. Garvin Warden as the team's interim chief executive officer. A corporate turnaround specialist who oversaw the 1996 bankruptcy of the Latrobe (Pennsylvania-based Italian Oven restaurant chain)

Warden was seen as a possible quarterback for a similar move by the hockey team.

Meanwhile, the Penguins were sued by SMG, which accused the team of defaulting on a $1 million loan in 1997. Fox Sports Network also sued the Penguins for nonpayment of advertising fees and won a $1.1 million judgement against the team.

By the start of the 1998–99 season the Penguins payroll had reached the $26 million level but the bad news emerged on October 13, 1998 when the franchise filed for bankruptcy. I was covering the Pittsburgh–New Jersey game at Continental Airlines Arena that day when the word was passed before the Devils and Penguins held their morning skate.

"Yes, I got my paycheck and I'm very happy about it," said captain Jaromir Jagr. "Roger Marino promised that we'd get them and we got them."

At the time, the long-term fear was that the club would have to be moved to another city with a brand new arena; one such as Portland, Oregon. The optimists hoped that the fiscal wrangling would ultimately lead them to a new Pittsburgh arena to replace the aging Civic Center.

"Our reason for doing this was to keep the Penguins viable and in Pittsburgh," said Marino. "When you're in protection, you're able to put money into the team rather than worrying about who else is going to come and grab it. That's what this team needs right now in the short term."

Baldwin's point—again well-taken—was that the Penguins desperately needed a new rink. The 37-year-old Civic Arena was the NHL's oldest building as of 1999.

From the bankruptcy declaration in October 1998 through the Spring of 1999 the Pittsburgh hockey scene was pockmarked with charges and countercharges as Lemieux sought to retrieve his lost millions and attempts were made to salvage the torpedoed franchise. In the end the hero would be Mario himself although the salvation would not come easy. On March 18, 1999, Lemieux submitted a reorganization plan in U.S. Bankruptcy Court to keep the team in Pittsburgh. *Le Grand Magnifique*, who had saved the hockey club so many times on the ice, was now preparing to save it before a judge.

My hope was to interview Lemieux. As it happened, our Fox Sports New York television team was in Pittsburgh for a Devils-Penguins game and Mario was in the building. My producer, Roland Dratch, was determined that we at least reach Lemieux at his seat but he was down near the ice and we were up at the top of the stairs. We had two choices; either brazen our way down the dozen steps and face the possibility of security guards throwing us out before we reached our quarry, or asking the security guard to walk down to Mario and ask him if he would agree to an interview.

I chose the latter course and then held my breath. Step by step, the security man headed toward Lemieux, finally reached him and whispered in his ear. Mario turned around, saw me and we made eye contact. Then, he waved and said, "C'mon down!"

The cameraman and I trotted down to a step adjacent to Mario's seat. He was warm and engaging. He told us as much as he could about the proceedings and it all made it to the air. It was a little coup, so to speak, but a coup nonetheless. I was very grateful to Mario. So were the citizens of Pittsburgh. As if stick-handling through an endless sudden death overtime game, Lemieux and his aides targetted a solution to the bankruptcy mess and finally reached a conclusion a week after the Stanley Cup playoffs had ended.

The deal essentially allowed Lemieux to recover some of the monies owed to him while he became a major leader of the team. Lemieux and his investors would chip in $50 million to operate the club. Furthermore, Penguins games would continue to be played in the Civic Arena and broadcast on Fox Sports Net Pittsburgh. Radio rights would be sold directly to WDVE-FM, the previous broadcaster.

"He's going to be just great," Craig Patrick said about Lemieux. "The one thing that everybody knows about him is that he's got a great hockey mind, and that's something that's going to be a great help to us."

Mario's bid was secured in the nick of time when a major creditor, Bank of America National Trust and Savings Association, agreed to a $2 million cut in their owed payment. According to the bank's attorney, that arrangement gave Lemieux and his group some very important leverage when dealing with other creditors.

Bill Daly, the NHL's senior vice president, expressed the opinions of the league. "We are extremely pleased," he said. "We realize it took an enormous effort that required a lot of hard work and dedication, and we congratulate Mario and his advisers for showing the tenacity to ensure the future of hockey in Pittsburgh."

Bettman, Inc. was tickled because the commissioner had supported the Lemieux plan from the get-go. Mario's image remained immense in Pittsburgh and his bid was sufficient to dilute much of the bad press that had accrued throughout the 1998–99 season.

But the league held a trump card in the event that Lemieux's blueprint had been rejected. Early in the Spring of 1999 it had been revealed that the league was nurturing an alternate plan in which the Penguins would be sold for a reported $85 million to Seattle billionaire Paul Allen. In that event, the Penguins would be moved to a relatively new arena, called the Rose Garden, in Oregon.

Even with the Lemieux plan in the bag, Portland remained a potential site for any other endangered NHL franchise. If nothing else, Bettman was thinking ahead.

BIG LEAGUE HOCKEY
Where Does It Go From Here?

"**W**hy Professional Hockey Is Its Own Worst Enemy"
"Winter Game, Spring Identity Crisis"
"NHL Sows Seeds for Failure"
"Big Ratings Missing; Big Names Gone, Too"
"Is Anyone Watching?"

The headlines all appeared in major American publications during a very short period in 1998 and were repeated again, in a different form, a year later. They represent unparalleled criticism of the National Hockey League from the most respected journals on the continent, from the *New York Times* to New York's *Newsday*.

In most cases, the negative response to big-league hockey was the result of a six-year buildup to a letdown that began with a glowing *Sports Illustrated* feature on June 20, 1994, which unabashedly forecast that the NHL would become *the* sport of the next decade.

"The NHL is hot," proclaimed *Sports Illustrated* in its cover story, "and the NBA is not."

When NHL Commissioner Gary Bettman saw the piece, he turned to his vice president, Steve Solomon, and shook his head. "This is too much, too soon," said Bettman.

He was right, although big-league hockey's picture was so rosy at the time it was difficult not to be optimistic.

Fox Network underlined the point with a $155 million investment in the NHL by acquiring broadcast rights in 1994. The five-year pact was not for NBA- or NFL-type numbers but it was a start and fueled hopes that exposure would lead to higher ratings and an even better pact the next time around.

The NHL's decision to break the Olympic ice for the first time and dispatch big-leaguers to the Winter Games in Nagano was viewed as yet another potential catalyst for the sport, especially because Canada and the United States had excellent chances to reach the finals.

Adding to the crescendo of enthusiasm was a wave of new, young stars, including the Canadian Paul Kariya, the American Keith Tkachuk, the Czech Jaromir Jagr, the Russian Sergei Fedorov, the Slovak Zigmund Palffy, and the Finn Teemu Selanne.

Why, then, has the NHL been so badly dumped upon by critics such as Joe Lapointe of the *New York Times* and Roy MacGregor of the *Ottawa Citizen*, each of whom professes a love of the sport?

To understand the answer, one must begin with hockey's television debacle.

Ever since TV came to the NHL, producers and directors have been challenged to find ways and means to enable American audiences to (1) better understand The Game; (2) learn how to follow the elusive puck; and (3) know and enjoy marquee players.

When Fox took over in 1994 its creative corps decided to ignore the traditional methods used by their hockey-savvy brethren. "I don't want to knock the way 'Hockey Night in Canada' does it," said Sandy Grossman, the director of "NHL on Fox," "but they've been covering hockey the same way for 50 years."

Fox radicalized coverage, starting with visualization of the puck. Because the black, six-ounce hunk of vulcanized rubber travels at speeds of up to 100 miles per hour and zigzags with no apparent rhyme or reason, Fox had a problem on its hands.

The "solution" became as controversial as any electronic novelty ever introduced to a sports audience. Network engineers invented "Fox Trax," a metallically doctored puck that glowed on the screen.

Microchip powered, the infrared-looking puck first streaked across the screens during the 1996 NHL All-Star Game. The response from purists was so negative that the network received death threats.

Not only were the blue and red streaks distracting, but the technology was faulty to the extent that when the real puck skimmed along the boards, the Fox puck appeared to be flying over—and cutting off—the heads of people in the stands.

"Try and tell fans that Fox Trax adds viewers and you will be met with laughter," said Las Vegas hockey analyst and author Bobby Bryde. "The magic puck detracts from the game, making it harder to follow the puck. Why can't Fox admit that?"

For one thing, Fox was willing to gamble that diehards, such as Bryde, would continue watching the NHL because they wanted hockey no matter what; and for another, the network believed it was on the right track with Fox Trax.

"The main problem with television hockey coverage is the speed the puck travels," explained Grossman, who had directed the CBS Olympic hockey coverage in 1992 and 1994. "But I didn't want to change for change's sake. I was changing because I thought the game needed to be presented to the American people in a slightly different manner. When it comes to hockey, the American public needs to be spoon-fed a little bit more than Canadians."

True, and through the 1995, 1996, and 1997 playoffs, the American public had time to acclimatize itself not only to the Fox productions, but those of ESPN and ESPN2, which also networked the NHL.

Some sports-TV critics, such as Phil Mushnick of the *New York Post*, had a positive response. "At least the NHL was trying," said Mushnick. "I liked their network presentation of hockey better than football's, and the kids do watch. The ratings numbers are not there but I'd be patient with the process."

NHL spin doctors attempted to glorify their numbers but their response sounded like a chapter from the book *How to Lie with Statistics*. *USA Today*'s Michael Hiestand responded: "Let's say you have a rating of 0.8 and it goes up to 1.6. Theoretically, some people would write it as a ratings increase of 100 percent. But if I had a nickel in my pocket and now I have a dime, I am up 100 percent but I still only have a dime."

Undaunted, Fox continued its efforts to improve the product. In 1997–98 it equipped its cameramen with joy-sticks to control the robotic camera behind each goal judge and also positioned a robotic camera high at each end of the ice to show action on power plays.

"When we got the NHL contract, the mandate was to make the game more intimate," said "NHL on Fox" executive producer and 13-time Emmy Award–winner Ed Goren. "So much of what we had done has been accepted and even expected by hockey fans now that you sometimes forget how radical it once was.

"We created a climate where no idea was a bad idea and Rupert Murdoch provided us with the financial tools to make those ideas reality at a time when the other networks were cutting back on spending. But there was almost a collective spirit that we could change the way hockey was broadcast and make it better."

The intention was noble but the response was thumbs-down in key areas. Writing in the *New York Times*, Joe Lapointe observed: "Why are the national television ratings dwindling? One reason might be the bizarre, low-ice camera angles. A sport thought difficult to televise does not become more telegenic when directors make it even harder to follow."

Also writing in the *Times*, former NHL broadcasting director Stu Hackel asserted that longtime fans were being driven away from the TV set. He blamed "Fox's vacuous studio show, its nonstop switching camera angles, a claustrophobic game-lengthening commercial inventory, the noisy ambience, the ever-shifting schedule, and those dancing Fox hockey robots."

Otherwise, he liked it. Fox, of course, did not. To critics such as Lapointe and Hackel, the network had an answer and it was provided by Fox Senior Vice President of Communications Vince Wladika.

"We are dumbfounded [about the ratings] and the Lapointe article was absurd," Wladika told me. "It is commonly known that hockey is a sport best viewed live and we have used things such as better stereo-surround sound and putting microphones on the coaches and referees to help create that feeling. As for the lower camera angles, most fans would rather sit behind the glass than 70 feet up.

"If Fox is hockey's main problem, the NHL should have such problems. We've put hockey on free television for the first time in 25 years and created a prime-time forum for the Stanley Cup Finals."

Wladika claimed that long intermissions hurt the ratings. "In the arenas, you have a captive audience. Between periods, they buy hot dogs and return to the game. At home, you're giving the viewer an opportunity to do something else from which they may not come back to watching the game. Fifteen minutes is a long time in television."

At one point Fox President David Hill suggested that The Game be changed from its traditional three-period sequence to a four-quarter affair. "I will keep bugging away," Hill promised. "I believe that as a television spectacle the game would be better as four quarters as every other game in the history of the world."

Like others at Fox, Hill had expected that ratings would continue an upward movement as the NHL contract wound down to its fifth year. "When you see our contract end," he insisted in December 1995, "the bidding rights for hockey will be pretty fast and furious."

But when the ratings began arriving during the 1998 playoffs, they were hardly numbers that Fox had coveted. *Boston Herald* sports-TV critic Jim Baker opined: "Game one of the finals on Fox achieved a 3.3 rating, down from 4.0 last season. ESPN has averaged a 1.2 cable rating (855,580 homes) through 30 games, down from last season's 1.5 average (1,088,713 homes) for 24 games.

"The video-game approach has not worked for the NHL. It has turned off many traditional viewers. The league has to do something and since next year is the last year of its contract with Fox, I imagine big things happening.

"But the NHL has not seen interest from competing networks. The season was stretched too long and there was no building drama in the finals."

Despite the low ratings, ABC–Disney–ESPN bid $600 million and won a five-year contract starting with the 1999–2000 season.

This was an amazing bit of luck, but it could not conceal the fact that the NHL continued to get clobbered elsewhere.

Disturbing to some observers was the attitude of many in the mainstream sports media. Hockey, to them, seems always to be the easiest sport to kick around. Allen Barra, who writes about sports for the *Wall Street Journal* and ESPN *Magazine*, was typical of that genre.

"There is a simple irrefutable fact about hockey that the past year in broadcasting ought to have made obvious even to TV executives and it's this: Americans really don't like hockey very much," said Barra.

Although hockey haters like Barra are not uncommon in the media, the question of why they dump on The Game remains unanswered. I decided it was worthwhile to probe a cross-section of hockey minds to determine what inspires such attacks and what could be done about them.

"Hockey has inherent problems," said Madison Avenue marketing expert Marty Blackman. "It has tremendous competition and is only an indoor sport, which means you can't have 70,000 people watching the games. While the NBA can't either, basketball is an inner-city sport. Hockey has to be organized and can be expensive to play. It isn't really inner-city appealing nor is it accessible."

Howard Dolgon, owner of the AHL Syracuse Crunch, warns the NHL against worrying about its rivals."Hockey should look at where it was 10 or 15 years ago, not where the NBA or NFL is now," he told me. "The strides hockey has made recently fall second only to the NBA. But the NHL will never get a TV deal like the NFL has. Hockey shouldn't see itself as competing with other leagues. The NHL should compete with itself to top the advances it has already made."

Antihockey media lynch mobs are nothing new according to Stan Saplin, former Rangers publicist and NHL writer for the now-defunct *New York Journal-American.* "Hockey has never been widely regarded by the public," Saplin explained. "It has always appealed to a very narrow group of people. You have never been able to talk about hockey in a living room setting."

Critics finger the 1998 U.S. Olympic failure, expansion, and talent dilution as some reasons for hockey's relatively low esteem. But it is all relative.

"It's absurd to think that any sport does or does not have inherent mass appeal," Andy Bernstein of *Street and Smith's Sports Business Journal* explained. "Look at soccer. In the United States, it's a low-rated sport but in other parts of the world, it's the biggest sport there is. But if you don't get the ratings, you're not a player."

Some observers, such as freelance sports business writer Steve Viuker, believe the NHL suffers from a lack of national identification. "Hockey is doing the best it can, but there are no marquee franchises," said Viuker. "There's no Chicago Bulls. There's no Michael Jordan. There's no old Canadiens anymore. The Colorado-Florida Stanley Cup Final [in 1996] was the ultimate 'Who?' championship."

"Hockey will always be the fourth of the four major sports," added Blackman. "The United States is not, psychologically, a winter sport country. Skiing is big, but winter doesn't exist in half the country and building rinks in those places doesn't mean people will flock to them. Winter sports here are seen as recreational."

"Look at how many people dump on Major League Baseball," said former International Hockey League Vice President of Communications Bill Jamieson. "But MLB is working its way back. Baseball is baseball. Right now we could be in the infancy of a major boom in hockey. Who knows where the sport will be 50 years from now?"

Can Bettman reverse the antihockey thinking?

Dolgon: "Gary Bettman has been a great choice for commissioner because he was an outsider and saw things differently. But he shouldn't worry about getting a billion-dollar TV deal. The NHL should take all its corporate partners and reinvest the money in promoting the players. They should use their national sponsors such as Nike and Mastercard to get a better presence in the marketplace."

Jamieson, who has won many awards as a hockey PR man, sees light at the end of the Zamboni tunnel.

"In the fifties youth hockey programs were taking off even though very few Americans were playing in the NHL," Jamieson notes. "Now, one or two generations later, we have an influx of good American players, whose parents grew up during that era.

"With the youth hockey programs that are in place now, such as Hockey in Harlem, in 20 years we may see a strong influx of African American or Latino players. Who knows? The league MVP could be from Raleigh, North Carolina, or be black or Hispanic. And if he's not, the fans will be."

American-born hockey players were expected to get a boost from Uncle Sam's entry into the 1998 Olympiad, particularly following the triumph over Canada in the 1997 World Cup. It was expected that a rematch would follow in 1998 and that the positives in terms of exposure would outweigh the negatives that would come from interrupting the NHL schedule for an unprecedented 17 days.

Then, there was the embarrassment of having televised Olympic hockey available in the United States only after midnight, which guaranteed low viewership. What few could anticipate was the abject play of the Americans and—even worse—the miniscandal that enveloped star-spangled skaters after they were defeated at Nagano.

In the aftermath of their elimination, some players returned to their rooms and what followed remains sketchy to this day. However, it is known that at least one suite occupied by players was trashed and that a fire extinguisher was hurled over a balcony. "It was not that terrible an episode compared to what other athletes have done in other situations," an NHL player agent told me, "but the fact that no one owned up to it enabled a small story to mushroom into a major journalistic event."

Therein was the problem. From the moment Olympic authorities discovered the mess, teammates buttoned their lips. The longer they kept quiet, the more the media made of the marauders.

"Rather than act responsibly and reveal which players mauled the rooms, sprayed goalie Mike Richter with harmful fire extinguisher juice, and threw a fire extinguisher and pieces of broken chairs out of a fifth-floor window, they have protected the guilty and said nothing," commented *Chicago Sun-Times* columnist Jay Mariotti. "It's something out of mob life, or more to the point, out of seventh-grade recess."

Weeks after the event none of the culprits stepped forward. During a face-to-face interview I conducted with Bettman and NHL Players' Association boss Bob Goodenow, I put the question to them. Was there a cover-up?

Goodenow replied: "Chris Chelios [Team USA captain] apologized. We don't know who did it and we don't condone it. It wasn't handled properly. It's been dealt with. It's unfortunate but it's behind us."

I turned to Bettman and asked why we still had not learned who trashed the room.

Bettman: "We didn't have access to the athletes' village and nobody talked. We are glad that Chris apologized although I would rather have had the individuals involved apologize. It's too bad all the hockey players' images are tainted because of a few. Someday we'll know."

It was wishful thinking. Apart from the general Chelios apology, nobody stepped forward. "The case, as they say at the cop shop, is ongoing," noted *Calgary Sun* columnist Jim Taylor, "and ever likely to be."

New York Daily News columnist Filip Bondy capsulized it best by describing Uncle Sam's Olympians as "the Black Sox of Hockey."

Apparently sworn to silence, the players returned to NHL action after the Czech Republic upset both Canada and the United States to win the gold medal in what was at the very least a minor upset. Canada, favored to come home with some medal, was beaten by Finland—minus Teemu Selanne—for the bronze medal.

As a group, though, NHLPA members were laughing as never before. Despite a collective bargaining agreement that ostensibly would curb inflation, the average salary continued climbing over $1 million.

Detroit Red Wings' owner Mike Ilitch put it this way, "You go through cycles. It's OK for a while, and then when Paul Kariya signs, it sets a new plateau. It's the same thing as in baseball—you can see it coming in hockey.

"But the difference in hockey is that we don't have the owners in hockey to sustain that kind of heat. They're not getting anything out of national TV, so you've only got your gate, basically."

In my face-to-face interview with the commissioner and the union leader, I asked them how high the salaries can continue climbing.

Goodenow's view: "Salaries are a reflection of the overall growth in the business. Water finds its own level. I don't think they will continue to grow at a certain pace. What we're seeing is simply a reflection of developments in the industry as a whole."

Bettman: "When we get to the end of this collective bargaining agreement, we will look at two things—growth in salaries and growth in revenues. If they kept pace, it worked. If they don't, one way or another there will have to be an adjustment going forward. That's why it's too early to tell. We have the most restrictive player movement system and I like how it works. There are trade-offs, though. If there were a salary cap, Bob would insist on complete free agency but I don't think it works in our team sport. Highest payroll does not equate to success or the best teams."

The most successful team in the late nineties was the Detroit Red Wings, winners of the Stanley Cup in 1997 and 1998. Directed by Mike and Marian Ilitch along with lieutenants Jimmy Devellano and Ken Holland, the Wings also proved most successful on the ledger. Detroit led the league in paid admissions—the Carolina Hurricanes were last—both seasons.

Despite the team's fiscal success, the Ilitches and their ilk remain concerned about runaway salaries. Goodenow continued claiming through the late nineties that if the NHL is in trouble, the problem is not the players. "It's not an issue of players' salaries," Goodenow insisted. "The issue is revenue."

Because of talent dilution, players who in another era would have been considered washed-up were commanding astronomical salaries. In 1998 the Red Wings won the championship with four such retread defensemen. Slava Fetisov was considered washed-up as a New Jersey Devil in 1994 and yet he was still a Detroit regular in 1998. Larry Murphy was booed out of Washington and Toronto but emerged as the Red Wings' best backliner. Jamie Macoun, one of the lowest men on the Leafs totem pole, moved on to Detroit and helped the Wings to a Stanley Cup.

Never was the absurdity of salary inflation more apparent than in July 1998. Rival general managers had promised Les Canadiens Rejean Houle that they would hold the line. They must have been kidding him. In the first week of the free-agent market at the beginning of the summer, the general managers indicated that they weren't being serious with Houle.

"NHL salary escalation far outstripped the North American inflation rate of 1.5 percent," noted Montreal *Gazette* columnist Pat Hickey. The examples were staggering:

- Doug Gilmour: his annual salary jumped from $3.55 million to $6 million.
- Uwe Krupp: awarded a 167 percent pay increase when he signed a four-year, $16.4 million deal with the Red Wings.
- Marc Bureau: new three-year contract with Philadelphia is worth $1.2 million per season, a 144 percent increase.
- Jyrki Lumme: Phoenix doubled his annual salary from $1.685 million to $3.4 million a season.

Bettman says not to worry and perhaps he's right.

The NHL has survived crises before.

Its footprint is more evident across America than ever and will continue to grow with the recent addition of Nashville, Tennessee and future expansion teams in Atlanta, Georgia; St. Paul, Minnesota; and Columbus, Ohio.

What's more, minor league hockey is booming in such unlikely precincts as Reno, Nevada; Boise, Idaho; Macon, Georgia; and Lincoln, Nebraska—to name a few.

Even more encouraging is the growth in the street and in-line areas. In Florida, the Panthers Street Cats program has skyrocketed from 300 participants to more than 8,000 in just three years.

"This is such a tremendous game," concluded Bruins longtime general manager Harry Sinden. "All of us who screw it up are depending on the game to save us."

Certainly, the NHL has responded to its critics in many ways. New rules have been written to address the dearth of goals as well as the inability of superstars to play to their potential.

Ownership remains firmly convinced that Bettman will successfully lead the NHL into the twenty-first century. And the commissioner remains steadfast that a brave, new hockey world will come—if only the critics will remain patient.

"There is an ebb and flow to sports, and you have to deal with cycles," Bettman concludes. "That's why there are no shortcuts. There are no Band Aids. You must build a foundation. If you were looking for a quick hit and were able to say 'Look at this, they've conquered the world,' that's not what it's all about. Try conquering the world. If you're not doing it on a good foundation, your world will crumble quickly."

But as the 1998–99 season concluded, the collective bargaining agreement, which Bettman had negotiated with Bob Goodenow in 1995, had turned into a disaster for ownership. By June 1999 the annual player's salary had zoomed to an all-time high of $1.4 million.

Television ratings in the United States remained tepid. And while no ratings are provided by newspaper coverage, it was evident to the naked eye that hockey was being relegated to the garbage dump of the sports sections. New York's *Newsday*, one of the nation's largest newspapers, did not even send a beat reporter to cover the 1999 Stanley Cup Finals.

As the 1999 playoffs unfolded, it appeared that once and for all, the NHL would get a break. Many of the preliminary series exceeded expectations and in one—Pittsburgh versus New Jersey—there were moments of exceptionally high drama as Penguins ace

Jaromir Jagr recovered from a debilitating injury to lead his team to an upset victory over the Devils.

Even after the defending champion Detroit Red Wings had been eliminated as well as the exceptionally talented Colorado Avalanche, a high degree of excitement was maintained.

The Finals pitted the aging, overpaid Dallas Stars against the Buffalo Sabres, whose goalie Dominik Hasek, was generally considered to be the world's best at his position. It also was a case of fat-cat big market team against a tight-budgeted small market club whose only marquee attraction was Hasek. In the end, the series proved so typical of the NHL; a potentially wonderful advertisement for The Game turned into yet another public relations disaster.

Unlike the previous four finals which ended in four-game sweeps, this one extended to a sixth game at Buffalo's Marine Midland Arena. Furthermore, there was every reason to believe that it could have gone to seven games, lifting excitement to the limit.

The game offered a delightfully dramatic touch. Visiting Dallas took the lead but the Sabres pounded away at the aging Stars' defense and finally tied the game at one apiece, sending it into overtime. Back and forth the teams battled through the first overtime but neither Hasek nor his counterpart Ed Belfour would crack. At one point it appeared as if Buffalo had won when a James Patrick slapshot from just inside the blue line beat Belfour cleanly but clanged off the crossbar and out of danger.

By the time the third overtime had begun it had become apparent that neither referee, Bill McCreary nor Terry Gregson, was prepared to call a penalty. Play had slowed to a crawl and uncalled infraction after uncalled infraction made a mockery of the rulebook. It was now almost 1:30 a.m. and there were those in the press box who feared that the game could go on forever. Then *IT* happened; a goal that would cause an inordinate amount of mockery directed at Bettman, Inc.

Following a scramble in front of the Sabres' net, Brett Hull of Dallas fired the puck past Hasek. The goal, which many to this day believe should not have been counted, was tallied at 54:51 of overtime.

That was the good news.

The bad news was as follows:

- Hull's foot was in the crease.
- In dozens of similar situations during the season, that type of foot-in-the-crease goal was disallowed.

- The capacity crowd was not even advised that the goal was under review—which it was.
- The NHL had sent a memo regarding such crease conflicts to various teams in March 1999 but never gave any to the media. Thus none of the hundreds of reporters could understand why the goal was allowed.

The very bad news was that minutes after the on-ice cele-brations were held both Buffalo coach Lindy Ruff and media members examined the replays and were convinced the goal should have been disallowed. Livid, Ruff sought out and found Bettman, demanding an explanation. Bettman walked away. Sabres' captain Michael Peca confronted the commissioner on the ice. "Gary," said Peca, "the guy's foot was in the crease." According to Peca, the commissioner walked away. Bettman later told *Sports Illustrated* he was not approached by Peca and that Ruff's "conduct was out of control and inappropriate."

In the Sabres' dressing room Hasek watched the replay as well. The goalie immediately put his sweater back on, convinced that the game would be resumed because of an illegal goal. "It's not a goal," said Hasek. But the netminder was told that the game would not continue.

During the post–game press conferences, Ruff continued to challenge the ruling. Answering the charges, Bryan Lewis, the league's director of officiating, insisted the replays were dutifully checked after the goal. He asserted that the goal, in his estima-tion, was legal. He supported his claim by citing a league direc-tive submitted on March 25, 1999. It stated that an attacking player can stay in the crease even if the puck leaves the area as long as he maintains control of the puck. Nobody in the media ever saw the memo because it was kept within NHL confines. This was among many mistakes; another being the failure to alert the live and TV audience that the goal was under review; something that was done innumerable times during the regular season.

The fallout for the NHL was horrendous. *Sports Illustrated* head-lined it as a "dubious goal" that "tarnished what had been the best final series in years." Reporter Michael Farber concluded: "This series should have revived a showcase event but instead left a worse taste than a champagne bender."

Writing in Toronto's *Globe and Mail*, Alan Maki said the Hull goal "was about as legal as a three-dollar coin."

Explanations by Bettman, Lewis, and other NHL cronies in some cases fell on deaf media ears.

"No one believes a word these people say," noted *Toronto Star* columnist Damien Cox. "The sport—not Bettman's little empire, but the sport—is in worse shape today than when he came to power. Now, Bettman's drifting administration has visited a travesty upon the game worse than the blue-streaked TV puck, depriving a champion of the integrity that comes with winning fair and square. The Dallas Stars deserve better. Bettman should be held responsible."

The commissioner's response was swift. Less than two days after the tainted goal fiasco, the NHL eliminated the use of video replay to determine crease violations on goals. The responsibility was shifted back to the on-ice officials.

In addition, the league further tinkered with its product with the following changes:

- In regular season play, each team will earn a point if a game is tied after 60 minutes of play. A team that scores in the five-minute overtime will earn an extra point.
- Teams will play four on four in regular season overtime instead of five on five.

One owner who attended the NHL meeting in New York which wrought the changes walked out in disgust. Many media critics charged that the league was overreacting and that allowing the referees to call the crease plays would lead to chaos.

But as the NHL prepared to enter a new century, rule-tinkering and botched replay calls were small potatoes compared to the matter intrinsic to the life or death of the league. By the time the Entry Draft was held late in June 1999, the Hull goal had been forgotten, having given way to the ultimate issue, spiraling costs.

Testifying in the Penguins' bankruptcy case, NHL senior vice-president William Daly asserted that 20 of 26 teams lost money in 1997–98 with two breaking even and only four showing a profit. The dismal fiscal picture had not changed as the 20th century came to a close.

Meanwhile, both the union and the league were fattening their war chests in the event that a strike or lockout were to take place. Peace seems impossible to those who know the leaders because as one insider told us, "Gary and Bob simply don't like each other."

Let us hope that each will like the game of hockey enough to make peace before it's too late.

EPILOGUE

An old friend named Eddie Howe, from the town of Shandaken in New York State's Catskill Mountains, had an excellent bit of advice for Gary Bettman and his NHL grey suits: Stop trying to be like Major League Baseball, the National Football League or the National Basketball Association.

"The NHL should accept itself as it is," said Howe. "As a hockey fan, I have no problem with the NHL being the fourth-ranked team sport. Personally, I don't care if it's number one or not."

Howe, who has watched more hockey than most of my friends and media colleagues, makes a good point. But sometimes the NHL doesn't know when to stop. My concern is whether big-league hockey can retain fourth place against ever-growing competition.

Womens basketball, which had trouble getting an inch in the newspapers a decade ago, has, at times, pushed the NHL aside in the headline derby the way big-time collegiate basketball sometimes does. And with the retirement of Wayne Gretzky in the Spring of 1999, Bettman, Inc. was left without a single major marquee name that would appeal to the marketing community.

Meanwhile, the talent pool has dramatically changed in the past decade. European players such as Dominik Hasek, Jaromir Jagr and Peter Forsberg have become dominant big-league performers while the traditional Canadian production line is losing its strength. Artistically, this may be commendable but in an area where the NHL is sorely hurting—marketing-public relations—it is a major debit.

European players are much more difficult to sell to the public. The language barrier makes it almost impossible to conduct an articulate, in-depth interview with the likes of a Jagr who supposedly has taken the torch from the interview-friendly Gretzky. As more and more non-English speaking players come to the NHL—the top four 1999 Entry Draft picks were Europeans—the PR problem will inevitably become even more difficult with no solution in sight.

Ironically, the European influx brings yet another problem in terms of style. Players from Scandinavian countries as well as Russia, Slovakia, and the Czech Republic are accustomed to playing on a larger, Olympic-size ice surface, the kind which the NHL refuses to adopt. When these skilled Europeans skate on the cramped NHL 85 by 200-foot rink they tend to alter their repertoire, to adjust to the conventional and more boring defensive "trap" formula, commonplace in big-league North American hockey.

Gretzky was one of the precious few virtuosos able to surmount the mundane, up-and-down brand of hockey that resulted in lower scores and pleas for help. The Great One's exit, in the minds of some experts, could signal the end of what remained of a creative era.

The perceptive *New York Post* hockey columnist Larry Brooks noted at the conclusion of the 1999 playoffs that the current NHL era is suffering from comparatively fewer stars than at any time in memory.

"Those with great ability," said Brooks, "those flamboyant talents who report to training camp as square pegs, these players are immediately reshaped by coaches for pounding into prefabricated round holes. It is the NHL, once featuring the fastest, most creative entertainment vehicle on earth, as an assembly line operation featuring interchangeable parts.

"We wonder how far an 18-year-old Gretzky would have gotten with his game, playing in this era for a (trapping) Ken Hitchcock or a Jacques Lemaire. Systems may win titles, but fans aren't drawn either to the rink or out of their seats by systems. Fans are drawn to the rink and lifted out of their seats by athletes with speed and skill and the ability to set up and score goals; athletes with charisma."

Such athletes are so few in the NHL, one can actually count them—Eric Lindros, Brian Leetch, Peter Forsberg, Dominik Hasek, Jaromir Jagr—on the fingers of one's hands.

What the NHL has done to inhibit its attractive flow that once earned the title of "Fastest Game on Earth" is allow goaltenders unlimited freedom to roam. The way hockey was meant to be played, there were three distinct positions and each had a specific function. Forwards were to score; defensemen were to thwart scorers and goaltenders were to stop the puck from going into the net; no more, no less.

But when Jacques Plante, as a top Montreal Canadiens goalie in the late 1950s, began roaming from his crease to trap and pass the puck, he not only added another body to the already crowded ice but also disrupted the normal flow of the game.

Rather than writing a rule that would have limited the goalie to his crease era—which should have been done immediately—the league overlooked this major disruption. Soon other goaltenders began aping Plante's success—his team won five consecutive Stanley Cups between 1956 and 1960—and the roaming goalie became very much *de rigeuer* in the NHL.

Decade upon decade, league rulesmakers continued to favor the puckstopper through the 1990s. By 1995 goalies were employing such oversized pads, gloves, and shoulder guards that it became more and more difficult to see the space behind the goalie. Yet, such abuses were virtually ignored until the end of the decade when some minor equipment regulations were written into the rules. But the primary problem—allowing goalies to roam anywhere in their end of the rink just like other skaters—continued to be a disruptive aspect that eluded the Bettman's think tank.

When the Commissioner succeeded John Ziegler and his interim replacement, Gil Stein, Bettman argued for time. As my father once told me, "Rome wasn't built in a day," so, too, Bettman insisted that the positive changes would be evident not in a matter of months but in years.

More than six years after dumping Ziegler-Stein and beatifying Bettman, one owner told me in June 1999 that the Commissioner who came out of the NBA was not the godsend that showed such promise in 1993.

"He's spent a lot of money and expanded his office," the owner declared mournfully, "but I don't see that John Ziegler couldn't have done the same thing."

Imported principally to neutralize the NHL Players' Association and its boss, Bob Goodenow, Bettman has done anything but achieve that goal.

While the league has added teams and expanded its footprint—a favorite Bettman expression—into new areas, it was able to do the same under Ziegler, so what's the big deal about expansion?

Bettman brags at a June 1999 press conference that fighting is down in the league while acknowledging that a *Hockey News* poll revealed that fans love fighting in hockey. So, why remove an attractive aspect of the game?

As the league prepares for the new century it faces a good news-bad news scenario.

The bad news is that salary escalation has forced ownership to hike ticket prices beyond the means of a large segment of fans. What's more, salary inflation threatens to kill franchises—

particularly the small market franchises—while leaving others hanging by a gossamer string. This could result in a fight-to-the-finish lockout which could kill the NHL as we know it.

The good news is that hockey has thrived in such expansion sites as Sunrise, Florida and Nashville, Tennesee. It is expected to do likewise when a new venues open for the 1999–2000 season in Raleigh, North Carolina and Atlanta, Georgia. St.Paul, Minnesota and Columbus, Ohio are NHL-franchises-in-the-making for the 21st century.

As bleak as the major league hockey picture may look from one prism, it looks as rosy from another. If nothing else, Bettman, Inc. *IS* trying to make the game better and the irrefutable fact is that the NHL has survived crises in the past.

I believe the concerns are genuine and must be addressed. The NHL does not like to hear such criticism but those of us with a stake in the game believe the problems must be addressed.

We are not alone. In 1998, Jeff Z. Klein and Karl-Eric Reiff authored a critical tome called *The Death of Hockey*. Upon receipt of the work, I walked over to my bookshelf and found a somewhat tattered hardcover edition written by Bruce Kidd and John MacFarlane two decades earlier. Oddly enough, it too was titled, *The Death of Hockey*.

I suspect that the reported death in each case was not only premature but erroneous. As we know, hockey has long been known as "a game of mistakes," and Klein, Reiff, Kidd, and MacFarlane merely made another puckchasing error.

There will be a brave, new world of NHL hockey in the 21st century. How brave and how new it will be remains to be seen.

About the only thing we can guarantee is that it won't be run by John Ziegler!